D0536861

The CHILDES Project

Tools for Analyzing Talk, Third Edition
Volume II: The Datatbase

The CHILDES Project

Tools for Analyzing Talk, Third Edition
Volume II: The Database

Brian MacWhinney
Carnegie Mellon University

LEA LAWRENCE ERLBAUM ASSOCIATES, PUBLISHERS
2000 Mahwah, New Jersey   London

LB1139
.L3
M24
2000
v. 2

43403520

Copyright © 2000 by Lawrence Erlbaum Associates, Inc.
   All rights reserved. No part of this book may be reproduced in any
   form, by photostat, microfilm, retrieval system, or any other
   means, without the prior written permission of the publisher.

Lawrence Erlbaum Associates, Inc., Publishers
10 Industrial Avenue
Mahwah, New Jersey 07430-2262

Library of Congress Cataloging-in-Publication Data

MacWhinney, Brian
      The CHILDES project : tools for analyzing talk / Brian
   MacWhinney.—3rd ed.
         p. cm.
      Includes bibliographical references and index.
      Contents: v. 1. Transcription format and programs — v. 2. The data-
   base.
      ISBN 0-8058-2995-4 (v. 1 : alk. paper) — 0-8058-3572-5 (v. 2 : alk.
   paper)
      1. Children—Language—Data processing. 2. Language acquisi-
   tion—Research—Data processing. I. Title: Child Language Data Exchange System project. II. Title.
   LB1139.L3 M24 2000
   155.4'136'0285—dc21   00-024971

Books published by Lawrence Erlbaum Associates are printed on acid-free
paper, and their bindings are chosen for strength and durability

Printed in the United States of America
10 9 8 7 6 5 4 3 2 1

Contents

1: Introduction

This book is the second volume of a two-volume set. The first volume provided a general introduction to the use of computational tools for studying language learning. It also gave specific instructions for transcribing and analyzing language acquisition data using the framework of the Child Language Data Exchange System (CHILDES) system. Transcription was done using the CLAN transcription system and analysis was done using the CLAN programs. CHAT and CLAN are two of the three components of the CHILDES system.

The third component of CHILDES is the database. This book provides detailed documentation of the database. The data files themselves are included on an accompanying CD-ROM. Researchers who plan to make use of these data are required to read and understand the documentation provided here and to cite the sources provided by the contributors of the individual corpora.

This database includes a rich variety of computerized transcripts from language learners. Most of these transcripts record spontaneous conversational interactions. The speakers involved are often young monolingual, normally developing children conversing with their parents or siblings. However, there are also transcripts from bilingual children, older school-aged children, adult second-language learners, children with various types of language disabilities, and aphasics who are trying to recover from language loss. The transcripts include data on the learning of 26 different languages.

The transcript files described here are included in the accompanying CD-ROM. The CD-ROM includes a directory of data files for Windows, a directory of identical data files for Macintosh, and a directory of materials that can be read on both systems. Updates to the files can be retrieved over the Internet from http://childes.psy.cmu.edu. This manual is the sole source for documentation of the contents of the database. It includes information on the participants, their ages, other family members, the recording conditions, interactional contexts, transcription conventions, and coding methods. All users of the materials in the CHILDES database should be familiar with this manual and should adhere to the following guidelines.

Guidelines

The fact that so many students of language learning have freely contributed the hard-won results of such time-intensive work to this database is a moving testimony to the vibrancy and openness of the entire language learning community. These scholars deserve our thanks and respect for their important contributions. To express this respect, it is crucial that researchers obey the following guidelines.

Researchers who publish articles based on the use of these data must include citations to publications by the contributors of the corpora. The specific citations are listed at the end of the description of each corpus. It is absolutely imperative that publications include at least one reference to a listed article and more where appropriate. In addition, articles using CHILDES data should include a citation to this book: MacWhinney, B. (2000). *The CHILDES database: Tools for analyzing talk. 3rd Edition. Vol 2: The Database.* Mahwah, NJ: Lawrence Erlbaum Associates. Drafts and preprints of articles based on the use of corpora should be sent to the contributors using the addresses given at the beginning of the description of each corpus. It is extremely important that these procedures be followed exactly, in order to respect the rights of the contributors.

All participants in the corpora are identified with pseudonyms, except in cases where the participants are the children of the investigators. All participants have given permission to have their transcripts included in the database. We would like to request that all analyses of the data respect the dignity of the people being recorded, whether or not pseudonyms are provided.

Support for the construction of the database has comes from the National Institute of Child Health and Human Development (NIH-NICHD) and the National Science Foundation Linguistics Program. To document ongoing requests for support, we need to show that the CHILDES tools are being used productively. This means that we need to receive detailed feedback regarding published articles that have used the programs and database. This information should be sent to: Brian MacWhinney, Department of Psychology, Carnegie Mellon University, Pittsburgh PA 15213 USA or to macw@cmu.edu through electronic mail.

Data-Sharing

The database can be of vital importance in understanding the process of language learning. These data can be used in a wide variety of ways. For example, a researcher may wish to examine the interaction between language type and pronoun omission in order to evaluate the claims of parameter-setting models. Another researcher may be interested in finding out whether children with Downs syndrome are responsive to maternal requests. Another group of researchers may wish to determine the ways in which children first learn mental state verbs such as "remember" or "know." For each of these problems, conducting an analysis on a small and unrepresentative sample may lead to incorrect conclusions. Because child language data are so time-consuming to collect and to process, many researchers may actually avoid using empirical data to test their theoretical predictions. Or they may try to find one or two sentences that illustrate their ideas, without considering the extent to which their predictions are important for the whole of the child's language. In the case of studies of pronoun omission, early claims based on the use of a few examples were reversed when researchers took a broader look at larger quantities of transcript data.

Having access to a database in which many children are included also provides us with a way of generalizing our initial results. In some cases, conclusions about individual differences in child language have been based on analysis of as few as two children, and rarely on groups larger than 25. Because statistical tests based on three or four participants have very little power, researchers may avoid the use of statistics altogether in corpora-based studies. This problem arises in a particularly clear form when linguistic or psycholinguistic theory make predictions regarding the occurrence and distribution of rare events such as dative passives or certain types of NP-movement. Because of the rarity of such events, large amounts of data must be examined to find out exactly how often they occur in the input and in the child's speech. In these and other cases, researchers who are trying to focus on theoretical analyses are faced with the dilemma of having to commit their time to basic empirical work, rather than being able to focus on the development of acquisitional theory.

There is now a realistic solution to this dilemma. Using the CHILDES database, a researcher can access data from a number of research projects. The database includes a wide variety of language samples from a wide range of ages and situations. Although more than half of the data comes from English speakers, there is also a significant component of non-English data. The total size of the database is now approximately 300 million characters (300 megabytes). The corpora are divided into five major directories: English data, non-English data, narrative data, data from clinical populations, and data from bilingualism and second-language acquisition. In addition, the database includes a bibliography of work on child language and the MacArthur Communicative Development Inventory (CDI) database.

Confidentiality

For conventional transcripts, it has been relatively easy to maintain confidentiality by using pseudonyms and eliminating place names from transcripts. In the transcript database, all of the subjects' names are pseudonyms with a few important exceptions. There are several children who were studied by their parents. For these children, it is impossible to guarantee anonymity in any meaningful way. Therefore, we have asked these children to give us permission to use their names. All have agreed.

As we move from transcript data to multimodal data, it becomes increasingly difficult to maintain confidentiality through the simple use of pseudonyms. Researchers and subjects who would be happy to donate their transcript data to CHILDES might have concerns about donating the related audio or video data. One approach to this problem that has been implemented by many local IRB (Institutional Review Board) committees in the United States focuses on specifying varying levels of confidentiality. In these systems, the most restrictive level provides no access at all and the least restrictive level allows full Internet access. These levels would typically be applied on a corpus-by-corpus basis, so that any given database within the distributed database system could contain corpora at each of these nine levels:

1. Data are fully public (public speeches, public interviews, and so forth) and generally viewable and copyable over the Internet, although they may still be copyrighted.

2. Data are open to general viewing and listening by the public across the Internet, but watermarking and other techniques are used to block copying and redistribution.

3. Transcript data with pseudonyms will be made publicly available. However, the corresponding audio or video data, for which anonymity is more difficult to preserve, will be made available on one of the next six, more restrictive levels.

4. Data are only available to researchers who have signed a nondisclosure form. This form sets tight standards regarding avoidance of use of personal names when required. It allows some temporary copying or downloading of the data for local analysis, but requires that downloaded files be deleted after a specific period and never further copied or distributed. These requirements are enforced through watermarking and software blocks.

5. Access is restricted to researchers who have signed nondisclosure forms. In addition, copying is disallowed.

6. Data viewing requires explicit approval from the contributor of the data. This level would work much like a research laboratory that made copies of videotapes to send to other laboratories and required those laboratories to follow rules about nondistribution of data. However, unlike Level 6, this level would also include mechanisms for insuring that the data would not be copied or distributed.

7. This level would only allow viewing and listening in controlled conditions under direct on-line supervision. This level is needed for data of a highly personal or revealing nature. This level has been used in the past for the viewing of material from psychiatric interviews.

8. This level would only allow viewing and listening in controlled conditions under the direct, in person, supervision of the particular researcher. This level is needed for highly sensitive material.

9. These data would not be viewable, but would be archived in the format of the general system for use by the original investigator only. This level allows the investigator to use the tools of the analysis system without actually "contributing" the data.

This system corresponds closely to procedures currently in use by Human Subjects review committees at the University of Minnesota and the University of California at Berkeley. In addition to protecting subject confidentiality, this system of varying levels can be used to support the academic interests of the original data collector. For example, if a researcher has not finished publishing the results of a study, access can be set to a more restrictive level. Once the research papers have been published, access can be changed to a less restrictive level.

Some aspects of this system of levels of confidentiality protection can benefit from the development of technical processes. For example, it is possible to protect confidentiality by blurring audio and video images. This technology is generally unacceptable for the study of interactional processes, because facial expressions and intonation convey so many important components of communicative meaning. However, there are more sophisticated ways of morphing the face and the voice to images that are still communicatively adequate. Currently, the Linguistic Data Consortium (LDC) is using audio morphing to preserve confidentiality in the Corpus of Spoken American English (CSAE) collected by researchers at UC Santa Barbara. Also, the technique of "watermarking" can be used to prevent or discourage the unauthorized copying of images.

Documentation

With the exception of a few corpora of historical interest, all of the files in the CHILDES database are in CHAT format and have been run through the CHECK program to guarantee correct usage of the CHAT coding and transcription conventions. Many of the files have full documentation of the conversational context, although the documentation in others is far less complete. An attempt has been made to secure as much documentation as possible from the contributors. For editorial consistency, these descriptions have been edited into a common format, eliminating use of the first person and clarifying certain points. However, none of the factual elements of these documentation files have been changed.

None of the corpora collected before 1987 were transcribed initially in CHAT. Instead, we used optical scanning and computer programs to reformat these earlier corpora into the new standard. After reformatting, the transcripts were checked by hand. Since 1987, most of the corpora added to the database have been transcribed directly in CHAT. These new corpora have certain obvious advantages over the older corpora. First, the corpora that have been transcribed directly into CHAT make full use of the various contrasts available in CHAT coding. Second, because the new data did not go through a process of optical scanning and reformatting, no errors were introduced by these processes.

In continuing the construction of the CHILDES database, the overall goal is to achieve a continually higher standard of transcription accuracy and contextual documentation. In a sense, the current shape of the database is a statement both about the impressive size of our current child language database and also about the many ways in which that database must be expanded and improved. Recently, we have digitized the audiotapes for about half of the corpora. If sufficient resources become available, these digitized files will be made available over the Internet in the near future. Eventually, we plan to link these audio files to individual utterances in the transcripts.

Users who are ready to contribute their files to the database should first make sure that all files pass the CHECK program and that the 00readme.cdc file is complete and accurate. When this is done, all of the files should be combined into a single zip file. The zip file can then be transferred to CMU by sending it as an e-mail attachment to Brian MacWhinney at macw@cmu.edu. If the file is larger than 4MB, it should be sent instead by using anonymous FTP to childes.psy.cmu.edu with username "dropbox" and password "dropbox." Once you have transferred the data using FTP, please send an e-mail message to macw@cmu.edu to alert us about the transfer. We will then send you a written contribution form. The data will be rechecked and your 00readme.cdc file will then be included in the electronic form of this database guide, as well as in future published versions.

Using This Guide

There are two forms of this manual — electronic and hard copy. The electronic version is an Adobe Acrobat PDF file with blue underlined hypertext fields. By clicking on these fields, you can go directly to the corpora or subtables being mentioned. In addition, there are tabs on the side of the electronic document that you can use to navigate to the various corpora. The printed version of the manual does not include clickable links and tabs, but it does include a table of contents and frequent use of page number references that serve a similar function in facilitating movement through the manual.

The table below is the top level index to the database. It provides access to seven additional tables. If you are using the electronic version of the manual, you can click on one of the labels in the "Corpora Group" column of the table. This will take you to the table for the particular type of corpora. If you are using the printed version of the manual, just turn to that page. When you reach the table you need, you then repeat this process to find the description of the specific corpus. The other way of navigating about through this manual is to use the table of contents for the printed version or the thumbtabs at the left side of the electronic version.

Table 1: Groups of Corpora

Corpora Group	Description
English Corpora on page 8	Studies of normally developing children learning English
Bilingual Corpora on page 104	Studies of child and adult bilinguals and second-language learners
Clinical Corpora on page 174	Studies of children and adults with language impairments
Narrative Corpora on page 243	Studies of children's narratives
Germanic Languages on page 274	Studies of normally developing children learning Germanic and Nordic languages other than English
Romance Languages on page 324	Studies of normally developing children learning Romance languages
Other Languages on page 360	Studies of normally developing children learning languages from other language groups

2:   English Corpora

Table 2: English Corpora

Corpus	Age Range	N	Comments
Bates on page 11	0;10–0;13 1;8–2;4	27	Longitudinal study of language and symbolic development at four points
Belfast on page 13	2;4–4;5	8	Study of the role of input in Belfast English and Standard English
Bernstein-Ratner on page 18	1;1–1;11	9	Mother child dyads during the earliest stages of language with play sessions followed by parental interviews
Bliss on page 20	3–10	8	Control participants for a study of SLI
Bloom 1970 on page 21	1;4.21–2;10	1	Six samples from the development of one child
Bloom 1973 on page 22	1;9–3;2	3	A large longitudinal study of one child with a few samples for two other children
Bohannon on page 25	Nat 2;8 and 3;0 Baxter 3;0	2	Interactions in a laboratory setting of different adults with two children
Braine on page 27	first word combinations	8	12 small files containing early utterances. Only child utterances are entered. Includes Hebrew and Samoan
Brown on page 28	Adam 2;3–4;10 Eve 1;6–2;3 Sarah 2;3–5;1	3	Large longitudinal study of three children: Adam 55 files, Eve 20 and Sarah 139
Carterette and Jones on page 32	1st, 3rd, 5th grade students and adults	174	Speech sample taken in a simple social situation
Clark on page 34	2;2–3;2 (weekly)	1	The transcripts pay close attention to repetitions, hesitations, and retracings
Cornell on page 37	1;6–4;0	8	Small samples from various families for graduate student projects
Cruttenden on page 38	1;5–3;7	2	Dizygotic twins with phonologically transcribed data collected at monthly intervals

Table 2: English Corpora

Corpus	Age Range	N	Comments
Demetras Trevor on page 39	2;0–3:11	1	Father / son interaction during free play. Nine sets of 4–20 minute conversations over a period of 35 months
Demetras Working on page 40	Michael 2;2 Tim 2;1–2;2 Jimmy 2;2–2;9	3	Parent–child interaction during free play session in two families with working parents and a child in day care
Evans on page 41	first graders	32	Indoor play session of first grade children
Fletcher on page 42	3, 5, 7	72	Normative data on British children collected in an interview setting
Garvey on page 44	2;10–5;7	48	Cross-sectional study of dyad school dialogs with no adult present
Gathercole on page 47	2;9–6;6	14	Cross-sectional study of children having lunch on four separate occasions
Gathercole / Burns on page 49	3;0–6;4	12	Cross-sectional data collection during a structured play session
Gleason on page 50	2;1–5;2	24	Each child had three sessions: mother–child lab; father–child lab; and dinner with mother, father and child
Haggerty on page 54	2;6	1	A detailed account of what one child said in one day
Hall on page 55	4;6–5;0	39	A large data set from Black Professional, Black Working, White Professional, and White Working families
Higginson on page 59	0;11–2;11	3	Naturalistic short-term longitudinal observations of mother–child interactions in unstructured play sessions
Howe on page 61	1;6–1;8 1;11–2;1	16	Mother–child interaction during free play with data coded extensively for actions and situations at two time points
Korman on page 65	infants	6	Maternal speech interactions with preverbal infants
Kuczaj on page 70	2;4–5;0	1	Diary study in the home environment

Table 2: English Corpora

Corpus	Age Range	N	Comments
MacWhinney on page 73	Ross 2;6–8;0 Mark 0;7–5;6	2	Diary study of the development of two brothers recorded in spontaneous situations
Manchester on page 74	1;8–3;0	12	12 English children recorded weekly for the period of a year
Nelson on page 77	1;9–3;0	1	One child's crib monologs and dialogs
New England on page 78	1;2 1;8 2;3–5	52	Parent–child laboratory interactions at three ages. Each session included several structured activities
Peters / Wilson on page 81	1;7.0–4;1.0	1	Interactions between a father and his visually-impaired son
Post on page 82	lew 1;10.20–2;8.7 she 1;7,18–2;5.8 tow 1;7.5–2;5.3	3	10 free play sessions over a 9 month period in the child's home
Sachs on page 85	1;1–5;1	1	Longitudinal naturalistic study
Snow on page 87	2;3–3;9	1	Longitudinal study with lots of book reading
Suppes on page 88	1;11–3;11	1	Longitudinal study of a single child
Tardif on page 89	3	25	Comparison with a group of 25 Chinese
Valian on page 90	1;9.20–2;8.24	21	Compares English and Italian development in regard to subject deletion
Van Houten on page 91	2;0 3;0	61 52	Differences in mother–child interactions between adolescent and older mothers
Van Kleeck on page 96	3 years	37	Each child participated in two half-hour laboratory sessions
Warren-Leubecker on page 97	1;6–3;1 4;6–6;2	10 10	Parent–child interactions
Wells on page 98	1;6–5;0	32	Large study of the language of British preschool children collected at random intervals

Bates

Elizabeth Bates
Department of Psychology
University of California
La Jolla, CA 92093 USA
bates@amos.ucsd.edu

This corpus contains transcripts from the Bates/Bretherton Colorado longitudinal sample of middle-class children studied in Boulder, Colorado, between 1978 and 1980. There are four subdirectories: free20, free28, snack28, and story28. These names indicate the ages of the children in months and the nature of the activity in which they were engaged. Children were studied at four age levels: 10, 13, 20, and 28 months. The initial sample included 32 children, but only 27 participated at all four ages. At each age level, data were collected in two sessions. The first session was always held in the home, followed by a session in the laboratory no more than 7 days later. Detailed transcriptions are available only for the laboratory session. At 20 months, there are only transcripts of motherese sequence of structured procedures that followed. The three situations include: free play with the same instructions and the same toys used in the 20-month segment, reading of the book *Miffy in the Snow*, and a snack.

The children were all originally participants in a study of causal understanding in infancy (Carlson-Luden, 1979) involving an initial group of 48 infants with an average age of 0;10.11 (with a range from 0;10.0 to 0;10.28). At the end of the Carlson-Luden study, parents were asked if they would be willing to participate in our longitudinal study of language and symbolic development, up through 28 months of age. The parents of 32 children agreed, resulting in a starting sample of 16 boys and 16 girls. These infants were next seen at 13 months of age. Five children subsequently moved away. At 20 months, three new children were therefore invited to participate in the project, to bring the sample up to 15 boys and 15 girls. This sample of 30 children all participated in the final sessions at 28 months. Although the total sample varied from one session to another, 27 children participated at all four age levels. All the analyses in Bates, Bretherton, and Snyder (1988) are based on this constant sample of 27, including 13 boys and 14 girls. Thirteen children were first-born, 10 were second-born, and 4 were third-born or later. Their average birthweight was 7.2 pounds, with a range from 5.5 to 9.0 lbs. Average age in days at the initial 10-month session was 311, with a range from 300 to 324. At all subsequent sessions, children were within 2 weeks on either side of the target range.

A note regarding the demographic make-up of this sample: Although we did not select participants systematically on the basis of race or socioeconomic level, the demographic characteristics of Boulder, Colorado are such that these selection criteria resulted in a sample of middle- to upper-middle-class White children (with the exception of one Black child from a middle-class family). This was, then, a very homogeneous and privileged group of children, a fact that of course limits the generalizability of our findings to other groups.

Publications using these data should cite:

Bates, E., Bretherton, I., & Snyder, L. (1988). *From first words to grammar: Individual differences and dissociable mechanisms.* Cambridge, MA: Cambridge University Press.

Carlson-Luden, V. (1979). *Causal understanding in the 10-month-old.* Unpublished doctoral dissertation. University of Colorado at Boulder.

Belfast

Alison Henry
School of Behavioural and Social Sciences
University of Ulster
Newtownsabbey, County Antrim
BT37 0QB Northern Ireland
am.henry@ulst.ac.uk

This directory contains transcripts from a study of eight upper-working-class children acquiring English in Belfast, Northern Ireland between 1995 and 1998. The contributors to this project were Alison Henry, John Wilson, Cathy Finlay, and Sile Harrington. The goal of the study was to establish how children treated variable forms in the input, that is, cases where there was more than one possible realization for a form or construction. In terms of subject-verb agreement, Belfast English allows "The eggs is cracked" for standard English "The eggs are cracked." In regard to negative concord, it allows, "They didn't bring nothing" for "They brought nothing." In regard to optional inversion in embedded questions, it allows "I wondered where were they going" for "I wondered where they were going." In the past tense, it allows "I done that" for "I did that."

Participants

Eight children were recorded over a period of 3 years. Four children were male and four were female. Pseudonyms have been used for all the names of the children and parents and for names of extended family members, areas in Belfast, schools, teachers' names and so forth. Pseudonyms have not been used for the investigator's personal details or her own children's names.

In order to study the impact of variability, it was necessary to identify children who had variation in the input to acquisition. An initial study of variation in the community indicated that it was upper-working-class and lower-middle-class parents who in general exhibited variability in most or all of the areas of language under study. Of course, it would be impossible to know exactly what input the child is exposed to without recording all the language the child hears. However, we wished to develop a methodology that would allow us to ensure in so far as that was possible that the sample of adult language we obtained was representative of the child's total input. First, we decided that we should select children whose exposure to language was relatively homogeneous, not in the sense of excluding variability, but in the sense of having contact mainly with adults whose grammars were similar to one another. Thus, we decided to exclude children who spent extensive periods of time in day care, who spent much time with relatives or other adults who were from different dialect backgrounds, or who attended preschool groups outside their own areas. In order to exclude as far as practicable the possibility of the child being exposed to language that was radically different from that which we would record, we thus imposed the following requirements on subject selection:

1. Eldest or only children in the family (thus excluding the impact of older children bringing language from school or the wider community),

2. cared for mainly at home,

3. both parents and all adults with whom the child regularly spent time were local (thus excluding the introduction of another dialect and the possibility of "bidialectal" acquisition), and

4. if the child attended a nursery or playgroup, it was in the local area and staffed by speakers of the local variety of English.

By selecting children in this way, we hoped to be confident that the parental speech we recorded, together with other adult speech to the child which we were likely to be able to record, would give us a realistic picture of the child's total input. We also wanted to select adults and children from the same speech community, so that where frequencies of occurrence were low in individual adult–child pairs, we could pool the data across adults and children to see the overall picture without distorting the evidence. In order to avoid atypical acquisition patterns, we also imposed the requirement that the child should have no known hearing or language development problems. In addition, it was necessary that the parents were prepared to have recordings made in their home for at least a year on a regular basis.

Obtaining Participants

Identifying children who met this range of requirements took some time; the most effective means of recruitment turned out to be through mother-toddler groups in appropriate areas; the research officers visited a number of such groups in areas thought to contain speakers who were likely to use the variables concerned, and explained the need for participants in the study. Volunteers who appeared to meet the criteria were then visited in their own homes in order to obtain a clearer picture of the linguistic background to which the child was exposed, to make a recording in order to ensure that variability of the type under study was indeed present, and to explain the requirements of the study. Naturally, not all the features we were interested in would show up in a single recording, but the presence of key variables generally indicated that other aspects of variability would be present.

We also undertook a preliminary study, using children from a preschool day care facility. From this it became clear that reasonable numbers of occurrences of the variable elements we were interested in would not appear before around age 2;6, and some would not be evident until well over age 3. In order to obtain relevant data at an early stage, we therefore chose to begin studying two groups of children — one around 2;4 and the other around 3;4. We also started recording one child at 2;0 in order to have some earlier data available. We excluded younger children who, although their language is interesting for many other reasons, exhibited few of the structures under study (for example, plural participants were very rare so that the study of singular concord was not possible; nor were irregular past tenses). Where the parents were agreeable, recording continued until the child began to attend school (and thus we considered was exposed to a wider range of linguistic influences that we could not reliably record). One family with a child in the younger age group withdrew from the study when the child was 3;2.

Recording Sessions

Visits were made to each family once a month for approximately 1 hour. The recordings were carried out mainly by Cathy Finlay, who is a native speaker of Belfast English, had two young children of her own, and was considered to be an equal participant in the adult child-based conversations with mothers on topics such as toilet training, sleep problems and so forth. Sometimes other children were present (friends, cousins etc). In general, adult and child recordings were informal, particularly as the investigator became more of a friend than investigator, sometimes resulting in two of the children (David and Stuart) playing in the investigator's house with the investigator's children. Some self recordings were also made by the families, where a tape recorder was left with the family and the child was recorded at mealtimes, bedtime, bath time etc.

The investigator would bring along toys such as train sets, monster and dinosaur figures, books, and jigsaws. Role play was also encouraged using fire fighter hats, medical kits, dolls etc. Other types of play provided a more language-specific style of data, that is, elementary games, blocks, and coloring activities resulted in language about the task. Sometimes toys were too interesting and the child became engrossed in the game with little language. Also some children were naturally more outgoing and chatty than others.

Recording Equipment

A Sony™ Walkman Professional powered by batteries was used with a boundary microphone. This provided excellent clear sound recordings and freedom to move about at random and was generally reliable, though technical problems resulted in three blank recordings. Video recording was not used.

Transcription

A complete orthographic transcription of each recording was made using the CED editor. Most transcriptions were made by the investigator who carried out the recordings and those not transcribed by her initially were subsequently verified by her. In addition, samples of all transcriptions were verified by another member of the research team. Overlaps and interruptions were largely ignored in transcription to save time, as the research was primarily interested in syntax. A very small amount of data that might be particularly sensitive or personal has been removed from the transcripts.

Table 3: Belfast Children

Child	Birthdate	First Age	Last Age	Gender	Hours
Barbara	14-JUL-1993	2;4.9	4;1.18	Female	20
Michelle	6-JUL-1993	2;4.28	4;4.19	Female	17
Courtney	8-SEP-1992	3;4.0	4;0.11	Female	9
Rachel	9-JUN-1993	2;5.25	3;2.3	Female	11
Conor	5-JAN-1992	3;8.14	4;5.22	Male	22
Stuart	21-APR-1992	3;5.12	4;5.4	Male	17
Johnny	29-MAY-1993	3;5.29	4;4.1	Male	10
David	21-SEP-1993	2;0.3	4;2.3	Male	17

Table 4: Belfast Files

File	Barb	Mich	Court	Rach	Conor	Stuart	John	David
1	2;4.9	Blank	3;4.0	2;5.25	3;8.14	3;5.12	3;6.0	2;0.3
2	2;4.23	2;4.28	3;5.25	2;6.10	3;8.27	3;6.24	3;6.21	2;0.10
3	2;6.16	2;7.20	3;6.18	2;7.27	3;9.4	3;7.20	3;7.30	2;1.1
4	2;7.8	2;7.26	3;7.24	2;8.30	3;10.10	3;10.2	3;9.11	2;1.22
5	Blank	2;10.14	3;9.4	2;11.0	3;10.22	3;10.14	3;10.24	2;2.19
6	2;9.12	2;11.4	3;11.0	2;11.26	4;0.10	4;1.6	4;0.12	Blank
7	2;10.28	3;1.27	4;0.11	3;2.3	4;0.24	3;8.26	4;4.1	2;7.21
8	3;2.19	3;3.25		2;9.2	4;1.21	3;10.16		2;8.24
9	3;3.3	3;6.21		2;9.16	4;2.20	4;4.4		3;0.2
10	3;5.5	3;10.21			4;3.17	4;5.4		3;3.25
11	3;6.9	3;10.22			4;4.15	4;4.1		3;5.24
12	3;7.13	3;11.10			4;5.22			3;8.11
13	3;9.10	4;2.25			4;0.24			3;11.9
14	3;11.5				4;6.5			4;0.28
15	4;1.18							

The study was funded by a research grant from the Economic and Social Research Council to Alison Henry and John Wilson for the study of "Language Acquisition in Conditions of Variable Input" (Ref R000235802).

Publications using these data should cite:

Henry, A. (1995) *Belfast English and Standard English: Dialect variation and parameter setting.* New York: Oxford University Press.
Wilson, J. & Henry, A. (1998) "Parameter setting within a socially realistic linguistics" *Language in Society, 27,* 1–21.

For a descriptive outline of dialect features in the data see:

Henry, A. (1996). The syntax of Belfast English. In J. Kallen (Ed.) *Focus on Ireland.* Amsterdam: Benjamins.

Bernstein-Ratner

Nan Bernstein-Ratner
Hearing and Speech Sciences
LeFrak Hall
University of Maryland
College Park, MD 20742 USA
nratner@bss1.umd.edu

Participants

The participants were nine mother–child dyads who were followed for a period of 4 to 5 months each. Each dyad has three transcripts. The mothers were all college-educated women, who were native-born Americans with white-collar husbands. The children (all girls) ranged in age from 1;1 to 1;9 at first taping. The ages of each child are posted on the very first line of each transcript file. Three of the children began the study as prelinguistic infants (Kay, Amelia, and Dale). Three began as "holophrastic" language users (Alice, Cindy, and Marie). Three began and finished as multi-word utterance producers (Lena, Gail, and Annie). These names do not correspond to those listed in either Bernstein (1982) or some subsequent articles, due to the request by CHILDES to provide pseudonyms. Children in each of the first two groups made significant linguistic progress into higher language stages during the course of the study

Procedure

Children and their mothers played for approximately 45 minutes at each session with the same selection of toys (blocks, stuffed animals, puppets, books, and so forth). Most of the sessions were followed by a parental interview. These interviews are collected in a subdirectory entitled "interview." The purpose of the interview was to gather a sample of the mothers' speech for comparison against the mother–child condition. In order to obtain exemplars of mother-adult words to match to the mother–child condition, the questioning sometimes wandered. In addition, to save transcription time, the mothers' responses to the investigator's questions are provided, but the investigator's comments are omitted.

Recording

These transcripts were derived from reel-to-reel audiotaped interactions carried out in a sound-proof playroom at the Massachusetts Institute of Technology Research Laboratory of Electronics during 1979 and 1980. The original inquiry regarded phonetic characteristics of maternal speech. The quality of the audio recordings of both mothers and children is extremely fine. Mothers wore lavaliere microphones with Sony™ ECM-50s and the interactions were taped on a Revox™ A77. These tapes will be made available to any researcher who requests them, with the provisos that the researcher receive some sort of authorship credit for subsequent research derived from them, and that the costs of materials and labor to duplicate the tapes be borne by the requesting researcher.

The children's language skills were not a primary focus of any of the research carried out to date using these samples. As a result, although phonetic transcriptions of the children have been provided, they are very rough. Given the notorious difficulty of obtaining reliability in the transcription of prelinguistic and early child phonetic strings, it is recommended that any researcher interested in doing a phonological analysis of the children's data request the original audiotapes. The children are transcribed in UNIBET, with minimal fine detail. To create uniformity, and to read as little as possible into the children's output, most of the children are phonetically transcribed, even when their productions appear to correspond to adult forms. The majority of the children's productions are phonetic, rather than phonemic, given the ages of the children. Some of the older children's transcripts include regular English orthography.

Miscellaneous Notes

Amelia was a nonidentical twin. Her mother's speech to the other twin girl was also recorded for 6 months, but has not been provided. It is available on request. A series of three tapes of a mother conversing with a girl thought to be language-delayed and eliminated from the first and subsequent studies is available without transcript. Finally, a girl having linguistic skills similar to Lena, but with a more talkative mother, was taped for a manuscript in preparation and can be provided without transcription. Copies of the dissertation (Bernstein, 1982) can be obtained upon request, as can more information about particular participants or other issues. Please feel free to contact Dr. Bernstein-Ratner if you have questions regarding these samples.

Publications using these data should cite one or more of these articles:

Bernstein, N. (1982). *Acoustic study of mothers' speech to language-learning children: An analysis of vowel articulatory characteristics.* Unpublished doctoral dissertation. Boston University.

Bernstein-Ratner, N. (1984a). Patterns of vowel modification in motherese. *Journal of Child Language, 11,* 557–578.

Bernstein-Ratner, N. (1984b). Phonological rule usage in mother–child speech. *Journal of Phonetics, 12,* 245-254.

Bernstein-Ratner, N. (1985). Dissociations between vowel durations and formant frequency characteristics. *Journal of Speech and Hearing Research, 28,* 255–264.

Bernstein-Ratner, N. (1986). Durational cues which mark clause boundaries in mother child speech. *Journal of Phonetics, 14,* 303–309.

Bernstein-Ratner, N. (1987). The phonology of parent child speech. In K. Nelson & A. Van Kleeck (Eds.), *Children's Language: Vol. 6.* Hillsdale, NJ: Lawrence Erlbaum.

Bernstein-Ratner, N., & Pye, C. (1984). Higher pitch in baby talk is not universal: Acoustic evidence from Quiche Mayan. *Journal of Child Language,* 11, 515–522.

Bliss

The Bliss corpus compares normally developing children with children with specific language impairment (SLI) of the same chronological age. The normally developing control participants are in this directory. Their ages are given in this table:

Table 5: Bliss Control Children

Child	Age
Aimee	5;4.0
Gary	11;8.0
Justin	4;6.0
Marjorie	2;3.0
Melissa	3;4.0
Meredith	2;5.0
Trevor	4;3.0
Willie	6;1.0

Publications using these data should cite:

Bliss, L. (1988). The development of modals. *The Journal of Applied Developmental Psychology, 9*, 253–261.

Bloom 1970

Lois Bloom
Teachers College
Columbia University
525 West 120th St.
New York, NY 10027 USA
lmb32@columbia.edu

This directory contains files from three children. The children are Peter, Eric, and Gia. Peter was born on December 27, 1969; Eric was born on July 2, 1964; and Gia was born on February 5, 1965. The Peter subdirectory contains 20 files, recorded between the ages of 1;9 and 3;2. It was recorded during the years 1971 and 1973. Peter was one of the four participants studied in the context of the project reported upon in Bloom (1970). The other three children were recorded in the late 1960's, whereas Peter was recorded after the 1970 book was published. Additional data on hand-written sheets are available for Eric and Gia, as well as for a fourth child Kathryn. Peter was an upper-middle class white child with college-educated parents. He was a first-born child living in a university community in New York City.

Table 6: Peter Files

File	Age	File	Age	File	Age	File	Age
01	1;9.7	06	2;0.7	11	2;3.21	16	2;7.14
02	1;9.21	07	2;0.7	12	2;4.14	17	2;8.14
03	1;10.15	08	2;1.21	13	2;5.0	18	2;9.14
04	1;11.7	09	2;2.14	14	2;5.21	19	2;10.21
05	1;11.21	10	2;3.0	15	2;6.14	20	3;1.21

Eric and Gia were two of the three children studied in the context of the preparation of Bloom (1970). The files called "bookeric" and "bookgia" have the material reported in the book. The other files, beginning when Eric is 19 months old, have been entered from hand-written transcripts.

Publications using these data should cite one of these sources:

Bloom, L. (1970). *Language development: Form and function in emerging grammars.* Cambridge, MA: MIT Press.

Bloom, L., Hood, L., & Lightbown, P. (1974). Imitation in language development: If, when and why. *Cognitive Psychology, 6*, 380–420.

Bloom, L., Lightbown, P., & Hood, L. (1975). Structure and variation in child language. *Monographs of the Society for Research in Child Development, 40*, (Serial No. 160).

Bloom 1973

Lois Bloom
Teachers College
Columbia University
525 West 120th St.
New York, NY 10027 USA
lmb32@columbia.edu

This subdirectory contains a set of files contributed by Lois Bloom of Columbia University Teachers College. Allison was the participant of the study of language development reported in the appendices to Bloom (1973). Two additional files for Allison that did not appear in that book were contributed directly by Bloom (Allison5 and Allison6). The original collection and transcription of these data were made possible by research support provided by The National Institutes of Health to Lois Bloom. One copy of any published report or unpublished dissertation that makes use of these data is to be sent to Lois Bloom.

Methods

All of the video recordings took place in the Audio-Visual Studio at Teachers College, Columbia University. They were made using a Sony™ half-inch helical scan recorder, Model CV 2200. The setting consisted of three pieces of furniture and a rug in front of a blank wall. There was a big wooden Windsor-type double chair that could seat two people comfortably. This is referred to as the "big chair" in the transcription and it was center stage. To the right of it was a child-size molded plastic chair, and between the two chairs was a triangular low table.

Three simultaneous microphones were used in each session; the models varied from session to session, but their placement was as follows: (1) on the low table between the chairs or on the floor, depending on where the action was; (2) attached to a lavaliere around my neck; and (3) attached to an adjustable overhead boom arm that was maneuvered vertically and horizontally, again depending on Allison's movements. The photographer was instructed to focus the camera on Allison's activity — on what she was doing and what she was looking at. Virtually all of the film takes in Allison in full view. Each session included a snack with cookies, a container of apple juice, and several paper cups. A group of toys was brought to all of the sessions, and only the doll, a floppy rag doll, was Allison's own toy. The other toys were borrowed from the Speech and Hearing Center at Teachers College, and Allison knew them only in the context of the recording sessions: a metal dump truck about 12 inches long, and a set of rubber farm animals (bull, cow, calf, horse, colt, lamb and pig). Other toys were used in one or another of the sessions, but not in all of them. These included a jar of bubble liquid, a group of hand and finger puppets, a 5-inch plastic doll wrapped in a blanket and a photograph of a girl in a plastic frame. The snack was carried in a canvas tote bag ("the bag") which was Allison's own and which also contained an extra diaper and napkins.

Allison gave every indication of being relaxed and comfortable in the recording sessions. There was one aborted session, however, approximately two weeks before the second session, in which Allison was distressed and uncooperative. That tape was erased. The four tapes presented here were each filmed continuously from start to finish; there was no stopping, and they have not been edited. Each session lasted 40 minutes.

My interaction with Allison could be described as somewhat more investigator than mother. I tended to follow her lead and to respond to what she said or did. I waited for an utterance when there was a hint that something might be said. I waited for Allison to ask for help, rather than assisting as soon as she had a problem (for example, extracting a cookie from a plastic bag, or putting the doll upright on the truck). I frequently asked a quizzical "What?" or "Hm?" to encourage her to say more. I also frequently repeated what I thought she had said and, interestingly, I often misheard her. There were a few "set up" situations — instances in which I asked a leading question, for example, at 19,2 when I asked her to distinguish between the big and little chairs and the big and little cows. Nevertheless, there was considerable touching, smiling, and nose wiping. We both enjoyed the sessions.

The video recordings were transcribed originally, with description of context, by Lois Hood, who also did the original word counts. One year later, the recordings and the first transcription were reviewed and compared by Lois Hood, Patsy Lightbown, Maxine Kenin and Lynn Streeter working in pairs, and this resulted in a second transcription. Five months later, I reviewed all of the recordings with the second transcription, working in groups of three with all four research assistants. This resulted in the third and final transcription. Our procedure for the third transcription included one assistant controlling the monitor playback and describing the video picture, a second assistant reading the transcription, and myself coordinating the video and audio records with the transcription. Considerably more of the situational context was added in the final version and the final transcription took approximately 6 hours' time for each 40-minute session. Part of the reason for this was the fact that we were finding new material in the tapes — behavior that none of us had noticed although the tapes had been viewed many, many times. This experience of transcribing the material so carefully and watching the recordings so closely has made us aware of the limitations in audio recording alone, and cautious of data that are not mechanically recorded at all so that they can be reviewed repeatedly before descriptions, judgments or interpretations are made. Werner Leopold's four-volume diary and several of the other diary studies that have become landmarks in the literature are even more impressive to us now, but at the same time we have an even sharper sense of how much they must have missed.

The numbers that appear in the transcriptions represent an attempt to divide the data into speech events primarily for the purpose of reference. The criterion used for the division was essentially a shift of topic or focus. All of the events were consecutive. What has not been captured is the time lapse between and within events. There were variable pauses throughout.

As can be seen, we have not completely analyzed the material in these transcriptions. The fourth sample at 22 months, when mean length of utterance was 1.73, is the Syntax Sample. The third sample at 20,3, with mean length of utterance 1.13, is the Transition Sample (between single-word utterances and syntax). The first two samples, at 16,3 and

19,2, represent what appears to have been two different stages among at least several stages in Allison's use of single-word utterances in the course of her language development from 9 to 22 months. Allison was born on July 12, 1968. Her ages in the six samples are as follows: 1;4.21, 1;7.14, 1;8.21, 1;10, 2;4.7, and 2;10.

Publications using these data should cite:

Bloom, L. (1973). *One word at a time: The use of single-word utterances before syntax.* The Hague: Mouton.

Bohannon

John Neil Bohannon III
Department of Psychology
Butler University
Indianapolis IN 46208 USA
bohannon@butler.edu

These transcripts show the interaction of different adults with one of two children, Nat and Baxter. There were 17 adults interacting with Nat and 10 interacting with Baxter. The adults include 15 undergraduates, 5 graduates and the participant's mother. The data were collected in 1976.

Participants

Twelve undergraduates and five graduate students participated in the experiment. Nat was 2;8 (MLU = 3.59 morphemes) when he interacted with the undergraduates. He was 3;0 (MLU = 3.73 morphemes) when he interacted with the graduate students. Nat was the son of a college professor and a college graduate and probably verbally precocious. No information is available about Baxter.

Procedure

Students were given minimal instructions concerning the experiment. They were simply told to converse with the child and to try to draw him into conversation. The undergraduate students were sent to Nat's home in six teams of two students and one team of three students. The students visiting Baxter's home went singly. During each interaction, the noninteracting team members took contextual notes while the other team member interacted. The mother was present during all interactions. They were also accompanied by an experimental assistant to run the tape recorder. All interactions were recorded on Realistic Super Tape by means of a Realistic CTR-29 cassette deck. During the interaction several play materials (i.e. blocks, stuffed animals, and books around the house) were made available for assisting conversations. The average interaction lasted about 15 minutes, with one group of undergraduate students going a full hour. These transcripts were checked against the tapes for accuracy by Nat's mother and the authors.

Response Codes

Six of the transcribed files are coded for adult response types, errors and MLU on a %cod tier. These files are claire.cha, dan.cha, elliott.cha, harvey.cha, ruth.cha, and stephani.cha. The coding for harvey.cha is not complete. Here are the codes and the format for these codes.

The first number on the line is the MLU count for the above speaker's utterance. It is coded in the form $MLU=4. The next letter is the utterance type ($UT) which is coded as one of these five values:

d	declarative
q	question
i	imperative
wf	well-formed
if	ill-formed

If the utterance is ill-formed (if), then one of these error codes will follow it:

pr	pragmatic
sm	semantic
sy	syntactic
ph	phonetic

Thus, there will be codes such as $UT=if:pr and $UT=if:sm. The final cluster of codes refers to the adult response type ($ART) which can be:

cc	child contingent
cd	child dependent
ad	adult dependent
nc	non contingent
corr	correction
app	approval
oth	other

Alternatively, the final codes may refer to repetition types ($RT) which can be:

sf	self follows
cf	child follows

Both the $ART and the $RT codes may be further described by these qualifiers:

exct	exact
elab	elaborate
rcst	recast
cont	continuation

Thus, there are codes such as $ART=cc:exct and $RT=sf:elab.

Publications using these data should cite:

Bohannon, J. N., & Marquis, A. L. (1977). Children's control of adult speech. *Child Development, 48*, 1002–1008.

Stine, E. L., & Bohannon III, J. N. (1983). I*mitations, interactions, and language acquisition.* Journal of Child Language, 10, 589–603.

Braine

Dr. Martin Braine
Professor of Psychology
New York University
deceased

The 12 small files in this directory contain the early utterances from Andrew, David, Johnathan, Kendall, Odi, Seppo, Sipili, and Tofi published in Braine (1976). Only the child's utterances are entered, because no parental input was reported.

Publications using these data should cite:

Braine, M. D. S. (1976). Children's first word combinations. *Monographs of the Society for Research in Child Development, 41*, (Whole No. 1).

Brown

Dr. Roger Brown
Professor of Psychology and Social Relations
Harvard University
deceased

This subdirectory contains the complete transcripts from the three participants Adam, Eve, and Sarah who were studied by Roger Brown and his students between 1962 and 1966. Adam was studied from 2;3 to 4;10, Eve from 1;6 to 2;3, and Sarah from 2;3 to 5;1. Brown (1973) summarized this research and provided detailed documentation regarding data collection, transcription, and analysis.

The corpus was scanned optically from the original typed sheets and then reformatted by program and extensively checked by hand. In addition to basic CHAT coding, the child's speech in the Adam and Eve corpora has also been coded for these five speech acts:

$RES	response
$IMIT	imitation
$EIMIT	elicited imitation
$MLR	metalinguistic reference
$IMP	imperative

Adam was the child of a minister and an elementary school teacher. His family was middle class and well educated. Though he was Black, he was not a speaker of American Black English, but of Standard American. There are 55 files in the Adam corpus and his age ranges from 2;3 to 4;10. Also included in the corpus is a file called "00lexicon.cdc" which contains some nonstandard lexical items that were used or invented by Adam.

Table 7: Adam Files

File	Age	File	Age	File	Age	File	Age
01	2;3.4	15	2;10.2	29	3;4.18	43	4;1.15
02	2;3.18	16	2;10.16	30	3;5.0	44	4;2.17
03	2;4.3	17	2;10.30	31	3;5.15	45	4;3.9
04	2;4.15	18	2;11.13	32	3;6.9	46	4;4.0
05	2;4.30	19	2;11.28	33	3;5.29	47	4;3.13
06	2;5.12	20	3;0.11	34	3;7.7	48	4;5.11
07	2;6.3	21	3;0.25	35	3;8.0	49	4;6.24
08	2;6.17	22	3;1.9	36	3;8.14	50	4;7.0

Table 7: Adam Files

File	Age	File	Age	File	Age	File	Age
09	2;6.17	23	3;1.26	37	3;8.26	51	4;7.29
10	2;7.14	24	3;2.9	38	3;9.16	52	5;2.12
11	2;8.0	25	3;2.21	39	3;10.15	53	4;9.2
12	2;8.16	26	3;3.4	40	3;11.0	54	4;10.2
13	2;9.4	27	3;3.18	41	3;11.14	55	4;10.23
14	2;9.18	28	3;4.1	42	4;0.14		

Eve was a linguistically precocious child. Unfortunately for the study, her family moved away from the Cambridge area after only 20 sessions were completed. Her speech developed very rapidly over these 9 months. In spite of the small amount of data, her record is especially rich. She began the study when she was 1;6 and left the study when she was 2;3. Included with the Eve data are two files, "00lexicon.cdc" and "00proper.cdc". The 00lexicon.cdc outlines nonstandard lexical items and the 00proper.cdc file shows the proper nouns used by Eve. Eve's approximate ages in each of the 20 files are as follows:

Table 8: Eve Files

File	Age	File	Age	File	Age	File	Age
01	1;6	06	1;9	11	1;11	16	2;1
02	1;6	07	1;9	12	1;11	17	2;2
03	1;7	08	1;9	13	1;12	18	2;2
04	1;7	09	1;10	14	2;0	19	2;3
05	1;8	10	1;10	15	2;1	20	2;3

Sarah was the child of a working class family. There are 139 files in the Sarah corpus covering the ages 2;3 to 5;1. There is also a "00lexicon.cdc" file outlining nonstandard lexical items used by Sarah. Sarah's approximate ages for each of the 139 files are as follows:

Table 9: Sarah Files

File	Age	File	Age	File	Age	File	Age
001	2;3.5	036	2;11.2	071	3;7.30	106	4;4.25

Table 9: Sarah Files

File	Age	File	Age	File	Age	File	Age
002	2;3.7	037	2;11.17	072	3;8.6	107	4;5.4
003	2;3.19	038	2;11.23	073	3;8.12	108	4;5.8
004	2;3.22	039	2;11.30	074	3;8.20	109	4;5.14
005	2;3.26	040	3;0.18	075	3;8.27	110	4;5.22
006	2;3.28	041	3;0.18	076	3;9.3	111	4;5.29
007	2;4.10	042	3;0.27	077	3;9.18	112	4;6.5
008	2;4.12	043	3;1.3	078	3;9.26	113	4;6.11
009	2;4.17	044	3;1.10	079	3;9.26	114	4;6.17
010	2;4.19	045	3;1.17	080	3;10.1	115	4;6.24
011	2;4.26	046	3;1.24	081	3;10.9	116	4;7.0
012	2;5.7	047	3;2.2	082	3;10.16	117	4;7.11
013	2;5.15	048	3;2.10	083	3;10.30	118	4;7.17
014	2;5.25	049	3;2.16	084	3;11.9	119	4;7.24
015	2;5.30	050	3;2.23	085	3;11.16	120	4;8.7
016	2;6.4	051	3;3.7	086	3;11.29	121	4;8.13
017	2;6.13	052	3;3.7	087	4;0.5	122	4;8.20
018	2;6.20	053	3;3.13	088	4;0.14	123	4;9.4
019	2;6.30	054	3;3.20	089	4;0.28	124	4;9.12
020	2;7.5	055	3;3.28	090	4;1.4	125	4;9.19
021	2;7.12	056	3;4.1	091	4;1.11	126	4;9.26
022	2;7.18	057	3;4.9	092	4;1.18	127	4;10.6
023	2;7.28	058	3;4.16	093	4;1.28	128	4;10.21
024	2;8.2	059	3;4.26	094	4;2.1	129	4;10.27
025	2;8.25	060	3;5.1	095	4;2.9	130	4;11.4
026	2;8.25	061	3;5.7	096	4;2.16	131	4;11.13
027	2;9.0	062	3;5.13	097	4;2.23	132	4;11.19
028	2;9.6	063	3;5.20	098	4;2.28	133	4;11.26

Table 9: Sarah Files

File	Age	File	Age	File	Age	File	Age
029	2;9.14	064	3;6.6	099	4;3.7	134	5;0.2
030	2;9.20	065	3;6.16	100	4;3.13	135	5;0.10
031	2;9.29	066	3;6.23	101	4;3.19	136	5;0.16
032	2;10.5	067	3;6.30	102	4;3.26	137	5;0.25
033	2;10.11	68	3;7.9	103	4;4.1	138	5;0.30
034	2;10.20	69	3;7.16	104	4;4.11	139	5;1.6
035	2;10.24	70	3;7.23	105	4;4.18		

Publications using these data should cite:

Brown, R. (1973). *A first language: The early stages*. Cambridge, MA: Harvard University Press.

Carterette and Jones

Edward Carterette
Department of Psychology
University of California
Los Angeles, CA 90024

This subdirectory contains the full text of the speech corpus in Carterette and Jones (1974) donated to the CHILDES by Edward Carterette of the University of California at Los Angeles in 1985. The data were taken from a computer tape from which the book had been made. The characters on that tape were translated first into ASCII and then into UN-IBET. The book is composed of a standard orthographic transcription of conversations and the corresponding text in phonetic orthography on the facing page.

Participants

The data were collected from first-, third- and fifth-grade students as well as adults. The adult sample was similar to the child samples in community, national and regional origin, and socioeconomic status. It was obtained from junior college classes of a city college in California. There were 54 first graders, 48 third graders, 48 fifth graders, and 24 adults. First graders did more giggling, interrupting, and drowning each other out, so more participants were needed to provide a comparable amount of material.

Children from two different schools were used to reduce possible biases of unsuspected sorts. Both schools had children drawn largely from the middle socioeconomic level. The investigation of the effect of socioeconomic status on language development is an important one, but not the subject under investigation here. Moreover, it also requires a norm. It was just this norm for studies of language development of all sorts that this database provides. The sample used all children in a grade who were present when called and who were not excused by reason of foreign language background, marked non-California dialect, or speech impediments. Because regions of the country differ in the phonemes used in speech, it was judged more in keeping with the aims of the study to include only one type of regional speech, which happened to be Southern Californian.

Data Collection Situation

A simple social situation was used. Three children were seated around a small table with a young, friendly adult. The adult greeted the children by name, told them she wanted to find out what children in their grade were interested in, and asked them to talk to each other about anything they wanted to talk about. Some groups required somewhat more encouragement; if so, the adult asked a question or two: "What do you do after school?" or "How many in your family?" Thereafter she said nothing. After the initial warm-up period, which was discarded for the transcription, the speech appeared to be children's normal speech. It was rapid; there were interruptions; it covered every conceivable topic; it was full of slang and noise words; there was give-and-take. This, then, was the situation in which all the child speech samples were recorded.

For the adults, the situation was structured differently. The participants were from elementary psychology classes, so their knowledge of psychological jargon was flattered. They were told that the experiment was investigating small group processes and that the situation was to be completely nondirective. Then they were introduced by first names and told they were at a party. The experimenter excused himself (psychologically) to get the snacks. Again groups of three were always used. Most of the adults did not know each other, whereas the children did. The three-person interaction proved as useful for adults as for children, and the language produced was judged to be normal, everyday conversation, as rapid, slangy, and diverse as any in an unrecorded situation.

As many individuals and as many groups as possible were included, in order to reduce the effect of idiosyncrasies of vocabulary, topic, sentence constructions, pronunciation, and various aspects peculiar to spoken language. However, it was also important to allow sufficient time for each group to warm up and then become thoroughly engrossed in conversation, for otherwise many aspects of oral language suffer.

Jones and Carterette (1963) showed that at least 6,000 words are necessary for stable statistical results, so the goal for the size of each sample was set at 10,000 words per level. It was felt that more than this would require too much time for phonemic transcription, which is very slow. Well over 10,000 words per level were actually transcribed, but more material than that was collected and remains untranscribed.

Transcription

Each tape was first transcribed by a typist, listening with binaural earphones. The instructions were to include all consecutive material, but if some part was incomprehensible to omit the entire utterance. Similarly, if some person was interrupted and did not pick up the thread of the utterance, the whole utterance was to be omitted, but if he or she did resume, then the interruption was to be omitted. The second step was to have the letter transcriptions checked by a research assistant. Next the phoneticians took over. Two formal reliability checks were made. The %pho lines are missing from the last 15% of the adult.cha file. These are in the book and will have to be reentered eventually by hand.

Publications that use these data should cite:

Carterette, E. C., & Jones, M. H. (1974). *Informal Speech: Alphabetic and Phonemic texts with statistical analyses and tables.* Berkeley, CA: University of California Press.
Jones, M. H., & Carterette, E. C. (1963). Redundancy in children's free-reading choices. *Journal of Verbal Learning and Verbal Behavior, 2,* 489–493.

Clark

Eve Clark
Department of Linguistics
Stanford University
Building 100
Stanford, CA 94305 USA
eclark@psych.stanford.edu

This subdirectory contains files from a short-term longitudinal study conducted by Eve Clark during 1976 two-year-old child. The transcripts pay close attention to repetitions, hesitations, and retracings.

Shem was seen on a nearly weekly basis by an observer (Cindy) who became a friend of the family over the course of the year's recording. The recordings were made at Shem's home, except on a few occasions when the parents made the recording because either Cindy or they were away on vacation so Shem would have missed more than one session. The child's name, his home address, his sister's name, the names of his parents, and the observer's name have been changed to preserve their confidentiality. The names of nearby places and institutions remain unchanged.

Shem was from a middle- to upper-middle-class professional family in the Palo Alto area. He was an only child until just after the recordings began when his first sister, Ana, was born. He attended a local day care center (Little Kids' Place) in the mornings, and occasionally went there for a short time in the afternoon. Most of the recording sessions took place at his home. Shem's age and the date (month and day) is noted at the top of each transcript. His date of birth was February 5, 1974. For convenience, the ages for each session are summarized here:

Table 10: Shem Files

Session	Age	Session	Age
shem01	2;2.16	shem21	2;8.15
shem02	2;2.23	shem22	2;8.20
shem03	2;3.2	shem23	2;8.29
shem04	2;3.16	shem24	2;9.1
shem05	2;3.21	shem25	2;9.10
shem06	2;3.28	shem26	2;9.19
shem07	2;4.4	shem27	2;9.27
shem08	2;4.20	shem28	2;10.2

Table 10: Shem Files

Session	Age	Session	Age
shem09	2;4.25	shem29	2;10.14/20
shem10	2;5.2	shem30	2;10.25
shem11	2;5.9	shem31	2;11.1
shem12	2;5.16	shem32	2;11.10
shem13	2;5.23	shem33	2;11.28
shem14	2;5.30	shem34	3;0.5
shem15	2;6.6	shem35	3;0.13
shem16	2;6.27/28	shem36	3;0.20
shem17	2;7.10	shem37	3;1.5
shem18	2;7.18	shem38	3;1.13
shem19	2;7.26	shem39	3;1.27
shem20	2;8.3	shem40	3;2.2

A few sessions are split into two parts if they lasted longer than usual. Most sessions lasted an hour.

Phonology

Shem's pronunciation at the beginning of the recording period was often unclear, and he frequently made more than one attempt to get himself understood. In the transcripts, all repairs are noted, but Shem's pronunciation has been largely normalized for representation in English orthography, except where his meaning remained unclear, or his pronunciation was critical to the overall form of an interchange. Typical features were voicing of intervocalic voiceless stops (whether or not at word boundaries); omission of voiced final stops; voicing of voiceless initial stops; substitutions among fricatives; great variation in vowel quality; extensive reliance on schwa or syllabic /n/ for function words (the syllabic /n/ was typically, but not always a locative preposition); simplification of clusters with loss of postconsonantal /l/ and /r/; initial /l/ often /y/; initial /s/ often /d ~ t/; final /s/ often /t/; final voiced stops often /n/ (e.g., /birn/ for "bird," /wen/ for "red," /bun/ or /bung/ for "bug"); voiceless final stops often replaced by glottal stops (especially /t/, and often /k/); and occasional homorganic voiceless stops as releases to final nasals (e.g., /lawnt/ for "lawn").

Intonation is indicated by punctuation, with a period marking a terminal fall, a question mark marking interrogative rise, an exclamation mark indicating emphatic tone, and a comma indicating continuing or listing contour (slight pause, with sustained level tone, or slight falling but nonterminal tone). The bulk of the transcription is in English orthography for ease of reading, but a few persistent forms are left with glosses more or less in the form Shem produced them. On a few tapes, background conversations (e.g., on the telephone) are omitted from the final transcription.

The data collection was supported by an NSF grant (BNS 75-17126) to E. V. Clark.

Publications using these data should cite one or more of these publications:

Clark, E. V. (1978a). Awareness of language: Some evidence from what children say and do. In R. J. A. Sinclair & W. Levelt (Eds.), *The child's conception of language*. Berlin: Springer Verlag.

Clark, E. V. (1978b). Discovering what words can do. In W. J. D. Farkas & K. Todrys (Eds.), *Papers from the parasession on the lexicon*. Chicago: Chicago Linguistic Society.

Clark, E. (1979). Building a vocabulary: Words for objects, actions and relations. In P. Fletcher & M. Garman (Eds.), *Language acquisition: Studies in first language development*. New York: Cambridge University Press.

Clark, E. V. (1982a). Language change during language acquisition. In M. E. Lamb & A. L. Brown (Eds.), *Advances in child development: Vol. 2*. Hillsdale, NJ: Lawrence Erlbaum Associates.

Clark, E. V. (1982b). The young word maker: A case study of innovation in the child's lexicon. In E. Wanner & L. R. Gleitman (Eds.), *Language acquisition: The state of the art*. Cambridge, MA: Cambridge University Press.

Cornell

Hayes, Donald
346 Uris Hall
Sociology Department
Cornell University
Ithaca, NY 14853 USA

These files are derived from a larger corpus of written and spoken transcripts collected by Donald Hayes and his students. This smaller set of files is the segment of the database that deals specifically with young children learning language. The files can be grouped into several types:

1. **Haas files.** These tapes were recorded to determine how lexical pitch changes across the first months of a child's speech. Taping began at 1;6 and ends at 1;8.

2. **Horn files.** These are samples of speech from two working-class Black families with a three-year-old.

3. **LSNO.** These are files from the Levin-Snow project studying parent–child interaction in the hospital.

4. **MOM files.** These files track several working mothers with their children.

5. **Moore files.** These are dialogs between a male graduate student and his male child aged 1.6.

6. **Nurse files.** These files record nurses in the nursery rooms.

7. **Schacter data.** These three files, beginning with sch*, look at mothers from different social classes.

8. **Wooten data.** These files record a mother with her 4-year-old from Aberdeen, Scotland.

Cruttenden

Alan Cruttenden
Department of Linguistics
University of Manchester
Manchester M13 9PL England
cruttenden@manchester.ac.uk

Alan Cruttenden of the University of Manchester has contributed phonologically transcribed data from two dizygotic twins, Jane and Lucy, from age 1;5 to 3;7. The transcription uses the IPA font. The data were collected at monthly intervals for a total of 25 files for each child. No data were collected from months 4 and 5 and data collected from month 23 onwards is sparse. The data were collected by direct notation and no audiotapes were made.

Error coding has only partially been carried out on these data. Errors that are clearly phonological have been systematically indicated but not coded. Inflectional errors have been indicated but no judgments have been made as to whether they are morphologically or phonologically induced. Syntactic errors have generally been indicated from the stage when the appropriate correct syntax was being used in other utterances. Comments on stress have been included on a comments line where this information is available.

Publications that use these data should cite:

Cruttenden, A. (1978). Assimilation in child language and elsewhere. *Journal of Child Language,* 5, 373–378.

Demetras Trevor

Marty Demetras
Arizona University Affiliated Program
2600 N. Wyatt
Tucson, AZ 85712
demetras@ccit.arizona.edu

This corpus contains 27 files of data collected by M. J. Demetras and John Umbreit between 1985 and 1987 from their son Trevor. Nine sets of four 20-minute conversations between Trevor and his father were recorded over a period of 35 months for a total of 28 sessions. All but one session were transcribed and included as part of this corpus. The context was free play and the participants used a somewhat standard set of toys through the duration of the recordings. Trevor was fairly intelligible and verbal at this stage in development. He also experienced two episodes of disfluency during this period, which was partially captured in the data. Trevor was born on June 3, 1983. Files 15 and 22 are missing.

Table 11: Trevor Files

File	Age	File	Age
01	2;0.27	15*	2;11.13
02	2;0.28	16	2;11.14
03	2;0.29	17	3;0.7
04	2;1.5	18	3;0.8
05	2;6.4	19	3;0.9
06	2;6.5	20	3;1.17
07	2;6.6	21	3;3.4
08	2;6.12	22*	3;3.10
09	2;8.3	23	3;3.12
10	2;8.5	24	3;10.22
11	2;8.7	25	3;10.23
12	2;8.10	26	3;10.24
13	2;10.4	27	3;11.27
14	2;11.11	28	3;11.27

Publications using these data should cite:
Demetras, M. (1989). *Working parents conversational responses to their two-year-old sons.* Working paper. University of Arizona.

Demetras Working

Marty Demetras
Arizona University Affiliated Program
2600 N. Wyatt
Tucson, AZ 85712
demetras@ccit.arizona.edu

This directory contains data from three families, each of which had a 2-year-old son. In each family, both parents worked during the day and the children were in day care. Four 20-minute conversations between the boys and their parents were recorded within a 2-week period of time. The context was free play and the toys varied from session to session. Sessions 2, 3, and 4 were transcribed and included in this corpus. The other sessions are available for future transcription. For one of the families, three additional sets of data (12 sessions) were collected and included in Demetras' (1989) longitudinal analysis of grammatical development and parent–child interactions. Thirteen of the 16 sessions collected for this family were transcribed and included in this corpus.

Table 12: Demetras – Working Files

File	Age	File	Age	File	Age
Michael1	2;2.17	Jimmy1	2;2.13	Jimmy9	2;6.29
Michael2	2;2.18	Jimmy2	2;2.15	Jimmy10	2;7.2
Michael3	2;2.20	Jimmy3	2;2.20	Jimmy11	2;7.4
Michael4	2;2.22	Jimmy4	2;2.24	Jimmy12	2;7.5
		Jimmy5	2;4.26	Jimmy13	2;9.14
Tim1	2;1.27	Jimmy6	2;4.28	Jimmy14	2;9.16
Tim2	2;1.30	Jimmy7	2;4.29	Jimmy15	2;9.22
Tim3	2;2.1	Jimmy8	2;4.30	Jimmy16	2;9.23
Tim4	2;2.6			Jimmy11	2;7.4

Publications using these data should cite:

Demetras, M. (1989a). *Changes in parents' conversational responses: A function of grammatical development.* Paper presented at ASHA, St. Louis, MO.
Demetras, M. (1989b). *Working parents' conversational responses to their two-year-old sons.* University of Arizona.

Evans

Mary Ann Evans
Department of Psychology
University of Guelph
Guelph ON N1G 2W1 Canada
evans@psyadm.css.uoguelph.ca

These transcripts are from 16 dyads of first-grade children at indoor play. They were recorded by Mary Evans in Guelph, Ontario, Canada. The transcripts were prepared from 10 minutes of interaction in about the middle of each play session as specified on the transcripts. The children in the dyads do not represent a random sample of children. Rather, children with ID numbers under 43 were described by their teachers as verbally quiet in kindergarten, whereas other children were consistently verbal or became verbal across the kindergarten year.

Fletcher

Paul Fletcher
Department of Linguistic Science
University of Reading
PO Box 218
Reading RG6 2AA England
llsfletp@reading.ac.uk

This subdirectory contains the Reading corpus of transcripts from 72 British children ages 3, 5, and 7. The participants in the project were Paul Fletcher, Michael Garman, Michael Johnson, Christina Schelleter, and Louisette Stodel. The project was entitled "The standardization of an expressive language assessment procedure" and was supported by Medical Research Council grant no. 68306114N and NATO Collaborative Research grant no. RG84/0135. The aims of this project were as follows:

1. To establish a computer database of the expressive language of British children between 3;0 and 7;0.

2. To identify grammatical and lexical features of this database that were developmentally significant.

3. To apply this information in the identification, assessment, and remediation of language-impaired children. This goal, which arises out of earlier work on LARSP (Crystal, Fletcher, & Garman, 1989), affects all aspects of the database including choice of interlocutor, data collection methods, and transcription decisions.

Elicitation

All data were collected in an interview situation between a female adult and the child. This was a deliberate attempt to mimic the typical initial encounter between a speech therapist and a child who is being assessed. All interviews took place in a quiet area of the nursery or school the child was attending, and lasted for approximately 45 minutes. The elicitation protocol for these sessions included these techniques:

1. Stick-on game (SG). Conversation takes place around a game (supplied by UNISET), consisting of a picture of either a house interior or a farmyard, and an appropriate set of stickers to be located at various points on these pictures.

2. Free/guided conversation (FC). There are no props for this part of the interview. The experimenter asks questions about the child's school and home experiences, and about significant past and future events in the child's life (Christmas, holidays, birthdays, Bonfire Night, and so forth). The aim is to encourage the child to talk, in as spontaneous a way as is possible within the constraints of the situation).

3. Balloon story (BS). The balloon story is a brief picture story, devised by Annette Karmiloff-Smith, to examine children's pronominal reference in discourse (Karmiloff-Smith, 1986).

Transcription and Segmentation

Conventions for transcription were the product of much discussion in the project team; their formal implementation was the work of M. Johnson.

Publications using these data should cite:

Fletcher, P., & Garman, M. (1988). Normal language development and language impairment: Syntax and beyond. *Clinical Linguistics and Phonetics, 2,* 97–114.

Johnson, M. (1986). *A computer-based approach to the analysis of child language data.* University of Reading.

Additional relevant references include:

Crystal, D., Fletcher, P., & Garman, M. (1989). *The grammatical analysis of language disability.* (2nd ed.). London: Cole and Whurr.

Karmiloff-Smith, A. (1986). From meta-processes to conscious access: Evidence from children's metalinguistic and repair data. *Cognition, 23,* 95–147.

Garvey

Catherine Garvey
Route 1, Box 255
Brooksville, ME 04617 USA

This directory contains a set of children's conversational data collected by Catherine Garvey and donated to the CHILDES in 1986. The original corpus consists of 48 files of transcripts of dialogues between two children with no experimenter or other children present. All of the children's names have been replaced with pseudonyms. The children range in age from 2;10 to 5;7. In the original corpus, pairs of children belong to 16 triads of three children. Particular files are always dialogues between two members of each triad. Calling the children in a given triad A, B, and C, there are always three possible pairings: AB, AC, and BC. Data for triads 1, 3, 4, 6, 10, and 11 are not in the CHILDES database. Thus, the database contains only 30 files from 10 triads. There is a file for each of these three pairings for each of the 10 triads.

Table 13: Garvey Triads

Triad	Child	Ages	Files
1	Sue	4;4	suedon, suetim
	Don	3;9	suedon, dontim
	Tim	4;1	dontim, suetim
2	Amy	3;6	amywes, amyann
	Wes	4;1	amywes, wesann
	Ann	4;0	wesann, amyann
3	Hal	4;5	halpat, halivy
	Pat	4;10	halpat, pativy
	Ivy	4;9	halivy, pativy
4	Ari	5;1	arigay, ariken
	Gay	5;2	arigay, kengay
	Ken	5;2	ariken, kengay
5	Pia	4;9	piaval, piaabe
	Val	4;7	piaval, valabe
	Abe	4;9	valabe, piaabe
6	Glo	5;0	glojoy, globob

Table 13: Garvey Triads

Triad	Child	Ages	Files
	Joy	4;9	glojoy, joybob
	Bob	4;11	globob, joybob
7	Fay	5;3	fayjay, faymeg
	Jay	5;0	fayjay, jaymeg
	Meg	5;0	faymeg, jaymeg
8	Gus	4;0	gusleo, guseve
	Leo	4;0	gusleo, leoeve
	Eve	3;11	guseve, leoeve
9	Kay	3;6	kayben, kaydeb
	Ben	3;7	kayben, bendeb
	Deb	3;7	kaydeb, bendeb
10	Ned	5;2	nedima, nedmae
	Ima	5;4	nedima, imamae
	Mae	5;5	nedmae, imamae
11	Bev	5;7	bevflo, bevguy
	Flo	5;1	bevflo, floguy
	Guy	5;2	bevguy, floguy
12	Ida	5;1	idabud, idazoe
	Bud	5;1	idabud, budzoe
	Zoe	5;0	idazoe, budzoe
13	Peg	3;1	pegron, pegjan
	Ron	3;3	pegron, ronjan
	Jan	3;1	pegjan, ronjan
14	Sam	2;11	samian, samava
	Ian	2;10	samian, ianava
	Ava	3;2	samava, ianava
15	Max	3;1	maxnan, maxjim

Table 13: Garvey Triads

Triad	Child	Ages	Files
	Nan	2;10	maxnan, nanjim
	Jim	3;0	maxjim, nanjim
16	Roy	3;2	roykim, royada
	Kim	3;0	roykim, kimada
	Ada	3;3	royada, kimada

The narrative section indicates when an interruption took place; it was sometimes necessary for the observers to intervene, to bring in another bag of toys, to turn on the light switch and caution the children not to turn off the light, or to take one or both children to the bathroom. Speech during these interruptions was not recorded. Conventional orthography is used with a few exceptions such as "gonna," "gotta," and "wanna." Some clearly distorted pronunciations are indicated, such as "beebe bottel" for "baby bottle." When periods, commas, or question marks appear in the text, they indicate utterance final intonation, nonterminal intonation, and interrogatory illocutionary force, respectively. In many scripts however, these punctuation marks are missing, as there was an unfulfilled plan to add transcription for intonation. The transcripts are heavily coded for actions, gestures, proxemics, timing, and intonation. The timing marks are missing for triad #4. Time is indicated in minutes and seconds with a colon separating the minutes and the seconds.

The file "0stats.cdc" gives a variety of statistics computed for these 48 files by Catherine Garvey. These include total time, total words, total utterances, rate of utterance, percentage utterances in an exchange, percentage time in focused interaction, and number of episodes that are longer than nine exchanges. For each child in the pair, this file reports number of words, number of utterances, and words per utterance. A frequent code that occurs on the %com line is $CFA, which stands for "common focus of attention." The symbol $/= followed by a number is used to indicate that some event or focus of attention continues for a certain number of lines.

Publications that use these data should cite:

Garvey, C. (1979). An approach to the study of children's role play. *The Quarterly Newsletter of the Laboratory of Comparative Human Cognition, 12*.
Garvey, C., & Hogan, R. (1973). Social speech and social interaction: Egocentrism revisited. *Child Development, 44*, 562–568.

Gathercole

Virginia C. Gathercole
School of Psychology
University of Wales
Bangor, Gwynedd LL57 2DG UK
v.c.gathercole@bangor.ac.uk

This directory consists of 16 files of cross-sectional data of children aged 2;9 to 6;6 donated to the CHILDES by Virginia Gathercole in 1987. There are four children at each age. These four children were observed at school while eating lunch with an experimenter present on four separate occasions. These data are arranged into files, named by date of collection. Dr. Gathercole would like those researchers requesting the data to contact her to discuss the use of the data. The following is a list of the target participants in these files by age:

Table 14: Gathercole Children

Child	Sex	Age	Sample	Child	Sex	Age	Sample
BRI	M	5;11	04	LUK	M	4;11	02
		6;2.15	07			5;2	06
		6;4.15	12			5;3	09
		6;6	16			5;5	14
ERI	M	3;2	11	MAT	M	4;7	02
		3;3	16			4;10	06
ERK	M	4;6	02			4;11	09
ERN	F	2;10	01			5;1	14
		3;0	05	MEG	F	3;6	03
		3;3	11			3;9	08
		3;4	13			3;10	10
GIL	M	4;3	02			4;0	15
		4;6	06	MIC	M	2;10	01
		4;7	09			3;0.15	05
		4;9	14			3;3	11
JEF	M	2;9	01			3;4	13

Table 14: Gathercole Children

Child	Sex	Age	Sample	Child	Sex	Age	Sample
		2;11	05	NIC	F	5;4	04
LIL	F	3;10	03			5;7	07
		4;2	08			5;9	12
		4;3	10			5;10	16
		4;5	15	SAA	F	5;8	04
SAR	F	3;6	03			6;1	07
		3;9	08			6;0.15	12
		3;10	10			6;2	16
		4;0	15				

In addition, the files contain speech by various other nontargeted children and adults. Precise ages for these additional speakers have not been provided.

Table 15: Nontargeted Children

Child	Sex	Samples	Adult	Sex	Samples
BRY	M	03,06,07,09,12,16	BOB	F	all except 02
SHA	?	02	PAT	F	05,10
RAC	F	01-04,06-08,12,16	LLE	F	01-04,06,09
ALY	F	15	GAY	F	04,08
KEN	M	13	VIR	F	all (investigator)
KEI	M	01,04,05,09	TEA	?	08,10,12,13
NAT	M	07,16	MOT	M	04
ALI	M	06	CHI	?	01,03,04,06,07
CON	F	01,08	UNC	?	02,04,11,15
CHR	?	01,02,06			

Publications that use these data should cite:
Gathercole, V. (1980). *Birdies like birdseed the bester than buns: A study of relational comparatives and their acquisition.* Unpublished doctoral dissertation. University of Kansas.

Gathercole / Burns

Virginia C. Gathercole
School of Psychology
University of Wales
Bangor, Gwynedd LL57 2DG UK
v.c.gathercole@bangor.ac.uk

Burns, Rebecca
School of Education
University of Miami
5202 University Drive, Merrick 312
Coral Gables, Fl 33124
rburns@umiami.ir.miami.edu

Cross-sectional data were collected from 12 Scottish children aged 3:0 to 6;4 at the Nursery of the Department of Psychology at the University of Edinburgh. There are four children at each of three age levels: 3-year-olds (mean age 3;2.15), 4-year-olds (mean age: 4;2), 5-year-olds (mean age: 5;0). Four Scottish adults interacted with the children: two of the children's teachers, one sevitor of the nursery, and one mother of one of the children. The first three had educations through secondary school; the last had attended college. Each group of four Scottish children was videotaped in 8 half-hour sessions for a total of 24 sessions. Each adult participated in two sessions with each group. The structured sessions involved block tasks and art tasks. All utterances were transcribed from the videotapes, along with extensive information on the nonlinguistic contexts of the utterances. The data were reformatted into CHAT by Rebecca Burns.

Publications using these data should cite:

Gathercole, V. (1986). The acquisition of the present perfect: explaining differences in the speech of Scottish and American children. *Journal of Child Language, 13*, 537–560.

Gleason

Jean Berko Gleason
Department of Psychology
Boston University
64 Cummington St.
Boston MA 02215 USA
gleason@bu.edu

This directory contains files donated to the CHILDES in 1988 by Jean Berko Gleason. The data were collected in the context of project called "Studies in the Acquisition of Communicative Competence," which was funded for 3 years by NSF grant #BNS 75-21909 to Jean Berko Gleason at Boston University. The participants are 24 children aged 2;1 to 5;2 who were recorded in interactions (a) with their mother, (b) with their father, and (c) at the dinner table. The 24 participants were recruited through nursery schools and similar networks, and were from middle-class families in the greater Boston area. There were 12 boys and 12 girls. All families were White, and English was spoken as a first language in all families. Each child was seen three times: once in the laboratory with the mother; once in the laboratory with the father; and once at dinner with both mother and father. The laboratory sessions were videotaped and audiotaped, and the dinners were only audiotaped. Laboratory sessions included: (a) play with a toy auto, (b) reading a picture book, and (c) playing store.

The parent was encouraged to divide each 30-minute lab session about evenly among these activities. In addition, each child was presented with a small gift during the lab session, and the gift-giving interchange was also recorded.

Table 16: Gleason Files

S#	Visit#	Date	Type	Child	Birth	Age
1	1	6/11/76	Father	Andy	5/23/72	4;0.18
	2	6/25/76	Mother			4;1.2
	3	6/23/76	Dinner			4;2.0
2	1	6/15/76	Mother	Bobby	4/27/72	4;1.19
	2	9/24/76	Father			4;4.28
	3	6/28/76	Home			4;2.1
3	1	6/23/76	Father	Charlie	7/6/73	2;11.17
	2	7/14/76	Mother			3;0.8
	3	7/7/76	Dinner			3;0.1
4	1	6/26/76	Father	David	5/7/72	4;1.19

Table 16: Gleason Files

S#	Visit#	Date	Type	Child	Birth	Age
	2	7/10/76	Mother			4;2.3
	3	7/8/76	Dinner			4;2.1
5	1	7/13/76	Mother	Edward	4/1/72	4;3.12
	2	8/7/76	Father			4;4.6
	3	8/4/76	Dinner			4;4.3
6	1	7/14/76	Mother	Frank	5/14/71	5;2.0
	2	7/24/76	Father			5;2.10
	3	7/21/76	Dinner			5;2.7
7	1	7/23/76	Mother	Guy	7/3/73	3;0.20
	2	8/7/76	Father			3;1.4
	3	7/8/76	Dinner			3;0.5
8	1	7/27/76	Mother	Helen	8/25/71	4;11.2
	2	8/4/76	Father			4;11.10
	3	1/8/76	Dinner			4;4.14
9	1	9/22/76	Mother	Isadora	3/15/73	3;6.7
	2	10/16/76	Father			3;7.1
	3	10/6/76	Dinner			3;6.21
10	1	9/28/76	Mother	John	8/10/72	4;1.18
	2	10/27/76	Father			4;2.17
	3	11/2/76	Dinner			4;2.23
11	1	9/29/76	Mother	Katie	7/27/73	3;2.2
	2	10/18/76	Father			3;2.21
	3	unknown	Dinner			
12	1	9/30/76	Mother	Laurel	10/24/73	2;11.6
	2	11/13/76	Father			3;0.20
	3	11/16/76	Dinner			3;0.23
13	1	10/6/76	Mother	Martin	4/11/74	2;5.26

Table 16: Gleason Files

S#	Visit#	Date	Type	Child	Birth	Age
	2	10/23/76	Father			2;6.12
	3	11/3/76	Dinner			2;6.23
14	1	10/7/76	Mother	Nanette	9/3/74	2;1.4
	2	10/23/76	Father			2;1.20
	3	11/9/76	Dinner			2;2.6
15	1	10/16/76	Father	Olivia	8/4/73	3;2.12
	2	11/20/76	Mother			3;3.16
	3	11/2/76	Dinner			3;2.29
16	1	10/27/76	Mother	Patricia	5/18/74	2;5.9
	2	11/18/76	Father			2;6.0
	3	11/17/76	Dinner			2;5.30
17	1	10/28/76	Mother	Richard	2/10/74	2;8.18
	2	11/30/76	Father			2;9.20
	3	12/2/76	Dinner	(no file)		2;9.22
18	1	1/14/77	Father	Susan	11/11/73	3;2.3
	2	2/1/77	Mother			3;2.21
	3	unknown	Dinner			
19	1	2/24/77	Mother	Theresa	2/24/73	4;0.0
	2	5/14/77	Father			4;2.20
	3	unknown	Dinner			
20	1	4/19/77	Father	Ursula	9/19/73	3;7.0
	2	5/14/77	Mother			3;7.25
	3	?	Dinner	(no file)		
21	1	4/11/77	Mother	Victor	12/20/74	2;3.22
	2	5/23/77	Father			2;5.3
	3	unknown	Dinner			
22	1	5/3/77	Father	Wanda	5/10/73	3;11.22

Table 16: Gleason Files

S#	Visit#	Date	Type	Child	Birth	Age
	2	5/21/77	Mother			4;0.11
	3	unknown	Dinner			
23	1	2/15/78	Mother	William	11/27/75	2;2.16
	2	3/18/78	Father			2;3.22
	3	3/17/78	Dinner			2;3.21
24	1	3/4/79	Mother	Xavia		
	2	17/7/79	Father			
	3	12/9/79	Dinner			

Publications that make use of this corpus should cite one or more of these publications:

Bellinger, D., & Gleason, J. (1982). Sex differences in parental directives to young children. *Journal of Sex Roles, 8*, 1123–1139.

Gleason, J. B. (1980). The acquisition of social speech and politeness formulae. In H. Giles, W. P. Robinson, & S. M. P. (Eds.), *Language: Social psychological perspectives*. Oxford: UK: Pergamon.

Gleason, J. B., & Greif, E. (1983). Men's speech to young children. In B. Thorne, C. Kramerae, & N. Henley (Eds.), *Language, Gender and Society*. Rowley, MA: Newbury.

Gleason, J. B., Perlmann, R. Y., & Greif, E. B. (1984). What's the magic word? Learning language through routines. *Discourse Processes, 6*, 493–502.

Greif, E. B., & Gleason, J. B. (1980). Hi, thanks and goodbye: More routine information. *Language in Society, 9*, 159-166.

Masur, E., & Gleason, J. B. (1980). Parent–child interaction and the acquisition of lexical information during play. *Developmental Psychology, 16*, 404–409.

Menn, L., & Gleason, J. B. (1986). Babytalk as a stereotype and register: Adult reports of children's speech patterns. In J. A. Fishman (Ed.), *The Fergusonian Impact, Volume I*. Berlin: Mouton de Gruyter.

Haggerty

This directory contains a single file with data taken from Haggerty (1929). This source is a published article which records what a 2-year-old child said in a day. Haggerty was on the faculty of the Department of Educational Psychology of the University of Minnesota. The child, Helen, was born in 1903 and thus this file also has a certain historical interest. The data were recorded by hand by the researcher and two assistants over the approximately 9.5 waking hours in Helen's day. The following passage is taken from Haggerty's introduction to the article.

The writer in the following pages reports the exact conversation carried on in the length of one day by her daughter, Helen, who was two years, seven and a half months old at the time. Helen was born in Anderson, Indiana, April 24, 1903. This record was made December 12, 1905. The record begins at seven o'clock in the morning when Helen awakened, and is continuous throughout the entire day, excepting for the period of the afternoon nap which occurred between 12:45 P.M. and 3:45 P.M. The record closes at 7:30 P.M., when Helen went to sleep for the night. With the aid of two others who gave occasional assistance, the writer was able to record every word uttered by Helen during the day. This record therefore represents in entirety the linguistic expression of a two-and-a-half-year-old child during the approximate nine and a half hours of her waking day. This day was a representative day in Helen's life and was not unlike other days in that period of her life. The persons most frequently referred to were her father and mother, her baby sister, Margaret, who was one year and four days old, her grandmother, who was present, Carrie, a high school girl who lived in the home, and Nancy, a young seamstress, who took great interest in the children, and who was frequently employed in the home.

Publications using this data should cite:

Haggerty, L. (1929). What a two-and-one-half-year-old child said in one day. *Journal of Genetic Psychology, 38*, 75–100.

Hall

William S. Hall
Department of Psychology
University of Maryland
College Park, MD 20742 USA
hall@bss3.umd.edu

This directory contains a large database of conversational interactions from 39 children aged 4;6 to 5;0. The files were computerized by Bill Hall of the University of Maryland and donated to the CHILDES in 1984. They were first placed into CHAT format in 1987, but this work was redone from the originals in 1991 to clear up additional problems. Although the conversion to CHAT was generally straightforward, it was not possible to code overlaps by pairs. Instead, the overlap marked was coded by using the [%^] sign for without any attempt to indicate the matches between overlap markers.

The corpus was collected with the purpose of providing a solid basis for comparing vocabulary usage in different socioeconomic and ethnic groups. This section describes how the corpus was collected in a way to ensure that spontaneous speech would be recorded in a variety of natural situations. These situations are characterized in as much detail as possible, to provide users of these data with an accurate picture of the conditions under which they were collected.

Participants were 39 preschool children (4;6 to 5;0) divided approximately equally according to race and socioeconomic status (SES) as follows: middle-class Black, middle-class White, working-class Black, and working-class White. The working-class children in our sample were attending federally-funded preschools: the middle-class children were in private preschools. The working-class Black children were in all-Black classes, with Black teachers, whereas the middle-class Black children were in interracial classes with both Black and White teachers. None of the Black target children were in the same classes as any of the White target children in our sample.

Language samples were collected over 2 consecutive days for each child. On each day, an average of about 150 minutes of conversation were recorded, distributed among different situations. Most importantly, the situations in which the data were gathered were both natural and varied. Conversations were taped in a variety of situations at home, at school, and en route between the two. The children and their families were aware that they were being taped, but this seems to have caused little if any disruptions of normal activities. There are occasional references (although relatively few) to the fact that the tape recorder is on; but the conversations are natural. Reading the transcripts, one can clearly sense that the families are not "putting on an act" for the tape recorder; they tend to ignore it almost completely. Even if the presence of the tape recorder does exert some effect, the fact remains that there is no other method, apart from deception, that would offer a less obtrusive way of obtaining natural data.

The taping equipment was also chosen to minimize any disruption of normal conversation or activities. The children wore vests with wireless microphones sewn in; their movements were not restricted, and they seemed quickly to forget about having them on. The use of wireless microphones made possible the inclusion of speech by the target children that might not otherwise have been recorded, including monologues spoken while the child was out of the hearing of any visible listener. Field workers clipped microphones to their ties. Although other adults and nontarget children in the study did not wear microphones, the two microphones used were, in general, sensitive enough to pick up significant verbal interaction with the children in the study. Portable tape recorders enabled data collection in a number of different settings, for example, in homes, shops, moving cars, and on sidewalks. The mobility achieved in this way would not have been possible with videotapes; although videotapes would provide more complete data in some respects, their use would have been far more disruptive.

The effects of the experimenter's race were minimized by using a Black field worker with Black families and a White field worker with White families. In the collection of data, the field workers tried to be as unobtrusive as possible. They rarely initiated conversations, but if spoken to, attempted to respond naturally. One of the field worker's responsibilities was to provide a verbal description of the context. For the purposes of this research, the context included: where the recording took place, where the participant was, who the interactants were and what they were doing. Descriptions of context often included what happened prior and subsequent to, as well as simultaneous with, the verbal interaction.

In order to sample situational variations in language, each child was recorded in a series of 10 temporal situations, which can be grouped into three basic categories: Home, School, and Transition. The Home data consists of tapes made in the following situations: prior to school in the morning, arriving home from school, before dinner, during dinner, and before bed. Each of these took place in or near the child's home, and includes approximately 30 minutes of conversation (15 minutes on each of the days taping was done). Particular segments of activities are missing from particular files. In BOO, the dinner segment was taped outside on the street. In TOS there is no dinner segment. In JAF and ANC there are no directed-activity segments. The target children were between 4;6 and 5;0 during the taping. In each of the four groups, there were more male than female target children. The makeup of the families differs somewhat from one group to another. The social class and ethnic status of the children is as follows: Participants GRC, LEA, and GAS in the White Profession-

Table 17: Hall Children

Class/Status	Target Children
White Prof	ZOR, GRC, MAA, JUB, TOH, GAT, TOS, JOB, ROB, LEA, GAS
Black Prof	JAF, ANC, KIF, REF,VOH, MIM, BOM, BRD, DED, TRH, CHJ
White Work	SUT, STL, BOO, BRH, KAO, DAL, SAT, MIG, KAG
Black Work	ROG, ANL, TRC, KMF, KIG, PAG, DEG, ROJ, MIS, LEF

al group have taperecordings, but no transcripts yet. A speaker is considered present if there are more than 100 words spoken at home by speaker or speakers in that category. For example, there was a brother of the target child present in 5 of the 11 Black middle-class families in our sample, that is, in 45% of these families, but only in 3 (that is 33%) of the White working-class families. In all the families in our sample, both the experimenter and the target child spoke more than 100 words at home.

Table 18: Other Hall Participants

Speaker Categories	Black Middle Class (N=11)	White Middle Class (N=9)	Black Working Class (N=10)	White Working Class (N=9)
Brother	5 (45)	4 (44)	6 (60)	3 (33)
Sister	4 (36)	0 (0)	6 (60)	1 (11)
Male Child	3 (27)	1 (11)	4 (40)	5 (56)
Female Child	3 (27)	0 (0)	3 (30)	2 (22)
Mother	10 (91)	9 (100)	10 (100)	8 (89)
Father	8 (73)	6 (67)	3 (30)	4 (44)
Grandmother	0 (0)	1 (11)	4 (40)	1 (11)
Grandfather	0 (0)	1 (11)	0 (0)	0 (0)
Male Adult	1 (9)	1 (11)	4 (40)	3 (33)
Female Adult		2 (22)	3 (30)	5 (56)

Participants GRC, LEA, and GAS in the White Professional group have taperecordings, but no transcripts yet. A speaker is considered present if there are more than 100 words spoken at home by speaker or speakers in that category. For example, there was a brother of the target child present in 5 of the 11 Black middle-class families in our sample, that is, in 45% of these families, but only in 3 (that is 33%) of the White working-class families. In all the families in our sample, both the experimenter and the target child spoke more than 100 words at home

These transcripts were not coded originally in the CHAT format. Please use caution when using the CLAN programs, because it is possible that some divergences from CHAT could lead to inaccuracies in certain analyses. A special code, <original text> [*] [new text], is used to indicate any of three types of structures in this corpus:

1.   errors

2.   preferred speech (i.e., standard English for nonstandard forms)

3.   estimated intent

When reformatting the data into CHAT, it was impossible to distinguish these three types of codings from one another. It is clear that many of these notations in the corpus refer to alternatives rather than errors. In addition, the phonological transcriptions have not yet been changed to UNIBET. Overlaps were marked in the original, but the direction of the overlap was not marked. We have used the CHAT symbol [<>] for these overlaps. It means unclear overlap and not "overlap both precedes and follows" in this particular corpus

Publications using these data should cite:

Hall, W. S., Nagy, W. E., & Linn, R. (1984). *Spoken words: Effects of situation and social group on oral word usage and frequency*. Hillsdale, NJ: Erlbaum.

Hall, W. S., Nagy, W. E., & Nottenburg, G. (1981). *Situational variation in the use of internal state words*. Champaign, IL: University of Illinois.

Hall, W. S., & Tirre, W. C. (1979). *The communicative environment of young children: Social class, ethnic and situational differences*. Champaign, IL: University of Illinois.

Higginson

Roy P. Higginson
77750 Calle Nogales
La Quinta, CA 92253-3311
rhigginson@ucsd.edu

This corpus contains 21 files, recorded in 1983 and 1984. The files are named according to the date they were recorded. All of the children's utterances are coded phonetically on the %pho tier and lexically on the main tier.

The project was funded in part by the Department of Anthropology at Washington State University, in part by the Sigma Xi Scientific Research Society, and in part from private funds of the researcher. The goals of the project were to examine the earliest stages of language development and to investigate the processes that children use to establish their lexica. Data was collected by making audio and video recordings of children in natural, unstructured play sessions in their homes. Each recording session was approximately 45 minutes long. First draft transcriptions were made from the video recordings by the researcher and these were then checked against the audio recordings to verify the transcripts. Phonetic transcriptions of the children's utterances were then prepared from the audio recordings and inserted into the transcripts at the appropriate places.

April was born April 22, 1981. She was studied between ages 1;10 and 2;11. She was the only child of an undergraduate student. Her mother and father were divorced; she lived with her mother at the university. Her mother was a native English speaker. There are 3.15 hours of natural observations in the participant's home.

May was born March 14, 1982. She was 0;11 at the beginning of the study. She was the only child of graduate students. Her mother was well on in her second pregnancy. Both parents were native English speakers. They were both graduate students working on masters' degrees. There are 1.75 hours of natural observations in the participant's home.

Table 19: Higginson Files

File	Age	File	Age	File	Age	File	Age
apr01	1;10	may01	0;11	jun05	1;5	jun10	1;7
apr02	2;1	may02	0;11	jun06	1;5	jun11	1;8
apr03	2;1	jun01	1;3	jun07	1;6	jun12	1;8
apr04	2;9	jun02	1;4	jun08	1;7	jun13	1;8
apr05	2;10	jun03	1;4	jun09	1;7	jun14	1;9
apr06	2;11	jun04	1;5				

June was born August 16, 1982. She was 1;3 at the beginning of the study and 1;9 at the end. She was the only child of graduate students. Both her mother and father were native English speakers. There are 12 hours of natural observations in the participant's home, which is in university accommodations

Phonetic Transcriptions

A computerized version of a modified IPA is used throughout the transcriptions. Wherever possible the standard character has been used to represent the modified IPA symbol. Exceptions to this are:

@ = mid, central, lax vowel	%= mid, central, tense vowel
O = mid, back, lax vowel	E = mid, front, lax vowel
A = low, front, tense vowel	U = high, back, lax vowel
Q = mid, front, lax, rounded vowel	

S = voiceless, palatal fricative	Z = voiced, palatal fricative
C = voiceless, palatal affricate	J = voiced, palatal affricate
T = voiceless, interdental fricative	6 = voiced, interdental fricative
P = voiceless, bilabial fricative	B = voiced, bilabial fricative
9 = voiced, velar nasal	? = glottal stop

V(n) = vowel nasalization	C. = syllabic consonant
C(w) = consonant labialization	C' = unreleased consonant
V(w) = vowel rounding/raising	

Aspiration of voiceless stops is assumed and, therefore, not included in normal transcription. When the expected aspiration is absent it is noted on the %com tier. When the aspiration is unusually heavy it is marked in the transcription by C(h). Stress is only commented upon when it deviates from the normal English stress pattern. Information about stress, pitch, and intonation appears on the %com tier. Throughout the phonetic transcriptions, indecipherable segments are shown as dashes.

Publications using these data should cite:

Higginson, R. P. (1985). *Fixing-assimilation in language acquisition.* Unpublished doctoral dissertation. Washington State University.

Howe

Christine Howe
Department of Psychology
Strathclyde University
155 George Street
Glasgow GIIRDUK Scotland

This directory contains transcripts from 16 of the 24 Scottish mother–child pairs observed by Christine Howe while playing with toys in their homes in Glasgow. Each pair was recorded twice and the recordings are 40 minutes in duration. The data was coded extensively for actions and situations. The children are aged 1;6 to 1;8 at the first recording and 1;11 to 2;1 at the second recording. There are two files per participant, thus the corpus contains 32 data files.

The procedure for participant recruitment was to place a notice in the local newspaper. The most straightforward method of obtaining a reasonable sample of mothers and children would have been random or quota sampling from a local authority list. Unfortunately, the local authority in question refused to cooperate and more indirect methods had to be used. As a start, an article was written for the local newspaper explaining the aims of the study in deliberately vague terms and asking mothers to volunteer children in the age range of 15 to 18 months. Notices making similar requests were posted in likely public places, including doctors' waiting rooms, baby clinics, university common rooms and centers for further education. A social worker persuaded one of her clients to take part. Finally, a month after recruitment had started, health visitors from two of the baby clinics made contact with offers of help. One suggested sitting in on an afternoon session and asking attending mothers to participate. This was done. The other offered names and addresses of every mother with a child of the right age in her area. The first eight in the alphabetical list were contacted and six said they were interested in taking part. By this time, some of the first volunteers had marshaled their friends into participating, and at the end of the period available for sampling, 33 mothers had volunteered their children. Two mothers were considered unsuitable because they had delegated childcare to a grandmother and an employed nanny. The remaining mothers had volunteered children in the age range of 13 to 21 months. It seemed sensible to choose the mothers with the 24 children nearest in age to the mean of 17 months and use others for pilot work.

Most of the final group lived in a small university town or nearby villages. Despite the fact that sampling was anything but random, the group was represented well by gender, birth order, and social class of family. Twelve children were boys and 12 were girls. Seven were only children, seven were the youngest of two, four were the oldest of two, four were the youngest of three, and two were twins without other siblings. The fathers of 13 children had professional or managerial occupations, whereas the fathers of the remaining 11 children had skilled or semiskilled manual occupations. The first group was designated "middle class" and the second group "working class," The following table shows the sex, birth order, social class, and recruitment method for the children (all identified by pseudonyms).

Table 20: Howe Children

Name	Sex	Birth Order	Social Class	Method
Barry	Male	3rd of 3	Working	Clinic
Eileen	Female	Only	Working	Clinic
Faye	Female	1st of 2	Middle	Other Mother
Graham	Male	1st of 2	Middle	Notice
Ian	Male	2nd of 2	Working	Article
Jason	Male	1st of 2	Middle	Notice
Kevin	Male	2nd of 2	Middle	Article
Lucy	Female	2nd of 2	Middle	Other Mother
Melanie	Female	1st of 2	Working	Clinic
Nicola	Female	3rd of 3	Working	Clinic
Oliver	Male	Only	Middle	Other Mother
Philip	Male	2nd of 2	Working	Article
Richard	Male	2nd of 2	Middle	Article
Sally	Female	Only	Middle	Article
Wayne	Male	Only	Working	Article
Yvonne	Female	Only	Working	Social Worker

Each session was videotaped in the home. The first 20 minutes consisted of a play session with the children's own toys and the second 20 minutes consisted of a play session with a special set of toys presented in the following order:

1. jigsaw puzzle,
2. plastic postbox with holes in the top for geometric shapes,
3. plastic doll with clothes, teaset, cot, and brush,
4. lorry,
5. jeep and horsebox,
6. model zoo animals with fences, cages, and keeper,
7. interchangeable heads, arms, and legs which could be assembled into postmen, firemen, and policemen,
8. cardboard building blocks with pictures on every face,

9.   fluffy puppet, and

10. picture story.

Once recording sessions were completed, the tapes were immediately transcribed. The videotapes were played back in the order of recording on a video taperecorder connected to a television screen and an audio taperecorder. The transcriber sat 6 feet from the screen holding an electrically powered pad that moved paper across a frame at the rate of 6 inches per minute. The rolls of paper used with this device had lines at 1/4-inch intervals. Thus, it was possible to know within 2 1/2 seconds when any mark on the paper was made, and 2 1/2 seconds became the basic time interval for analysis.

The moving paper device, the audio taperecorder set to record and the video taperecorder set to playback were started in that order. Watching only the child, the transcriber noted changes of action and object using a short-hand code. The code essentially used hieroglyphics to represent actions, including gaze, and the first two letters of names to represent the objects of actions. Every time the child vocalized, a dash was drawn on the left of the paper to be filled in later. Every vocalization was being re-recorded on audiotape. The second tape was replayed and the child's behavior transcribed in the same way. Then the audio taperecorder was switched off and the whole procedure repeated for the mother. The transcription of all other participants required a third run.

The next stage was transcribing the vocalizations and inserting them in the behavioral record. English words were transcribed as English words and other sounds were transcribed with some attempt to represent them using English syllables. Speakers varied in their intelligibility and the tapes varied in the amount of background noise. The mean percent of intelligible utterances was 94% for the children and 98% for the mothers. Reliability of transcription and coding completed a year later, resulted in 91% agreement for transcription and 83% agreement for the nonvocal behavior and speech in every 2.5 second period where speech occurred. Mean Length of Utterances and Type–Token Ratios for each recording session are presented below:

Table 21: Howe MLU and TTR

Name	1st Recording		2nd Recording	
	MLU	TTR	MLU	TTR
Barry	1.30	0.27	2.56	0.20
Eileen	1.47	0.18	1.57	0.38
Faye	1.27	0.17	1.65	0.23
Graham	1.09	0.26	1.32	0.51
Ian	1.53	0.38	2.04	0.41
Jason	1.00	0.17	1.17	0.40
Kevin	1.16	0.45	1.87	0.50

Table 21: Howe MLU and TTR

Lucy	1.09	0.17	1.15	0.23
Melanie	1.19	0.43	1.55	0.41
Nicola	1.21	0.21	1.67	0.55
Oliver	1.53	0.23	2.04	0.23
Philip	1.22	0.17	1.54	0.26
Richard	1.30	0.16	2.13	0.19
Sally	1.33	0.39	1.98	0.44
Wayne	1.33	0.18	1.39	0.26
Yvonne	1.72	0.36	1.69	0.37

Publications using these data should cite:

Howe, C. (1981). *Acquiring language in a conversational context*. New York: Academic Press.

Korman

Myron Korman
4218 State Street
Erie, PA 16508 USA

This subdirectory contains the speech of British mothers to infants during the infant's first year. These data are from the Myron Korman's doctoral dissertation. The project focused on maternal speech interactions with preverbal infants. The data were collected in Britain from middle-class mothers with their first children. The children ranged in age from 6 weeks at the outset to 16 weeks at the end of the project.

These data focus on the language of mothers of infant children. They are useful for understanding the input to the infant, but not for studying the child's vocalizations, because these vocalizations are quite primitive and there is no attempt to capture the vocalizations in phonetic detail. Rather the focus is on the functions and pause characteristics of the maternal input.

The data were reformatted into CHAT in 1992. There are five files from each of the six mothers. The ages of the child for these five files are 6, 7, 11, 15, and 16 weeks. The main tier has utterances that are marked either as ATT for "attentional" or TUR for "turn-constructional." The codes for the %spa tier are given in the 0funct.cdc file. In addition, the codes $t and $c indicate repetitions of content or temporal structure. The recordings at 7, 11, and 15 weeks have a %tim tier that contains two types of timing information. The first number gives the length of phrase in seconds; the second number gives the length of the pause after the utterance in seconds. When the mother is not talking and the tape recorder goes on and off, an @New Episode marker is inserted.

Participants

Participants were six primiparous mothers from the greater Nottingham community. They had been contacted through introductions and referrals made by health visitors serving health centers local to their area. Mothers were told that the experimenter was interested in the development of their infant's vocalization over time.

Every effort was made to acquire a homogeneous but balanced study sample. All mothers were in their 20s and all were middle class. All (save one who had been completing a first degree) had worked prior to marriage and pregnancy. Three were breast feeders and three used a bottle. The infants were three boys and three girls. The following table provides an account of various vital statistics of each family in the study.

Table 22: Korman Mother Characteristics

	La.	Gl.	Cr.	Hi.	St.	Gi.
Mother's Age	27	26	23	25	27	25
Occupation	Teacher	Clerical	Student	Nurse	Teacher	Chemist
Feeding	Breast	Breast	Bottle	Bottle	Bottle	Breast
Husband	Police	Chemist	Clerk	Plumber	Photog	Chemist
Infant's Sex	Female	Female	Female	Male	Male	Male

Data Collection

Recordings were made of each infant's auditory experience in the home for the whole of 24-hour periods. These recordings were made without an experimenter present and included a continuous record of the whole of all mothers throughout the day. Video recordings were made of the mother in the home. Videotapings were limited to three monthly sessions nearest to the end, the midpoint, and the beginning of the period under investigation (at 7, 11, and 15 weeks). Audio records were made at fortnightly intervals beginning at 6 and ending at 16 weeks. The recording apparatus consisted of a Revox 4000 reel-to-reel tape recorder, a voice key, a small lavaliere microphone, and 50 feet of thin wire.

Audio Sessions

Audio records were made at weeks 6, 8, 10, 12, 14, and 16. The sample was split into two groups of three infants each, and the groups were recorded on alternate weeks. It was explained that the study concerned the development of the infant's vocalization over time. Mothers were shown the operation of the device and asked to keep the microphone pinned near to the infant at all times. The apparatus was usually dropped off in mid-morning and picked up the following day at approximately the same time. In each household, a hiding place was found and the equipment, except for the wire and microphone, was always out of view. All households were on two floors and in each instance the length of wire was checked to see if it allowed access to all floors and rooms before recording began.

Video Sessions

Videotaping took place in the participants' homes in a room of their own choosing (usually a front or "best" room). Sessions were held at a time of day that each mother had indicated their infant would be most alert and active. Most sessions took place around midday. Mothers were asked to "play with the baby as you would normally do" and no other instructions were given or restrictions imposed. There was no attempt to "standardize" the location of taping sessions or the positioning of mother and infant. Mothers were never discouraged from stopping to chat with the experimenter and short breaks in the play activity were common. Each mother was simply asked to play with the baby in their normal manner wherever, whenever, and however it suited them to do so. This is not to say that the purpose of these sessions was not clear to each mother (i.e., to play with the baby), but to point up the fact that control of the activity in each session was left as much as possible in the hands of the mothers. The sessions themselves were intended to be as relaxed and non-restrictive as possible so as not to constrict or inhibit the mothers' natural responsiveness under the circumstances. Three toys were offered to provide an interactive alternative (a monkey hand puppet, a rattle, and a pop-up toy), but mothers were not encouraged to use them. In each session mothers could use their infants' own toys, which were usually close at hand. The play sessions were, for the most part, friendly social visits during which the mother was asked to play or interact with her infant while a video record was made. A typical session might consist of the experimenter and mother first having coffee and a chat, the mother preparing the area and the baby for play, the recorded play sessions themselves, which stopped at the mothers' convenience or the infant's continuance, and then perhaps another cup of coffee and a further casual discussion of the activity just finished, the infant's responsivity and growth generally, or the cost of coffee at Sainsbury's.

Pause Analysis

A pause was defined as "any maternal silence of longer than 300 ms which ended at: (a) another maternal utterance, (b) an interruption from the experimenter, or (c) an intruding and other than vocal interactive sound produced by the mother, such as rattle shaking or tapping noises." As a consequence, this procedure resulted in the scoring of certain maternal pauses whose duration, although long, was nonetheless populated with some form of interactive behavior from one or the other of the partners in any exchange. Those especially long pauses that are scored will be made up of: a maternal vocal silence in anticipation of, or in response to, some infant behavior or some maternal activity that was done in complete silence.

Timing Procedures

The following timing procedures were used in analysis of the eighteen video observations of the present study. Videotaped interactions were copied onto audiotape cassettes and timings were then undertaken with a hand held stop watch and a tape recorder. Maternal vocal behavior was timed from the perceived end of a phrase to the end of the next sequential phrase. Pauses were then timed from the end of the same first phrase to the onset of the second phrase and the durations of each sequential phrase and pause determined. Each set of timings was undertaken for a minimum of three trials until the experimenter was familiar with the sequence and satisfied with his result. The procedure was designed to familiarize the experimenter with the rhythmic and temporal patterning of the phrase/pause sequence about to be timed, and to help reduce the amount of time that might have been lost through guessing at the onset of a sequential vocalization. Average adult serial reaction time to auditory stimuli at irregular intervals is 335 ms to intervals of 500 ms. All transcription and timing was later checked against the videotapes themselves to assess contextual accuracy.

Reliability

Three raters (undergraduates) were asked to transcribe 100 sequential vocalizations of the same mother selected at random from available audio observations. That transcription resulted in a 97% agreement with the content and segmentation of the original transcript produced by the experimenter.

Six 30-second exchanges were selected at random and the mothers' speech segmented and timed by the research assistant (an average of 21 phrases and pauses per mother; 126 in all). The resulting segmentation and the durations of phrases and pauses were then compared with measures of the experimenter. A comparison of segmentation resulted in 88.8% agreement. Those instances in which segmentation did not coincide (i.e., instances where two phrases were separated or joined by differing measurement of the same pause criteria) were later discarded from the final comparison of temporal durations (discarded were 14 phrases and 7 pauses of the original transcription). That final temporal analysis resulted in a comparison of 112 phrases and 119 pauses overall. In the measurement of phrase durations, agreement was 95.5% to within 300 ms and 84.8% agreement to within 200 ms.

Table 23: Korman Functional Utterance Types

Code	Function	Code	Function
STQ	tag questions	TC	turn-constructional
Bc	back-channel	Aux	auxiliary utterances
Ex	exhortations	ST	statements
Ph	phatics	Co	commands
Gr	greetings	Wh	wh-questions
Pe	performance	Y-N	yes-no questions
TQ	tag question	RI	rising intonation
PC	post completer		

This taxonomy is an attempt to define and describe the uses and functions of mothers' language as an interactive phenomenon. It is predicated on the assumption that maternal speech in any interaction is not only a mode of expression, but that it also constitutes a form of social organization whose overall structure is largely based in the coordination of engagement relative to the behavior of a prelinguistic infant. Its purpose is to provide a catalog of frequently occurring interactive uses or "functions" in maternal speech. Its goal is to provide insight into the ways a mother will integrate her language in the organization of an engagement — how she will cultivate and eventually achieve a framework of mutual orientation necessary for successful interaction; the vocal alternatives that are open to her in any exchange; and how her individual vocalizations are organized within an engagement to both exchange information and help keep it going.

It will be assumed a priori that maternal language in interaction is organized to both offer communication (whether it be real or imagined) and to assist in the interactive flow of behavior in any prelinguistic engagement. To define and distinguish those communicative vocalizations from those that perform an interactive (and/or regulative) function, a distinction had to be made between those vocal constituents intended as actual communication and those constructions having a "metacommunicative" or supportive role in engagements. In other words, we have to distinguish when a mother is "talking" to her infant using communicative constructions which indicate she is taking a "turn" at speaking and when her vocal behavior is simply something that is used to get or keep the infant's attention. The terms that will\ be used to identify these two general types of interactive function are turn-constructional utterances (TC), and auxiliary utterances (Aux).

A turn-constructional utterance is one in which a mother takes a turn at verbally communicating or "saying" something to her infant. The utterance she makes is intended to convey information, request it, or to direct an infant to a specific activity. In other words, the utterance is used to "construct" a mother's turn at speaking whose purpose is an exchange of verbal information in some form. For this group of mothers, this type of meaningful utterance was identified in three frequently occurring forms that are fundamentally standard English constructions: statements, commands, and interrogative questions.

Kuczaj

Kuczaj, Stan
Center for Comparative Cognition
211 Old Santa Fe Trail
Santa Fe, NM 87501
skuczaj@ocean.st.usm.edu

This corpus consists of 210 files containing the diary study (1973–75) of Stan Kuczaj's son, Abe. From age 2;4 to 4;1, two 30 minutes sessions of Abe's spontaneous speech were recorded each week in the home. From 4;1 to 5;0, one 30-minute sample was taken weekly.

Table 24: Kuczaj Files

File	Age	File	Age	File	Age	File	Age
001	2;4.24	053	2;11.2	105	3;5.29	157	4;1.0
002	2;5.0	054	2;11.6	106	3;6.3	158	4;1.5
003	2;5.7	055	2;11.10	107	3;6.4	159	4;1.9
004	2;5.10	056	2;11.13	108	3;6.10	160	4;1.15
005	2;5.14	057	2;11.18	109	3;6.13	161	4;1.20
006	2;5.16	058	2;11.21	110	3;6.16	162	4;1.24
007	2;5.20	059	2;11.25	111	3;6.19	163	4;1.29
008	2;5.22	060	2;11.30	112	3;6.22	164	4;2.2
009	2;5.23	061	3;0.7	113	3;6.26	165	4;2.9
010	2;5.26	062	3;0.16	114	3;6.29	166	4;2.13
011	2;5.29	063	3;0.25	115	3;7.4	167	4;2.19
012	2;6.4	064	3;0.29	116	3;7.5	168	4;2.24
013	2;6.6	065	3;1.1	117	3;7.15	169	4;3.1
014	2;6.10	066	3;1.5	118	3;7.21	170	4;3.7
015	2;6.14	067	3;1.8	119	3;7.22	171	4;3.11
016	2;6.14	068	3;1.11	120	3;7.28	172	4;3.15
017	2;6.16	069	3;1.15	121	3;8.1	173	4;3.21
018	2;6.18	070	3;1.18	122	3;8.5	174	4;4.1
019	2;7.0	071	3;1.22	123	3;8.8	175	4;4.4

Table 24: Kuczaj Files

File	Age	File	Age	File	Age	File	Age
020	2;7.4	072	3;1.26	124	3;8.11	176	4;4.21
021	2;7.7	073	3;1.28	125	3;8.16	177	4;5.3
022	2;7.11	074	3;2.1	126	3;8.17	178	4;5.14
023	2;7.14	075	3;2.5	127	3;8.21	179	4;5.20
024	2;7.15	076	3;2.7	128	3;8.23	180	4;5.28
025	2;7.18	077	3;2.9	129	3;8.28	181	4;6.1
026	2;7.26	078	3;2.18	130	3;9.0	182	4;6.5
027	2;8.1	079	3;2.21	131	3;9.5	183	4;6.12
028	2;8.6	080	3;2.26	132	3;9.6	184	4;6.14
029	2;8.8	081	3;2.29	133	3;9.12	185	4;6.19
030	2;8.14	082	3;3.1	134	3;9.14	186	4;6.27
031	2;8.18	083	3;3.4	135	3;9.19	187	4;7.3
032	2;8.22	084	3;3.8	136	3;9.23	188	4;7.5
033	2;8.25	085	3;3.11	137	3;9.25	189	4;7.11
034	2;8.29	086	3;3.15	138	3;9.27	190	4;8.0
035	2;9.1	087	3;3.18	139	3;10.3	191	4;8.2
036	2;9.5	088	3;3.25	140	3;10.7	192	4;8.7
037	2;9.8	089	3;3.28	141	3;10.9	193	4;8.14
038	2;9.11	090	3;4.1	142	3;10.14	194	4;8.20
039	2;9.16	091	3;4.4	143	3;10.15	195	4;8.27
040	2;9.19	092	3;4.8	144	3;10.18	196	4;9.0
041	2;9.23	093	3;4.12	145	3;10.25	197	4;9.12
042	2;9.27	094	3;4.15	146	3;11.0	198	4;9.19
043	2;9.30	095	3;4.19	147	3;11.2	199	4;9.24
044	2;10.3	096	3;4.26	148	3;11.6	200	4;10.1
045	2;10.6	097	3;4.26	149	3;11.11	201	4;10.9
046	2;10.7	098	3;4.30	150	3;11.12	202	4;10.15

Table 24: Kuczaj Files

File	Age	File	Age	File	Age	File	Age
047	2;10.12	099	3;5.3	151	3;11.16	203	4;10.22
048	2;10.15	100	3;5.6	152	3;11.25	204	4;10.29
049	2;10.20	101	3;5.13	153	4;0.3	205	4;11.5
050	2;10.22	102	3;5.17	154	4;0.15	206	4;11.13
051	2;10.27	103	3;5.23	155	4;0.16	207	4;11.21
052	2;10.30	104	3;5.24	156	4;0.25	208	4;11.27
						209	5;0.4
						210	5;0.11

Publications using these data should cite:

Kuczaj, S. (1976a). *-ing, -s and -ed: A study of the acquisition of certain verb inflections.* Unpublished doctoral dissertation, University of Minnesota.

That dissertation includes a complete description of the project. Additional relevant publications include:

Kuczaj, S. A. (1976b). Arguments against Hurford's 'Aux copying rule'. *Journal of Child Language, 3,* 423–427.

Kuczaj, S. (1977). The acquisition of regular and irregular past tense forms. *Journal of Verbal Learning and Verbal Behavior, 16,* 589–600.

Kuczaj, S. A. (1978). Why do children fail to generalize the progressive inflection? *Journal of Child Language, 5,* 167–171.

Kuczaj, S. (1979). The influence of contractibility on the acquisition of be: Substantial, meager, or unknown? *Journal of Psycholinguistic Research, 8,* 1–11.

Kuczaj, S. A. (1980). Old and new forms, old and new meanings: The form-function hypothesis revisited. *First Language, 3,* 55–61.

Kuczaj, S. A. (1986). General developmental patterns and individual differences in the acquisition of copula and auxiliary be forms. *First Language, 6,* 111–117.

Kuczaj, S., & Daly, M. (1979). The development of hypothetical reference in the speech of young children. *Journal of Child Language, 6,* 563–579.

Kuczaj, S., & Maratsos, M. (1983). Initial Verbs of yes-no questions: A different kind of general grammatical category. *Developmental Psychology, 19,* 440–444.

Kuczaj, S. A., & Maratsos, M. P. (1975). What children can say before they will. *Merrill-Palmer Quarterly, 21,* 89–111.

MacWhinney

Brian MacWhinney
Department of Psychology
Carnegie Mellon University
Pittsburgh PA 15213 USA
macw@cmu.edu

This directory contains transcripts from MacWhinney's diary study of the development of his two sons, Ross and Mark. Ross was born on December 25, 1977 and Mark was born on November 19, 1979. Ross was recorded between the ages of 2;6 and 8;0 and Mark was recorded between 0;7 and 5;6. Because the experimenter is also the boys' father, these data represent a fairly natural record of the family's interactions. Some of the transcriptions are still in a preliminary state and several files are not yet transcribed. Although they are available for public use, users should be aware of their preliminary state. In particular, there is much descriptive information that has not yet been included in these files.

The files with the label "boys" include 29 files from Ross between the ages of 5;6 and 8;0 and from Mark between the ages of 3;6 and 6;0. The files with the label "ross" include 38 files from Ross between 2;6 and 5;4, when Mark is between 0;7 and 3;5. There is also a file (Ross01) that chronicles Ross's very early development. There is also a directory of 29 unfinished files from Ross and Mark that is called "unfinished." Data were collected from 5;0 to 9;0, but they are not yet transcribed.

Publications using these data should cite this manual.

Manchester

Elena V. M. Lieven
Max Planck Institute for
Evolutionary Anthropology
Inselstrasses 22
D-04103 Leipzig Germany
lieven@eva.mpg.de

Julian Pine
Department of Psychology
University of Nottingham
NE7 2RCD Nottingham, UK
jp@psyc.nott.ac.uk

Caroline Rowland
Institute of Behavioural Sciences
Mickleover Site
University of Derby
DE3 5GX Derby, UK
c.rowland@derby.ac.uk

Anna Theakston
Department of Psychology
University of Manchester
Oxford Rd
M13 9PL Manchester, UK
theaksto@fs4.psy.man.ac.uk

This corpus consists of transcripts of audio recordings from a longitudinal study of 12 English-speaking children between the ages of approximately 2 and 3 years. The children were recruited through newspaper advertisements and local nurseries. All the children were first borns, monolingual and were cared for primarily by their mothers. Although socioeconomic status was not taken into account with respect to recruitment, the children were from predominantly middle-class families. There were six boys and six girls, half from Manchester and half from Nottingham. At the beginning of the study, the children ranged in age from 1;8.22 to 2;0.25 with MLUs ranging between 1.06 to 2.27 in morphemes. The children's dates of birth and ages are available in the headers to each transcript. The transcripts for each child are numbered from 1 to 34 corresponding to the tape number and labeled (a) and (b) to correspond to the two 30-minute sessions within each recording. The following recording sessions were missed and therefore have no corresponding transcript: Aran14a/b, Carl14b, Carl24a/b, John15a/b, John16a/b, Ruth4a/b, Warren3b.

Procedure

The children were audiotaped in their homes for an hour on two separate occasions in every 3-week period for one year. They engaged in normal play activities with their mothers. For the first 30 minutes of each hour they played with their own toys whilst for the second 30 minutes, toys provided by the experimenter were available to the child. For the duration of the recordings, the experimenter attempted as far as possible to remain in the background to allow contextual notes to be taken.

Transcription

All speech was transcribed with the exception of speech not directed to the child(i.e. speech between adults, telephone calls etc.). However, if the child produced an utterance in response to such speech, the relevant utterances were transcribed. Generally speaking, contextual information was added only when the utterance would otherwise be unclear. Of course, because the children were not videotaped, we had only the experimenter's notes for such information. Punctuation was kept to a minimum – double commas indicate tag questions and single commas were used to indicate vocatives.

Phonological Forms

The data were collected with the intention of looking specifically at early grammatical development. We were not interested in the specific phonological forms the children used. Therefore, unless the child used what appeared to be child-specific forms, the target word was transcribed rather than an approximation of the child's phonological form. This also helped with coding using the MOR program.

Morphemicization

On the main line the data were morphemicized for plurals (except irregular forms), possessives, progressive -ing, regular past tense -ed, and third person singular main verbs. Third person singular auxiliaries were not morphemicized. Contracted auxiliary and main verb forms were morphemicized, as in we-'re or you-'ve. We also morphemicized contracted markers of negation, as in can-'nt or does-'nt. Contracted main verbs 'have' and 'be' and contracted auxiliaries 'have', 'be' were transcribed in full form, as in it-'is, it-'has , and she-'is.

Postcodes

The children's data were coded for imitation [+ I], self-repetition [+ SR], partially intelligible utterances [+ PI], incomplete utterances [+ IN] and routines [+ R]. The mothers' data were coded for partially intelligible utterances, incomplete utterances, and routines.

Imitations were considered to be utterances where all components of the child's speech occurred in one of another speaker's preceding five utterances unless more than 10 seconds removed in time. This guideline was adhered to even if the mother's utterance encoded different semantics or illocutionary force. If the child added anything to the utterance (e.g., an extra word or morpheme), this was not coded as imitation.

Self-repetitions were considered to be utterances where all components of the child's speech occurred in one of his or her preceding five utterances unless more than 10 seconds removed in time, even if the two utterances in question functioned as independent communicative acts. If the child added anything to the utterance this was not coded as self-repetition. Incomplete utterances were those where the speaker trailed off, was interrupted, self-interrupted, or completed an earlier utterance.Partially intelligible utterances were those where a part of the utterance was unintelligible and transcribed as xxx. Routines included counting, nursery rhymes, the alphabet and so forth. However, if the child added nonroutine material, as in "one two three bricks" the utterance was not coded as a routine.

Error Coding

The data were coded for the following errors (where '0' indicates a missing speech component). For all of the errors the marker [*] was added to the main line and a dependent tier was added showing the correct form.

Missing morphemes	two dog-0s, he's go-0ing
Case errors	her do it, me get it
Missing auxiliaries	it 0is going there, I 0am getting a drink
Word Class Errors	a that one
Agreement errors	a bricks, does she likes it?, it don't go there
Pronominal Errors	carry you (when the child wants to be carried)
Wrong word	I put it off (where the context indicates take is appropriate)
Overgeneralisations	it broked, I stayed it on there.

Although we have attempted to be consistent in coding, errors may have been missed. In particular, missing auxiliaries and copulas have often not been coded. Where it was impossible to identify exactly what the error was, the error was simply marked on the main line with [*]. Anyone wishing to work on particular error types should carry out a detailed analysis of the child's use of a particular system (e.g., pronoun case marking) rather than relying on pulling out errors by searching for the [*] error marker.

Publications using these data should cite:

Theakston, A. L., Lieven, E. V. M., Pine, J. M. & Rowland, C. F. (in press). The role of performance limitations in the acquisition of 'mixed' verb-argument structure at stage 1. In M. Perkins & S. Howard (Eds.) *New Directions in Language Development and Disorders*. New York: Plenum.

Nelson

Katherine Nelson
Developmental Psychology
City University of New York Graduate Center
33 West 42nd St.
New York, NY 10036
knelson@email.gc.cuny.edu

This data set was collected over a 15-month period (November 1981 to February 1983) when the child Emily was 21 to 36 months old. The child's parents recorded their conversations and the child's spontaneous speech while alone after they left her room at night or at nap time. The recordings were done under the direction of Katherine Nelson. Recording was done by casette recorder placed under Emily's crib. Tape recordings were made more frequently in the first few months. Tapes were reviewed and commented upon by the child's mother, and were initially transcribed by both the mother and the researcher. Later tapes were reviewed by different researchers studying them over a 2-year period. The final transcription made available to CHILDES has revised some of the original versions for consistency and accuracy. The data have been reported in a number of previous publications, and the study is documented more fully in Nelson (1989). There may be minor discrepancies in the version delivered to CHILDES compared with published excerpts. Such discrepancies are to be expected given the difficulties of interpreting speech of a child talking to herself at this age. The tapes contain many references to individuals in addition to parents and child, including baby-sitter (Tanta), grandmother (Mormor); baby brother (Stephen), and friend Carl. The names of other friends and relations have been changed for confidentiality, and are not necessarily consistent with the names used in previous publications (which were also substitutes). Last names have been consistently deleted, although in some cases this interrupts the rhythmic quality of the talk. Permission to use the data for research must be obtained before publication is contemplated.

Publications using these data should cite:

Nelson, K. (Ed.) (1989). *Narratives from the crib.* Cambridge, MA: Harvard University Press.

New England

Barbara Pan
Harvard Graduate School of Education
Larsen Hall, Appian Way
Cambridge, MA 02138
snowbp@hugse1.harvard.edu

Catherine Snow
Harvard Graduate School of Education
Larsen Hall, Appian Way
Cambridge, MA 02138 USA
catherine_snow@harvard.edu

Participants

This directory contains longitudinal data on 52 children whose language development was studied by Catherine Snow, Barbara Pan, and colleagues as part of the project "Foundations for Language Assessment in Spontaneous Speech," funded by the National Institutes of Health. Participants were chosen from a larger sample of 100 children on whom language and other data were available from the MacArthur Individual Differences Project. A description of participant solicitation and other information about the original sample can be found in Snow (1989) and Dale, Bates, Reznick, and Morisset (1989). The present sample of 52 children from English-speaking families was chosen to include half girls and half boys, and equal proportions of children from families of lower-middle and upper-middle socioeconomic status. Children with indications of medical or other developmental problems were excluded.

Procedure

Each child–parent (mother–child) dyad was brought to the laboratory at three ages: at 14 months, at 20 months, and again between the ages of 27 and 32 months. Transcripts at 14 and 20 months reflect spontaneous language data collected during a 5-minute warm up and several subsequent activities, each of which is described briefly here.

1. Warm-up. For the warm-up period, the mother and child were left alone in a small room with some toys, and the mother was instructed to take a few minutes to let her child become accustomed to the setting.
2. Toy play. Next there was a 5-minute period during which the child was given a variety of small toys to play with (Small-Scale Activity) while the mother was filling out a form at a nearby table. Because the mother was instructed not to initiate interaction with the child during this period, this portion of the videotaped protocol was not transcribed.

3. Forbidden object. In the next task, the mother was seated beside the child at the table and instructed to try and keep the child from touching an attractive, moving object (Forbidden Object). Users of these transcripts should be aware that this part of the transcribed data involved some triadic (examiner–parent–child) interaction, and thus for certain analyses may not be comparable to the dyadic (parent–child) interaction that makes up the rest of the transcript.

4. Boxes. Finally, the mother was asked to spend about 10 minutes playing with her child using the contents of four successive boxes. She was not instructed how long should be spent on each box, but was told to try to get to all four, and to have only one box open at a time. The boxes contained, in order, a ball, a cloth for peekaboo, paper and crayons, and a book. The entire transcribed parent–child interaction averaged 20 to 25 minutes in duration.

The protocol for parent–child interaction at the third data point (age 27-32 months) involved only four boxes (no warm-up or forbidden object), and two substitutions were made to make the activities more age-appropriate: hand puppets and a Fisher-Price™ toy house replaced the ball and peekaboo cloth. Parent and child were videotaped by means of a camera located either at ceiling level in one corner of the room and operated by remote control, or located on the other side of a one-way mirror.

Transcription and Coding

The transcripts in this corpus were prepared from the videotaped parent–child interaction by transcribers trained in the CHAT conventions. Users should note several specific transcription guidelines that were followed. Utterance boundaries were based on intonation contour. No attempt was made to distinguish the number of unintelligible words in a string; therefore xxx and yyy (rather than xx and yy) are used throughout. Where the phonological form could be represented, yyy was followed by a %pho tier and UNIBET transcription. Other nonverbal vocalizations were represented as 0 [=! vocalizes]. The audio quality of videotapes did not permit phonetic transcription. In general, no attempt was made to represent possible word omissions, nor to distinguish child-invented forms, family-specific forms, and phonologically consistent forms; rather the generic @ was used for all three. Pauses were transcribed as either # or #long, rather than in terms of precise duration. Words on the main tier were morphemicized so that MLU could be automatically computed in morphemes, and so that inflected forms of nouns and verbs would be counted not as separate word types, but as tokens of the uninflected stem.

Because it was anticipated that looking behaviors, especially in the 14 month olds, would often be used to direct the adult's attention and would therefore be important to consider in coding infants' nonverbal communicative acts, it was decided that all looking behaviors (as well as points, head nods, and so forth.) would be recorded on %gpx tiers. Time at the beginning of each activity and the passage of each subsequent full minute were recorded on %tim tiers.

Codes on the %spa tier are based on the Inventory of Communicative Acts Abridged (INCA-A), a shortened and modified version of the system developed by Ninio and Wheeler (1984). For fuller discussions of this coding scheme, see Ninio, Snow, Pan, & Rollins, (1994) and Snow, Pan, Imbens-Bailey, & Herman (1996).

Publications using these data should cite:

Ninio, A., Snow, C., Pan, B., & Rollins, P. (1994). Classifying communicative acts in children's interactions. *Journal of Communications Disorders, 27*, 157-188.

Additional relevant references are:

Dale, P., Bates, E., Reznick, S., & Morisset, C. (1989). The validity of a parent report instrument. *Journal of Child Language, 16*, 239–249.
Ninio, A., & Wheeler, P. (1984). A manual for classifying verbal communicative functions in mother-infant interaction. Working Papers in Developmental Psychology, No. 1. Jerusalem: The Martin and Vivian Levin Center, Hebrew University.
Snow, C. E. (1989). Imitativeness: a trait or a skill? In G. Speidel & K. Nelson (Eds.), *The many faces of imitation*. New York: Reidel.
Snow, C., Pan, B., Imbens-Bailey, A., & Herman, J. (1996). Learning how to say what one means: A longitudinal study of children's speech act use. *Social Development, 5*, 56–84.

Peters / Wilson

Ann Peters
Department of Linguistics
University of Hawaii
1890 East West Road
Honolulu, HI 96822
ann@hawaii.edu

Bob Wilson
Department of State/FSI
1400 Key Blvd.
Suite 901
Arlington, VA 22209
statefsi@guvax.bitnet

These are transcripts of audiotapes made by Dr. Bob Wilson of himself and his son Seth, who was born October 18, 1980. Although Wilson has placed this material in the public domain, it has not been censored as to personally sensitive material. Please be careful of this when using these transcripts and do not quote any questionable material. Wilson has chosen not to have the names changed. For coding conventions for the %spa line see the files "00spa.fat" and "00spa.chi" for the father and the child. The file "00coding.cdc" has special codes for the %gls lines for Seth and for phonological forms placed on the main line for Seth. The files were reformatted into CHAT in June 1992 by Brian MacWhinney. They were then rechecked in 1994 by Ann Peters.

The CHAT versions of these transcripts were made under the supervision of Dr. Ann Peters of the University of Hawai'i, with financial assistance from NSF grant BNS84-18272. Reference to these materials in documents to be circulated (published or unpublished) should acknowledge the above sources. Seth has a severe visual impairment. Researchers using these data should cite:

Peters, A. (1987). The role of imitation in the developing syntax of a blind child. *Text, 7,* 289–311.

Wilson, B., & Peters, A. M. (1988). What are you cookin' on a hot?: Movement constraints in the speech of a three-year-old blind child. *Language, 64,* 249–273.

Post

Kathy Post
134 Ridgeview Circle
Glenshaw, PA 15116 USA

This study examined children from families living in Suwannee County, Florida. This area was chosen because it fits the criterion of being a rural, Southern community that has a predominantly white, working-class population. It is also the family home of this investigator's parents and numerous aunts, uncles, and cousins. Through work on the qualifying paper, contacts had already been established at the Suwannee County Health Department to obtain access to the immunization records. In addition, the investigator's shared regional accent and shared cultural experiences allowed easy access to and ready acceptance by the study families.

Participants

The participants were three girls and their families. Two of the girls were approximately 19 months of age at the time of selection and the third was 22 months. One participant was the second-born, one was the third-born, and the third participant was the fourth-born child in the family. The next-oldest sibling in each family was approximately 18 months older than the third- and fourth-born participants and the older sibling was 2 years older than the second-born participant. All of the participants were the products of normal pregnancies, were healthy at the time of taping and had no apparent hearing, speech or mental deficiencies. They were located through immunization records obtained from the Suwannee County Health Department and the records of a pediatrician in Live Oak. The mothers were contacted by telephone and a meeting arranged to ascertain if the family met the criteria for the study.

Recruitment

At the initial meeting the mothers were told that the investigator was interested in observing how children change or develop over time. Because the families were selected according to the age of the younger child, the younger child was called the target child. It was emphasized, however, that we were interested in how both children developed over time, not just the younger one. It was explained to the families that they were entering a long-term commitment to the study. It was agreed that the sum of $100.00 would be paid to the families as an incentive to complete the study. Fifty dollars was paid to each family at the end of the first taping session and the remaining $50.00 was paid at the end of the final taping session. In addition, at the end of the fifth taping session, the investigator took the families out to lunch. The mothers also signed a consent form. The mothers were interviewed periodically and asked their views on child rearing, how their children spend the day, methods of discipline, goals for their children, and other related issues. They were asked more specific questions on how they thought their children learn language, how the parents affect their children's language learning, how important language learning is, how they thought their children will do in school, what they thought their children should be able to do by the time they enter kindergarten, and what they perceived as the long-term and short-term effects of their children's education. In addition, the mothers were asked how they felt about their children watching television and if it should be regulated or not. In the ethnographic tradition, detailed descriptions of the community and the children and their families are provided. The descriptions help the reader understand the environment in which these children are learning language. The purpose of these portraits is to add a richness and completeness to the data.

Data Collection

Within one week of the initial meeting a taping session was conducted in each participant's home. Taping was accomplished with a Sony™ Video 8 AF portable videocassette recorder. Prior to the taping the recording equipment was brought into the participants' homes to allow the children to examine the equipment to lessen the disruptive influence on the normal interaction. Occasionally, during the taping sessions, one of the children would come over to examine the camera, but generally, the camera was ignored once the toys were introduced. Each taping session lasted approximately 60 minutes. A toy bag provided by the investigator was introduced at the beginning of the session and the family played with whatever interested them. The toys were appropriate for the ages of the children and included such items as books, blocks, action figures, puzzles, pull-toys, and one playset. New toys and books were added over the taping sessions to maintain interest. Occasionally the participants would bring out a favorite toy or book of their own. Taping sessions were scheduled at times which the mothers deemed most convenient and most likely to have the children in a receptive mood. Taping took place approximately every four weeks. Because of illness or vacations, occasionally the sessions were scheduled a little farther apart. A total of 10 sessions was recorded for each family. Thus the language development of these three children was followed over a period of about 9 months during the latter part of their second year and the early part of their third year. This age was chosen because during this time the child's language is expanding greatly in complexity of syntax and size of vocabulary.

The investigator was present for all of the tapings and made contextual notes to aid in transcription. The presence of an outsider and recording equipment no doubt affects the interaction among the family members. For this reason one "practice" taping session was made with each family, the data from which was not included in later analyses. It was observed that with repeated exposure to the taping situation the disruptive effects of the data collection methods were minimal.

Data Coding

Transcripts of the tapes were made as soon as possible after the session by the investigator. The data was transcribed in CHAT. In determining how to divide up maternal utterances, it was decided to use breath groups. That is, what the mother said on one breath was considered to be one utterance. One of the mothers tended to have longer utterances than the other two. On occasion, this mother (Darla) might take a quick supplemental breath, but the pause would be less than one second and it was clear that she was continuing the same utterance. The feedback data were obtained using the modified coding scheme described in Demetras, Post, and Snow (1986).

Publications using these data should cite:

Demetras, M., Post, K., & Snow, C. (1986). Feedback to first-language learners. *Journal of Child Language, 13,* 275–292.

Post, K. (1992). *The language learning environment of laterborns in a rural Florida community.* Unpublished doctoral dissertation. Harvard University.

Post, K. (1994). Negative evidence. In J. Sokolov & C. Snow (Eds.), *Handbook of Research in Language Development Using CHILDES,* (pp. 132–173). Hillsdale, NJ: Lawrence Erlbaum Associates.

Sachs

Jacqueline Sachs
Department of Psychology
University of Connecticut U-85
Storrs, CT 06268 USA
jsachs@psych.psy.uconn.edu

This corpus consists of Jacqueline Sachs' longitudinal study of her daughter, Naomi, who was born June 8, 1968. The transcripts cover the time from age 1;1 to 5;1. There is also a "0lexicon.cdc" file, which is a list of nonstandard forms present in the data. The data on the various MLU ranges are as follows:

Table 25: MLU Ranges

MLU	Utterances	Age
1-2	1340	1;8.0 to 1;10.17
2-2.5	1730	1;8.18 to 1;9.11
2.5-3	2300	1;9.12 to 2;2.0
3-3.5	920	2;2.25 to 2;4.0
3.5-4	3030	2;4.6 to 3;3.27
4-4.5	900	3;4.0 to 3;5.12
4-5;5	1050	3;6.0 to 3;8.19
5 up	730	4;7.28 to 5;1.20

Naomi's ages for the various files are as follows:

Table 26: Naomi Files

File	Age	File	Age	File	Age	File	Age
01	1;2.29	24	1;11.9	47	2;1.17	70	2;8.23
02	1;6.16	25	1;11.11	48	2;1.25	71	2;9.9
03	1;8.6	26	1;11.12	49	2;1.26	72	2;9.11
04	1;8.0	27	1;11.17	50	2;2.0	73	2;11.8
05	1;8.29	28	1;11.16	51	2;2.25	74	2;11.10
06	1;9.7	29	1;11.18	52	2;3.0	75	2;11.11

Table 26: Naomi Files

File	Age	File	Age	File	Age	File	Age
07	1;9.10	30	1;11.20	53	2;3.17	76	2;11.12
08	1;9.26	31	1;11.21	54	2;3.19	77	2;11.13
09	1;10.3	32	1;11.23	55	2;3.21	78	2;11.17
10	1;10.10	33	1;11.29	56	2;3.29	79	2;11.18
11	1;10.10	34	1;11.30	57	2;4.4	80	2;11.24
12	1;10.11	35	2;0.2	58	2;4.5	81	3;2.10
13	1;10.14	36	2;0.3	59	2;4.13	82	3;3.26
14	1;10.17	37	2;0.5	60	2;4.30	83	3;3.27
15	1;10.18	38	2;0.18	61	2;5.3	84	3;4.0
16	1;10.19	39	2;0.19	62	2;5.8	85	3;4.18
17	1;10.20	40	2;0.26	63	2;5.9	86	3;5.3
18	1;10.23	41	2;0.27	64	2;5.21	87	3;5.4
19	1;10.25	42	2;0.28	65	2;6.4	88	3;5.6
20	1;10.28	43	2;1.0	66	2;6.5	89	3;5.7
21	1;11.2	44	2;1.1	67	2;7.13	90	3;8.19
22	1;11.3	45	2;1.7	68	2;7.16	91	4;7.28
23	1;11.6	46	2;1.9	69	2;8.14	92	4;7.29
						93	4;9.3

Publications using these data should cite:

Sachs, J. (1983). Talking about the there and then: The emergence of displaced reference in parent–child discourse. In K. E. Nelson (Ed.), *Children's language, Vol. 4,* Hillsdale, NJ: Lawrence Erlbaum Associates.

Snow

Snow, Catherine
Harvard Graduate School of Education
Larsen Hall, Appian Way
Cambridge MA 02138 USA
catherine_snow@harvard.edu

This corpus contains 30 files of data collected by Catherine Snow between 1979 and 1980 in Brookline, MA. The participant was her son, Nathaniel. He was 2;5 at the start of the study and 3;9 at the end. Before using the data, please check with Catherine Snow. Nathaniel was, at this stage of development, a particularly unintelligible child. He also used many empty or semi-empty forms mixed with meaningful speech, such as duh-duh, da-da, dede. Accordingly, many of his transcribed utterances include syllables that were broadly phonetically transcribed, either because they had no meaning, or because they could not be interpreted. His mispronunciations had in some cases standardized themselves into lexical or semilexicalized items, used either standardly in the family (see 0lexicon.cdc) or transiently within certain conversations (see 0lexicon.cdc). Unintelligible and empty syllables have been indicated in the text line by a yyy and the phonetic transcription is indicated on the %pho: tier.

Table 27: Nathaniel Files

File	Age	File	Age	File	Age	File	Age
01	2;5.18	08	2;6.25	15	3;0.19	23	3;4.10
02	2;6.0	09	2;7.1	16	3;0.22	24	3;4.10
03	2;6.0	10	-	17	3;1.6	25	3;4.18
04	2;6.0	11	-	18	3;2.27	26	3;4.21
05	2;6.3	12	-	19	3;4.8	27	3;4.21
06	2;6.19	13	-	20	3;4.8	28	3;7.14
07	2;6.19	14	2;8.20	21	3;4.9	29	3;9.2
				22	3;4.9	30	3;9.4

Publications using these data should cite this manual.

Suppes

Patrick Suppes
Department of Philosophy
Stanford University
Stanford, CA 94305 USA

These data were contributed by Patrick Suppes. The child under study, named Nina, was 1;11 when the study began and 3;3 when it ended. The 52 files (4 were not included), consisting of 102,230 tokens, were collected between 1972 and 1973.

Table 28: Nina Files

File	Age	File	Age	File	Age	File	Age
01	1;11.16	15	2;2.28	31	2;5.28	44	3;0.16
02	1;11.24	16	2;3.5	32	2;9.13	45	3;0.24
03	1;11.29	17	2;3.14	33	2;9.21	46	3;1.4
04	2;0.3	18	2;3.18	34	2;9.26	47	3;1.5
05	2;0.10	19	2;3.28	35	2;10.6	48	3;1.6
06	2;0.17	20	2;4.6	36	2;10.13	49	3;1.7
07	2;0.24	21	2;4.12	37	2;10.21	50	3;2.4
09	2;1.6	22	2;4.18	38	2;10.28	51	3;2.12
10	2;1.15	23	2;4.26	39	2;11.6	52	3;2.16
11	2;1.22	27	2;5.24	40	2;11.12	53	3;2.24
12	2;1.29	28	2;5.25	41	2;11.16	54	3;3.1
13	2;2.6	29	2;5.26	42	3;0.3	55	3;3.8
14	2;2.12	30	2;5.27	43	3;0.10	56	3;3.21

Publications using these data should cite:

Suppes, P. (1974). The semantics of children's language. *American Psychologist, 29,* 103–114.

Tardif

This corpus includes a set of 25 files from English-speaking children used as controls for a study of Chinese language development and noun use. For details on this study, please consult the description of Tardif's Mandarin "Context" study.

Valian

Virginia Valian
Department of Psychology
Hunter College
695 Park Ave.
New York, NY 10021
vvvhc@cunyvm.cuny.edu

These data were contributed by Virginia Valian in 1995 and reformatted into CHAT later in that year. They were used as the empirical basis for Valian (1991) which compared English and Italian development. However, only the English data are available here. The corpus includes two samples each from 21 children distributed across the following levels of MLU:

Table 29: Valian MLU Levels

Child	MLU	Child	MLU
01	1.53	11	3.07
02	1.74	12	3.15
03	1.79	13	3.16
04	1.81	14	3.31
05	1.99	15	3.34
06	2.24	16	3.62
07	2.28	17	3.68
08	2.52	18	3.72
09	2.66	19	4.12
10	2.76	20	4.17
		21	4.38

Utterances that were fully enclosed in parentheses in the original were marked with the postcode [+V] in the reformatted version. It is not clear why these utterances were placed entirely in parentheses in the original. Strings of one or two words that were enclosed in parentheses are marked in the form [%v material]. It is not clear why this material was placed in parentheses.

Publications using these data should cite:
Valian, V. (1991). Syntactic subjects in the early speech of American and Italian children. *Cognition, 40,* 21–81.

Van Houten

Lori Van Houten
School of Education
Stanford University
Stanford, CA 94305 USA
inquiry@pacbell.net

These data were obtained from Lori Van Houten's doctoral dissertation, which studied differences in mother–child interaction between adolescent and older mothers. The dissertation work was a part of a larger study, conducted by Cynthia Garcia-Coll of Department of Education at Brown University.

The mothers were followed from the time of the birth of their children. Data were collected at 4 months, 8 months, 2 years, and 3 years. Only the 2 year and 3 year data is on the computer.

Two Year Data

The two year data are in the subdirectory "twos." The children were studied at home in three different situational contexts in which the mother attempted to teach the child a task, and a free play situation. First there is a 3-minute segment of interaction while the child eats lunch. Videotaped for a half hour, mothers were instructed to try to ignore the camera and do whatever they would normally do during lunch. If the child finished lunch before the half hour was up mothers were instructed to do whatever they would normally do after eating lunch. The 3 minutes of tape following the first minute of interaction were transcribed for this study.

The second session was a teaching session in which the mother was instructed to teach the child three tasks from the Bayley Scales of Infant Development which were considered too difficult for the child's age. Mothers did not know the task was too difficult for the child. The tasks were: placing a block in specific locations (on, in, under, and so forth) around a cup and a small chair, stringing beads, and sorting black and white buttons. The mothers were given one task at a time. The task was explained and the mother was given 3 minutes to teach each one. Only the first 2 minutes of the bead stringing and 1 minute of the sorting buttons task are transcribed.

The third session consisted of a half hour of play with a box of experimenter-provided toys. Among the toys were: cloth books, a tea set, a truck with different-shaped blocks which fit in holes in the side of the truck, a miniature playground set with small characters, giant Legos, Ernie and Cookie Monster puppets, and a chalk board/magnetic board with chalk and magnetic pieces. Mother and child played in an area in which they usually interacted. Also, mothers were requested to play only with the experimenter provided toys. The 3 minutes of interaction following the first minute of tape is transcribed.

Three Year Data

The files for these data are in the subdirectory "threes." The children in this part of the study were between 3;2 and 3;7. In this segment of the study, 27 children were recorded during a free-play situation, and 25 children were recorded during a teaching activity in which the child attempts to teach the mother a simple task.

Thirteen of the children were children of adolescent mothers. All of the children, with the exception of Goose, have data at the 2-year level as well. Wilson, Doll, Dean, and Valley have 2-year transcripts but no 3-year data. The participant Park has two free-play tapes. The child was generally uncooperative using the toys provided by the experimenter. A second file, entitled "Bestpark" is probably more representative of the child's true linguistic abilities as the child plays with his own toys. The reader will have to decide whether to opt for a more controlled sample on the same topic as the other files or for a more representative linguistic sample.

The children were seen in their homes by two experimenters. The mother was taken to another room where she was given a standard IQ test by one of the examiners. The child remained with the other examiner and the McCarthy Scales of Children's Abilities and the Rhode Island Test of Language Structure were administered. The children's scores for each of these tests (McCarthy verbal and cognitive scores, RITLS number of errors out of 100) are given in the headers for each file. With the RITLS in particular, it sometimes took more than one visit to complete the test.

Free play

Following the tests, the examiner and the child engaged in at least 5 minutes of free play with an experimenter-provided toy. The toy was a miniature park set including a slide, merry-go-round, park bench, some small figures, and a mother figure with a baby in a stroller. These interactions were audiotaped only. The goal of the interaction was to elicit a reasonable language sample in a fairly controlled setting. The examiner tried to use the same line of conversation with each child. Some of the children, however, responded better to some forms of conversation than others. For example, some children preferred to act out a story with the characters and others preferred to merely talk about the characters. The free-play sessions were transcribed and coded using the same procedures used with the 2-year data.

Teaching

The second transcript for each child, and the last activity to take place during the home visit, consists of audiotapes of the child trying to teach the mother a given activity. The mother joined the experimenter and child. The mother was instructed to "close her eyes and cover her ears" while the examiner taught the child a simple task. The examiner taught the child the task (manipulating the small characters from the park set and stringing beads) in such a way as to ensure that the child could perform the task, and to offer a verbal model of how to teach the task. The child was then told to teach the mother the task. Throughout the teaching the investigator encouraged the child to teach the mother the task and then have the mother perform the task. The investigator again tried to use similar procedures and utterances with each child. We were interested in looking at whether the child chose to demonstrate the task, to teach it verbally, or used a combination of the two techniques. The final goal was to compare the child's teaching technique with what the mothers had done at 2 years in a similar situation. These teaching segments were not timed and each transcript may be of a different length. A separate coding system was devised for this segment.

Coding System for Twos

This coding system is appropriate for use with children from approximately Stage 1 to about 4 years. It is based on the premise that there are elements of interaction beyond the sentence level that may affect the course and rate of language acquisition. There are three main components to the coding system: Structural Complexity (MLU and Number of Main Verbs), Discourse Role (Initiate, Respond, Continue Turn, and so forth) and Pragmatic Role (Request Information, Report, Clarification, Control/Restrict, and so forth). These are coded for both mother and child (although some of the pragmatic variables pertain only to the mother or child) in an attempt to characterize the reciprocal nature of the interaction. The codes are basically the same as those used in the INCA coding system and in the New England corpus.

Coding for Threes

The coding system used for the teaching situation at 3 years is different from that used with free play. It was designed specifically for use with these transcripts with several questions in mind. First, how well does the child adhere to the teaching procedure in terms of the type of utterances used and the structure of the teaching situation? Secondly, what role do the adults play in this interaction? Finally, how do the utterances in teaching differ from those used in free play? Based on these questions, a coding system was developed that included rough measures of grammatical complexity, variables representing the various segments of the teaching situation, and variables coding the pragmatic role of both the adult's and the child's utterances. The following is a list of the variable names and the three-letter codes used for each. This is followed by a description of each variable:

The interaction is divided in terms of who is teaching whom and, in general, what the purpose of the interaction is. To this end, the following segments are used:

1. Teach Mother (Tmo): By far the largest portion of the interaction, this segment includes all utterances by the examiner and mother exhorting the child to teach the mother, all the child's utterances surrounding the teaching process, and all utterances evaluating the mother's performance of the task.
2. Teach Child (Tch): Some children forget what they are supposed to teach. The examiner interrupts the interaction to teach the child the task again.

3. Closing (Clo): Includes any closing statements, usually evaluations of the child's teaching techniques, following the teaching of the task.

These segment markers are the third item entered on the coding line following the two grammatical complexity measures. The final measure considers the pragmatic role of the individual utterance.

Headers

In addition to the standard CHAT headers such as Participants, Sex, and Situation, there are some project-specific headers.

1. Mother's Age Group: The mother's status as an adolescent or older mother is provided.

2. Mother's SES: Socioeconomic status based on the Hollingshead four factor index is given for each mother. The information necessary for calculating SES was collected when the child was 8 months old.

3. Mother's Education: Maternal educational level. 1 = completed junior high, 2 = completed high school, 3 = some post-secondary education. Again this is based on the mother's educational status at 8 months. Not too many of the adolescents had continued with school after the birth of their child and none of the older mothers were students. Therefore, these figures can be considered reasonably accurate.

4. McCarthy-Cognitive: (3 year data only) The child's IQ based on his or her performance on the McCarthy Scales of Infant Development.

5. McCarthy-Verbal: (3 year data only) The child's scaled score on the verbal portion of the McCarthy Scales of Infant Development.

6. RITLS: (3 year data only) The total number of errors out of 100 on the Rhode Island Test of Language Structure, a standardized test of comprehension of various simple and complex syntactic structures. Utilizing a picture identification task, the test requires children to choose from an array of three the one picture that most closely exemplifies the examiner's stimulus sentence.

Results

The repeated measures ANOVAs at both age levels demonstrate main effects for maternal age but no significant interactions between maternal age and situation. At 2 years, teenage mothers confirmed or acknowledged children's utterances significantly less and had fewer teaching utterances. These results, combined with other trends in the data, suggest that adolescent mothers did not differ significantly from children of older mothers in their general linguistic competencies. Thus, despite differences in the nature of their input, adolescent and older mothers provided at least the minimum amount of the right kind of input to ensure that acquisition proceeded at a "normal" rate. A review of mother's instructional strategies revealed that teenage mothers were less likely to use the decontextualized, syntactically complex, language of the classroom. Lack of familiarity with this form of discourse may have contributed to the children's poor performance. Thus, adolescent mothers' communicative strategies with their language learning children could be associated with the children's lack of success in school and school-related tasks.

Publications using these data should cite:

Van Houten, L. (1986). *Role of maternal input in the acquisition process: The communicative strategies of adolescent and older mothers with their language learning children.* Paper presented at the Boston University Conference on Language Development, Boston.

Van Kleeck

Anne Van Kleeck
Department of Speech Communication
University of Texas
Austin, TX 78712-1089
avkleeck@utxvm.cc.utexas.edu

These data were contributed by Anne Van Kleeck of the University of Texas at Austin. They are from 37 normal 3-year-olds in a laboratory setting. The children are from the Austin area and are native English speakers. This sample was not controlled for race or socio-economic status.

We have received only a small amount of information concerning the files. Each individual file is headed with identifying information on the child, the file names represent the child's name (usually first, but last initial or name has been used where there is duplication of the first name), and the session number. Each child participated in two one-half hour sessions, creating the first file (Bree1) for the first session and the second file (Bree2) for the second session. We hope to eventually receive further details regarding the participants and data collection procedures.

Warren-Leubecker

Amye Warren-Leubecker
Department of Psychology
University of Tennessee
615 McCallie Ave
Chattanooga, TN 37403

This subdirectory contains data from 20 children interacting either with their mothers or their fathers. The families are White and middle-class, but nonprofessionals. One group of children was aged 1;6 to 3;1 and the other group was aged 4;6 to 6;2. Ten of the children were in the "older" group, (Mean age of 64.7 months, SD = 8.25, range from 4;6 to 6;2) and ten are in a "younger" group (Mean age of 26.5 months, SD = 5.99, range from 1;6 to 3;1). Half of the children in each age group were boys and half were girls. Each child spoke to his or her mother and father in successive dyadic, separate sessions. The order in which they spoke to mother or father was randomized. The sessions took place in the child's home, normally in a living room or den area, with the child's own toys or books present to facilitate conversation. The experimenter was either not present in the room (set up the tape recorder and left it behind) or was in an isolated part of the room where the child could not easily see her. Parents were instructed to play with or talk to their children as naturally as possible. They were instructed to bring out the child in conversation, and the only limitation was that neither child or parent was to actually read to the other.

The parents were told that the experimenter was interested in how language develops, and thus was tape recording children of various ages for a project. Actually, the purpose of the project was to examine the fundamental voice frequencies used by mothers versus fathers when speaking to children, and the parents were subsequently informed that the experimenter was less interested in the child's speech than in their own. Because voice frequency was the primary measure to be used, the recording had to be high quality. A Revox reel-to-reel recorder and omnidirectional microphone were used and all home background noise was eliminated. Each session with mother or father lasted at least 15 minutes, possibly up to half an hour. Thus, each child conversed for at least half an hour. The recordings were transcribed verbatim by the experimenter using the common English alphabet. Phonetic approximations were used for any uninterpretable speech segments, and for common "slang" phrases (e.g., "gonna," "wanna,""doin," and "uh-huh"). Moreover, care was taken to approximate dialectical variation in pronunciation. All of the parents lived in the suburbs of Atlanta, Georgia, but did not have "Southern" accents. None of the parents or children had any obvious speech disfluencies, and none of the children were language delayed. The transcripts were compared for mother-directed speech.

Publications using these data should cite:

Warren-Leubecker, A. (1982). *Sex differences in speech to children.* Unpublished doctoral dissertation. Georgia Institute of Technology.

Warren-Leubecker, A., & Bohannon, J. N. (1984). Intonation patterns in child-directed speech: Mother-father speech. *Child Development, 55,* 1379–1385.

Wells

Gordon Wells
OISE
252 Bloor St. West
Toronto ON M5S 1V6 Canada
gwells@oise.utoronto.ca

This extensive corpus contains 299 files from 32 British children (16 girls and 16 boys) aged 1;6 to 5;0, recorded in a naturalistic setting. The data are taken from a project by Gordon Wells and colleagues entitled "The Bristol language development study: language development in preschool children" (1973). The original intent of the study was to provide a normative survey of British children growing up in an urban environment. The samples were recorded by tape recorders that turned on for 90-second intervals and then automatically turned off.

Approximately 1000 names were drawn at random from the record of births held by the City Medical Officer, and the families of all these children were approached initially by health visitors and subsequently by members of the research team. Details relevant to the classification of family background were obtained from all families, including a small minority who declined to take part in the study. At the same time, information was obtained that allowed us to exclude a number of categories of children: multiple births, children with known handicaps, those in full-time day care and those whose parents did not speak English as their native language. These categories were excluded, not out of any lack of interest in the problems that such children might be expected to encounter, but because their numbers in a sample of this size could not be expected to be large enough to permit meaningful comparisons to be made with the "normal" population.

Then, finally, names of those children whose families had agreed to take part were picked at random to fill the cells in the sample design, and a number of reserves were picked in a similar manner. During the following 4 years several families withdrew from the study, but when the schedule of recordings was finally completed, the sample still numbered 129 children.

Each child was observed a total of 10 times at three-monthly intervals, each observation consisting of a recording in the child's home and the administration of a number of tests at the Research Unit in the university. In addition, the parents of each child were interviewed when he or she was aged 3;6, to obtain information about the long-term environment provided by the home and about the parents' beliefs and practices concerning their role in the upbringing of their children.

The recording of spontaneous occurring conversation was the main part of each observation. The decision was made at the outset to obtain recordings in conditions that reduced to the minimum the possibly distorting effect of the actual observation process. To this end, special equipment was constructed that could be delivered to the child's home on the day before the observation was to be made and left there to work quite automatically until after the observation was completed. In the morning, when the child was being dressed for the day, a lightweight harness containing a radio microphone was put under the child's top garment. This transmitted continuously all speech produced by the child and any speech by others that was loud enough for the child to hear. It also, of course, picked up and transmitted a large range of other noises, such as doors shutting, footsteps, and even the bubbles of the goldfish in the aquarium. Because the microphone was linked to the tape recorder by radio, it caused no impediment to the child's freedom to move around, and reception remained good up to a range of 100 meters.

At the other end of the radio link in an out-of-the-way room or cupboard was a box containing the rest of the equipment: a radio receiver, a tape recorder, and a rather complex timing mechanism that was programmed to record 24 examples of 90 seconds' duration at approximately 20-minute intervals between 9 a.m. and 6 p.m. The intervals between samples were irregular so that parents would not be tempted to plan activities in regular 20-minute cycles. In fact, they were completely unaware of the precise time at which recordings were to be made, and the program was changed for each observation. The result was that, as far as is humanly possible within the limits set by ethical considerations, we recorded samples of these families' normal spontaneous conversation without their being aware that they were being observed.

There was, of course, a price to be paid. By choosing to give priority to naturalness, we had to forgo the making of on-the-spot notes about the context in which the conversations occurred. To a considerable extent we were able to compensate for this by playing the recording back to the parents in the evening and asking them to recall, in as much detail as possible, the location, participants, and activity for each of the recorded 90-second samples. An experiment carried out to compare this procedure with the more traditional procedure of a researcher being present during the recording revealed little difference in terms of the amount of contextual information that could be recovered; in some cases the mother was able to make more sense of an episode when she listened to it in the evening than the observer had been able to do while it was actually occurring. Once the observation had been made, the recording was transcribed and checked and then each child utterance was analyzed using the framework described earlier.

Table 30: Wells Files

Sample	Age	Sample	Age	Sample	Age
abigai02	1;5.28	geofre04	2;2.29	nancy08	3;0.6
abigai03	1;8.27	geofre05	2;2.29	nancy09	3;3.3
abigai04	2;0.1	geofre06	2;5.29	neil02	1;6.4
abigai05	2;3.0	geofre07	2;9.4	neil03	1;9.5
abigai06	2;6.2	geofre08	3;0.12	neil04	1;11.28
abigai07	2;9.3	geofre09	3;3.9	neil05	2;2.25

Table 30: Wells Files

Sample	Age	Sample	Age	Sample	Age
abigai08	3;0.2	geofre10	3;6.11	neil06	2;6.1
abigai09	3;3.0	geofre21	4;11.22	neil08	3;0.2
abigai10	3;6.6	gerald02	1;6.6	neil09	3;3.1
abigai21	4;8	gerald03	1;8.29	neil10	3;6.1
benjam02	1;5.21	gerald04	2;0.15	nevill02	1;5.25
benjam03	1;8.27	gerald05	2;3.5	nevill03	1;9.15
benjam04	1;11.30	gerald06	2;6.5	nevill04	2;0.7
benjam05	2;3.3	gerald07	2;9.1	nevill05	2;3.0
benjam06	2;5.28	gerald08	2;11.26	nevill06	2;5.21
benjam07	2;9.1	gerald10	3;5.0	nevill07	2;9.0
benjam08	2;11.29	gerald21	4;9.5	nevill08	3;0.1
benjam09	3;2.29	harrie02	1;6.2	nevill09	3;4.12
benjam10	3;6.3	harrie03	1;9.1	nevill10	3;5.27
benjam21	5;0.24	harrie04	2;0.1	olivia02	1;6.0
betty02	1;6.3	harrie05	2;3.2	olivia03	1;9.4
betty03	1;9.4	harrie06	2;6.1	olivia04	1;11.27
betty04	2;0.3	harrie07	2;9.0	olivia05	2;3.5
betty05	2;3.2	harrie08	3;0.0	olivia06	2;5.25
betty06	2;5.28	harrie09	3;3.0	olivia07	2;8.21
betty07	2;8.27	harrie10	3;6.1	olivia08	2;11.26
betty08	3;0.9	harrie21	4;10.3	olivia09	3;3.10
betty09	3;3.2	iris02	1;6.0	olivia10	3;5.22
betty21	4;11.2	iris03	1;8.5	penny02	1;6.9
darren02	1;6.2	iris04	2;0.2	penny03	2;9.5
darren03	1;9.0	iris05	2;2.30	penny04	1;11.27
darren04	2;0.6	iris06	2;3/2;9?	penny05	2;3.0
darren05	2;2.26	iris07	2;9.13	penny06	2;6.0

Table 30: Wells Files

Sample	Age	Sample	Age	Sample	Age
darren06	2;6.1	iris08	3;0.6	penny07	2;9.18
darren07	2;8.29	iris09	3;2.29	penny08	2;11.27
darren08	3;0.3	iris10	3;5.27	penny09	3;3.7
darren09	3;3.11	iris21	4;8.4	penny10	3;5.26
darren10	3;6.4	jack02	1;5.26	rosie02	1;5.29
darren21	4;10.6	jack03	1;9.4	rosie03	1;9.19
debbie02	1;6.9	jack04	2;0.2	rosie04	2;0.13
debbie03	1;8.30	jack05	2;2.25	rosie05	2;2.27
debbie04	1;11.29	jack06	2;5.13	rosie06	2;6.3
debbie05	2;3.20	jack07	2;9.24	rosie07	2;9.10
debbie06	2;6.6	jack08	2;11.26	rosie08	0;0.3
debbie07	2;9.5	jack09	3;3.8	rosie09	3;3.0
debbie08	3;11.28	jack10	3;5.23	rosie10	3;6.11
debbie09	3;3.4	jack21	4;9.1	samant02	1;6.6
debbie10	3;6.24	jason02	1;6.0	samant03	1;9.7
debbie21	1;11.25?	jason03	1;9.0	samant04	1;11.30
ellen02	1;5.26	jason04	2;0.8	samant05	2;2.29
ellen03	1;9.0	jason05	2;3.1	samant06	2;6.0
ellen04	1;11.29	jason06	2;6.1	samant07	2;9.3
ellen05	2;2.21	jason07	2;9.29	samant08	3;0.4
ellen06	2;5.21	jason08	3;0.2	samant09	3;2.27
ellen07	2;8.30	jason09	3;3.6	samant10	3;6.11
ellen08	2;11.28	jason10	3;5.30	sean02	1;6.11
ellen09	3;3.4	jason21	5;0.19	sean03	1;8.30
ellen10	3;6.1	jonath0	1;6.5	sean04	1;11.29
ellen21	4;9.22	jonath03	1;8.26	sean05	2;2.28
elspet02	1;5.30	jonath04	1;11.29	sean06	2;6.5

Table 30: Wells Files

Sample	Age	Sample	Age	Sample	Age
elspet03	1;8.23	jonath05	2;2.26	sean07	2;9.4
elspet04	2;0.2	jonath06	2;6.2	sean08	3;0.11
elspet05	2;2.29	jonath07	2;9.1	sean09	3;2.28
elspet06	2;6.6	jonath0	2;11.29	sean10	3;6.9
elspet07	2;8.28	jonath	3;2.28	sheila02	1;11.25?
elspet08	3;0.4	jonath	3;5.24	sheila03	1;9.2
elspet09	3;2.30	jonath	4;7.14	sheila04	1;11.30
elspet10	3;6.5	laura02	1;6.1	sheila05	2;3.4
elspet21	5;0.3	laura03	1;9.7	sheila06	2;5.27
frances02	1;6.1	laura04	2;0.6	sheila07	2;9.0
frances03	1;8.30	laura05	2;4.16	sheila08	2;11.28
frances04	2;0.1	laura06	2;6.3	sheila09	3;3.4
frances05	2;3.2	laura07	2;9.13	sheila10	3;6.25
frances06	2;6.3	laura08	3;0.7	simon02	1;5.21
frances07	2;8.30	laura09	3;3.0	simon03	1;9.2
frances08	2;11.28	laura10	3;6.2	simon04	1;11.13
frances09	3;3.0	lee02	1;5.28	simon05	2;3.5
frances10	3;6.0	lee03	2;2.3	simon06	2;6.0
frances21	4;10.8	lee04	1;11.26	simon07	1;9.1
gary02	1;6.0	lee05	2;3.1	simon08	3;0.1
gary03	1;9.2	lee06	2;6.1	simon09	3;3.9
gary04	2;0.4	lee07	2;9.24	simon10	3;5.22
gary05	2;3.4	lee08	3;0.1	stella02	1;6.8
gary06	2;6.3	lee09	3;3.0	stella03	1;9.3
gary07	2;9.5	lee10	3;5.29	stella05	2;2.30
gary08	3;0.4	martin02	1;5.26	stella06	2;6.2
gary09	3;3.3	martin03	1;9.2	stella07	2;8.25

Table 30: Wells Files

Sample	Age	Sample	Age	Sample	Age
gary10	3;5.25	martin04	2;0.8	stella08	2;11.27
gary21	4;9.0	martin05	2;3.3	stella09	3;3.7
gavin02	1;6.21	martin06	2;5.26	stella10	3;5.30
gavin03	1;9.4	martin07	2;8.24	tony02	1;5.26
gavin04	1;11.30	martin08	3;0.4	tony03	1;8.26
gavin05	2;4.4	martin09	3;3.5	tony04	1;11.14
gavin07	2;10.5	martin10	3;5.28	tony05	2;3.10
gavin08	3;0.6	nancy02	1;6.2	tony06	2;5.26
gavin09	3;3.19	nancy03	1;9.4	tony07	2;9.2
gavin10	3;7.27	nancy04	2;0.1	tony08	2;11.23
gavin21	4;9.18	nancy05	2;3.12	tony09	3;3.21
geofre02	1;6.0	nancy06	2;5.27	tony10	3;6.8
geofre03	1;9.6	nancy07	2;8.25		

Publications using these data should cite:

Wells, C. G. (1981). *Learning through interaction: The study of language development.* Cambridge, UK: Cambridge University Press.

3: Bilingual Corpora

Table 31: Bilingual Corpora

Corpus	Age Range	N	Comments
Aarssen/Bos on page 105	4–10	1021 files	Arabic-Dutch bilinguals, Turkish-Dutch bilinguals, and monolingual control groups for Arabic, Dutch, and Turkish
Blum / Snow on page 107	3;1–17;2	24 families	Study of Israeli, American Israeli, and American Jewish families at dinner
De Houwer on page 111	2;7–3;4	1	Longitudinal study of an English-Dutch bilingual child over an 8-month period.
Deuchar on page 130	1;3–3;3	1	Longitudinal study of a Spanish-English bilingual child in England
Guthrie on page 133	6;4–8;0	14	Classroom interactions of Chinese-English bilingual students
Hatzidaki on page 144	14–29	34	Interactions of French-Greek bilingual young adults in group environments
Hayashi on page 148	0;12–2;5	1	Study of a Japanese-Danish bilingual child in Denmark
Ionin on page 151	2;4–12;5	22	Russian immigrant children learning English
Krupa on page 155	6;2–8	1	Study of a Polish boy learning English as a second language
Langman on page 159	adults	11	Chinese immigrants to Hungary, learning Hungarian in natural contexts
Reading on page 161	16 years	34	Cross sectional study of English speaking students learning French
Serra / Sole on page 165	0;10–4;3	4	Catalan-Spanish bilingual children
Snow / Velasco on page 166	3rd and 5th graders	80	Oral language performance of bilingual children in both Spanish and English were assessed using two different tasks
Vila on page 170	1;9–5;4	1	Bilingual Spanish-Catalan girl with 50 monthly recordings
Watkins on page 171	1;9–7;2	7	French-English bilingual children studied for their use of deixis

Aarssen / Bos

Jeroen Aarssen
Petra Bos
Tilburg University–BABYLON,
Center for Studies on Multilingualism in the Multicultural Society
P.O. Box 90153
5000 LE Tilburg
The Netherlands
J.Aarssen@kub.nl
P.H.F.Bos@kub.nl

This database contains 1021 transcripts collected in the Netherlands, Turkey, and Morocco by Jeroen Aarssen and Petra Bos, Tilburg University. Bilingual data (either Turkish-Dutch or Moroccan Arabic-Dutch) were collected within the framework of a longitudinal study into development of bilingualism among Turkish and Moroccan children in the Netherlands.

The age range of the bilingual informants was from 4 to 10. The design of the study is pseudo-longitudinal with two consecutive cohorts of 25 informants. The younger cohort was followed for four rounds (from age 4 to age 7) and the older cohort for three rounds (from 8 to 10). The first round of data collection took place in 1991, and data collection was repeated in 1992, 1993, and 1994. The interval between subsequent rounds of data collection was about 1 year.

Turkish, Moroccan Arabic, and Dutch monolingual control data were collected as well in Turkey, Morocco, and The Netherlands, respectively. The Dutch control data were collected according to the same pseudo-longitudinal design as described above. The Turkish and Moroccan control data, however, were collected cross-sectionally from three different age groups (ages 5, 7, and 9).

Each transcript contains retellings of six short six-picture stories and the frog story (Mayer, 1969). The six short stories were constructed according to the following set-up: two stories with a clearly identifiable main character; two with two equivalent main characters; and two without a clearly identifiable main character.

The file names use the following code. First comes the child's pseudonym. Next comes a number for the child's age group. These numbers are often off by a year, so please rely on the ages as given inside the files. Then comes a letter for the language of the interaction (t=Turkish, m=Moroccan Arabic, n=Dutch). For the monolingual children, no letter is given. The files are structured into five directories:

ArabBiling: 350 files, ages 4–10
ArabMono: 71 files, ages 5, 7, 9
DutchMono: 175 files, ages 4–10
TurkBiling: 350 files, ages 4–10

TurkMono: 75 files, ages 5, 7, 9

Some adjustments were made in order to represent some special Turkish and Moroccan Arabic characters in standard ASCII:

Table 32: Aarssen/Bos Special Characters

Language	Character	Code	Language	Character	Code
Turkish	c-cedille	c1	Arabic	pharyngealized h	h2
Turkish	yumusak g	g1	Arabic	emphatic t	t2
Turkish	i without dot	i1	Arabic	emphatic s	s2
Turkish	o umlaut	o1	Arabic	emphatic d	d2
Arabic	ch of "loch"	x	Arabic	uvular r	gh
Arabic	j	j	Arabic	ayn	c

This research was supported by the Linguistic Research Foundation (Grant No. 300-172-002), which is funded by the Netherlands Organization for Scientific Research, NWO. This research resulted into the two doctoral theses cited below.

Publications using these data should cite:

Aarssen, J. (1996). Relating events in two languages: Acquisition of cohesive devices by Turkish-Dutch bilingual children at school age. *Studies in Multilingualism, Vol. 2*. Tilburg: Tilburg University Press.
Bos, P. (1997) Development of bilingualism: A study of school-age Moroccan children in the Netherlands. *Studies in Multilingualism, Vol. 8*. Tilburg: Tilburg University Press.
Mayer, M. (1969). *Frog, where are you?* New York: Dial Press.

Blum / Snow

Shoshana Blum-Kulka
Department of Communications
Hebrew University
91905 Jerusalem, Israel

Catherine Snow
Harvard Graduate School of Education
Larsen Hall, Appian Way
Cambridge, MA 02138 USA
catherine_snow@harvard.edu

This corpus includes data from the Family Discourse Project, carried out in two stages between 1985 to 1988 and 1989 to 1992. The research was funded by two grants from the Israeli-American Binational Science Foundation, grant No. 82-3422 to Shoshana Blum-Kulka, David Gordon, Susan Ervin-Tripp, and Catherine Snow as consultant, and grant 87-00167/1 to Shoshana Blum-Kulka and Catherine Snow. Three groups of families were involved in the project: native born Israeli families from Jerusalem, American-born Israeli families living in Israel, and American-born Jewish families living in Boston. The project was carried out in two stages. Stage one included 34 families and stage two included 24 families.

A monograph by Blum-Kulka (1997) is devoted to the analysis of these data. The book demonstrates the ways talk at dinner constructs, reflects, and invokes familial, social and cultural identities and provides social support for children to become members of their parents' culture. The groups studied are shown to differ in the ways they negotiate issues of power, independence and involvement through speech activities such as the choice and initiation of topics, conversational story-telling, naming practices, metapragmatic discourse, politeness, language choice, and code-switching. The transcripts in the CHILDES database include two types of files from stage two:

1. The first type includes transcripts of one dinner table conversation per family from eight native Israeli and eight American Israeli families. The families were taped in their homes in Jerusalem (Blum-Kulka).

2. The second type includes transcripts of one dinner table conversation per family from eightJewish American families. The families were taped in their homes in Boston (Blum-Kulka and Snow).

Families are identified by group and number, and participants are identified by role for adults and by name for children. The names of the children in the corpus are pseudonyms.

Family Backgrounds

The families in the project were middle-class and upper-middle-class, white-collar professional, nonobservant Jewish families from a European background from Israel and the

United States. All parents were at least college educated and were occupied professionally outside the home. Most parents were at the time of data collection in their late 30s or early 40s (mean age 41, range 34 to 54). Families had two, three or four children; the ages of children ranged from 3;1 to 17;2. By design most children are at the school-age of 6;1 to 13;5. Further information about the ages of the children is given below.

Data Collection

Data were collected by a participant observer who participated in and taped three family dinners over a period of 2 to 3 months. Recording started when the family began to gather around the table and stopped when they left the table. Meals lasted on the average from 1 to 1.5 hours. One meal per family was transcribed in CHAT.

Group 1: Native Israeli Families

The parents in this group are all Israeli born. The language spoken at dinner is Hebrew.

Table 33: Native Israeli Children

Family #	Children's Age and Sex
1	12;0 m, 10; 5 m
2	13;2 m, 11.4 m, 5;2 f
4	16;1 m, 12.2 f, 8;6 m
5	13;1 m, 10;8 m, 4;0 f
6	6;2 f, 6;2 f
8	10;5 f, 8;7 m
9	8;8 m, 5;6 m
10	11;5 f, 8;3 f, 3;2 m

Group 2: American Israeli Families

The adults in the American-Israeli families were born in the United States and lived in Israel for more than 9 years at the time of the study. Twenty-five of the children were born in Israel and four in the United States. All members of the family are competent bilinguals. Both English and Hebrew are used; the rate of English varies by family from 30% to 96%.

Group 3: Jewish-American Families

This set includes dinner conversations in English from eightmiddle-class Jewish Amer-

Table 34: American Israeli Children

Family #	Children's Age and Sex
1	11;4 m, 7;2 f
2	8;0 m, 6;1 m
3	9;0 m, 6;3 m
4	17;2 m, 13;4 f, 9;4 f, 7;5 f
6	15;10 m, 13;11 f, 5;5 f
7	13;11 f, 12;4 f, 9;0 f
8	12;9 f, 9;5 m, 5;8 m
12	12;2 m, 8;4 f

ican families from Boston. The families were taped in their homes.

Table 35: Jewish-American Children

Family #	Children's Age and Sex
1	15;5 f, 13;5 f
2	8;5 m, 6;1 m 4;4 m
3	10;0 m, 5;11 m
4	7;5 m, 4;3 m
9	9;5 m, 7;3 f
10	10;4 m, 8;2 f, 3;1 m
11	11;7 m, 9;6 f
12	13;4 f, 10;1 f, 4;1 m

The coding schemes developed for the analysis of family discourse include:

1. The Topical Actions Code (analyzes conversational topical actions such as the introduction, change, and shift of topics);
2. The Request Code (analyzes the speech act of directives);
3. The Narrative-Event Code (analyzes narrative segments from both the interactive and structural perspectives);
4. The Metapragmatic Comments Code (analyzes metapragmatic comments made with regard to turn-taking, conversational norms, and language).

The full set of codes is available on request from Shoshana Blum-Kulka.

Publications using these data should cite:

Blum-Kulka, S. (1997). Dinner-talk: Cultural patterns of sociability and socialization in family discourse. Mahwah, NJ: Lawrence Erlbaum Associates.

Additional relevant references include:

Blum-Kulka, S. (1990). "You don't touch lettuce with your fingers": Parental politeness in family discourse. *Journal of Pragmatics, 14,* 259–289.

Blum-Kulka, S. (1993). "You gotta know how to tell a story": Telling, tales and tellers in American and Israeli narrative events at dinner. *Language in Society, 22,* 361–402.

Blum-Kulka, S. (1994). The dynamics of family dinner-talk: Cultural contexts for children's passages to adult discourse. *Research on Language and Social Interaction, 27,* 1–51.

Blum-Kulka, S. (1996). Cultural patterns in dinner talk. In W. Senn (Ed.), *SPELL, Swiss Papers in English Language and Literature. Vol.9: Families* (pp. 77–107). Tübingen, Germany: Gunter Narr.

Blum-Kulka, S., & Katriel, T. (1991). Nicknaming practices in families: A cross-cultural perspective. In S. Ting-Toomey & F. Korseny (Eds.), *Cross Cultural Interpersonal Communication: International and Intercultural Communication Manual Vol. 15,* 58–77. London: Sage Publications.

Blum-Kulka, S., & Snow, C. (1992). Developing autonomy for tellers, tales and telling in family narrative-events. *Journal of Narrative and Life History, 2,* 187–217.

Olshtain, E., & Blum-Kulka, S. (1989). Happy Hebrish: Mixing and switching in American-Israeli family interaction. In S. Gass, C. Madden, & D. Presto Selinker (Eds.), *Variation in Second Language Acquisition Volume 1: Discourse and Pragmatics* (pp. 59–84). Philadelphia: Multilingual Matters.

De Houwer

Annick DeHouwer
Communicatiewetenschap
PSW – UIA
Universiteitsplein 1
2610 Antwerp, Belgium
vhouwer@uia.ua.ac.be

The child featured in this corpus is an only child who we will call Kate. Kate's first exposure to Dutch and English occurred within the period of a week after her birth, and exposure to two languages was regular up to and including the period of investigation.

Kate was born of an American mother and a Flemish father in a hospital near Antwerp, Belgium, where the language used by the nursing staff in conversations with patients is a standard-like variety of Dutch as spoken in Flanders. Kate roomed in with her English-speaking mother, who stayed in hospital for a week. Kate's Dutch-speaking father was present at the birth and afterwards visited daily. In her first days of life, Kate heard English spoken to her by her mother, and Dutch by her father and various members of the nursing staff. Thus, first exposure to two languages occurred within the period of a week.

Kate lived with both her parents up to and including the period of investigation and was usually addressed in a different language by each parent. Apart from short intervals when one of the parents was away on a trip, or when both Kate and her mother were in the United States without Kate's father, exposure to two languages was a pseudo-daily occurrence. Kate's mother, who is also her most regular care-giver, almost always addresses Kate in mainstream American English with a slight Midwestern accent. The term "mainstream American English" here is meant to refer to that variety of English that on the morphosyntactic level is not substantially different from the type of language used on national United States television. Kate's father almost always addressed Kate in standard Dutch with a slight Ghent accent. The term "standard Dutch" here refers to the supraregional variant of the language spoken in the Belgian region of Flanders and in most of the Netherlands.

Both parents are university graduates and hold prestigious jobs: Kate's mother was a part-time free-lance journalist for a variety of international publications, and Kate's father was a university professor. Kate's social background thus could be described as upper middle class. Kate's parents spoke English with each other, because Kate's mother spoke a heavily accented, often ungrammatical Dutch (she understood a lot more than she could produce herself), whereas Kate's father spoke English with a close to native competence.

At the beginning of the study, Kate's mother was asked to fill out a form with questions about the child's language background up to the time of the study. The information obtained is represented below.

Table 36: Countries Visited by Kate

Age	Country	Duration
birth-0;4	Belgium (Antwerp)	3 months
0;4-0;9	Australia (Canberra)	6 months
0;10-0;10	USA and Great Britain	3 weeks
0;10-1;6	Belgium (Antwerp)	8 months
1;7-1;8	USA	5 weeks
1;8-2;5	Belgium (Antwerp)	9 months
2;5-2;5	USA	2 weeks
2;6-3;4	Belgium (Antwerp)	11 months

The family's home base was mostly Antwerp, a large city in Belgium with much international activity mainly due to the presence of a major seaport and a large diamond industry. Many languages are spoken in the streets but the language of the local inhabitants is a distinct local dialect that is significantly different from standard Dutch on the phonological, lexical, and morphosyntactic levels. Kate had little contact with speakers of this Antwerp dialect, and it can be said to be of little importance in a discussion of her language background. Before the age of 3;4, Kate spent 8 months in an English-speaking country compared to about 2 years and 7 months in a Dutch-speaking region. The local environment was thus mainly Dutch-speaking. The type of Dutch that nonrelatives (including peers) would tend to use with Kate is fairly standard, with regionally colored accents. The media use standard Dutch. In the English-speaking environments, Kate was exposed to a variety of regional dialects ranging from Australian to British to American.

On weekdays, English was heard by the child much more often than Dutch, with an average of about 10 hours of English versus about 4 hours of Dutch a day. This was mainly due to the fact that Kate went to an English-speaking preschool, a small private school with a low pupil to teacher ratio. Before Kate started going to school at age 2;6, the input for both languages on week-days was about equal: for three mornings a week she was cared for by a Dutch-speaking neighbor.

On weekends, Dutch was heard more often than English, because Kate's father spends more time with her then, and this is mostly the time when the grandparents were present. Also visits to Dutch-speaking acquaintances and friends tended to take place on the weekends. Kate occasionally spent a week alone with her monolingual Dutch-speaking grandparents in the holidays or during the school-term when her parents were away on business trips.

Table 37: Kate's Language Environment (2;5–3;4)

Input type	Language	Frequency
mother	English	average 6 hrs. a day
father	Dutch	average 4.5 hrs. a day
paternal grandparents	Dutch	average 5 days a month
neighbor baby-sitter	Dutch	irregularly
most visitors	English	average 5 hrs. a week
some visitors	Dutch	irregularly
most people visited	English	average 5 hrs. a week
some people visited	Dutch	irregularly
peers outside school	Dutch	irregularly
preschool	English	average 20 hrs. a week
playgroup	English	3 hrs. a week
television	Dutch & English	average 1 hour a day
shops and services	Dutch	short periods daily

On the whole, it might be said that for the period from 2;5 to 3;4, Kate had slightly more contact with English than with Dutch. For both languages, she was exposed to a wide variety of accents. Most of the people that Kate met addressed her in only one language, and certainly her caregivers used mainly one language with her. Kate had thus grown up in a one person/one language situation.

On the information form filled out by her mother, Kate was described as a talkative child "in both languages." From my own observation of the child I can confirm this. In addition, Kate was a healthy child with no history of hospitalization or illnesses. She had never had to stay away from school because of a cold or other ailment. Kate was used to meeting a lot of different people from various ethnic backgrounds and was not shy in communicating with them. There is no reason to assume that she is exceptionally intelligent or has lower than normal intelligence. Finally, a word should be said about the attitudes in the child's environment towards her developing bilingualism. Although no formal investigation of this issue was carried out, informal observation during the study, as well as before and after it, showed there to be strong negative or positive attitudes present. Rather, the child's bilingualism at the age period studied seemed to be accepted by the environment at large as a matter of course, which was not commented on in either positive or negative terms. Kate's parents themselves only mentioned their daughter's bilingualism to outsiders when they were proudly recounting her "bilingual jokes." Bilingual individuals who were in regular contact with the child, however, were made aware by Kate's parents that they preferred that person to use mainly one language with her.

History of Data Collection

The data that form the core of the Kate corpus were collected independently from any institution using personal funds while the investigator, who had been trained as a linguist specializing in Dutch and English linguistics and held a Master's degree in Germanic Philology, was enrolled in a one-year graduate program in Psycholinguistics at the University of Leuven, Belgium. The data were transcribed as soon as possible after data collection using a typewriter. At the time of data collection no real plan existed as to what was going to happen with these data, and at the time the investigator had only a superficial knowledge of the field of child language. This soon changed after the investigator spent the year after data collection as an independent graduate student at Stanford University, studying mainly under Professor Eve Clark. When the investigator returned to Belgium she decided to use Kate's data as a basis for a doctoral thesis on bilingual children's language acquisition. This thesis was prepared over a 6-year period while the investigator was a lecturer in English linguistics at the Free University of Brussels, Belgium. The advisor was Professor Hugo Baetens Beardsmore of the Free University of Brussels, who is a specialist on bilingualism. During the summer and fall of 1990, the computerized corpus was transferred to CHAT format and the adult utterances from the original transcript were added to the computerized corpus. The investigator did this work while she was a Visiting Scholar at Carnegie Mellon University.

More About Data Collection

The investigator (INV) first met Kate about 6 months before data collection began and was in regular contact with her after the initial meeting. The child saw INV as a close friend of the family's and seemed to feel totally at ease with her. The investigator, a native speaker of Dutch, used Dutch with Kate most of the time throughout the initial acquaintanceship and the recording period. When data collection began, the child was not aware that her language use was of any particular interest to INV. There was no observable difference between Kate's behavior towards INV before data collection began and afterwards.

In total, 19 one-hour recordings were made. The age period studied covers the eight months from 2;7 to 3;4. Although the aim was to make one recording a week, the sessions ended up being irregularly spaced due to the family's unexpected absences or visitors which made data collection impossible. Data collection was carried out in the child's home using a good quality portable cassette-recorder with a built-in multidirectional microphone. This recorder was placed on the floor or on a table close to where interaction was taking place and received little interest from the child, except on some infrequent occasions when INV or Kate's mother was asked to "turn the music on." There is no reason to believe that the interaction was influenced by the presence of the recorder.

Transcription

The tapes were transcribed orthographically by the investigator as soon as possible after their recording. Contextual information was added from memory where deemed necessary for later disambiguation. Unfortunately much needed contextual information is still lacking, so that interactions are sometimes uninterpretable. In reformatting the corpus into CHAT, overlap information was omitted altogether, and bits of IPA transcriptions were translated into UNIBET.

All child-adult interactions were transcribed in full (including hesitations, false starts, repetitions, self–made songs, and nonsense utterances). Extended conversations between the adults that did not include the child in any way were not transcribed (this was indicated by a comment), but all other adult utterances were included in the transcription. The adult utterances in the corpus should be interpreted as being addressed to the child or to the child and the other adult(s) present unless specifically noted otherwise. The boundaries of both child and adult utterances were determined intuitively on the basis of intonation contours (this procedure is unfortunately far from ideal). Utterances were separated from one another using full stops unless there was clear question intonation (in which case a question mark was used), or unless the utterance was uttered in a fairly loud and/or excited voice (in which case an exclamation point was used).

The transcriber was trained in linguistics and phonetics and was quite proficient in both the language varieties that Kate was exposed to. Every effort was made to carry out the transcriptions as meticulously as possible, but for practical and financial reasons it was unfortunately impossible to engage a second transcriber for verification purposes.

The Recording Sessions

The overall description of the recording sessions is given in this table:

Table 38: Kate Recording Sessions

Tape	Age	Dutch	English	Mixed	NLS	Totals
1	2;7.12	68.8	23.4	7.8	0.0	77
2	2;7.17	42.7	38.2	18.8	0.3	335
3	2;8.8	45.9	27.0	21.6	5.4	37
4	2;9.0	94.7	0.5	3.2	1.6	374
5	2;10.5	60.8	36.6	0.9	1.7	232
6	2;10.13	95.8	0.4	3.6	0.2	527
7	2;10.28	69.3	26.1	4.1	0.4	241

Table 38: Kate Recording Sessions

Tape	Age	Dutch	English	Mixed	NLS	Totals
8	2;11.14	72.5	20.8	6.7	0.0	284
9	3;0.6	52.3	38.6	9.1	0.0	88
10	3;0.11	52.3	36.2	11.5	0.0	130
11	3;0.17	16.2	68.4	15.4	0.0	117
12	3;1.6	45.2	48.8	6.0	0.0	84
13	3;1.12	52.7	45.1	2.2	0.0	91
14	3;1.13	5.2	85.8	6.7	2.2	134
15	3;1.18	10.7	77.2	5.4	6.7	224
16	3;1.26	53.5	36.0	3.5	7.0	258
17	3;2.7	55.9	38.8	3.3	2.0	245
18	3;3.9	88.3	1.1	5.5	5.1	274
19	3;3.16	89.3	2.6	7.9	0.3	392
Totals		65.2	26.5	6.5	1.7	4144

Frequently, interactions were recorded while Kate was playing with INV in the kitchen and Kate's mother was cooking. Thus, at most of the recording sessions both languages were present, but because MOT was busy cooking and INV was usually Kate's focus of attention (after all, INV was there "to play with her," as MOT frequently told Kate), interactions between MOT and Kate were rather less frequent than interactions between INV and Kate. On many of the tapes, then, there are three speakers present, and each of these may interact with either one of the others. This situation, by the way, was quite usual in Kate's life: her parents had visitors almost daily, and the very hospitable atmosphere in Kate's house meant that more often than not, a visitor stayed for lunch or dinner.

Favorite games played during the recording sessions included "flying," in which Kate would repeatedly ask INV to lift her high up in the air; playing with an animal farm; pretending to be a lion or some other animal; making pretend "dinner" and "tea"; and naming colors. In MOT's interactions with Kate during the recording sessions discussions of past and future events featured prominently (again nothing unusual in Kate's life: every day before going to bed Kate had a conversation with MOT about the events of that day or the next). Other interaction between Kate and her mother frequently concerned the eating or preparing of food. There are not many examples of playing between Kate and her mother. As MOT has reported to INV, she does not usually play with Kate, except when Kate needs someone to give pretend "tea" or "dinner" to.

There were a few recording sessions where Kate's father (FAT) was present as well. In addition, Kate's aunt Elaine, her grandparents, and a colleague of her father's were present at some sessions. Overall, the data consist of mainly Dutch interactions between Kate and INV, and mainly English interactions between Kate and MOT. The language used between INV and MOT is English.

The table below lists the main activities that Kate engaged in during the recording sessions, together with an indication of who the major interacting adult was for each activity and which language they tended to use in addressing the child.

Table 39: Kate's Activities and Interlocutors

Tape	Activity	Person	Language
1	Naming colors	INV	Dutch
	General conversation	INV	Dutch
2	Recounting a visit	INV	Dutch
	Arranging cushions	INV	Dutch
	Naming colors	INV	Dutch
	Discussing imaginary events	MOT	English
3	Acting out boating scene	INV	Dutch
4	Pretending to be cooking	INV	Dutch
	Pretending to be sleeping	INV	Dutch
	Pretending to be a sick lion	INV	Dutch
	Pretending to shoot a bird	INV	Dutch
5	Requesting candy	MOT	English
	Being thrown up in the air	FAT/INV	Dutch
	Hiding game		Dutch
	Pretending to be a fish	INV	Dutch
6	Playing with animal farm	INV	Dutch
	Singing		Dutch
	General conversation	INV	Dutch
	Pretending to an animal	INV	Dutch
7	Discussing school events	INV/MOT	Dutch
	Discussing museum	INV/MOT	English/Dutch

Table 39: Kate's Activities and Interlocutors

Tape	Activity	Person	Language
	Singing	INV	Dutch
	Requesting and insisting	MOT	English
	Pretending to be a rooster	INV	Dutch
8	Drawing	FAT/INV	Dutch
	Making and serving	MOT/INV	English/Dutch
	Requesting and insisting	MOT	English
	Playing with animal farm	INV	Dutch
9	Naming colors	INV	Dutch
	Playing with a doll	INV	Dutch
	Requesting food stuffs	MOT	English
10	Playing in the bath tub	INV	Dutch
	Getting dressed	MOT	English
11	Discussing past events	MOT/INV	English/Dutch
	Joking around		English/Dutch
	Making and serving	MOT/INV	English/Dutch
12	Playing in the bath tub	MOT/INV	English/Dutch
	Getting dressed	MOT	English
	Discussing food	MOT	English
13	Discussing a trip	MOT/INV	English/Dutch
	Discussing the weekend	MOT/INV	English/Dutch
	"Helping" M prepare food	MOT	English
	Discussing food	FAT	Dutch
14	Making matches "dance"	MOT	English
	Learning about food stuffs	MOT	English
	Learning about cooking	MOT	English
	Singing		English
	General conversation	MOT	English

Table 39: Kate's Activities and Interlocutors

Tape	Activity	Person	Language
	Chattering nonsense	FAT	Dutch
15	Discussing school events	MOT	English
	General conversation	MOT	English
	Requesting food stuffs	MOT	English
	Riding tricycle		English
	Discussing upcoming trip	MOT	English
	Discussing trip to the seaside	INV	Dutch
	Bedtime monologue	-	-
16	Being thrown up in the air	INV	Dutch
	Hiding game		Dutch
	Naming colors	INV	Dutch
	Requesting food stuffs	MOT	English
	General conversation	MOT	English
17	General conversation	MOT	English
	Cutting up strawberries	INV	Dutch
	Requesting food to cut up	MOT	English
18	Playing at "dinner"	FAT/INV	Dutch
	Discussing school event	INV	Dutch
	Conversation and joking	FAT/INV	Dutch
19	Hiding games	FAT/INV	Dutch
	Playing with a ball	FAT/INV	Dutch
	General conversation	FAT/INV	Dutch
	Pretend dinner	FAT/INV	Dutch
	Discussing upcoming trip	FAT/INV	Dutch

The Codes

Each child utterance in the Kate corpus can in principle be followed by four coding lines (%gl1, %mph, %gl2 and %stx), but is always followed by a minimum of three coding lines (%mph, %gl1 and %gl2). Coding lines %gl1 and %gl2 contain codes that refer to characteristics of the relevant utterance as a whole (hence gl for "global"). Coding lines %mph and %stx contain word-per-word codes on the morphological and syntactic levels respectively. For more detailed information on the procedures used to construct the morphological and syntactic code systems used here, see De Houwer (1987).

Global Coding Line 1 — the %gl1 tier

The %gl1 tier consists of a language-use code, a morpheme count, and one or more optional utterance characterization codes (in this order).

Language-use code

The language-use codes used to characterize each child utterance contain three elements: the first refers to the language used by Kate, the second to the language that Kate's utterance was a response to (if Kate's utterance was not a clear response to any utterance by an interlocutor the second element was coded as "I" for initiation), and the third element defines the interlocutor. First we discuss the language used by Kate.

A child utterance was coded as being English (E) or Dutch (D) if all the lexical items and bound morphemes in it were unambiguously and fully English or Dutch. One phonetic feature from the other language was allowed to occur. It should be noted that the few linguistic forms that in principle could belong to either Dutch or English were not taken into account in deciding which language an utterance was. An utterance was coded as Mixed (M) if there was a lexical item consisting of one English and one Dutch morpheme, if there was a Dutch lexical item next to an English one, or if the utterance contained a "blend," that is, a free morpheme which without any doubt combined phonological elements from both languages (only two of these occur in the entire corpus).

In a few cases Kate produced nonadult morphemes that could belong to either language. In these instances it was decided to consider the bound morphemes as belonging to the same language as the free morphemes they were attached to. A final subgrouping is that of the "non-language-specific" utterances. A "non-language-specific" (X) utterance contains no elements referable to either English or Dutch, but consists only of gibberish or onomatopoeic sounds.

The second element in the language use code refers to the language that Kate's utterance was a reaction to. There are two main categories here: initiations and responses. An utterance was coded as an "initiation" if (1) it occurred after a lull in the conversation and could not be considered a delayed response to an adult's query, or (2) Kate had inserted an utterance in the middle of a conversation by adults and the utterance had both semantically and structurally no connection to what any adult was saying, or (3) the utterance was a response to a nonverbal action by an adult. An utterance was considered to be a "response" in all other cases, and was given the code English, Dutch, or Mixed as second element.

These codes refer to the language used by the interlocutor in the utterance preceding the child's utterance. The criteria for deciding between the three "language" groups are the same as the ones for the first element in the language use code.

This brings us to the third element of the language-use code — the interlocutor code. There are three possibilities for the interlocutor (IC) code: the IC is a Dutch or an English speaker (codes D and E), or the IC code is X, which means that the IC could be either a Dutch or English speaker. By definition, an IC code X can only follow an initiation code, except when Kate is talking to herself. The IC codes D and E were used only when through the context or elements in the child's utterance (such as Vocatives) it was quite clear what type of speaker the utterance was directed at. In this study the child's mother (MOT) and aunt were categorized as being English speakers, whereas all others were categorized as being Dutch speakers.

Below are the language-use codes. These codes consist of three parts. The first term is the language:

D	Dutch
E	English
M	Mixed
X	Non-language-specific

The second term is an initiation code (no clear response to an interlocutor's preceding utterance):

ID	Directed at a Dutch speaker.
IE	Directed at an English speaker.
IX	Addressee could be either an English or a Dutch speaker.

The third term is the response to an interlocutor's preceding utterance:

DD	In response to a Dutch utterance by a Dutch speaker.
DE	In response to a Dutch utterance by an English speaker.
MD	In response to a mixed utterance by a Dutch speaker.
ME	In response to a mixed utterance by an English speaker.
ED	In response to an English utterance by a Dutch speaker.
EE	In response to an English utterance by an English speaker.

Morpheme count

The language use code in %gl1 is followed by a morpheme count. For various reasons, Brown's (1973) criteria for counting morphemes were not followed (see DeHouwer 1987). Instead, for the Kate data an adult-oriented morphemic analysis was adopted for both languages, but of course no claim is made that a form used by the child has the same analytical value that it might have for an adult. The minimum morpheme count was 1, so even total nonsense utterances were given a morpheme count of 1.

Optional utterance characterization codes

These codes refer to general, nonsyntactic characteristics of the utterance or pertain to its more "performance" oriented aspects. A %gl1 may contain none, some or all of the following codes:

hes	A clear disfluency (hesitation).
rep	An element that repeats a previous element within the utterance.
corr1	Part of the utterance is retraced and changed.
Corr2:	Part of the child's previous utterance is repeated and changed.
Double	The utterance seems to consist of two completely divergent utterances.
Incompl	The child stops talking in the middle of an utterance.
Formula	The utterance is totally formulaic in nature (e.g., bye-bye, thank you).

Global Coding Line 2 — The %gl2 tier

The second global coding line includes four classes of codes. The four classes are constituents, structures, judgments, and ellipses.

Constituent codes

Every child utterance has one of the following nine mutually exclusive constituent codes:

ZZ	The utterance has a morphological code consisting only of one or more of the following: den, aff, sound, nons, interj, excl.
ZS	The utterance consists of a single constituent and is a short response to a previous utterance by the interacting adult (but not a repetition).
ZR	The utterance consists of a single constituent and is a (partial) repetition of the previous utterance by the interacting adult.
ZY	The utterance consists of a single constituent and is not a short response to or a (partial) repetition of the previous utterance by the interacting adult.
ZX	The utterance is totally unclear.
UA	The utterance consists of more than one constituent and contains no negative particle or rising (question) intonation, except in tag questions.
UN	The utterance consists of more than one constituent and contains a negative particle but no rising (question) intonation, except in tag questions.
UY	The utterance consists of more than one constituent, and at least one clause in it (but not a tag question) has rising (question) intonation and has the form of a Yes/No question.
UW	The utterance consists of more than one constituent, and at least one clause in it (but not a tag question) has rising (question) intonation and has the form of a Wh-question.

If an utterance has a code ZZ, ZS, ZR, ZY or ZX, it gets no other syntactic codes and there will be no %stx coding line. It is possible, though, that besides a Z-code there is a "transcription unclear" flag WT code after the Z-code.

If an utterance has a code UA, UN, UY, or UW, then it must receive a "Structure code" (and only one).

Structure codes

CS	The utterance is a simple sentence consisting of a single independent clause.
C2	The utterance is a compound sentence with or without a tag question.
C1	The utterance is a complex sentence with or without a tag question.
CQ	The utterance consists of a simple sentence and a tag question.
CY	Any other type of sentence ("rest" category).

Utterances which were given as first code UA, UN, UY or UW may get one or more of the following codes, all of which refer to some "special" syntactic aspect of the utterance in question.

Judgment codes

These codes evaluate the child utterance and comment on form that are not adultlike.

NI	Word-order error: there is inversion where it is not appropriate.
NN	Word-order error: there is no inversion although there should have been.
ND	Direct object placed outside VP containing at least two parts.
NA	Inappropriate placement of negative adverbial.
NY	Word order error different from the above.
NE	Ellipsis that is not adultlike.
NF	No ellipsis, where expected.
NS	Other syntactic error not covered by the above.

Ellipsis codes

ED	Adult-like discourse ellipsis.
EG	Adult-like grammatical ellipsis.
EY	Other type of adult-like ellipsis.

If there is an ellipsis code NE, ED, EG, or EY, it must be followed by one or more of the following codes specifying which element was elided:

XS	Subject elided.
XD	Direct Object elided.
XI	Indirect Object elided.
XV	Verb element elided.
XT	Time Adverbial elided.
XP	Place Adverbial elided.
XW	Manner Adverbial elided.
XM	Sentence Modifier elided.
XG	Subject Complement elided.
XC	Clause Connector elided.
XY	Anything not covered above elided.

If more than one syllable was unclearly transcribed, the utterance gets an "unclear" flag WT. If the utterance contains syntactic aspects not covered by the coding scheme that are worth looking at, it gets a code WS if the utterance also contains a semantic anomaly and the code WY in all other cases.

Morphological Coding Line — %mph

This coding line is always present and labels each word in the preceding child utterance on the morphological level. This is also the place where the status of word-items in the utterance can be commented on, using "special" codes. Note that any number of codes can be combined for any one word by using slashes (but no spaces!) between each code. These slashes indicate that just one of the codes applies, but the coder is not sure which, in which case the slashes function as logical OR operators and the special code "doubt" should be part of the code constellation, or the slashes indicate that all of the codes in the code constellation apply, in which case the slashes function as logical AND operators.

Special codes

XX	The word is uncodable, although fully transcribed; this code cannot be combined with any other code.
absent	The word is uncodable, because it is not fully transcribed; this code cannot be with any other code.
nons	The "word" to be coded is nonsense; this code cannot be combined with any other code except the code "doubt."
sound	The "word" is onomatopoeic; this code cannot be combined with any other code except the code "doubt".
doubt	This code is always used in combination with another code and means that the other codes linked to it are doubtful, e.g., doubt/Nprop.
greet	The word forms part of a greeting.
song	The word forms part of a memorized (in contrast to self-made) song.
excl	The word is an exclamation, e.g., voila, oh!
polite	The word is or is part of a politeness formula other than a greeting.

Singular nouns

Nprop	Proper noun.
NpropGEN	Proper noun, genitive form.
title	Mrs., Miss, Mr., meneer, mevrouw, juffrouw, and the like.
NED	Common noun (English); nonneuter common noun (Dutch).
neut	Common noun, neuter, nondiminutive (Dutch only).
NDIM	Common noun, neuter, diminutive (Dutch only).

Plural Nouns

NPL	Common noun, plural, nondiminutive, adult form.
NDIMPL	Common noun, plural, diminutive, adult form (Dutch only).

NPLx   Common noun, plural, nonadult-like form.

Adjectives modifying a noun

Adj	Cositive, root form, not a color term or negative adjective.
Adjdecl	Positive, root + {-e} form, not a color term or negative adjective (Dutch).
Adjcol	Root form, color term.
Adjdeclcol	Root + {-e} form, color term (Dutch only).
Adjneg	Negative adjective (GEEN or NO).
Adjcomp	Comparative.
Adjsup	Superlative.
Adjpp	Past participle form.

Adjectives used predicatively

AdjI	Positive, root form, not a numeral, color term or negative adjective AdjIdecl =positive, root + {-e} form, not a color term or negative adjective (Dutch only).
AdjIcol	Root form, color term.
AdjIdeclcol	Root + {-e} form, color term (Dutch only).
AdjIcomp	Comparative.
AdjsupI	Superlative.
AdjIDIM	Diminutive form of adjective.
AdjIpp	Past participle form used attributively in Subject Complement position.

Numerals

num	Used in prenoun position.
numI	Not used in prenoun position.

Adverbs

adv	Root form, consisting of a single lexical item.
advcomp	Comparative form.
aff	Affirmative sentence adverb (YES/JA and variations, e.g., OK).
den	Negative sentence adverb (NO/NEE and variations).

Particles

neg	Negative particle (NIET/NOT and variations).
part	Other particle (Dutch only).

Articles

0art	Zero article: no modifier or determiner present in front of a noun or adjective used as head of a noun phrase.
THE	Definite article (English only).
DE	Definite article, nonneuter or plural (Dutch only).

HET   Definite article, neuter (Dutch only).
EEN   Indefinite article

Personal pronouns

1psg   First person singular, used in Subject position (English: I; Dutch: IK).
2psg   Second person singular, used in Subject position (English: YOU;
                Dutch:JIJ/JE/GIJ/GE/U).
3psg   Third person singular, used in Subject position (English: HE/SHE;
                Dutch:HIJ/ZIJ /ZE).
impro   Third person singular, used in any position (English: IT; Dutch: HET/'T).
1ppl   First person plural Subject (English: WE; Dutch: WIJ/WE).
3ppl   Third person plural Subject (English: THEY; Dutch: ZIJ/ZE).
perspro   Any personal pronoun other than the ones listed above, regardless of its po-
                sition, or any personal pronoun listed above (except impro) not occurring in
                subject position.

Possessive pronouns

possD   Used as modifier, root form.
possDdecl   Used as modifier, appears in root + {-e} form (Dutch only).
possI   Not used as modifier, root form.
possIdecl   Not used as modifier, appears in root + {-e} form (Dutch only).

Demonstrative pronouns

demproD   Used as modifier.
demproI   Not used as modifier.

Interrogative pronouns

intproD   Used as modifier.
intproI   Not used as modifier.

Other pronouns

indpro   Indefinite pronoun.
relpro   Relative pronoun.
one   The pro-form ONE (English) or EEN (Dutch).
onedim   The diminutive pro-form EENTJE (Dutch only).

Verbs finite

These codes are used for those verb forms appearing closest to the Subject, or, if there is an
unambiguous, but elided Subject, used for those verb forms which in adult usage would appear closest to the Subject if it were overtly present.

Lexical verbs

VFPrstem	Stem form (Dutch) or UVF form (English).
VFPrstems	Stem + {-t} form (Dutch) or UVF + {-s} form (English).
VFPrstemn	Stem/UVF form + {-en}.
VFPrirr	Adult irregular form not formed by stem/UVF + bound morpheme.
VFPrx	Nonexisting form, no clear past or future reference.
VFPast	Adult-like form that is formally marked as past.

Copula and auxiliaries

VFPrcop	Copula in adult-like, present tense form.
VFPrDO	English DO used as an auxiliary in adult-like, nonpast form.
VFPraux	Temporal/aspectual auxiliary in adult-like, nonpast form.
VFPastcop	Copula in adult-like, past form.
VFPastDO	English DO used as an auxiliary in adult-like, past form.
VFPastaux	Temporal/aspectual auxiliary (not DO) in adult-like, past form.

Imperatives

VFim	Adult form.
Vfimx	Form nonexisting in adult usage.

Modal verbs

VFPrstemMod	Stem/UVF form, with nonfinite element in rest of verb phrase.
VFPrstemModI	Stem/UVF form, only verb element in VP.
VFPrstemtMod	Stem/UVF + {-t} form, with nonfinite element in rest of VP.
VFPrstemtModI	Stem/UVF + {-t} form, only verb element in VP.
VFPrstemsModI	Stem/UVF + {-s} form, only verb element in VP.
VFPrstemnMod	Stem/UVF form + {-en}, with nonfinite element in rest of VP.
VFPrstemnModI	Stem/UVF form + {-en}, only verb element in VP.
VFPrirrMod	Irregular form, with nonfinite element in rest of VP.
VFPrirrModI	Irregular form, only verb element in VP.
VFPrxMod	Nonexisting form, with nonfinite element in rest of VP.
VFPrxModI	Nonexisting form, only verb element in VP.
VFPastModI	Adult-like form formally marked as past, only verb element in VP.
VFPastMod	Adult-like form marked as past, with nonfinite element in VP.

Nonfinite

(verb elements used in clauses containing at least one finite verb form)

VNFp	Past participle.
VNFinf	Infinitive (=stem + {-en} or UVF).
VNFing	-ing participle (=UVF + {-ing}; English only).
VNFstem	Stem form (Dutch only).
VNFpast	Finite past form used in a nonfinite manner.

VNFx   Form not relatable to any form in adult usage.

Other verb elements that are not clearly finite or nonfinite

pp   Past participle form used in clauses containing no finite verb.
inf   Infinitive (= stem + {-en} for Dutch or UVF for English) used in clauses with a single verb form and no detectable Subject.
ing   ing-form (= UVF + {-ing}; English only) in clauses without a finite verb.
stem   verb stem (Dutch only) used in clauses with a single verb form and no detectable Subject.

Other parts of speech

prep   Preposition
conj   Conjunction
interj   Interjection

%stx: Word-Per-Word Syntactic Coding Line

This coding line is absent if the first code on the %gl2 code line is a Z-code but is present if the first code on the %gl2 code line is a U-code. The word-per-word syntactic coding line labels each word in the preceding child utterance on the syntactic level. Every syntactic code minimally consists of a constituent code, but it can also be more complex, and can consist of a constituent code followed by a position code or repetition code, or both. The minimum number of characters for each syntactic code is one, and the maximum is four.

Constituent codes

S   Subject
D   Direct Object
G   Subject Complement
O   Object Complement
I   Indirect Object
F   Sentence Modifier
V   Intransitive or Copular Verb
VT   Monotransitive Verb
VD   Ditransitive Verb
VX   Complex-transitive Verb
T   Optional Time Adverbial
M   Optional Manner Adverbial
P   Optional Place Adverbial
A   Optional Adverbial (other than Time, Manner or Place)
LL   Clause Connector
BB   Vocative
YY   Residue code: anything not covered above

Constituent position codes

Every constituent code that is not part of the first main clause in the utterance is followed by a position code indicating what type of clause the constituent belongs to. Note that for the verb codes VT, VD, and VX any position code comes directly after the V-part of the code.

S   The constituent is part of a subordinate clause.
2   The constituent is part of the second main clause in the utterance.
Y   The constituent is part of some unit other than the ones covered before.

Repetition code

Any constituent code may be followed by a repetition code R indicating that the lexical item filling that constituent is a repetition of a lexical item occurring in the interlocutor's preceding utterance. The repetition must be exact on the free morpheme level. Note that for the verb codes VT,VD and VX the repetition code comes directly after the V-part of the code if there is no position code, or after the position code if there is one.

Publications using these should cite:

De Houwer, A. (1987) *Two at a Time: An Exploration of How Children Acquire Two Languages from Birth*. Unpublished doctoral dissertation, Vrije Universiteit Brussel.

De Houwer, A. (1990).*The acquisition of two languages: A case study*. New York: Cambridge University Press.

Deuchar

Margaret Deuchar
Department of Linguistics
University of Wales
Bangor, Gwynedd LL57 2DG United Kingdom
mdeuchar@bangor.ac.uk

This corpus is a study of Manuela, a girl born in Brighton, England on 24-JUN-1985. Manuela lived in Brighton and was an only child during the period under investigation. Her mother, Margaret Deuchar, was the investigator, and is a linguist. Her father is a civil engineer. Her mother was born and brought up in England, speaking English, and learned Spanish in early adulthood. Her English was standard with an RP accent slightly modified by southern English features (most of her childhood was spent in Hampshire). Her father was born in Cuba where he lived until age 7, after which he lived mostly in the Dominican Republic and Panama, most of that time being spent in the latter until early adulthood, when he moved to England. He was brought up by Cuban parents speaking Cuban Spanish; his Spanish was also influenced by that spoken in Panama, where he spent his middle and later childhood. He learned English as a second language, starting in secondary school. From the time of their marriage (four years before Manuela's birth) the parents spoke Spanish with one another. During the period of data collection, Manuela was exposed to Spanish from both parents in the home. She was exposed to English from caretakers in the creche and from her maternal grandmother, who spent one day per week with her. The grandmother spoke standard English with a fairly conservative RP accent. At age 1;3, Manuela heard, on the average, English 48% of the time, and Spanish 52% of the time (calculated on the basis of 12 waking hours per day, 7 days per week).

Data Collection

Video and audio recordings were made weekly of spontaneous interactions between Manuela and her Spanish-speaking father on one hand, and Manuela and her English-speaking grandmother on the other. Manuela's mother was also present at some of the recordings in both languages. In addition to the weekly recording, studio-quality audio recordings were made at age 1;11 and monthly from age 2;3 onwards in order to obtain elicited data of sufficient quality for the voicing study. Daily diary records were also kept by Manuela's mother when interacting with Manuela and were supplemented by observations in the creche attended by Manuela. Most of the recordings took place at home in a rectangular room – half of which was the living room and half, the dining room. There was no partition separating the two areas.

Sampling Procedure

The corpus here represents only a small sample of the recordings made, of which there are in total 95 made with an English-speaking interlocutor, mostly the maternal grandmother, and 125 with a Spanish-speaking interlocutor, mostly the father. These recordings were made weekly over a 2-year period from age 1;3 to 3;3. Many of the recordings have not yet been transcribed; others, although transcribed, do not yet meet the CHAT conventions. Diary and creche records are also not yet available in the CHAT format.

Warnings

1. In %pho: lines the $ symbol is used inconsistently to indicate word boundaries.
2. There is a tendency for Manuela's utterances to be represented as "yyy" in the main tier.
3. The form "ae" should be changed to "&" and "ao" should be changed to "Q" in the %pho tier in all files.
4. The form "Manuela" is used invariably in the main tier of the child's speech, pronunciation of this being given in %pho tier as "m i n a." In adult speech, where no %pho tier is included, the actual pronunciation of "Manuela" is indicated by the spelling.
5. Adult sentences are in general very long, as many sentences have been linked by pause symbols (#) instead of being delimited by utterance terminators.
6. Pseudonyms were not used. All adults involved gave informed consent for the use of their data.

Goals of the Project

The major goal was to determine, by means of a case study of an infant acquiring English and Spanish simultaneously between the ages of 1;3 and 3;3, whether the child had an initial linguistic system which subsequently divided into two, or whether a division corresponding to the two sources of linguistic input could be ascertained from the beginning of linguistic production.

Transcription

Recorded data were transcribed, using phonetic transcription in PHONASCII for the child utterances. The transcriber was competent in English and Spanish and phonetic transcription, and was trained in the CHAT conventions. Transcriptions were typed directly into computer files while videotapes were viewed and audiotapes listened to. The transcriber operated computer, video recorder and audio recorder at the same time while doing transcription. The %pho tier was the only one recorded for each utterance by Manuela; other tiers, such as those coding nonverbal or situational information, were included when the transcriber judged that they gave useful additional information. Prosody was not transcribed. In the Spanish transcriptions, each utterance was given a tier with a translation into English. Random spot reliability checks were done. However, these affected only a small portion of the data. The only file checked and corrected in exhaustive detail is 861002eg.cha. No project-specific codes were used.

Table 40: Deuchar Transcripts

Language	File	Date	Age
English	861002eg.cha	2-OCT-1986	1;3.8
English	861023eg.cha	23-OCT-1986	1;3.29
English	861127eg.cha	27-NOV-1986	1;5.3
English	870205eg.cha	5-FEB-1987	1;7.12
English	870402eg.cha	2-APR-1987	1;9.9
English	870528eg.cha	28-MAY-1987	1;11.4
English	870728er.cha	28-JUL-1987	2;1.4
English	870823ej.cha	23-AUG-1987	2;1.30
English	871126eg.cha	26-NOV-1987	2;5.2
English	880114eg.cha	14-JAN-1988	2;6.21
Spanish	860928sf.cha	28-SEP-1986	1;3.4
Spanish	861025sf.cha	25-OCT-1986	1;4.1
Spanish	870201sf.cha	1-FEB-1987	1;7.8
Spanish	870329sf.cha	29-MAR-1987	1;9.5
Spanish	870531sf.cha	31-MAY-1987	1;11.7
Spanish	870720sk.cha	20-JULY-1987	2;0.26
Spanish	870829sp.cha	29-AUG-1987	2;2.5
Spanish	871129sf.cha	29-NOV-1987	2;5.5
Spanish	871226sf.cha		2;6.2

The labels "s" or "e" in the file names refer to the language spoken by the adult in the recording session. Copies of articles that make use of the data should be sent to Margaret Deuchar. This project was supported by grants from the Economic and Social Research Council (ref. no. C00232393) and the British Academy. Publications using these data should cite:

Deuchar, M., & Quay, S. (1992). *Bilingual acquisition: Theoretical implications of a case study.* Oxford, UK: Oxford University Press.

Guthrie

Larry F. Guthrie
Far West Laboratory
1855 Folsom St.
San Francisco, CA 94103 USA

This subdirectory contains data from a detailed examination of the language use of a group of Chinese-American first-graders and their two teachers. The files were collected by Larry Guthrie of the Far Western Research Laboratory and donated to the CHILDES in 1985. They were reformatted into CHAT in 1986.

Goals

Although considerable information is available on language use in monolingual classrooms, and to a lesser extent on that in Hispanic bilingual situations, very little is known about how Chinese children and their teachers construct interactions. The focus of the research was a bilingual class of students that alternated each half-day between a Chinese bilingual teacher and a teacher who did not speak Chinese. This provided the unique opportunity to examine the language of the same Limited-English-Speaking (LES) children with two different teachers. The first of these teachers not only spoke the students' first language, Cantonese, but was also of the same cultural background. A woman in her early twenties, she had immigrated to the United States at the age of 9. Both her Cantonese and English were native-like. The other teacher was an Anglo male who had taught in Spanish-English bilingual programs, but had little prior experience with Chinese students.

Three basic questions directed the research. The first of these sought an in-depth description of the classroom interaction between Chinese-American children and their teachers. How do teachers orchestrate lessons and how, in turn, do students respond? What variation, in both teacher and student language, is found across student English language proficiency groups? Second, we compared the interaction in the two classrooms. What differences occur between the ways in which the two teachers orchestrate lessons? What differences emerge in student language use? How do these differences compare across linguistic proficiency groups? Third, we asked what variations in teacher and student language might be found when this group of children moved on to second grade. Did these students experience difficulty in crossing the "border" between first and second grade, or in adjusting to the rule system of the new teacher?

Method

Sociolinguistic methods were used to seek answers to these questions and to uncover the ways in which Cantonese-speaking children and their teachers constructed their interactions and used language. The study was conducted in three phases. In the first phase, target students and speech events (lessons) were identified. In the second phase, recordings of sample lessons were collected, transcribed, and analyzed. The third phase involved additional recording in reading lessons after target students had progressed to second grade. The procedures employed within each phase are described in more detail later. First, however, is a description of the setting in which the study was conducted.

Participants

The setting for the study was an elementary school with a predominantly Chinese population. The school was located near a large Chinatown community on the West Coast. There were approximately 644 students enrolled in Chinatown Elementary at the time of this study. The school population is relatively stable, but there are periodic influxes of new immigrant and refugee populations. Almost half (44.6%) of the school population was Chinese; the remainder of the students were largely Hispanic (19.9%), other Asian (20.5%), and Black (11.6%). Because of the ethnic quota system operative within the district, the school is now officially "closed" to new Chinese students, except those who live within the most immediate neighborhood. Most of the Chinese students at Chinatown Elementary are classified as either Limited-English-Speaking (LES, 28%) or nonEnglish-speaking (NES, 61%). These students, in turn, are placed in either a bilingual or regular class.

Within the Chinese community, the school has a good reputation. Most Chinese parents seem to feel more secure if their children are attending a school that is predominantly Chinese and has Chinese teachers. There have been reports of parents who submitted a falsified address, or used that of a relative, in order that their child might be allowed to attend the school.

The participants in Phase One were eleven first-grade Chinese-American students, selected on the basis of English-language proficiency. Prior to data collection, each teacher was asked to rank all students in the class on a four-point scale of oral English language proficiency. The bilingual teacher also provided similar information on students' Chinese proficiency. These judgments were then verified through observations of potential target students. In this way, five students ranking at the low end of the scale (1-2), four ranking at the middle of the scale (3), and two fluent English speakers were selected.

Lessons

As mentioned earlier, the two participating teachers in the study taught in a half-day alternation bilingual program. Each teacher met with the students in the target class for half of each school day, and alternated between mornings and afternoons. One teacher was bilingual and biliterate in Chinese and English, and although the other spoke no Chinese, he did speak Spanish and had taught a self-contained Spanish bilingual class the year before. Both teachers had several years of experience.

Two types of lessons were selected for analysis in this report — reading with the bilingual teacher and oral language with the Anglo teacher's class. All of the lessons in the

CHILDES database are in English. Although the lesson content and focus differed some-what across the teachers' lessons, they were in many respects comparable. For two weeks prior to taping, classroom observers took descriptive field notes and coded for activity structures. These two lessons were found to be compatible in that they were both teacher-directed, student membership was approximately the same, and both teachers organized lessons around a basic question/answer format. Descriptions of the typical organization of each teacher's lesson follow.

Reading

The bilingual teacher divided students into four instructional groups for reading: Flint-stones, Roadrunners, Bugs Bunnies, and Snoopies. Each group met with the teacher for 15 to 20 minutes during each reading period, rotating according to the schedule set up by the teacher. Reading lessons were conducted in much the same way with each group. The teacher usually began by writing a list of vocabulary words on the board near the reading table. She then would introduce each word and ask students to read and say the words as a group. Individual students were then called on to read all the vocabulary words aloud. The next activity included story posters. Each poster contained a picture on the top and a story below. When she used the poster, the teacher would ask the students to look at the picture first, then ask them to describe the picture. Together, they would then read the story on the poster. When she used the book, she adopted the same approach as with the poster, begin-ning with a description of the picture, followed by reading. The final step in the typical reading lesson would be to ask the children to read the text silently, after which she asked them comprehension questions. To answer these, students were allowed to read an appro-priate phrase or sentence from the text. Throughout the reading lesson, if students stumbled over a word, the teacher read it out and asked the student to repeat it.

Oral Language

The Anglo teacher divided his class for oral language into two instructional groups on the basis of oral English proficiency: Low and a combination of Middle and High. Howev-er, during the oral language period, only that group being taught by the teacher remained in the classroom; the other group met with another instructor in a different room. The over-all procedures employed with each group were much the same. The Low group consisted of six students who sat in their assigned seats. For oral language, the teacher would join the group by pulling up an additional chair. Very often the lesson began with picture flash-cards, which students were required to identify and describe. The Middle/High group was composed of nine students. They all sat at a table in the center of the room, where only the Middle group students normally sat. The teacher brought his own chair when he joined the group. Once again, the teacher usually began with picture flashcards, which the students were to identify. Chinese lessons taught by the bilingual teacher as well as seat work in the other teacher's class were recorded as well.

Phase Two

In Phase Two, teachers and target students were recorded in different lessons: oral language and seat work in the Anglo teacher's class and reading and Chinese in the bilingual teacher's class. These were transcribed, coded, and analyzed. The following is an overall description of the activities within this phase of the study. Audiotape recordings were made through the use of a Marantz recorder, with two lavaliere microphones placed in the middle of each group's table. All data collection for Phase Two was conducted over a 2-month period in the spring of 1982.

Two data collectors were present during each taping session, both fluent speakers of Cantonese, Mandarin, and English. One data collector took field notes on the activities of the focal group, recording information on the physical arrangement of the group, important nonverbal behaviors, the text and materials used, and other contextual information. The other data collector, meanwhile, monitored the audiotape through earphones. Because of incidental noise in the class and the voices of students in other groups, the earphones enabled the data collector to hear the speech of the teacher and target students much better. This data collector wrote down names and utterance fragments of speakers throughout the interaction to aid in subsequent transcription.

The audiotape recording of each lesson was transcribed by the data collector who monitored that taping session. The handwritten transcript was then entered into an IBM-PC used for the analysis. Those utterances in Chinese were transcribed in Chinese, and an English translation was provided in brackets. Descriptions of nonverbal behavior were included in parentheses.

Recordings took place between February 1982 and October 1982. Lessons 1 to 28 were recorded while students were in first grade. Lessons 30 to 38 were recorded while students were in second grade. The following tables list the target children, additional children in the classrooms, and the adults in the classrooms.

Table 41: Guthrie Children

Code	Child's name	Sex	Age
*WYM	Wyman	M	7;8
*PHU	Phung Ngoc	F	6;11
*AHT	Ah Tay	F	?
*AHN	Ah Ngat	F	6;10
*AHP	Ah Phang	F	6;6
*MEO	Mei Oanh	F	8;0
*STE	Steven	F	7;5

Table 41: Guthrie Children

Code	Child's name	Sex	Age
*HOW	Howie	M	7;10
*HIE	Hieu Nghi	F	6;7
*ANT	Anton	M	?
*CAO	Carolina	F	6;5
*JAC	Jackie	F	6;4
*CHR	Christopher	M	7;1
*CLI	Clifton	M	?

Table 42: Guthrie — Other Children

Code	Child's Name	Sex
*AMY	Amy	F
*MEN	Mei-Ngoc	F
*LIS	Lisa	F
*JUS	Justin	M
*JOS	Joseph	M
*KEA	Kearny	M
*YVO	Yvonne	F
*ANH	Anh Tu	F
*WAI	Wai Yee	F
*CAL	Carletta	F
*HEN	Henrietta	F
*SUB	Subnum	F
*STU	Unidentified Student 1	
*STU	Unidentified Student 2	
*SEV	Several	

Table 43: Guthrie — Adults

Code	Adult's Name	Description
*MAR	Mary	(bilingual teacher A)
*LAR	Larry	(Teacher B)
*ELA	Elaine	(Mary's aide)
*ELL	Ellen	(Larry's aide)
*TRA	Tracy	(Mary's student teacher)
*JUN	June	
*BEA	Beatrice	
*FOO	Miss Foo	

Files

There are three subdirectories. The "Larry" subdirectory contains the files from the monolingual Anglo teacher's class of first graders. The "Mary" subdirectory contains the files from the first grade class of the bilingual teacher. The "Maisie" subdirectory contains the files from the second grade teacher's class in the follow-up study. The teacher was observed on three different days with three reading groups on each day. For the "Maisie" subdirectory, the following speakers were present:

Table 44: Speakers in the Maisie Data

Speaker	Code Name	Identity
MAI	Maisie Dea	Teacher
QUO	Quoc-Hung	Student
SAM	Sam-Day	Student
ELI	Elizabeth	Student
XYZ	*	Student
KIM	Kim-Lien	Student
RIT	Rita	Student
CHI	Chin	Student
EDW	Edwin	Student
TIN	Tina	Student

Table 44: Speakers in the Maisie Data

Speaker	Code Name	Identity
ANG	Angela	Student
PUI	Pui-Chin	Student
NGH	Nghi-Ma	Student
VEL	Velma	Student
STU	Unknown	Student
STU	Unknown	Student
STU	Unknown	Student
SEV	Several	Students

*There is no positive identification of speaker XYZ's name, however the speaker may be "Sui-Wai"

Coding

Utterances were coded using a system of conversational acts (C-acts) developed by Dore (1977). C-acts represent a taxonomy of speech act types that code utterances according to (1) the grammatical structure of the utterance, (2) its illocutionary properties, and (3) its general semantic or propositional content. Because of the different nature and focus of the present research, some modifications were made in the system as used in previous studies. These included both the addition and deletion of certain codes.

Forty-nine separate speech acts, each assigned a three-letter code, constitute the conversational act system. These are grouped into six broad function types: (1) Assertions, which solicit information or actions; (2) Organizational Devices, which control personal contact and conversational flow; (3) Performatives, which accomplish acts by being said; (4) Requests, which solicit information or actions; and (6) Responses, which supply solicited information or acknowledge remarks (Dore et al., 1978, pp. 372-3). An additional category of special speech acts that codes activities such as microphone talk, laughing, and singing is also included. Conversational acts serving the Request function, for example, include Requests for Action (QAC), Product Requests (QPR), and Requests for Permission (QPM).

Coding proceeded as follows. First, the grammatical form and its literal semantic meaning were determined. Then a judgment was made as to the conventional force, or purpose, of the utterance. In this step, sequencing, reference, and other conversational cues, such as marked illocutionary devices and intonation, were taken into consideration. Utterances were thus placed first within the six broad function types, and then categorized as an individual conversational act. Throughout the coding, the contextual information contained in field notes provided an addition check for the validity.

Initial coding was conducted by the data collector who observed a particular lesson. To ensure inter-coder agreement, each taped session was then coded a second time by another member of the research team, all of whom had engaged in two weeks of training and practice. Discrepancies were resolved through discussion. Throughout the coding process, inter-coder agreement for individual lessons ranged from 0.90 to 0.96. It should be noted that conversational act coding has been shown to be highly reliable in other studies as well, with inter-coder reliability approaching 0.90.

Although utterances in Chinese were translated into English and entered as data, all coding was done on the original Chinese. In several instances, this procedure proved to be crucial, because the English translation would have received a different code.

Cicourel has compared three prevalent models of discourse: the speech act model, the expansion model, and the problem-solving model. His conclusion was that any one of these models in isolation is inadequate; some sort of integration is required. The method used in the present study represents an attempt at such an integration. By including both quantitative and qualitative analyses, the speech-act and expansion models were to some extent combined. This integration also helped to meet some of the criticisms leveled by Cicourel against the speech-act approach. Cicourel faulted the speech act model because it cannot easily account for 1) organizational features of interaction; 2) participant's strategies, such as plans for elaboration; 3) the situated nature of discourse, such as situated meaning and context; and 4) the multiple functions of utterances. The present study overcomes these weaknesses by incorporating the following methodologies:

1. First, organizational features of interaction or participant structures were identified in the Phase I observations. These guided the selection of episodes (lessons) for taping in Phase Two. All coding and analysis was done with regard to the participant structures.

2. Second, attention was given to participants' local strategies and plans for elaboration in ways of speaking. Because coding was done not on single sentences or utterances but on stretches of discourse, taking the course and development of the conversation into consideration, the actor's strategies and intentions were included. In addition, the qualitative analysis in many respects focused on just this aspect of discourse. Particular attention was given to the questioning strategies each teacher employed in conducting particular lessons.

3. Third, because all coding was done on relatively large stretches of language, situational meanings were taken into account. In coding the data, consideration was given to the speakers' utterances in context. What was said before, after, and in contexts more removed in time was taken into account in the coding.

3. Finally, the present study was sensitive to the multiple functions of utterances in context. The C-act system allows for multiple coding so that important meanings and intentions are not lost. Further, in this study, the observers' field notes provided a running description of the context which contributed to the coder's knowledge of

and sensitivity to the interaction. The fact that the data collectors conducted the coding also contributed to its validity.

The use of conversational acts rather than other coding systems contributed to a mitigation of some of the other weaknesses Cicourel identified in speech-act analyses. First, because conversational acts are sensitive to grammatical form, semantic content, and illocutionary force, and not just one of these, they provide a link between form and function. As Cole, Dore, Hall, and Dowley (1978) pointed out, conversational acts mediate between the grammatical and the social, between the "grammatical forms and the interactional purpose for which they are used" (p.74). In other words, they integrate speakers' interests and purposes.

Definitions and Examples of Conversational-Acts

Assertive Devices

ASS	Assertives report facts, state rules, convey attitudes, and so forth.
AAT	Attributions report beliefs about another's internal state: "He does not know the answer."; "He wants to"; "He can't do it."
ADC	Descriptions predicate events, properties, and locations of objects or people: "The car is red"; "It fell on the floor"; "We did it"; "We have a boat."
AEV	Evaluations express personal judgments or attitudes: "That's good."
AEX	Explanations state reasons, causes, justifications, and predictions: "I did it because it's fun"; "It won't stay up there."
AID	Identifications label objects, events, and people: "That's a car"; "I'm Robin."
AIR	Internal Reports express emotions, sensations, intents, and other mental events: "I like it"; "It hurts"; "I'll do it"; "I know."
APR	Predictives state expectations about future events or actions: "I'll give it to you tomorrow"; "It'll arrive later this week."
ARU	Rules state procedures and definitions: "It goes in here"; "We don't fight in school"; "That happens later."

Organizational Devices

OAC	Accompaniments maintain contact by supplying information redundant with respect to some contextual feature: "Here you are"; "There you go."
OAG	Attention Getters solicit attention: "Hey!"; "John!"; "Look!"
OBM	Boundary Markers indicate openings, closings, and shifts in the conversation "Okay"; "All right"; "By the way."
OCO	Clarification Questions seek clarification of prior remark: "What?"
OEX	Exclamations express surprise, delight, or other attitudes: "Oh!"; "Wow!"
OFL	Fillers enable a speaker to maintain a turn: "...well...", "...and uh..."

OFS	False Starts indicate aborted utterances: "We... they"
OPM	Politeness Markers indicate ostensible politeness: "Please."
ORQ	Rhetorical Questions seek acknowledgment to continue: "Know what?"
OSS	Speaker Selections label speaker of next turn: "John"; "You."
OVP	Verbal Play indicates language in which meaning is secondary to play.

Performatives

PBT	Bets express conviction about a future event: "I bet you can't do it."
PCL	Claims establish rights for speaker: "That's mine"; "I'm first."
PJD	Jokes cause humorous effect by stating incongruous information, usually patently false: "We throwed the soup in the ceiling."
PPR	Protests express objections to hearer's behavior: "Stop!"; "No!"
PTE	Teasing annoys, taunts, or playfully provokes a hearer: "You can't get me."
PWA	Warnings alert hearer of impending harm: "Watch out!"; "Be careful!"

Requestives solicit information or actions.

QAC	Action Requests seek the performance of an action by hearer: "Give me it!"; "Put the toy down!"
QCH	Choice questions seek either-or judgments relative to propositions: "is this an apple?"; "Is it red or green?"; "Okay?"; "Right?"
QMA	Requests for Mental Action seek specific mental activity by the hearer: "Think"; "Remember."
QPC	Process questions seek extended descriptions or explanations: "Why did he go?"; "How did it happen?"; "What about him?"
QPM	Permission Requests seek permission to perform action: "May I go?"
QPR	Product Questions seek information relative to most wh-interrogatives: "Where's John?"; "What happened?"; "Who?" "When?"
QSU	Suggestions recommend the performance of an action by hearer or speaker or both: "Let's do it!"; "Why don't you do it?"; "You should do it."
QVB	Verbal Action Requests seek performance part of an instructional routine such as reading aloud, conducting language-learning exercises, repeating, or spelling: "Read this word"; "Repeat after me"; "I go, you go, he...."

Responsives

RAG	Agreements agree or disagree with prior nonrequestive act: "No, it is not!"; "I don't think you're right."
RAK	Acknowledgments recognize prior nonrequestives and are noncommittal: "Oh"; "Yeah."
RCH	Choice Answers provide solicited judgments of propositions: "Yes."
RCL	Clarification Responses provide solicited confirmations: "I said no."

RCO	Compliances express acceptance, denial, or acknowledgment of requests: "Okay"; "Yes"; "I'll do it."
RPC	Process Answers provide solicited explanations: "I wanted to."
RPR	Product Answers provide wh-information: "John's here"; "It fell."
RQL	Qualifications provide unsolicited information to requestives: "But I didn't do it"; "This is not an apple."
RVB	Response to Requests for Verbal Action provide solicited speech, such as reading aloud, repeating in chorus, or spelling.

Special Speech Acts

SAC	Counting indicates naming numerals or counting objects.
SAL	Laughing codes laughter.
SAS	Singing indicates singing, either words or sounds.
MKE	Microphone talk codes speech directed at the tape recorder microphone, often silly or nonsensical.
NVB	Nonverbals code important nonverbal acts.
TRA	Translation codes conscious, direct translations.

Publications using these data should cite:

Guthrie, L. F. (1983). *Learning to use a new language: Language functions and use by first grade Chinese-Americans*. Oakland, CA: ARC Associates.

Guthrie, L. F. (1984). Contrasts in teachers" language use in a Chinese-English bilingual classroom. In J. Hanscombe, R. Orem, & B. Taylor (Eds.), *On TESOL '83: The question of control*. Washington, DC: TESOL.

Guthrie, L. F., & Guthrie, G. P. (1988). Teacher language use in a Chinese bilingual classroom. In S. Goldman & H. Trueba (Eds.), *Becoming literate in English as a second language*. Norwood, NJ: Ablex.

Other references include:

Cole, M., Dore, J., Hall, W., & Dowley, G. (1978). Situation and task in young children's talk. *Discourse Processes, 4,* 119–176.

Dore, J. (1977). Children's illocutionary acts. In R. O. Freedle (Ed.), *Discourse production and comprehension*. Norwood, NJ: Ablex.

Dore, J., M. Gearhart, et al. (1978). The structure of nursery school conversation. In K. E. Nelson (Ed.) *Children's Language*. New York: Gardner Press.

Hatzidaki

Aspa Hatzidaki
Tripoleos 11
Kalamaria
Thessaloniki, 55131 Greece

The data contained in this corpus were used in Hatzidaki (1994). The purpose of the investigation which took place among the second-generation Greeks living in Brussels was to examine their linguistic behavior with a view to discovering to what degree they maintain the use of the ethnic language, and how they alternate between French and Greek in their daily interaction (to the extent that they do use Greek in spontaneous conversation). The data collection took place between January 1991 and October 1992 and consisted of three complementary techniques: the taperecording of speech events such as interviews, participant observation, and the compilation of network lists.

Thirty-four second-generation informants (19 male, 15 female) took part in the study. The following tables group participants together and provides information on their sex, age, and occupation at the time of the study.

Table 45: Hatzidaki Participants

Participant	Sex	Age	Occupation
Stefanos	M	14	High school student
Dimitris	M	16	High school student
Lazaros	M	16	Studying hotel management
Tassos	M	18	High school student
Pavlos	M	18	Studying hotel management
Kostas	M	20	Studying car mechanics
Nikos	M	20	Studying chemistry
Fotis	M	21	Technician
Andreas	M	21	Running bookshop, studying PoliSci
Spiros	M	22	Car mechanic, cook
Yannis	M	22	Studying computers, waiter
Orestis	M	23	Studying car mechanics
Yorgos	M	23	Physiotherapist
Vassilis	M	24	Physiotherapist

Table 45: Hatzidaki Participants

Participant	Sex	Age	Occupation
Ilias	M	24	Cook
Michalis	M	24	Studying Economics
Miltos	M	24	Telecommunications engineer
Christos	M	29	Degree in Economics
Petros	M	29	Mechanical Engineering
Thalia	F	14	High school student
Zoe	F	15	High school student
Roula	F	16	High school student
Natasa	F	18	Studying linguistics
Vera	F	19	Studying linguistics
Sofia	F	20	Studying linguistics
Katerina	F	20	Studying linguistics
Maria	F	21	Studying accounting
Voula	F	21	Going to secretarial school
Olga	F	21	Studying linguistics
Fani	F	23	Secretary
Alexandra	F	25	Translator
Elissavet	F	25	Ergonomics, unemployed
Irene	F	26	Studying pharmaceutics
Despina	F	28	Beautician

All our informants belonged to the category of "early bilinguals" (although two of them, Petros and his sister Irene, were not born in Belgium but acquired the French language in their early school years). It is difficult to be more precise and to place the informants in the category of "consecutive" or "successive" bilinguals, because they were not always able to provide reliable answers to the question of how they learned their two languages and when they started using one or the other for the first time. Differences in their learning experiences, differences in time and type of language exposure time all together made it difficult to say with certainty what their first language was. On the whole, most of our informants seemed to have experienced a positive, additive form of bilingualism, even though the Greek spoken by the majority is not comparable to Standard Greek in many ways; the speech of second-generation Greeks is markedly different from the norm for

Modern Greek, as their variety of the ethnic language manifests certain distinctive features on all linguistic levels. Some of these features even appear with a certain systematicity.

Irrespective of the structural deviations from the norm, the participants' overall competence in Greek was sufficient for communication purposes. The active involvement of Greek authorities and the Greek Orthodox Church, frequent visits to Greece, and the availability of Greek-language press and media provided ample opportunity to develop oral and literacy skills in the ethnic language. If our informants' competence in Greek varied from poor to very good, their competence in French was higher, by their own admission. They could be safely considered French-dominant bilinguals, something which is true for the totality of second-generation Greeks in Brussels (apart from those few who have been educated in Dutch, of course). This means that French was the language which served most functions in their everyday life, the language they felt more comfortable in, and the language they mastered best. The dominance of the French language was due to the nature of the children's socialization and the functions fulfilled by the two codes in question. For those who still attended Mother Tongue Classes, Greek was the language of instruction for a few hours twice a week. Apart from that, they used it with family and friends to varying degrees. All other linguistic activity, be it receptive or productive, took place in French. This functional separation of codes, which they experienced since their infancy, firmly established the dominance of French. They definitely did not speak Greek as well as they spoke French. Their French is as good as that of any native speaker of their background.

Informants were asked to rate their Greek proficiency on two aspects, and the mean of the score for oral proficiency and literacy skills gave the informant's proficiency score. It was decided to consider as "more proficient speakers" those informants who gave themselves between 2.5 and 4 and "less proficient speakers" those who rated themselves between 1 and 2.5. When the mean turned out to be exactly 2.5, the final placement of the informant was left to the researcher's discretion. The criteria on which this judgment was based were the following: A "more proficient" speaker of Greek did not manifest disfluency phenomena indicating incompetence, made very few or no grammatical mistakes, used the appropriate words most of the time, and did not switch frequently out of incompetence. On the other hand, the speech of "less proficient" speakers of Greek manifested more clearly the dominance of French. In contrast to "more proficient" speakers, it was fraught with pauses, hesitations, grammatical mistakes, poor word selection, and competence-related code-switching. The more proficient speakers were Miltos, Lazaros, Orestis, Katerina, Elissavet, Ilias, Petros, Alexandra, Yannia, Andreas, Vassilis, Yorgos, Fotis, and Nikos. The other speakers can be classed as less proficient.

The participants came from several social groups. These included the Sphynx Café group, the Hellenic Community group, the Association group, the foursome group, the students group, and Orestis and Alexandra. Full details regarding the social structure and language usage in these different groups is given in Hatzidaki (1994).

The results of the quantitative study of language choice in our data led to the conclusion that more proficient speakers used significantly more Greek during monitored situations (mean: 91%) than their less proficient counterparts (mean: 60%). This discrepancy can be attributed to the former group's higher competence and greater practice in the ethnic language, which permitted them to conduct a long conversation with almost no French elements. Less proficient speakers in our sample, on the other hand, rarely found themselves in situations where the use of Greek was called for. However, the number of speakers on whom data are available is too small to draw any significant conclusions. Again, more proficient speakers manifest a more homogeneous behavior, which is natural in view of their consistency in using Greek.

Publications using these data should cite:

Hatzidaki, A. (1994). *Ethnic language use among second-generation Greeks in Brussels.* Unpublished doctoral dissertation. Vrije Universiteit, Brussels.

Hayashi

Mariko Hayashi
Institute of Psychology
University of Århus
Asylvej 4
Risskov, Denmark
ostmh@hum.aau.dk

This corpus includes longitudinal data from a child growing up in a Japanese-Danish bilingual family in the age range of 12 to 29 months. The data were collected by Mariko Hayashi, University of Aarhus, Denmark, in the context of her doctoral study investigating language development in bilingual children. Pseudonyms have been used to preserve informant anonymity. The child is called "Anders." Anders was a first-born boy, and had no siblings during the period studied. The father had an university education, the mother college education, thus the family belonged to the educated middle class.

Anders' mother was Japanese and his father was Danish. The family resided in Denmark, where the community language is Danish. The parents spoke their respective native tongue to the child from the beginning. Occasional code-switching, especially by the father, occurred to a certain extent. The parents spoke mainly English, and occasionally Japanese and Danish to each other. Anders and his mother spent summer vacation in Japan at the child's age of 21 to 23 months. In this period, Anders was exposed exclusively to Japanese.

Anders was taken care of by his mother in the day time. He had a couple of Danish-speaking playmates he was occasionally together with. In the evenings and the weekends the father took care of the child as well. The father's parents, who spoke Danish, lived in the neighborhood and visited the family regularly. People who visited the mother spoke either Japanese or English to her, as the mother did not understand much Danish. The father and the mother, as mentioned above, spoke mainly English to each other. Otherwise, the child was not exposed to English.

The language Anders was exposed most to was Japanese, as it was the mother who took care of him in the day time. He also spent a three-month summer vacation in Japan, where he was exposed exclusively to Japanese. In his productive vocabulary Japanese began to be dominant at 20 months. The dominance of the Japanese language became especially clear during and after his visit to Japan. Although Anders did not show any clear sign for comprehending English, he did pick up a few English expressions such as "see you" and "two."

Monthly videotapings of the child of about an hour's duration were made in the age range of 11 to 38 months. All recordings were made in the child's own home by Hayashi. With a few exceptions, both parents were present at each session. Each visit included until a certain time testing on the Uzgiris-Hunt Infant Assessment Scales (1978) as well. For a certain period, the parents kept a record of lexical items, which was used as a supplement to the videotapings. The mother made audio recordings during their stay in Japan as well.

Thirty minutes of each session were transcribed based on standard orthography by Hayashi, who is a native speaker of Japanese as well as a fluent speaker of Danish. All transcripts were checked by a native speaker of Danish. Three or four different situations, typically dinner, free play, and book reading, were selected for transcription. Furthermore, care was taken so that the mother and the father were more or less equally included in the portion of recording to be transcribed. Utterances are identified after prosodic criteria such as intonation and pauses, whereas utterances themselves are divided into units based on clarity of articulation and fluency. Limited attention is paid to overlapping, retracings, and hesitations. A deviated phonological form is described in the phonetic tier. However, it does not provide a precise phonetic analysis. Speech errors are not coded.

The corpus contains the following 17 files:

Table 46: Hayashi Files

File	Date of recording	Age of Child
and03.cha	02-NOV-1986	1;0.15
and04.cha	07-DEC-1986	1;1.20
and05.cha	18-JAN-1987	1;3.1
and06.cha	15-FEB-1987	1;3.28
and07.cha	08-MAR-1987	1;4.21
and08.cha	12-APR-1987	1;5.25
and09.cha	04-MAY-1987	1;6.17
and10.cha	31-MAY-1987	1;7.14
and11.cha	29-JUN-1987	1;8.12
and12.cha	03-AUG-1987	1;9.16
and13.cha	05-SEP-1987	1;10.18
and14.cha	31-OCT-1987	2;0.14
and15.cha	28-NOV-1987	2;1.11
and16.cha	07-JAN-1988	2;2.20
and17.cha	14-FEB-1988	2;3.27
and18.cha	17-MAR-1988	2,5.0
and19.cha	15-APR-1988	2;5.28

Warnings

1. Overlapping is not accurately transcribed in these data.
2. Retracings and hesitations are not accurately transcribed in these data.
3. These data contain limited information regarding the context.
4. Repetitions of identical units/utterances are transcribed twice at most.
5. Productive units within an utterance are identified on the basis of articulation and fluency criteria.
6. The phonetic tier is used to describe more accurately the child's pronunciation of a given sound. However, it does not provide a precise phonetic analysis.
7. Regular inflections of nouns and verbs are preceded by a dash in the main text line. Irregularly inflected nouns and verbs are not divided into morphemes.
8. Two (or more) different words, which are spelled identically, are distinguished by @ followed by English explanation. Note that only the one word of the two in each pair, which is assumed to be used less often, is marked. @d stands for Danish word, @j for Japanese word, and @fp for final particle.
9. There are three letters of the Danish alphabet that cannot be typed onto the computer using ASCII codes. Based on the conventional method, these letters are replaced by ae, oe, and aa.

Publications using these data should cite:

Hayashi, M. (1993). *A longitudinal study of the language development in bilingual children.* Unpublished doctoral dissertation, University of Aarhus.
Klausen, T., Subritzky, M. S., & Hayashi, M. (1992). Initial production of inflections in bilingual children. In G. Turner & D. Messer (Eds.), *Critical influences on language acquisition and development.* London: Macmillan.

Ionin

Tania Ionin
NE20-410
Massachusetts Institute of Technology
77 Massachusetts Ave.
Cambridge, MA 02139
tionin@mit.edu

The data in this corpus come from 22 children residing in the United States who either spoke Russian as their first language or were born in Russian-speaking families. Most children also acquired English as their first or second language. The Russian and/or English utterances of the children were collected as part of a 15-month study by Tania Ionin, an undergraduate student in linguistics at the University of Michigan, under the supervision of Dr. Teresa Satterfield. The primary goal of this project was to examine the emergence of verb finiteness and overt participants in the children's acquisition of Russian and English. Another goal of this project was to look for effects of age on the pattern of second-language acquisition.

All of the data were collected by Tania Ionin in a series of taped interactions with the children. Each taping session took place in an informal setting such as the child's home and involved such activities as playing with toys, looking at picture books, and interacting with parents, other caretakers, peers, and/or the experimenter. No particular elicitation methods were used. All of the children resided in Michigan at the time of the study, most in the Ann Arbor area, but some in Flint or Southfield. The following are detailed descriptions of the participants in each taping session and their relationships to each other. The investigator in each taping session is Tania Ionin.

1. **Arkady (12;4)** and **Roma (12;4)** are twin brothers from Flint who were born in Russia and emigrated to the United States with their parents 1 month prior to their taping session of 17-JAN-1998. Russian was the only language spoken at home. The twins had studied English in Russia for about six months and were studying English in school during the course of the study. Other participants include Svetlana, their mother, and Tania, the investigator.

2. **Aysel (10;1)**, a girl from Ann Arbor, was born in Azerbaijan into a family that spoke both Azerbaijani and Russian. Russian was the primary language spoken at home. Aysel, an only child, emigrated to the United States with her parents 2 months prior to her first taping session of 1-NOV-1997. She spoke no English prior to arrival, and was studying it in school during the course of the study. At the session of 20-JAN-1998, she had been in the United States for 5 months.

3. **Borya (2;4)** and **Luba (11;10)**, sister and brother living in Ann Arbor, were born in Russia and emigrated to the United States with their widowed mother 4 months prior to the first taping session. **Sasha (8;10),** their first cousin, had emigrated to the United States with his parents and grandmother 6 months earlier. Luba had studied English intensively in Rus-

sia for 4 years. Both Luba and Sasha were studying English in school during the course of the study, while Borya was sporadically attending an English-speaking preschool and was speaking only Russian. Russian was the only language spoken in the children's homes. All of the taping sessions took place in Luba and Borya's home. Sasha was present during the first session only. The two later sessions were conducted with Borya only, although Luba was present for the first of those sessions. Luba and Borya were living with their mother and maternal grandmother, and Sasha, an only child, was living with his parents and maternal grandmother, who was also Luba and Borya's paternal grandmother.

1. 19-OCT-1997. Time in the United States: Luba and Borya: 4 months; Sasha: 10 months. Participants: Luba (11;10); Borya (2;4); Sasha (8;10); Iraida, the mother of Luba and Borya; Tamara, the maternal grandmother of Sasha and also the paternal grandmother of Luba and Borya; and Tania, the investigator.

2. 6-DEC-1997. Time in the United States: 6 months. Participants: Luba (12;0); Borya (2;6); Iraida, their mother; Gita, their maternal grandmother; Tamara, their paternal grandmother; and Tania, the investigator.

3. 6-FEB-1998. Time in the United States: 8 months.Participants: Borya (2;8); Gita, his maternal grandmother; and Tania, the investigator.

4. **David (3;9)** , a boy from Ann Arbor, was born in the United States to a Russian-speaking family temporarily residing in the United States Russian was the primary language spoken at home, although David's older sister (not present during the taping session) spoke primarily English. During the course of the study, David was attending an English-speaking preschool full-time. Participants include David (3;9); Luné, his mother; and Tania, the investigator.

5. **Hanna (3;1)**, a girl from Ann Arbor, was born in the United States to an immigrant Russian-speaking family. Russian was the primary language spoken at home by Hanna's parents and older brother, but Hanna spoke only English. During the course of the study, Hanna was attending an English-speaking preschool full-time. Taping was done on 21-SEP-1997 and 15-NOV-1997.

6. **Lisa (5;4)** , a girl from Ann Arbor, was born in Russia and, after losing her parents as a baby, grew up in a Russian orphanage. Lisa was adopted by an American family 1 year and 4 months prior to the study. At the session on 5-AUG-1997, Lisa was living with her adoptive parents, who spoke no Russian, and attending an English-speaking preschool full-time. She spoke only English.

7. **Yulya (12;5)** and **Roma (7;7),** sister and brother from Southfield, were born in a Russian-speaking family in Kazakhstan and emigrated to the United States with their parents four months prior to their first taping session. They had not studied English prior to arriving in the United States. The first taping session was conducted for Yulya and Roma in their home. The second taping session was conducted for Roma and Masha in Roma's apartment; Yulya was also present for that session. The last two sessions were conducted separately for Roma and Masha in their respective homes; Yulya was present during Roma's taping session.For the recording on 8-NOV1997, Yulya and Roma had been in the

United States 4 months. For the recording on 23-JAN-1998, they had been in the United States 7 months. For 19-FEB-1998. Yulya and Roma had been in the United States 8 months. Other participants include Sergey, Yulya and Roma's father; Slava; their neighbor Masha; Masha's father; and Tania, the investigator.

8. **Masha (7;4)**, a girl from Southfield, was born in a Russian-speaking family in Uzbekistan and emigrated to the United States with her parents and older brother 4 months after Yulya and Roma. She was a neighbor of Yulya and Roma. At the session of 23-JAN-1998 she had been in the United States 3 months. At the session of 19-FEB-1998 she had been in the United States 4 months.

9. **Ola (6;10)** and **Maya (5;3)**, two sisters from Ann Arbor, were born in Russia and orphaned as young children. They spent 10 months in a Russian orphanage, and were adopted by an American family 5 months prior to their first taping session. At the time of the study, Ola and Maya were residing with their adoptive parents and older sister, none of whom spoke Russian, and were attending an English-speaking school. Ola and Maya spoke only English throughout the course of the study.

1. 12-AUG-1997. Time in the United States: 5 months. Participants: Ola (6;10); Maya (5;3); Melanie, their adoptive mother; Amy, their 8-year-old adopted sister; and Tania, the investigator.

2. 27-OCT-1997. Time in the United States: 7 months.Participants: Ola (7;0); Maya (5;5); and Tania, the investigator.

10. **Valeria (5;0)** and **Nastya (6;7)**, two girls from Ann Arbor, were born in Russia. Valeria spent her infancy in France, and came to the United States as a toddler with her parents. Nastya came to the United States with her parents 9 months prior to the taping session. The parents of both girls were temporarily residing in the United States on work visas. Russian was the primary language spoken in both girls' homes. Both Valeria and Nastya were attending English-speaking schools. Both girls were only children. The families of the two girls were friends, and the taping session was conducted in Valeria's home, with Nastya over for a visit. At the session of 10-SEP-1997 Valeria had been in the United States about 3.5 years and Nastya had been in the United States about 9 months. Other participants include Nastya's friend, Marina; Valeria's mother; Andrei, Valeria's father; Oxana, Nastya's mother; and Tania, the investigator.

11. **Vanya (4;11) and Lisa (2;4)**, a brother and sister from Flint, were living in an immigrant Russian family. Vanya was born in Russia and came to the United States as a toddler, while Lisa was born in the United States. Russian was the primary language spoken by the children's parents and grandmother. During the course of the study, Vanya attended an English-speaking preschool full-time, while Lisa stayed home with her grandmother and spoke only Russian. At the session of 12-JUN-1997 Vanya had been in the United States about 2.5 years and Lisa had been in the United States since birth. Other participants include Yulya, their mother; their paternal grandmother; and Tania, the investigator.

12. **Yasha (4;7) and Gulia (2;11)**, a brother and sister from Ann Arbor, were born in

the United States to parents who had emigrated from Russia. Russian was the primary language spoken at home by the children's parents and grandmother. Throughout the period of the first five tapings, Yasha and Gulia did not attend preschool but stayed in the home of an English-speaking baby-sitter a few hours a week. During the period of the last taping session, Gulia was attending an English-speaking preschool regularly, and Yasha attended kindergarten.

1. 10-JAN-1997 (at home). Participants: Yasha (4;7); Gulia (2;11); Anna, their mother; their maternal grandmother; and Tania, the investigator.

2. 27-JAN-1997 (at the baby-sitter's). Participants: Yasha (4;7); Gulia (2;11); Debra, their baby-sitter; Jasmine, Debra's two-year-old daughter; Alexander, Yasha and Gulia's father who comes to take them home from the baby-sitter's; and Tania, the investigator.

3. 13-FEB-1997 (at home). Participants: Yasha (4;8); Gulia (3;0); Anna, their mother; their maternal grandmother; and Tania, the investigator.

4. 19-MAR-1997 (at the baby-sitter's). Participants: Yasha (4;9); Gulia (3;1); Debra, their baby-sitter; Jasmine, Debra's three-year-old daughter; and Tania, the investigator.

5. 13-APR-1997 (at home). Participants: Yasha (4;10); Gulia (3;2); Anna, their mother; Teresa, a friend of Anna; Julian, Teresa's four-year-old son, a friend of Yasha; and Tania, the investigator.

6. 23-NOV-1997 (at home). Participants: Yasha (5;5); Gulia (3;9); their maternal grandmother; and Tania, the investigator.

13. **Yulya (8;9) and Anya (5;2)**, two sisters from Ann Arbor, were born in Russia and emigrated to the United States with their parents 2 and a half years prior to the taping session of 26-JUN-1997. At the time of the study, both sisters were attending English-speaking schools. Russian was the primary language spoken at home.

Krupa

Magda Krupa-Kwiatkowska
Neuropsychology Laboratory
San Diego State University
6330 Alvarado Court, Suite 201
San Diego, CA 92182-1850
phone: (619) 594-8669
magda@crl.ucsd.edu

This directory contains data from a longitudinal, ethnographic case study of a Polish boy learning English as a second language. The study examined selected aspects of language acquisition within the context of the child's socialization in a new culture and microscopic observation as the technique of data collection was therefore considered crucial. These data were collected and transcribed by M. Krupa-Kwiatkowska, from her son, Martin.

They are selected from a 2-year observational record, which started in September 1992, 1 month after the boy first arrived in the United States, and ended in August 1994, during his first summer vacation in Poland. Twenty-two of the 31 sessions videotaped in the United States were transcribed and included in this corpus. Sessions recorded in Poland are still to be transcribed.

Target Child

When the observations began, Martin was 6 years and 2 months old and had just arrived in the United States, following his mother, who was there studying towards her doctoral degree in second language education. Two weeks after his arrival in the United States, Martin began to attend first grade in a Buffalo, New York, elementary school. His prior education included 4 years of kindergarten and preschool in Poland, where he was born and brought up until then. Except for sporadic instruction in English at the age of 5, when he was taught approximately 50 to 100 words and short phrases, this was his first encounter with the English language and American culture. Martin was the only child and was raised by his mother. He was born on July 7, 1986.

Other Children

The other children invited to participate in the play sessions with Martin were selected in such a way as to reflect a plethora of combinations of personal and cultural features that could be potentially accountable for different patterns of interactional behavior. The original criterion for contrasting the boy's behavior in peer interactions was the availability of language as a medium of interaction. Therefore, three kinds of situations were recorded: (a) the boy's interactions with American children who spoke only English, (b) the boy's interactions with Polish-American children who spoke both languages, and (c) the boy's interactions with a Latin-American girl who spoke Spanish and little English, with very few shared linguistic resources. The data in this corpus include sessions with six children, who were Martin's most frequent playmates at that time: Basia, Sarah, Scott, Justin, Robert, and Gabi.

Basia was one year older than Martin. She was Polish and came to the United States a year and a half before the period covered by this report. Her father was a research associate at one of the research institutions in the area. Her family lived in the same neighborhood as Martin, which made their frequent contacts possible. She attended the same elementary school as Martin. She spoke Polish better than English, but, as all the Polish children in the study, preferred to use English in contacts with other bilingual children.

Sarah was 2 years older than Martin. She was American and spoke only English. She also lived in the same neighborhood and attended the same school as Martin. Her mother was a graduate student at the university where Martin's mother studied.

Scott was 2 years older than Martin. He was the youngest child in a Polish-American family. His parents came to the States about 20 years before, settled and established a family. All their children were born in the United States. Although both languages were used in their home, at the time of the study English already prevailed and was the language of communication among the siblings. Scott spoke only English and understood only a little Polish. The family, however, maintained vivid ties with the Polish community in the area.

Justin was American and spoke only English. He was a year and a half younger than Martin. He was Martin's close neighbor and thus a frequent guest at the house. His mother was a graduate student at the university.

Robert was a year older than Martin. He was Polish. His father was a research associate at the University and his family also lived in the same neighborhood. Robert came to the United States at the age of 4, so when the study began, he had already been in the States for over 3 years. Polish was the predominant language used in Robert's home, although English could also be heard, particularly when addressed to the boy. Robert could speak both Polish and English, but showed preference for English. Martin considered him his best friend.

Gabi was a year older than Martin and, when the study began, she had been in the United States for 1 year. She lived with her family in the same neighborhood and her mother was a graduate student at the same University as Martin's mother. She spoke her native language, Spanish, and had just started to pick up some English.

Procedure

The observational sessions were typically held two or three times a month for the time of 1 hour. Most of them took place at Martin's house and a few at the house of the other child. The children were free to play wherever and whatever they wanted. They could move from one room to another and change the play topic according to their wishes. Although an attempt was made to conduct two to three hourly sessions monthly, the session schedule was not forced, but was dependent upon the boy's social calendar and followed the events as they occurred. These restrictions often limited the possibility of recording interactional events. Adult intervention was avoided unless asked for or necessary for safety reasons. A tripod was used to avoid adult's presence when it was not necessary. However, because of high mobility of the children, this was not often possible. All the sessions were videotaped by a person considered most neutral to the situation. Usually it was the parent of the hosting child, and because most sessions took place in Martin's home, it was typically the researcher herself.

Transcription

Out of these sessions, specimens of about 20 minutes considered to be most "interactive" were selected for transcription. Because there were large patches of non-interactive recorded data, such a selection criterion seemed most natural and justified. This material was then transcribed in the CHAT format. The transcripts include a verbatim record of the children's speech, paying close attention to such conversational features as repetitions, retracings, interruptions, noncompletions, and omissions, and to special forms of linguistic and quasi-linguistic activity, such as word play, syllabification, invented words, and onomatopoeic expressions. Whenever Polish was used, English translation was provided for the utterance. Utterances were transcribed using the standard alphabets of English and Polish, with the omissions of diacritics in Polish, as these were not then available in CHAT. Nonverbal expressions, such as nonsensical or incomprehensible words, whenever pronounced as in English, were transcribed using the UNIBET system. Unless otherwise marked, children's utterances should be interpreted as being addressed to the other child. Apart from the speech record, incorporated in the transcripts are the nonlinguistic data, involving the record of general activity, paralinguistic behavior, gestures and facial expressions, and other comments. These were transcribed whenever they were judged to constitute a communicative act on the part of the child. The record of paralinguistic behavior includes various kinds of vocalizations, like screams, sighs, groans, laughter, singsong, and the message conveyed by the tone of the voice, when it was apparent.

The following table contains basic information about each file in the corpus:

Table 47: Krupa Files

File	Date	Age	Part	Age	Part. L1	Length
mar01	29-SEP-1992	6;2	Gabi	7;	Spanish	36:00
mar02	04-OCT-1992	6;2	Scott	8;	English	17:30
mar03	04-OCT-1992	6;2	Scott	8;	English	14:30
mar04	10-OCT-1992	6;3	Sarah	8;	English	5:00

Table 47: Krupa Files

File	Date	Age	Part	Age	Part. L1	Length
mar05	21-FEB-1993	6;7	Gabi	7;	Spanish	22:00
mar06	21-FEB-1993	6;7	Basia	7;7	Polish	17:00
mar07	21-MAR-1993	6;8	Scott	8;	English	5:00
mar08	03-APR-1993	6;8	Sarah	8;	English	21:00
mar09	04-APR-1993	6;8	Robert	7;10	Polish	19:00
mar10	25-APR-1993	6;9	Justin	6;2	English	22:10
mar11	26-JUL-1993	7;0	Justin	6;5	English	16:30
mar12	27-JUL-1993	7;0	Basia	8;1	Polish	17:20
mar13	28-AUG-1993	7;1	Basia	8;2	Polish	22:50
mar14	31-AUG-1993	7;1	Justin	6;6	English	17:00
mar15	10-OCT-1993	7;3	Justin	6;8	English	22:00
mar16	10-OCT-1993	7;3	Robert	8;4	Polish	17:00
mar17	06-NOV-1993	7;3	Scott	9;	English	20:00
mar18	07-NOV-1993	7;4	Basia	8;4	Polish	20:40
mar19	27-DEC-1993	7;5	Justin	6;10	English	20:30
mar20	28-DEC-1993	7;5	Robert	8;7	Polish	20:40
mar21	12-FEB-1994	7;7	Basia	8;7	Polish	19:40
mar22	13-FEB-1994	7;7	Gabi	8;	Spanish	15:20

Publications using these data should cite:

Krupa-Kwiatkowska, M. (1997). *Second-language acquisition in the context of socialization: A case study of a Polish boy learning English.* Unpublished doctoral dissertation, State University of New York at Buffalo.

Langman

Dr. Juliet Langman
Division of Bicultural-Bilingual Studies
University of Texas at San Antonio
6900 North Loop, 1603 West
San Antonio, TX 78249
jlangman@lonestar.utsa.edu

This corpus is made up of 10 files consisting of interviews conducted in 1994 with 11 Chinese immigrants living in Hungary. The bulk of the conversation is in Hungarian, although in the case of those who speak English there is also English, and in the case of one transcript (KIN10) there are significant amounts of Chinese (with a Hungarian translation in a %tra dependent tier). Interviews focused on issues related to their arrival in Hungary as well as their daily life activities. With the exception of KIN2 and KIN10 none of the participants had had formal training in Hungarian. Interviewers were the researcher, as well as three different Hungarian undergraduates. Data were collected with two purposes in mind: the analyses of communicative strategies among adult second-language learners learning in a nonstructured environment, and the analysis of the acquisition of morphology of an agglutinative language. The following additional form markers have been used in the (*) speaker lines of the transcripts:

@e = english word, e.g., go@e
@c = chinese word, e.g., xie@c
@a = adult-invented word, e.g., pigyilni@a

The following special codes have been used on the %lan tier:

$MIX	utterances with some form of code-switching or borrowing
$CHI	utterance in Chinese (used only in KIN10)

The following special codes have been used on the %rep (repetition) tier to identify:
1. whose speech is repeated

SRP	self-repetition of immediately previous utterance
ORP	other repetition of immediately previous utterance
SRE	self-repetition of an utterance not immediately preceding
ORE	other repetition of an utterance not immediately preceding

2. the function of the repetition

MIS	misunderstanding, prompting, asking for clarification
VAL	validation repetition of previous utterance
EXP	explanation to ease understanding
COR	correction and language learning functions

3. the form of the repetition

PAR	partial
COM	exact
TRA	translation
PLU	repetition including additional information

These three types of codes could be combined as in: %rep: SRP:MIS:PAR

Error coding focused exclusively on morphology and is represented on two separate tiers, %err and %mor. The %mor tier shows the actual target form for each error marked. The %err tier marks the types of errors using the following codes:

$OMI:	omission
$OMI:PAR	partial omission
$INS:	insertion
$INS:PAR	partial insertion
$SWI	switched form
$SWI:PAR	partially switched form

Partial support for data collection and analysis was provided through a grant awarded to Dr. Csaba Pléh, OTKA grant T018173, A magyar morfológia pszicholingvistikai vizsgálata (The psycholinguistic study of Hungarian morphology).

Publications using these data should cite:

Langman, Juliet. (1998) "Aha" as Communication Strategy: Chinese speakers of Hungarian. In Regan, V. (ed.) *Contemporary Approaches to Second-language Acquisition in Social Context: Crosslinguistic Perspectives*. Dublin: University College Dublin Press, 32-45.

Langman, Juliet. (1997). Analyzing second-language learners' communication strategies: Chinese speakers of Hungarian. *Acta Linguistica Hungarica 44*, 277–299.

Langman, Juliet. (1995-1996). The role of code-switching in achieving understanding: Chinese speakers of Hungarian. *Acta Linguistica Hungarica, 43,* 323–344.

Reading

Brian Richards
Dept. of Arts and Humanities in Education
University of Reading
Bulmershe Court
Earley, Reading RG6 1HY United Kingdom
B.J.Richards@reading.ac.uk

These data on French foreign language oral interviews were transcribed as part of a study of the reliability and validity of oral assessment in modern foreign languages in the General Certificate of Secondary Education (GCSE). GCSE is a public examination normally taken by school children in the United Kingdom at the age of 16, i.e. after the 11 years of compulsory schooling. The 34 interviews constitute one part of the French oral examination: the so-called "free conversation." Here, students are interviewed by their French teacher, covering everyday topics such as school, home, family, holidays, future aspirations and hobbies, and interests. Other parts of the oral examination such as role-plays are not part of these data.

Our analyses have compared lexical and grammatical features of the children's language with teachers' expectations of foreign language learners of this age, and with the language of French native speakers in a similar interview setting (Chambers & Richards, 1995). We have also compared teachers' impressionistic assessments of the presence of qualities specified in the assessment criteria with our own objective counts using the CLAN software (Richards & Chambers, 1996). We are currently looking at teacher-student interaction, focusing on the teachers' accommodation strategies.

The Interviews

The oral examinations, including the interviews, are conducted by the teachers on set dates and on topics determined by the official examination board. Only one teacher and one student are present during each interview, the audio recording being made by the teacher. The teacher enters assessments on a mark sheet during the interview, and on completion of the examination the tapes and mark sheets are sent to the examination board. A sample of tapes is remarked by a moderator appointed by the examination board and the teachers' assessments adjusted if necessary. The average length of the interviews is 5 minutes 30 seconds. They range from 3 minutes to 12 minutes.

Participants

All 34 participants come from the same all-ability secondary school (11-18 comprehensive school) in an English-speaking area of South Wales. They are 16 years old and are native speakers of English who have been learning French for 5 years. All have also spent at least one year learning Welsh and some have had the opportunity to learn German.

The school is situated in a predominantly working-class area, but the students selected here cover a wide range of social background. It should be noted that students with the weakest performance in French were excluded from this sample because the focus of our study was the Higher Level examination. This part of the examination, which is taken in addition to Basic Level, gives students access to the highest grades. Students in the sample obtained pass grades ranging from Grade A (the highest) to Grade E. No students with Grades F and G were included.

Two teachers, one female and one male, are involved in the conduct of the interviews. Neither are native speakers of French; both are native speakers of British English who have learned French as a foreign language and have a degree in Modern Languages.

As a condition of using the school's tapes we promised that the identity of the school, teachers, and students would not be revealed. We have therefore used pseudonyms for these. In addition, we have changed the names of all locations mentioned on the tapes, as well as names of sports teams, and exchange schools in France and Germany. The tapes were transcribed in CHAT format initially by Francine Chambers who is a native speaker of French and were subsequently checked, edited and coded by Brian Richards. Final checking was carried out by Fiona Richards.

The following points should be noted:

1. In transcribing the French language we have followed the CHILDES manual (sections 4.5.14 and 27.4.1) in dealing with apostrophes and hyphens: apostrophes are followed by a space (l' aim, c' est); hyphens in compounds are replaced by a plus sign (le week+end); dashes between words (est-ce que) are replaced by spaces (est ce que).

2. It is difficult to draw a line between an English accent and a pronunciation error; because an assessment criterion of the GCSE examination is whether an utterance would be comprehensible to a "sympathetic native speaker," only those student errors that were serious enough to cause a breakdown of communication, or which were followed by a teacher correction, were coded. These were transcribed in UNIBET on the %err tier.

3. Some students answer questions in English or insert English words. Where the whole utterance is in English, a separate speaker tier for the student (*STE) has been created. English words inserted in French are marked with the @e suffix (father@e). Students who are also learning German sometimes use German words. These are marked with a @g suffix. Both the @e and @g symbols are contained in the 00DEPADD file.

4. Other additions to the 00DEPADD file are: +//? (self-interruption of a question) and +..? (question tailing off).

5. Acknowledgment tokens have been coded as back channels and are marked [+ bch]. These can be excluded from MLU and MLT counts using the -s"[+ bch]" switch.

6. The exclamations and interactional markers used are: "aah," "euh," "mm," and

"um." To omit these from analyses they can be placed in an exclude file.

List of Files

In the table below, the fourth column shows the combined total of points obtained by each student for the tests in Speaking, Listening, Reading, and Writing in the GCSE examination. A maximum of 7 points is awarded for each of these 4 skills, giving a possible total of 28 points. The fifth column shows the score for the whole oral test, including the interview and role-plays.

Table 48: Recordings and GSCE Scores

File number	Sex	Teacher Sex	Total GCSE Points	Points for Oral Test
W01.cha	male	male	19	4
W02.cha	male	male	17	3
W03.cha	female	female	16	2
W04.cha	female	female	11	3
W05.cha	female	male	16	4
W06.cha	male	male	19	4
W07.cha	male	male	18	4
W08.cha	female	male	22	5
W09.cha	male	male	15	4
W10.cha	female	female	14	3
W11.cha	female	male	20	4
W12.cha	male	male	17	4
W13.cha	male	female	12	2
W14.cha	male	male	12	3
W15.cha	male	male	19	4
W16.cha	female	female	11	2
W17.cha	male	female	16	4
W18.cha	female	male	23	6
W19.cha	male	male	23	6

Table 48: Recordings and GSCE Scores

File number	Sex	Teacher Sex	Total GCSE Points	Points for Oral Test
W20.cha	male	female	12	2
W21.cha	male	male	19	5
W22.cha	female	female	10	2
W23.cha	female	male	20	4
W24.cha	male	male	17	4
W25.cha	female	male	21	5
W26.cha	female	male	14	4
W27.cha	female	male	21	5
W28.cha	female	male	21	5
W29.cha	male	male	21	4
W30.cha	female	female	16	3
W31.cha	male	male	24	6
W32.cha	female	male	25	6
W33.cha	male	male	8	7
W34.cha	female	male	26	6

Acknowledgment

The "Oral Assessment in Modern Languages Project" was funded by the Research Endowment Trust Fund of the University of Reading.

Publications using these data should cite:

Chambers, F., & Richards, B. J. (1995). The "free conversation" and the assessment of oral proficiency. *Language Learning, 11*, 6–10.

Serra / Sole

Miquel Serra
Departament de Psicologia Basica
Universitat de Barcelona
Adolf Florensa s/n
Barcelona, 08028 Spain
mserra@psi.ub.es

The Serra–Sole longitudinal study includes 10 children. Five are monolingual Catalan, four are bilingual Catalan-Spanish, and one is monolingual Spanish. The Spanish-speaking child (#10) is included in the Spanish directory. The other children, including the four bilinguals, are in the Catalan directory. The children were videotaped monthly from 1 to 4 years of age, from 1986 to 1989. They were videotaped at their homes in spontaneous interaction with a familiar adult, usually the mother, in sessions of 30 to 45 minutes. All the children belong to middle-class families. The research project is entitled "Language acquisition in Catalan and Spanish children" and is directed by Miquel Serra (Universitat de Barcelona) and Rosa Sole (Universitat Autonoma de Barcelona). It has received support from the Spanish research council (Grants DGICYT PB84/0455; PB89/0317; PB91/0851; PB94/0886). The research assistants of the project have been: Montserrat Cortes, Connie Schultz, Elisabet Serrat, Vicens Torrents, and Melina Aparici. Cristina Vila and Montse Capdevila collaborated at various stages of the project.

Table 49: Catalan-Spanish Bilinguals

Participant	Name	# Files	Age	Sex
02	Antoni	23	1;4.1-3;0.24	M
06	Marti	24	0;10.14-4;0.13	M
07	Josep Andreu	24	0;10,1-4;0.3	M
12	Caterina	18	1;1.17-4;3.21	F

Snow / Velasco

Patricia Velasco
Apartado Postal 23 Comitan 44
San Cristobal de las Casas
Chiapas 29200, Mexico

Catherine Snow
Harvard Graduate School of Education
703 Larsen Hall, Appian Way
Cambridge MA 02138 USA
snowcat@hugse1.harvard.edu

Participants in this study were Puerto Rican bilinguals who were enrolled in the bilingual program at the public schools in New Haven, Connecticut. Participants were selected on the basis of teacher ratings. Teachers were asked to rate each of the children on their reading and writing skills, and on their speaking and listening skills on a five-point scale in both languages. Eighty children were selected for participation in this study; half were third graders and half were fifth graders. Half in each grade were identified as relatively poor readers (in Spanish) and the other half as good readers. All the children were born either in Puerto Rico or on the mainland to Puerto Rican parents, and all spoke Spanish predominantly or exclusively at home. The files are organized into four directories, each corresponding to a group of children:

Table 50: Snow/Velasco Files

File	Grade Level	Reading Skill
3PR	3rd grade	poor readers
3GR	3rd grade	good readers
5PR	5th grade	poor readers
5GR	5th grade	good readers

Within each directory, files are identified for the language used (S or E), the task (dpt = decontextualized picture description, def = definitions), and the participant number. Thus, to compare the English and Spanish files for one child one must select (for example) EDPT277.cha and SDPT277.cha.

The children were attending public school bilingual classrooms in a school system that had adopted a "pairing model" for bilingual education. Within this model, each child spends half the day with a Spanish-speaking teacher receiving instruction in Spanish, and the other half with an English-speaking teacher receiving instruction in English. The Spanish half of the day is devoted primarily to reading and content area instruction, whereas the English half of the day includes repetition in English of some of the content already presented in Spanish, English reading, and some ESL instruction. In the third grade the bilingual classrooms that the participants attended contained about 30 to 35 children. By fifth grade, classes were much smaller, because most of the normally progressing children had been mainstreamed. Fifth grade classes consisted of two groups: more recent arrivals from Puerto Rico and children with persistent difficulties in acquiring English. The selection criteria guaranteed that:

1. All students had been in this bilingual program for at least 2 years.

2. All students qualified for the free lunch program (indicator of poverty status, based on per capita family income). Parents were unskilled laborers or unemployed.

3. California Test of Basic Skills (Spanish) reading scores fell between the 60th to 89th percentile (for the good readers) or the 11th to 40th percentile (poor readers). Means (standard deviations) were: third grade poor readers 33 (7); third grade good readers 70 (9); fifth grade poor readers 30 (9); and fifth grade good readers 75 (10).

4. All participants had adequate (i.e., third grade equivalent) English decoding skills, as assessed by the Word Recognition Achievement Test.

Testing Procedure

Oral language performance in both Spanish and English was assessed using two different tasks. Testing was done in separate sessions for each language. Half of the participants in each grade was tested first in Spanish, half was tested first in English. Testing in both languages was carried out by Patricia Velasco, a fluent bilingual. The participants were also administered a reading comprehension test (Velasco, 1989).

Definitions

The definitions task was designed to test the child's ability to give formal definitions (Davidson, Kline, and Snow, 1986). The procedure is identical to that prescribed in the WISC-R instructions, and the first 10 nouns in the WISC-R were used. Specific instructions were: "What does __ mean?" The Spanish version of this is, "Qué quiere decir ___?"

Picture Description

To assess children's ability to respond to the needs of a distant listener, a picture description task was used. Children were shown a picture that included 3 to 4 children of the same gender engaged in play or household activities. Instructions were: "Please describe this picture so that another child that will be coming after you can draw a picture exactly like this one but without looking at it, just by listening to you." The Spanish version of this was, "Por favor describe lo que está pasando en este dibujo, para que el niño que venga después pueda hacer un dibujo iqual a este, pero sin verlo, solo escuchandote a ti."

The picture description files contain a coding line that reflects coding for various features presumed to be of importance in distinguishing more complete, more explicit, and more narrative descriptions from the rest. For complete coding instructions, see Davidson et al (1986). Briefly, the categories coded with their abbreviations were:

Table 51: Coding Categories

Abbreviations	Categories
VE	verb, present tense
VN	nonpresent tense verb
NP	noun phrase
LX	lexical noun phrase
AJ	adjective
UC	unusual conjunction (i.e., not "and" or "and then')
SL	specific locative
CM	clarificatory marker (post nominal clarification)
RL	relative clause
RE	revision, self correction
CO	communicatively effective revision
OP	opening — an explicitly narrative opening
TP	saying explicitly "this picture'
CL	closing — some conventional closing (the end; that's all)
NC	naming characters — assigning proper names to characters
XP	extrapictorial element — mention of something not in picture
IS	internal state — reference to internal state of character
CF	conversational features — intrusions of child as speaker
DI	dialogue — instances in which character is quoted directly
LS	language switch — word from other language
CW	creation of words — use of words not in Spanish or English

Publications using these data should cite:

Davidson, R., Kline, S., & Snow, C. E. (1986). Definitions and definite noun phrases: Indicators of children's decontextualized language skills. *Journal of Research in Childhood Education, 1,* 37–48.

Velasco, P. (1989). *The relationship between decontextualized oral language skills and reading comprehension in bilingual children.* Unpublished doctoral dissertation. Harvard Graduate School of Education.

Vila

Elisabet Serrat Sellabona
Department of Psychology
University of Girona
Pl. Sant Domenech, 9
17071 Girona, Spain
eli@zeus.udg.es

This is a corpus of data from Maria del Mar, a Spanish-Catalan bilingual girl who was audiotaped (with some gaps) from 1981 to 1984 from 1;9 to 5;4. Maria was born 16-FEB-1980. The project has been partially supported by a grant from the Spanish government (DGICYT PB89-0624-C02-01). The head of the project was Ignasi Vila, and the work was carried out in the ICE (Institute of Educational Sciences) in the University of Barcelona. Associate researchers were Montserrat Cortes, Montserrat Moreno, Carme Muñoz, and Elisabet Serrat. The collection and transcription of the data would have not been possible without the help of: Carme Mena, Ana Novella, and Joaquim Romero.

Table 52: Vila Files

File	Age	File	Age	File	Age
M01	1;09.14	M16	2;08.28	M36	4;05.02
M02	1;09.27	M17	2;09.09	M37	4;06.16
M03	1;10.18	M18	2;09.22	M38	4;07.08
M04	2;00.22	M19	2;10.16	M39	4;08.05
M05	2;01.15	M20	2;11.05	M40	4;08.20
M06	2;02.04	M22	2;11.27	M41	4;09.09
M07	2;02.26	M23	3;00.08	M42	4;09.23
M08	2;03.28	M24	3;01.02	M43	4;10.18
M09	2;04.04			M44	4;11.04
M10	2;04.19			M45	4;11.19
M11	2;04.26	M31	4;00.15	M46	5;00.01
M12	2;06.15	M32	4;01.15	M47	5;00.19
M13	2;07.03	M33	4;03.03	M48	5;02.15
M14	2;07.17	M34	4;03.26	M49	5;03.14
M15	2;08.01	M35	4;04.06	M50	5;04.16

Watkins

Charles Watkins
Université de Paris XIII
Avenue Jean-Baptiste Climent
93430 Villetaneuse France
watkins_charles@wanadoo.fr

This corpus was collated and scripted for a doctoral thesis in English Linguistics at the Université de Paris XIII entitled "The acquisition of deixis in English by children brought up in a bilingual environment." The focus of the reasearch is theoretical linguistics rather than psycholinguistics. The corpus is made up of scripted conversations in a naturalistic setting (often family videos not initially intended for research purposes) involving seven participants from three families over a range of ages between 1;9 to 7;2. The participants are all simultaneously bilingual, being exposed to both French and English from birth.

The corpus contains some 1400 child utterances in 72 CHAT files, each file corresponding to an uninterrupted sequence of dialogue. The transcript contains coding tags on the main line; coding tiers; and GEM markers for the purposes of the research project. All deictics are flagged on the main line with @ed (English deictic), @frd (French deictic), or @fred (Franco-English deictic) postcodes according to the phonetic form of the deictic. Two coding tiers, %dei (DEIctic) and %ana (pragmatic ANAlysis) further develop the analysis. The %ana line is not language specific and simply codes whether the deictic is used deictically (either symbolically or gesturally) or nondeictically (anaphorically or nonanaphorically). The %dei tier has the codes described in the following table which gives the codes for English. A parallel set of codes was also used for French.

Table 53: Watkins Deictic Codes

Part of Speech	Level 2	Level 3	Level 4	Examples
$EADV	:EDEM	:EPROX		here
			:ESHI	here vs. there
		:EDIST		there
			:ESHI	there vs. here
		:EPRESEN		here (we come)
		:EFORCLU		there (we are)
	:ETEMP	:EPRES		now
		:EPAST		then, ago, yesterday...
		:EFUT		then, soon, tomorrow....
	:EEXIST			there (is/are)
$EADJ	:EDEM	:EPROX		this+N/one

Table 53: Watkins Deictic Codes

Part of Speech	Level 2	Level 3	Level 4	Examples
			:ESHI	this+N/one vs. that+N/one
		:EDIST		that+N/one
			:ESHI	that+N/one vs. this+N/one
		:EPRESEN		There was this man, who....
		:EFORCLU		That's that job done
	:ETEMP	:EPAST		that afternoon, last year
		:EPRES		this moment, week
		:EFUT		this Thursday, next year
	:EPOS	:ESHI		my, your, our (exclusive)
		:EINC		our (inclusive)
		:ENONSPEC		your, one's
		:ETHIRD		his, her
$EPRO	:EDEFNEUT			it
	:EDEM	:EPROX		look at this
			:ESHI	this vs. that
		:EDIST		look at that
			:ESHI	that vs. this
		:EPRESEN		This might do the trick.
		:EFORCLU		That's that.
	:EPOS	:ESHI		mine, yours, ours (exclusive)
		:EINC		ours (inclusive)
		:ENONSPEC		yours, one's
		:ETHIRD		his, hers
	:ETEMP			Ow! That's my feet!
$EPER	:SUBJ	:ESHI		I, you, we exclusive
		:EINC		we inclusive
		:ENONSPEC		you, one
		:ETHIRD		he, she
	:NONSUBJ	:ESHI		me, you, us exclusive

Table 53: Watkins Deictic Codes

Part of Speech	Level 2	Level 3	Level 4	Examples
		:EINC		us inclusive
		:ENONSPEC		you, one
		:ETHIRD		him, her
$EVRB	:EVEN			come, bring
	:EAND			go, take

In addition to the deictic codes, there were a set of codes used on the GEM lines. These are given in the following list:

$AFFECT	nonlinguistic affect
$AMBIG	deictics in ambiguous utterances
$CATH	cathexis (investissement)
$CODESWITCH	deixis in code-switching
$CORR	correction by the interlocutor
$DET	determination of the noun phrase
$ECHO	deictics in echolalia
$EXISTCON	confusion in existential constructions
$EXISTMARG	marginally existential deictic
$FR	French
$GUESS	deictics in unclear material
$INTERROG	deictics in interrogatives
$L	the phoneme "l"
$LA	confusion of "la" and "that"
$LEXINT	lexical interference
$LOOK	gesture instead of deictic
$LYES	the phoneme /l/ in the yes of contradiction
$MARGDEIX	marginal use of deictic in a usual deictic form
$MARGGEST	marginally gestural use of deictic
$MARGTEMP	marginally temporal use of deictic
$NEGATIVE	deictic in negatives
$NONDEICTIC	utterance without deictics
$PHONCONF	phonetic confusion
$PHONINT	phonetic interference
$PROTO	protodeictics
$RETRACE	deictics in repetitions
$ROTE	deictics in rote forms
$SHIFT	shifter
$SYNINT	syntactic interference
$WANTLIKE	confusion of "want" and "like"
$WEIMP	impersonal use of "we"
$WEINC	inclusive use of "we"

4: Clinical Corpora

Table 54: Clinical Corpora

Corpus	Age Range	N	Comments
Beers on page 176	4;0–6;0	15 impaired	Cross-sectional study of phonologically impaired monolingual Dutch-speaking children
Bliss on page 184	3:0–11;8 2;3–11;8	8 normal 7impaired	Cross-sectional study of language-disordered children from different ages along with a normal comparisons group
Bol / Kuiken on page 185	4;1.16–8;1.17	20	Cross-sectional study of the morpho-syntax of Dutch children with specific language impairment (SLI)
CAP on page 188	English 25–71 yrs German 31–81 yrs Hung 18–76yrs	12 20 24	Cross-sectional study of English, German, and Hungarian aphasics along with normal controls. All of the aphasic participants had left lateral lesions
Conti-Ramsden 1 on page 194	4;0–9;0	5	Cross-sectional study of British SLI children and their younger MLU-matched siblings
Conti-Ramsden 2 on page 200	1;11–5;8	7	Cross-sectional study of British SLI children and their younger MLU-matched siblings
Feldman on page 204	1;2–3;0 xxx	4 sets of twins	Longitudinal study that examines the language development in twin sets with one suffering perinatal brain injury
Flusberg on page 211	xxx	6 Autism 6 Down	Longitudinal study of language development in children with autism and Down syndrome
Fujiki / Brinton on page 212	24 –77 years	42	Cross-sectional study of adults living in a residential setting with 2 conversational language samples elicited from each participant
Hargrove on page 214	3;0–6;0	6	Cross-sectional study with interviews between a speech therapist and children with SLI

Table 54: Clinical Corpora

Corpus	Age Range	N	Comments
Holland on page 215	19–93	42	Longitudinal study of early language recovery following a stroke
Hooshyar on page 218	1;4–2;11 3;2–11;6 2;8–5;9	40 normal 31 Downs 21 impaired	Cross-sectional study of language interactions between mothers and their nonhandicapped children, mothers and their Down syndrome children, and mothers and their language-impaired children
Leonard on page 225	3;8–5;7	11	Cross-sectional study of specifically language-impaired (SLI) children
Levy on page 226	1;10–8;4	14	Longitudinal study of Hebrew children with various developmental and/or medical disorders. A normal control population is included in this corpus
Malakoff / Mayes on page 227	2;0–2;22	76	46 children exposed to cocaine in utero and 22 control children, each sampled once
Oviedo on page 232	7–8	2	One SLI child and Williams Syndrome child, both speakers of Spanish
Rollins on page 234	2;2–3;1	5	Young boys with autism interviewed by a clinician
Rondal on page 237	3;0–12;1	21 Downs 21 controls	Cross-sectional study; Examines how mothers talk to their children with Down syndrome. Uses a comparison group of mothers talking with their normal children
Ulm on page 242	3;0–7;5	165	Longitudinal study of the development of stuttering in childhood. The transcribed language is not standard German but a Swabian dialect

Beers

Meike Beers
Institute for General Linguistics
Spruistraat 210
1012-VT Amsterdam, The Netherlands
mieke@alf.let.uva.nl

The data in these files were collected by Meike Beers and were originally used in Beers (1995). The data presented to CHILDES formed the input to a computer program which performed phonological analyses at the segment and the feature level of all consonants, vowels, and consonant clusters. These input files have been transformed into CHAT format by Steven Gillis and Masja Kempen from the University of Antwerp. The phonologically impaired children who took part in the project are described below. The data files and a description of the normally developing Dutch children from the same project can be found in the directory of Dutch corpora. General information on the selection, segmentation, and transcription of the items in the data files are similar for both groups of children.

Selection Criteria

Participants were also selected among children who had been diagnosed as specifically language impaired (SLI). The speech therapists from two schools for children with speech and language problems were asked to select children from among the SLI group for investigation in the present study using the following criteria:

1. The children lived in the Central Western part of the Netherlands, had native Dutch parents, and were monolingual Dutch-speaking.
2. The children had to be between 4;0 and 6;0.
3. The children had to be diagnosed as phonologically impaired.

Design

The period between 4;0 and 6;0 was divided into four age groups of 6 months each (4;0 to 4;6, 4;6 to 5;0, and so forth). The children were grouped together on the basis of their age in order to assure an even spread of participants across the age range of 4;0 to 6;0 years. From the phonologically impaired children, 24 spontaneous speech recordings were made of 15 children.

Data Collection

The data were collected from audio-recordings of spontaneous speech in a nonstructured, naturalistic setting. The recordings were made in a speech therapy room. All participants were selected and recorded in the course of the present study by the researcher. For

20 minutes the children were allowed to talk about any subject they liked. Television programs, pets, and toys were favorite topics of conversation. If the child could not come up with a topic, the speech therapist was allowed to use a picture book to prompt the child. The same picture book was used in these cases. At the end of each recording session, an evaluation was made by the child's speech therapist of the representativeness of the recording. The researcher was present at the recordings in order to make notes on the nonverbal contextual factors of the interaction.

Contextual information of each spontaneous speech recording was first reported using a standard form. From these standard forms items were selected that were to be analyzed phonologically. The first 10 minutes of each recording were not transcribed. This was done in order to let the children get used to the recording situation and materials (microphones and tape recorder). From a recording, transcription of realizations was carried out until 100 analyzable word realizations were found. FAN-analyses are based on data samples of 100 different word realizations. A word realization is defined as a unique articulation of a target word. The target word is the adult realization of a word and may be either a lexical item (dog, blue, sweet, and so forth) or a grammatical item (that, yes, we, and so forth). So, if a child has three different articulations of the target form for "kip" (chicken), for example, [kIp] -> [kI], [kIk], [pIp], these three realizations form three separate items for the analysis. If one of these child realizations turns up more than once in the sample, only three instances of these realization forms are included in the analysis. (The other occurrences can be entered in a separate box on the database chart, so that the information that this form is used very often by the child is not lost.)

Realizations of content words and function words were selected as analyzable from each utterance that was comprehensible and intelligible. Words from utterances with deviant word order and words from utterances that were partly unintelligible were analyzed. Furthermore, a FAN-analysis includes communicators such as *ja* "yes" and *nou* "well", as well as words selected from repetitions of whole utterances and imitated utterances. If parts of an utterance are unanalyzable these forms were excluded from the phonological analysis. Also excluded are: nonfunctional realizations, false starts, and vocalizations, such as "hm," "ah," and "oh" (cf. Bol & Kuiken, 1988, p.38).

In cases where the sampling norm of 100 realizations could not be reached on the basis of the 1-hour recording, analyses were performed based on the first 75 analyzable word realizations. From two of the impaired children only 75 analyzable realizations could be collected. In the case of one of these children only 10 minutes of recording time was available, the other child was just not very talkative.

Phonological Transcription

After transcriptions were made of the recordings the realizations of 100 different word tokens were transcribed phonologically. The phonological transcription of the word realizations was performed using the International Phonetic Alphabet (IPA, revised version 1979) supplemented with the phonetic symbols recommended by the project investigating

the Phonetic Representation of Disordered Speech (PRDS, 1983) to be found in the procedures for the Phonological Assessment of Child Speech (PACS, Grunwell, 1985). When
the child's pronunciation of a word was correct in relation to the adult target, the segments
of that word were transcribed broadly with IPA symbols. In the case of incorrect pronunciations of segments, transcription was as narrow as possible, using IPA and PRDS symbols.

In the case of transcription of target /s/-sounds we have followed a different procedure.
As has been found in studies of articulatory development for English (e.g., Templin 1957),
but also for Dutch (Peddemors-Boon, van der Meulen, & de Vries, 1977; van den Broecke,
Ruijters, & van der Meulen, 1984), the correct realization in terms of place of articulation
is acquired late in normal development. Errors, however, consist primarily of distortions of
/s/, and do not affect the contrastive function of this sound. In the Dutch studies, distortion
of /s/ in initial word position was found in children up to age 3;6, and in final word position
this occurred in children up to age 4;0. In Dutch, the coronal fricative is realized as a dental
alveolar. The majority of the distortions found in these studies of Dutch were interdental
realizations of /s/. Other distortions included realizations at the dental or at the alveolar position. Because in the present study we were primarily interested in the acquisition of the
contrastive use of segments, we did not distinguish between these variants of /s/ and have
transcribed them broadly.

CHAT Formatting

In the data files, the following information is available. The main tier is supposed to
contain the written form of each word uttered by the children. At present these forms are
supplied by M. Beers, together with an English gloss. On the main tier there is only the
symbol '0'. In addition, there are these dependent tiers:

1. The %mod tier contains the phonological form of the adult word attempted by the
    child (on the %mod tier).

2. The %rep tier contains the child's actual production in phonemes.

3. The %fam tier gives the original phonetic transcription of the adult target form.

4. The %far tier contains the child's phonetic rendition of the target word. In addition
    to a phonetic transcription of the child's utterance, this tier also contains a coding
    of the relevant phonological processes. These codes will be enumerated, explained,
    and exemplified below.

5. The %num tier stipulates the number of times a particular utterance occurred in the
    recording.

The segmental characters are based on the Dutch UNIBET given in the CHAT manual.
However, there are a few additional consonantal segments, as given in the following table.

Table 55: Consonants

Code	Definition	Code	Definition
W	labio-dental approximant	J	palatal plosive, voiced
P	labio-dental plosive, voiceless	$	palatal nasal
B	labio-dental plosive, voiced	c	palatal fricative, voiceless
M	labio-dental nasal	j	palatal approximant
F	bilabial fricative, voiceless	ij	palatal fricative, voiced
V	bilabial fricative, voiced	&	velar approximant
T	dental fricative, voiceless	K	uvular plosive, voiceless
D	dental fricative, voiced	R	uvular roll
L	lateral fricative	G	uvular plosive, voiced
r	alveolar roll	|	uvular nasal
"	dental-alveolar approximant	X	uvular fricative, voiceless
/	tap	%	uvular approximant
S	pal-alveolar fricative, voiceless	IJ	uvular fricative, voiced
C	palatal plosive, voiceless	h	glottal fricative
Z	pal-alveolar fricative, voiced	FE	pharyngeal plosive

On the %far tier the following symbols for phonological processes occur.

Table 56: Phonological Processes

Process	Symbol	mod	rep
insertion	{}	'la	'la{t}
cluster creation	({})	(s)are	(s{t})ar
deletion	0	'pot	'po0
medial C	=	p^=k-@	p^=k-@
diacritic addition	;x	'pOst	'pO;~cst
affricate notation	;^	'xap	'xap;^f
unclear sounds	.F.	'bos	'bo.F.
cluster insertion	{}	ok	'(st)ok
vowel insertion	{}	'(st)a	'(s{o}t)a
syllable insertion	{--}	b^l	b^w{-@-}
reduplication	-{--}00	Wa-t@r	Wa-{-Wa-}00
insertion and stress	{-'-}	'di	{-'t@-}ti
metathesis	[m:1] [m:2]	m[m:1]^k[m:2]	k[m:2]^m[m:1]
		rYp[m:1]s[m:2]	rYs[m:2]p[m:1]
regressive assimil.	[ra:1][ra:2]	'lo-p@	p[ra:1]o-p[ra:1]@
progressive assimil.	[pa:1][pa:2]	'W^l	'W[pa:1]^W[pa:1]
with deletion		'fOl	'l[ra:1]0O[ra:1]
C->V		'b^nt	'b^;~[ra:1]0[ra:1]t
in CCs		slop	0p[ra:1]op[ra:1]
syllable hopping	-[h:1]	'le-s[h:1]@	'les[h:1]-00
in CCs	-[h:1][h:2]	me-s[h:1]t[h:2]@	mes[h:1]t[h:2]-00
substitution		me-s[h:1]@	mef[h:1]-00
deletion and hopping		me-s[h:1]t[h:2]	me0[h:1]t[h:2]-00

On the %far tier the following diacritics are used.

Table 57: Diacritics: (preceded by ';')

Diacritic	Definition	Diacritic	Definition
-	devoiced	s	sibilance
h	aspirated	t	trill
d	dentalized	w	weak articulation
i	interdentalized	c	centralized vowel
l	labialized	`	shortened vowel
p	palatalized	.	half-long vowel
v	velarized	:	lengthened vowel
u	uvularized	+	heightened vowel
~	nasalized	T	lowered vowel
r	retroflex	f	fronted vowel
@	wet articulation	b	retracted vowel
>	ingressive airstream		

Segmentation

Segmentation of words into syllables in the case of polysyllabic words is based on morphological boundaries in compound words, for instance "voet-bal" (football), or derived forms, for instance "zij maak-ten" (they made). In the case of polysyllabic words that do not have a clear morphological boundary, for example, "appel" (apple), the word-medial consonants and clusters are considered as a separate category and are excluded from the sums of both the syllable-initial and the syllable-final consonants and consonant clusters (cf. Crystal 1982, p.63).

The category of Dutch medial consonants and consonant clusters were defined as ambisyllabic consonants based on proposals for syllabification in Dutch (Booij, 1981; Trommelen, 1984; van der Hulst, 1985). In Dutch, a final consonant is obligatory in syllables with a short vowel. At the same time, in polysyllabic words the Maximal Onset Principle (Selkirk, 1984) requires the word medial consonant(s) as the onset of the second syllable. Selkirk's Maximal Onset Principle is formulated as follows: "In the syllable structure of an utterance, the onsets of syllables are maximized, in conformance with the principles of basic syllable composition of the language (p. 359)". Therefore, in Dutch a word-medial consonant appearing after a short vowel is ambisyllabic: it can be syllabified as the final consonant of the first syllable as well as the initial consonant of the second syllable, as in "koffie" in (1). The exception to this rule is the case where a single consonant follows schwa. This consonant is then considered the initial consonant of the following syllable, as in (2), which often also has primary stress.

1.   /'k O = f - i/   koffie   coffee
2.   /b @ -'h ^ = N - @/   behangen   to wallpaper

The present analysis is theory-driven, and therefore differs from data-driven observations in perception-based studies (Gillis & de Schutter, 1996).

   In the case of word-medial consonant clusters of 2 consonants, the syllable boundary is also determined by the Maximal Onset Principle. After a long vowel, the cluster is syllabified as a syllable-initial cluster, as in "haasten" in (3), because in Dutch syllable-initial clusters of this type are allowed. After short vowels, the syllable boundary is located within the cluster. This means that after short vowels the first consonant of the cluster is syllabified as a syllable-final consonant and the second consonant as a syllable-initial consonant, as in "janken" in (4).

3.   /'h a: - s t @ n /   haasten   to hurry
4.   /'j ^ N - k @/   janken   to cry
5.   /'h ^ = s p - @ l]   haspel   reel
6.   /b @ -'s x @y t/   beschuit   rusk

   Medial consonant clusters were only found after short vowels in words as in (5), because in Dutch a cluster is ambisyllabic in that position. Again, after /@/, the consonant cluster was syllabified as the initial cluster of the following stressed vowel, as in "beschuit" in (6). In Dutch, clusters of 3 consonants are also found in word-medial position. In these cases, following Booij (1981) and Trommelen (1984), the clusters were syllabified as C-CC, but as CC-C if the last consonant was nasal. In general, the category of word-medial consonants and clusters is more restricted than in other word-based studies.

Publications using these data should cite:

Beers, M. (1995). The phonology of normally developing and language-impaired children. *Studies on Language and Language Use, 20*, Amsterdam: IFOTT.

Other relevant literature includes:

Bol, G. & Kuiken, F.(1988). *Grammatical Analyse van Taalontwikkelingsstoornissen.* Unpublished doctoral dissertation, University of Amsterdam.
Booij, G.E. (1981). *Generatieve Fonologie van het Nederlands.* Utrecht/Antwerpen: Het Spectrum.
Crystal, D. (1982). *Profiling linguistic disability.* London: Edward Arnold.
Gillis, S., & de Schutter, G. (1996). Intuitive syllabification: Universals and language specific constraints. *Journal of Child Language, 23,* 487–514.
Grunwell, P. (1985). *PACS: Phonological Assessment of Child Speech.* Windsor, UK: NFER Nelson.

Peddemors-Boon, M., Van der Meulen, Sj., & de Vries, A. K. (1977). *Utrechts Articulatie Underzook.* Lisse: Swets & Zeitlinger.

Selkirk, E. O. (1984). On the major class features and syllable theory. In M. Aronoff & R. Oehrle (Eds.), *Language Sound Structure.* Cambridge, MA: MIT Press.

Templin, M.C. (1957). *Certain language skills in children.* Minneapolis, MN: University of Minnesota Press.

Trommelen, M. (1984). *The syllable in Dutch.* Dordrecht, The Netherlands: Foris.

van den Broecke, M.P.R., Ruijters, S., van der Meulen, Sj. (1984). Verschillen in moeilijkheidsgraad in distinctieve kenmerken bij consonanten en consonant clusters. *Logopedie en Foniatrie 56*, 2–9.

van der Hulst, H. G. (1985). Ambisyllabicity in Dutch. In H. Bennis & F. Beukema (Eds.), *Linguistics in the Netherlands.* Dordrecht, The Netherlands: Foris.

Bliss

Lynn S. Bliss
Speech Communication
Wayne State University
585 Manoogian Hall
Detroit, MI 48202 USA
lbliss@cms.cc.wayne.edu

The Bliss directory consists of transcripts from seven language impaired children collected by Lynn Bliss at Wayne State University and formatted in CHAT. Comparable data from eight normally developing children can be found in the corpus in the English database. These data are not intended as comprehensive documentations of particular types of language disorders, but simply as illustrations of language-disordered children from different ages and their normal comparisons. Dr. Bliss would like researchers to provide her with the results of any analyses that use these data.

Table 58: Bliss Children

Impaired	Age
Denise	5;7.0
Fred	5;9.0
Jim	8;0.0
Joel	3;0.0
John	6;4.0
Sarah	11;8.0
Terra	4;11.0

Publications using these data should cite:

Bliss, L. (1988). The development of modals. *The Journal of Applied Developmental Psychology, 9,* 253–261.

Bol / Kuiken

Gerard Bol
General Linguistics
University of Groningen
9700-AS Groningen, The Netherlands
bol@let.rug.nl

This corpus includes data from the SLI children of the GRAMAT research, carried out by Gerard Bol and Folkert Kuiken between 1984 and 1988. This research was supported by a grant from the Praeventiefonds at The Hague in the Netherlands (Nr. 28-798).

The GRAMAT research aimed at two questions: 1) Is it possible to discern patterns in the morphosyntax of three groups of language-disordered children — children with SLI, with Down syndrome, and with hearing impairment, and 2) Can these patterns be related to the clinical characteristics of the children? Analysis of samples of spontaneous speech produced an affirmative answer to the first question. The answer to the second question is that the different clinical characteristics of the children did not lead so much to different kinds of language disorders as to differences in the degree of being language disordered. The three groups of children showed more commonalities than differences in producing morphosyntax.

Participants

The 20 Dutch SLI children (5 female and 15 male) in this research ranged in age from 4;01.16 to 8;01.17. The children all lacked sufficient intellectual or physiological impairment to account for their difficulties in language production. The IQ of the children has been tested (except for participant 16) and fell within normal ranges. The names of the children in the corpus are pseudonyms. Participants are identified by first names and with a five-digit code, indicating the age of the child in years, months, and days. Further information about the children is given below.

Data Collection

The speech of the 20 SLI children was audiotaped at their school, while they were playing with their speech therapist in a free-play situation. One of the two investigators was present in the room of the speech therapist. From time to time the investigator participated in the conversation. From each child 100 analyzable utterances were transcribed by the investigator that had been present at the recording. After that the utterances were analyzed according to the GRAMAT framework. GRAMAT (Grammatical Analysis of Developmental Language Disorders) is a Dutch adaptation of the descriptive morphosyntactic-framework used by Crystal, Fletcher and Garman (1976).

Table 59: Bol / Kuiken Files

Nr.	Name	Age	Sex	MLU	VC1	Articulation
01	Rinanda	40116	F	2.4	0;11	
02	Pierre	40720	M	4.4	0;00	phonol.problems
03	Renzo	40821	M	3.7	0;00	dyspraxia
04	Monique	40908	F	2.2	0;00	dyspraxia
05	Wilma	50102	F	3.7	0;00	phonol. problems
06	Diana	50104	F	3.9	0;00	phonol. problems
07	Lieneke	50307	F	3.2	1;09	
08	Pascal	50428	M	4.4	1;09	*
09	Mark	51122	M	4.4	1;07	dyspraxia *
10	Bertus	60010	M	3.3	1;07	slow phonol. dev.
11	Pim	60013	M	3.4	0;00	*
12	Hessel	60024	M	2.1	1;07	inconsist. conson.
13	Jelle	60113	M	4.4	n.t.	dyspraxia
14	Joep	60126	M	3.5	1;06	dyspraxia
15	Ramon	60210	M	2.5	1;06	
16	Joost	60722	M	2.8	1;05	inconsist. conson. *
17	Pjotr	70018	M	4.6	1;07	
18	Sjouke	70126	M	4.8	2;01	dyspraxia
19	Kees	70419	M	5.7	1;08	
20	Lennart	80117	M	4.2	2;11	

1. Verbal comprehension was tested with the Dutch adaptation of the Reynell Developmental Language Scales (Rev.), by Bomers & Mugge (1982). Indicated is the delay in years and months. If a child had not been tested, "n.t." is noted in the list.
2. Weak auditory memory is indicated by (*).
3. MLU is computed in morphemes (MLU-m).

Publications using these data should cite:

Bol, G. W. & Kuiken, F. (1990). Grammatical analysis of developmental language disorders: A study of the morphosyntax of children with specific language disorders, with hearing impairment and with Down's syndrome, *Clinical Linguistics and Phonetics, 4,* 77–86.

An additional reference is:

Crystal, D., Fletcher, P., & Garman, M. (1976). *The grammatical analysis of language disability*. London: Edward Arnold.

CAP

This subdirectory contains transcripts gathered from 60 English, German, and Hungarian aphasics along with normal controls in the Comparative Aphasia Project (CAP) directed by Elizabeth Bates. The transcripts are in CHAT format and large segments have full morphemic coding and error coding. Additional normal comparison groups for these data can be found in the MacWhinney / Bates 1 narrative corpus, which is the raw data from MacWhinney and Bates (1978). These comparison data are for English, Italian, and Hungarian children and adults.

Procedure

All of the data were collected using a common procedure, which is the "given-new" picture description task of MacWhinney and Bates (1978). This procedure was varied only slightly to allow the aphasic participants to see three pictures in a series at once. Participants saw nine sets of pictorial stimuli which could be described in terms of simple sentences. For example, Series 2 consists of three pictures of the same boy, which can be described by these sentences:

1. A boy is running.
2. A boy is skiing.
3. A boy is swimming.

Table 60: Sentence Structure

Series	Structure	Sentence
1	S V	A bear (mouse, bunny) is crying.
2	S V	A boy is running (swimming, skiing).
3	S V O	A monkey (squirrel, bunny) is eating a banana.
4	S V O	A boy is kissing (hugging, kicking) a dog.
5	S V O	A girl is eating an apple (cookie, ice cream).
6	S V L	A dog is in (on, under) a car.
7	S V L	A cat is on a table (bed, chair).
8	S V O I	A lady is giving a present (truck, mouse) to a girl.
9	S V O I	A cat is giving a flower to a boy (bunny, dog).

In this listing, these abbreviations are used for the major elements of a sentence: S=subject, V=verb, O=object, L=object of the locative preposition, and I=indirect object. The three pictures in each series are called frames. For example, (a) is the first frame, (b) is the second frame, and (c) is the third frame. In this particular series, the subject increases in givenness across the frames whereas the verb increases in newness. In Series 6 and 7, the verb is taken to include both the copular and the locative preposition. (In Hungarian, the locative is a postposition or suffix rather that a preposition.)

The order of the nine series of pictures was randomized. Following each series, a picture of a common object such as a bottle or a sailboat was inserted. This was done to break up any set (Einstellung) effects. Participants were examined individually. Each participant was seated next to the experimenter at a table. The participants were told that they would be asked to tell about what they saw in some pictures. The experimenter showed the pictures to each participant in groups of three, varying the placement of particular pictures left, middle, and right across participants. Two probes were used: "Tell me about this picture," and "What's happening in this picture?" Use of the two probes was also randomized. Each session was taperecorded in its entirety.

Participants

All of the participants were right-handed. All of the aphasic participants had left lateral lesions. The transcripts in the CHILDES database are from either Broca's aphasics, Wernicke aphasics, or anomics. The characterization of these syndromes is as follows:

1. Broca's aphasics are nonfluent patients, displaying an abnormal reduction in utterance length and sentence complexity, with marked errors of omission or substitution in grammatical morphology.

2. Wernicke's aphasics are patients suffering from marked comprehension deficits, despite fluent or hyper-fluent speech with an apparently normal melodic line; these patients are expected to display serious word-finding difficulties, usually with semantic and/or phonological paraphasias and occasional paragrammatisms.

3. Anomics are fluent patients, with apparently normal comprehension abilities in free conversation, suffering primarily from word-finding problems (in the absence of severe paraphasias or paragrammatism).

Patients were referred for testing by neurologists and speech pathologists at the respective research sites, with one of the above diagnoses. In support of each classification, we were provided with neurological records (including CT scans in many cases), together with the results of standard aphasia batteries that were used at the respective research sites, such as the Boston Diagnostic Aphasia Examination in the United States and the Aachen Aphasia Battery in Europe. To eliminate the possibility that a patient had changed status since the diagnosis provided at referral, patients were all screened in a biographical interview administered and recorded prior to testing. In addition, we excluded all patients with one or more of the following conditions:

1. history of multiple strokes,

2. significant hearing and/or visual disabilities,

3. severe gross motor disabilities,

4. severe motor-speech involvement such that less than 50% of the participant's

speech attempts were intelligible, or

5.   evidence that participant was neurologically or physically unstable and/or less than 3 months post onset.

Patient groups were defined within each language according to their fit to a prototype used by neurologists and speech pathologists in that community. For example, a prototypic Broca's aphasic would show reduced fluency and phrase length, and a tendency toward omission of functors. Hence patients were matched across languages only in the sense that they represented different degrees of deviation from a prototype developed out of observed variation within each language group. This permitted comparison of the "best" and the "worst" patients across languages, as well as those who fit the mean.

Table 61: English CAP Participants

File	Sex	Onset	Test Lag	Etiology	Ed.	Occupation
B1-71	M	58	2 years	CVA	12	telephone engineer
B2-73	M	31	1 year	CVA	16	engineer
B3-76	M	61	5 years	CVA	-	telephone repair
B4-66	M	43	8 years	CVA	18	accountant
B5-74	M	33	3 years	Trauma	15	electronics
B6-72	M	44	1 year	CVA	-	-
W1-82	M	47	2 months	CVA	16	insurance
W2-83	M	81	1 year	CVA	-	build. maintenance
W3-84	M	56	1 month	CVA	11	-
W4-81	M	53	1 year	CVA	16	parish priest
W5-85	M	61	3 weeks	CVA	18	army colonel

Table 62: German CAP Participants

File	Sex	Onset	Test Lag	Etiology	Ed.	Occupation
B08	F	57	2 months	CVA	13+	speech therapist
B41	F	55	1 year	CVA		
B42	F	42	4 years	CVA	13+	technician
B43	F	25	6 years	Trauma	9	sales clerk
B44	F	40	7 years	CVA	9	housewife

Table 62: German CAP Participants

File	Sex	Onset	Test Lag	Etiology	Ed.	Occupation
B45	F	59	2 years	CVA	9+	office clerk
B46	F	36	7 years	CVA	11	dressmaker
B47	F	52	20 months	CVA	9	kitchen help
B48	M	47	8 years	CVA	16	engineer
B161	M	62	9 years	CVA	9+	business
W31	F	43	8 years	Trauma	9+	office clerk
W32	M	52	11 years	CVA	9+	electrician
W33	M	70	20 months	CVA	9+	foundry worker
W34	F	36	8 years	Trauma	9+	sales clerk
W35	M	59	4 years	CVA	9+	accountant
W36	M	47	3 years	CVA	13+	merchant
W37	F	65	4 years	CVA	9	housewife
W38	M	64	5 years	CVA	9+	service manager
W39	M	71	3 years	CVA	9	
W40	F	49	7 weeks	CVA		housewife

Table 63: Hungarian CAP Participants

File	Sex	Etiology	Onset	Test Lag	Ed.	Occupation
B1	F	trauma	37	4 years	6	Worker
B2	M	CVA	36	7 months	8	Ironworker
B5	M	thrombosis	44	7.5 months	16	Engineer
B7	F	thrombosis	55	25 months	8	Accountant
B9	M	trauma	18	8 months	8	Student
B10	M	CVA	53	2 years	8	Ironworker
B11	M	trauma	26	4 years	8	Fireman
B12	M	thrombosis	55	7.5 years	16	Engineer
B13	F	CVA	34	4 months	8	Telex

Table 63: Hungarian CAP Participants

File	Sex	Etiology	Onset	Test Lag	Ed.	Occupation
B14	M	aneurism	41	5 months	8	Mechanic
W2	F	abscess	51	4 months	12	Teacher
W4	F	meningeoma	55	2 months	12	Clerk
W5	M	tumor	37	2 months	16	Engineer
W9	M	thrombosis	76	3 months	12	accountant
W11	F	ischemia	63	3 months	6	xeroxer
A1	F	vascular	39	<year	8	
A2	F	vascular	18	<year	12	
A3	F	vascular	48	<year	12	
A4	M	vascular	57	<year	8	
A5	M	trauma	18	<year	8	
A6	M	tumor	31	two years	12	
A7	M	vascular	64	<year	8	
A8	F	angioma	29	<year	8	
A10	F	tumor	57	<year	5	
A11	M	vascular	59	<year	8	

Table 64: Hungarian CAP Test Scores

File	Locus	WAB AQ	WAB Fluency	WAB Comp.
B1	centro-parietal	73	4	9.0
B2	MCA	50.2	4	6.4
B5	MCA	33.6	3	6.7
B7	MCA	70.8	4	8.2
B9	fronto-temporal	59.8	2	8.1
B10	MCA	45.4	5	6.9
B11	fronto-temporal	43.4	5	7.4
B12	fronto-temporal	65.4	6	8.6

Table 64: Hungarian CAP Test Scores

File	Locus	WAB AQ	WAB Fluency	WAB Comp.
B13	fronto-temporal	67.0	4	9.2
B14	fronto-temporal	66.6	4	6.4
W2	centro-parietal	33	6	6.6
W4	occipital	58	7	5.6
W5	ant-temporal	56	8	5.6
W9	MCA	51.2	8	5.5
W11	MCA	49.4	6	6.7

Publications using these data should cite one or more of these studies:

Bates, E., Friederici, A., & Wulfeck, B. (1987a). Grammatical morphology in aphasia: Evidence from three languages. *Cortex, 23,* 545–574.

Bates, E., Friederici, A., & Wulfeck, B. (1987b). Sentence comprehension in aphasia: A cross-linguistic study. *Brain and Language, 32,* 19–67.

Bates, E., Friederici, A., Wulfeck, B., & Juarez, L. (1988). On the preservation of word order in aphasia: Cross-linguistic evidence. *Brain and Language, 33,* 323–364.

Bates, E., Hamby, S., & Zurif, E. (1983). The effects of focal brain damage on pragmatic expression. *Canadian Journal of Psychology, 37,* 59–84.

Bates, E., & Wulfeck, B. (1989a). Comparative aphasiology: A crosslinguistic approach to language breakdown. *Aphasiology, 3,* 11–142.

Bates, E., & Wulfeck, B. (1989b). Crosslinguistic studies of aphasia. In B. MacWhinney & E. Bates (Eds.), *The crosslinguistic study of sentence processing*, (pp. 328–374). New York: Cambridge University Press.

MacWhinney, B., & Bates, E. (1978). Sentential devices for conveying givenness and newness: A cross-cultural developmental study. *Journal of Verbal Learning and Verbal Behavior, 17,* 539–558.

Wulfeck, B., Bates, E., Juarez, L., Opie, M., Friederici, A., MacWhinney, B., & Zurif, E. (1989). Pragmatics in aphasia: Crosslinguistic evidence. *Language and Speech, 32,* 315–336.

Conti-Ramsden 1

Gina Conti-Ramsden
Centre for Educational Guidance
Department of Education
University of Manchester
Manchester, England M13 9PL
gina.conti-ramsden@man.ac.uk

This corpus includes data from five British language-impaired children and their younger MLU-matched siblings in the age range from 4;0 to 9;0.

Participants

Two groups of children and their mothers participated in this study. Five participants were language-impaired children and five were their normally developing younger siblings. The families were drawn from a larger study of parent–child interaction conducted by Conti-Ramsden in England. The study had a two-stage screening procedure for the recruitment of participants. First, families were contacted through a network of speech therapists and professional colleagues who were informed by letter of the criteria for participation. Second, each language-impaired participant referred was matched with his or her younger, normally developing sibling on the basis of MLU during a home visit. This part of the screening consisted of audiotaping a language sample of each of the two children while playing at home in order to obtain a rough idea of their MLU. It is not often that one finds an older language-impaired child at the same expressive language stage as his or her younger normally developing sibling. For the Conti-Ramsden project in England 36 families were contacted of which only 5 met the standards of language match required in this study. The five families participating in this study were White, intact (both father and mother living together at home), and monolingual.

Table 65: Conti-Ramsden Families

FED	MED	FSEG	SE Group	Children
Secondary	Secondary	skilled manual	III(M)	Rick and Rose
Further	Secondary	managerial	II	Clay and Charles
Further	Secondary	managerial	II	Abe and Ann
Secondary	Secondary	manual	IV	Kate and Kale
Secondary	Secondary	skilled manual	III(M)	Sean and Susan

All parents had secondary education (two fathers had further education but did not hold university degrees). The mothers were all housewives. Based on the father's occupation, the families belonged to social class II (ancillary workers with occupations between professional and skilled), III (skilled manual workers), or IV (semiskilled manual workers), as indicated in the preceding table.

The language-impaired children ranged in age from 4;9 to 6;9 years. All five language-impaired children presented with severe expressive language delays as measured by MLU. The language-impaired children fell within Brown's (1973) Stage I and II of linguistic development, although according to their chronological age they should have been functioning post-Stage V. In addition, all language-impaired children appeared to have nonverbal abilities within normal limits as measured by the Leiter International Performance Scale (Leiter, 1969). These data, along with the child's sibling position in the family are as follows:

Table 66: Conti-Ramsden Children

Child	Group	Sex	Age	Position	M.A.	I.Q.
Rick	LI	M	6;9	3/4	6;6	101
Rose	SIB	F	3;2	4/4	3;3	108
Clay	LI	M	5;10	1/2	4;9	86
Charles	SIB	M	2;4	2/2	2;0	91
Abe	LI	M	5;3	2/3	5;9	115
Ann	SIB	F	1;11	3/3	1;10	101
Kate	LI	F	4;9	1/3	4;3	95
Kyle	SIB	M	2;4	3/3	2;3	101
Sid	LI	M	4;9	1/2	5;0	110
Susan	SIB	F	2;5	2/2	2;3	98

Interestingly, the children's comprehension status varied depending on which aspect of comprehension was being measured. The following table gives the results for three standardized tests. Results of the Preschool Language Scale (PLS-C) (Zimmerman, Steiner & Pond, 1979), a developmental test of auditory comprehension, revealed all language-impaired children to be functioning within normal limits (quotients ranging from 82 to 105). Results for the receptive vocabulary test, the British Picture Vocabulary Scale (BPVS) (Dunn, Dunn, Whetton, & Pintillie, 1982), a test in which the child points to one picture out of four choices, revealed all language-impaired children to have difficulties with receptive vocabulary (percentile scores ranging from 6% to 26%). Finally, findings of the Test of Reception of Grammar (TROG) (Bishop, 1982), a test of the comprehension of grammatical structures, revealed some language-impaired children to have difficulties in this area, although others appeared to be functioning normally (percentile scores ranging from no measurable comprehension of grammar to 50%).

The results on these three tests were as follows:

Table 67: Conti-Ramsden Test Scores

Child	Group	CA	PLS-C	BPVS	TROG
Rick	LI	6;9	6;6 (96)	4;6 (6%)	5;0 (10%)
Rose	SIB	3;2	2;9 (87)	2;8 (28%)	*
Clay	LI	5;10	5;4 (91)	4;7 (22%)	4;9 (20%)
Charles	SIB	2;4	2;4 (98)	*	*
Abe	LI	5;3	5;6 (105)	4;4 (26%)	5;0 (40%)
Ann	SIB	1;11	2;7 (131)	*	*
Kate	LI	4;9	3;10 (82)	3;0 (7%)	See note
Kyle	SIB	2;4	2;1 (91)	*	*
Sean	LI	4;9	4;10 (103)	2;10 (6%)	5;0 (50%)
Susan	SIB	2;5	2;3 (93)	*	*

* Too young to be tested.
Note: Kate (LI) did not reach the lowest age equivalent of 4;0 for the TROG test.

Younger siblings ranged in age from 1;11 to 3;2 years. All younger siblings appeared normally developing (IQ ranging from 91 to 108) with age-appropriate language in terms of MLU (MLU in Stages I and II) and general auditory comprehension (PLS-C quotients ranging from 87 to 131). All children participating in the study had hearing within normal limits as determined by pure tone audiometry screening bilaterally (at 500, 1,000 and 2,000 Hz at 25 dB). Through the use of a questionnaire and parent interview, it was ascertained that no child had a history of chronic middle ear problems that necessitated regular otological treatment. In addition, all children presented uneventful case histories with respect to severe neurological or emotional problems.

Furthermore, as can be seen in the following summary, all language-impaired children were receiving speech therapy in the clinic or were enrolled in language-based classrooms for specific language-disordered children (language units). In these classrooms, the children received help from their language teacher and speech-language pathologist who worked together to develop a program for each individual child. In England, both speech-language pathologists and teachers are in continual contact with the children's parents via home visits and visits by the parents to the clinic or the language units in the school. Nonetheless, none of the parents participating in this study had attended a parent training program.

Table 68: Conti-Ramsden Therapy Breakdown

Child	Started Therapy	Months in Therapy	Type of Provision
Rick	4;0	33	Clinic 4;0 to 5;3
			Language-Unit 5;3 to 6;9
Clay	2;6	44	Clinic 2;6 to 4;6
			Language Unit 4;6 to 5;8
Abe	3;0	27	Clinic 3;0 to 4;6
			L-Unit 4;6 to 5;3
Kate	4;6	3	Clinic 4;6 to 4;9
Sean	3;2	21	Clinic 3;2 to 4;2
			L-Unit 4;2 to 4;9

"Clinic" refers to weekly therapy in a clinic. Despite severe problems, Kate appears to have fallen through the health-service net as she was not referred to therapy until she attended nursery school.

Procedures

After a warm up period of 2 to 10 visits, each pair of language-impaired child and younger sibling was videotaped interacting individually with their mothers in a free play situation in the participants' home. The video recorder was not turned on until the participants were ready and playing comfortably. Each dyadic play interaction lasted approximately 15 minutes. The order of interactions was determined by each family given everyday restrictions such as older sibling's possible school attendance, children's willingness, and so forth. In addition, each family chose the toys they wanted to play with and were only instructed to "do what you normally do." The present project attempted to gather ecologically valid, everyday interactions; thus, it was desirable to minimize the amount of structure imposed on the families' everyday activities.

Transcription

The transcription process involved two phases. In the first phase, 10-minute samples of continuous play interaction were transcribed from the videotape recordings. Transcriptions included verbal and nonverbal events and the context in which these event occurred. These initial transcriptions were done by two native speakers of British English using paper and pencil. In the second phase, the paper and pencil transcriptions were computerized; verified; enriched with gestures, indications of nonverbal communicative activity, gaze, and some broad phonetic information required for the analyses; and formatted in accordance with CHAT.

Coding

The coding scheme aims to identify whether the partners in each dyadic interaction are a) engaged in a conversation, b) following their own separate foci of attention, or c) engaged in a mainly nonverbal episode of interaction. Further coding under each of these three main categories is then applied in order to identify more subtle aspects of the interaction.

Conversations

Conversations were defined according to Conti-Ramsden and Friel-Patti's (1987) definition: "Two or more turns linked together by a focus on a particular topic." Turns are defined as either verbal or nonverbal. Codes that indicate that a turn is part of a conversation are: $NEW, $CON, $END, and $NC (noncontingent). After each of these codes, further codes were added which vary according to whether the turn was that of parent or child, or alternatively mark the end of the conversation.

$END codes include:
NE	natural end
TCP	topic end, change of topic by parent
TCC	topic change by the child
TCO	topic change by some outside event

$CON codes include:
IMI	imitation
SR	simple recasts
CR	complex recasts
IN	requests or commands the parent makes to the child
RC	requests for clarification
COM	comments
ACK	acknowledgments
OTH	other
UN	unclear
RES	responsive utterances
INT	interactives that move the conversation forward

$NC codes include:
BTC	breakdown in topic change
BNA	breakdown nonacknowledgments
BIN	breakdown initiation, the child fails to respond to a command

BNA	breakdown requests for clarification
BCO	breakdown comments, which are not responded to by the child
BIM	breakdown imitations
BOT	breakdown other

Additional speech act codes are:

VI	verbal initiation
NVI	nonverbal initiation
VR	verbal response
NVR	nonverbal response
SV	verbal self-continuation
SNV	nonverbal self-continuation
NVE	nonverbal episode
COD	commands (parents only)
COM	comments (parents only)

Publications using these data should cite:

Conti-Ramsden, G., & Dykins, J. (1991). Mother–child interactions with language-impaired children and their siblings. *British Journal of Disorders of Communication, 26,* 337–354.

Other relevant publications include:

Bishop, D. V. M. (1982). *The test of reception of grammar*. University of Manchester, UK: Medical Research Council.

Brown, R. (1973). *A first language: The early stages*. Cambridge, MA: Harvard University Press.

Conti-Ramsden, G., & Friel-Patti, S. Situational variability in mother-child conversations. In *Children's language* K. Nelson and A. van Kleeck (Eds.) (pp. 43-64). Hillsdale, NJ: Lawrence Erlbaum Associates.

Dunn, L. M., Dunn, L. M., Whetton, C., & Pintillie, D. (1982). *The British Picture Vocabulary Scale*. Windsor, UK: NFER.

Leiter, R. G. (1969). *The Leiter International Performance Scale*. Chicago: Stoelting.

Zimmerman, I. L., Steiner, V. G., & Pond, R. E. (1979). *The preschool language scale*. London: Merrill.

Conti-Ramsden 2

Gina Conti-Ramsden
Centre for Educational Guidance
Department of Education
University of Manchester
Manchester, England M13 9PL
gina.conti-ramsden@man.ac.uk

This corpus contains transcripts from seven children with specific language impairment (SLI) and their younger normal siblings.

The Families of the Children With SLI

The families involved in this longitudinal study were part of a larger project investigating the language development of children with specific language impairment (SLI), and of their younger nonimpaired siblings (Conti-Ramsden & Dykins, 1991; Conti-Ramsden, Hutcheson, & Grove, 1995). Families were informed of the research project through the speech and language therapy services in the northwest of England, and asked if they would be willing for the research workers to visit them and discuss their possible involvement in more detail. During an initial visit, the research project was explained and parents were given the opportunity to opt for a longer longitudinal involvement of approximately 2 years. In addition, the researchers collected language samples, by means of an audio recording, from the child with SLI and, at a separate session, from the younger sibling. The first 50 child utterances were transcribed from the recordings in order to ascertain the mean length of utterance of the children, using Brown's (1973) criteria, with the modifications suggested by Miller (1981). From the outset, it was made clear to the parents that no identifying information would be revealed except to the research workers, and that the family could terminate their longitudinal involvement in the research project at any time. Accordingly, any data collected from the family at that point would be destroyed if desired. Three families agreed to participate in the longitudinal phase of the project. We examine the data obtained from these three children with SLI and their younger normal language learning siblings. The children with SLI were named Colin, Andrew, and Mark and the younger siblings were named Chris, Nina and Adam.

Characteristics of the Children

The characteristics of the children with SLI and their younger siblings at the beginning of the study are presented in the table that follows in terms of age and psychometric results. It can be seen that the participants with SLI were three expressively impaired children, all male, with severe problems (as can be seen from the discrepancy between their age and their MLU obtained on the language sample). The three children performed within one standard deviation of the mean in the Leiter International Performance Scale, which provided a measure of IQ. In addition, they were tested in a number of comprehension measures. These children had varying comprehension profiles with below-average vocabulary comprehension (as measured by the British Picture Vocabulary Scale (BPVS); 18 to 26 percentile rank), poor comprehension of grammar (as measured by the TROG; 20 to 40 percentile rank), but better overall auditory comprehension abilities (as measured by the Preschool Language Scale; results in Table 1). The younger siblings were two males and one female who ranged in age from 1;11 to 2;2 at the beginning of the study. The three siblings performed within one standard deviation of the mean in the measure of IQ. They also had expressive language and auditory comprehension skills well within normal limits. The siblings were too young to be tested for comprehension of grammar (TROG) or vocabulary comprehension (BPVS).

In addition, all six children had adequate hearing sensitivity as determined by pure-tone audiometry screening bilaterally at 500, 1000, and 2000 Hz at 25 dB (equivalent to pure tone thresholds of 25 dB HL, re: ANSI, 1989). The three children with SLI had eventful birth histories with the three children being anoxic at birth. Developmental histories ascertained by a questionnaire to parents revealed all developmental language milestones to be delayed in the three children with SLI. In addition, motor milestones appeared delayed for Colin and Andrew.

All six children spoke English in monolingual homes and came from intact (two parent) families. In all three families, the mothers remained at home as housewives while the fathers went out to work; all the parents had secondary education. All children with SLI were receiving speech therapy in a clinic or were enrolled in language-based classrooms for children with SLI (called "language units" in England).

Video Recordings

The video recording sessions lasted approximately 15 to 20 minutes and were conducted in the homes of the families using the play materials available there. In order to keep the parents as unconcerned as possible about the nature of their own speech, they were told that the research was primarily about the children's communicative development. The instructions given to the parents were "play as you normally do." The three families participated in a number of dyadic interactions including mother, father, and sibling. The present study mainly concerns itself with the mother–child play interactions although some father–child interactions were occasionally also used.

All the children were videotaped every 6 weeks, but illness and cancellations meant that video samples were, on average, once every 3 months over a 15 month period. A further sample was taken after approximately 10 to 16 months, completing a 2-year observation period. In the present study, we examined seven sessions over the two-year period for each of the three families. As the aim of the study was to examine the development of expressive language (in particular the early stages of verb use), MLU in words was thought to be a better indication of expressive language than MLU in morphemes. This was also a more appropriate measure for comparisons with the nonimpaired younger siblings as we were interested in what the children were doing at the point at which they were just starting to use multiword speech.

Transcription

The first 10 minutes of each of the seven mother–child sessions were transcribed. The transcriptions contained information about verbal and nonverbal interactions, and the context in which these events occurred. This was carried out in accordance with the CHILDES guidelines for CHAT. The computerized transcripts were then compared with the original videotaped data by an independent transcriber in order to verify their accuracy. This process resulted in 97.0% inter-transcriber reliability. Any disagreements concerning the transcription were resolved by re-examination until consensus was reached. The data from the present study are available in the CHILDES database.

The number of child utterances was noted for each MLU point for each child. We were able to include in the analysis 100 child utterances for each of the seven sessions for each child. Transcripts from the father–child interaction sessions (carried out on the same day) were used in some cases to supplement those mother–child sessions containing too few child utterances.

Table 69: Children at Beginning of Study

	CA	MLU	Performance IQ	PLS-AC	ACQ
Colin (SLI)	5;8	1.45	89	5;4	91
Chris (Sibling)	2;2	1.28	91	2;1	131
Andrew (SLI)	5;3	1.77	115	5;6	105
Nina (Sibling)	1;11	1.45	101	2;7	131
Mark (SLI)	3;9	1.28	105	3;10	103
Adam (Sibling)	1;11	1.51	96	2;0	104

PLS-AC = Preschool Language Scale Auditory Comprehension
ACQ = Auditory Comprehension Quotient

Publications using these data should cite:

Conti-Ramsden, G., & Dykins, J. (1991). Mother–child interactions with language-impaired children and their siblings. *British Journal of Disorders of Communication, 26,* 337–354.
Conti-Ramsden, G., Hutcheson, G. D., & Grove, J. (1995). Contingency and breakdown: Specific Language Impaired children's conversations with their mothers and fathers. *Journal of Speech and Hearing Research.*
Conti-Ramsden, G., & Jones, M. (1997). Verb use in specific language impairment. *Jour-*

nal of Speech and Hearing Research, 40, 1298-1313.

Additional references include:

Brown, R. (1973). *A first language: The early stages.* Cambridge, MA, Harvard University Press.

Miller, J. (1981). *Assessing language production in children: Experimental procedures.* Baltimore, University Park Press.

Feldman

Heidi Feldman
Child Development Unit
Children's Hospital
3705 Fifth Ave.
Pittsburgh, PA 15213 USA
feldmanh@vms.cis.pitt.edu

This corpus contains a set of files collected by Heidi Feldman and colleagues at Children's Hospital in Pittsburgh. The children included are either participants who have experienced some form of brain lesion or the normal controls for these children. There are two main studies. The first set of files is a part of the "narrative study" with children aged 4 to 7 that used picture book story-telling procedures to elicit narrative descriptions. The second study, the "PC" study, looked at younger children using the procedures of the New England study (Ninio, Snow, Pan, & Rollins, 1996). In addition to these two major studies, there was a study of two twin pairs with one child with using both the methods of the PC study and, later, the narrative tasks.

Table 70: Narrative Children

Name	Ages	Sex	Comments
CAL	4;0.15–6;11.20	M	Diffuse PVE injury
CAS	4;1.6–6;2.25	M	Bilateral injury in preterm infant
CES	4;1.10–7.2.20	M	Bilateral injury in preterm infant
CIO	4;1.19	M	Prenatal RH white matter stroke in full-term infant
DAV	4;2.12–6;0.	M	Right hemisphere porencephaly
DON	4;1.10–6;20	M	Diffuse injury in full-term infant
DOT	6;6	M	Right hemiparesis, LH lesion
FRI	5;0.25–8;2.29	F	Diffuse injury in preterm infant
GAM	5;0.19–8;2.25	M	Left cystic PVL in preterm infant
HIN	4;20–5;0.	M	Diffuse injury in preterm infant
MAC	4;0.15–6;2.7	M	Diffuse injury in preterm infant
MAT	4;0.12–6;1.9	F	Diffuse injury in preterm infant
MEC	4;6.0–5;2.18	M	Diffuse and LH injury in preterm infant

Table 70: Narrative Children

Name	Ages	Sex	Comments
SCO	4;1.10–7;0.8	F	Infantile hemiplegia in full-term infant; left cystic PVL
SLA	6;2.0	F	Diffuse lesion
SNO	4;0.25	M	Left hemisphere stroke at 1 month of age during catheterization
YUC	4;0.25–6;3.18	M	Diffuse white matter lesion in preterm infant
YUR	4;0.3–7;1.23	M	Diffuse lesion in near–term infant

Table 71: Narrative Controls

Name	Ages	Sex	Comments
BO2	4;0–5;0	F	Full-term healthy sibling of BOU
DR2	5;1.12–7–1.12	F	Full-term healthy sibling
GA3	4;1–5;1.22	M	Full-term healthy sibling of GAL
GR2	4;2.17–5;1.18	M	Full-term healthy sibling of GRA
LE2	5;5–6;1.0	F	Full-term healthy sibling of LEO
MA2	4;0–5;0	F	Full-term healthy sibling of MAT
MA3	4;0–5;0	F	Full-term healthy sibling of MAT
ME2	4;7.25–6;0	M	Full-term healthy sibling of MEY
PO2	4;0	M	Full-term healthy sibling of POR
ZI2	4;5.17–8;2.20	F	Full-term healthy sibling of ZIC

Table 72: PC Children

Code	Ages	Sex	Comments
BAR	1;6.0	M	Prenatal LH stroke
BEA	1;2.15–2;0.18	M	Right infarct
BEY	1;6.0–2;3.0	F	Focal left PVL
BLA	1;3.22–3;3.13	F	Right par–occipital porencephalic cyst with hydrocephalus, shunted
BOT	2;6.2–2;9.4	M	Acquired lesion at 1;9 during surgery, multiple infarcts
BRA	2;3.0–3;7.0	F	bilateral hypodensity lesion
CAL	2;6.0–3;6.0	M	Diffuse injury at term
CAS	2;3.0–3;6.0	M	Bilateral injury in preterm child
CES	2;7.0–3;6.0	M	Bilateral injury in preterm child
CHA	1;4.12–3;0.13	M	Diffuse PVE
CIC	1;2.22–2;6.25	F	Diffuse PVE l
CIO	3;3.9–3;9.3	M	Focal right PVL
DAN	1;6.0–3;1.7	F	Congenital lesion
DEB	1;6.10–2;6.10	M	Diffuse injury
DOR	1;11.25–3;0.18	F	Right Parietal Infarct
DUP	1;4.17–2;5.1	F	PVL lesion type
EDW	1;10.0–4;1.17	F	Lesion type is bi-PVE, R Cyst, Hydrocephalus; infection
FEI	1;3.7–2;4.16	F	Bilateral PVE lesion type
FLO	2;4.6–2;10.26	F	PVE lesion type
FRI	1;5.0–4;0.23	F	Focal right, frontal–parietal–occipital lesion
GAL	1;3.20–2;10.15	M	PVL lesion
GAM	1;3.0–4;6.0	M	Focal left parietal lesion
GAR	1;2.15–3;2.19	F	PVL–L fronto–parietal

Table 72: PC Children

Code	Ages	Sex	Comments
GIG	1;6.0–3;6.10	F	Focal right lesion
GLA	1;2.28–3;5.1	F	PVL-L lesion, porencephaly-R
GRA	1;3.23–3;0.1	F	Focal right lesion
HAL	1;6.0–3;3.17	F	Bilateral injury on ultrasound, spastic diplegia
HAP	1;4.0–2;2.7	M	PVE-L lesion, and right porencephalic cyst
HAT	1;5.10–3;0.	M	Large right hemisphere infarct
HIN	2;2.0–3;9.0	M	Noncystic PVL on ultrasound, spastic quadriplegia
LEO	1;3.17–2;8.14	F	Diffuse noncystic PVE
LIN	1;5.15–3;0.27	M	Diffuse PVL
MAC	2;6.0–4;0.15	M	Diffuse white matter disease; no motor or sensory impairment
MAG	4;0.15–5;3.14	F	Left MCA infarct
MAR	2;11.25–3;4.2	F	Left hydrocephalus
MAT	2;3.10–4;0.	F	Diffuse PVL
MEC	2;3.0–3;6.0	M	Diffuse+left temporal damage
MED	1;4.10–2;11.21	M	Left parietal hemmorhage
MEY	1;3.0–2;6.7	M	Bilateral injury
MYE	1;3.2–4;0.21	M	Right PVL lesion
NEA	1;4.25–2;1.29	M	LH porencephalic cyst
NOW	2;6.20–3;9.21	M	Bilateral PVL lesion
PLA	1;3.1–2;8.16	M	Right porencephalic cyst
POP	1;3.0–3;0.6	M	Right PVE lesion
ROM	1;3.27–3;0.25	M	Right parietal infarct
SCO	1;6.0–3;9.0	F	Infantile hemiplegia; Left cystic PVL
SHN	2;8.15–4;0.3	M	Right fronto–parietal infarct

Table 72: PC Children

Code	Ages	Sex	Comments
SNO	2;8.0–3;6.0		Focal left infarct
SUL	1;4.0–3;6.0	M	Diffuse injury
TRU	2;7.6	M	Diffuse injury
WAL	1;2.23–3;9.26	M	Right PVL lesion
WIX	1;3.0–3;9.	M	Diffuse injury
YUC	2;10.0–3;6.0	M	Diffuse PVL lesion
YUZ	4;1.4	M	Diffuse injury
ZIC	1;5.4–2;6.12	F	Bilateral PVL lesion

Most of the control children for the PC study were full-term infants. However, there are also files from eight preterm controls. The preterms files begin with "p" and the nonpreterm control files begin with "n."

Table 73: PC Controls

File	Code	Ages	Sex	Condition
nchi0127	IPP	2;3.0	F	Gestational age is 40 weeks
nchi0218	TAY	1;6. 2;3	F	Gestational age is 40 weeks
nchi0227	TAY	2;3.0	F	Gestational age is 40 weeks
nchi0318	JON	1;6.0	F	Gestational age is 40 weeks
nchi0321	JON	1;9.0	F	Gestational age is 40 weeks
nchi0342	JON	3;6.17	F	Gestational age is 40 weeks
nchi0415	DO3	1;4.0	M	Gestational age is 40 weeks
nchi0421	D03	1;9.2	M	Gestational age is 40 weeks
nchi0430	DO3	2;6	M	Gestational age is 40 weeks
nchi0439	DO3	3;3.0	M	Gestational age is 40 weeks
nchi0515	GID	1;3.0	M	Gestational age is 40 weeks
nchi0615	LO1	1;2.27	F	Gestational age is 40 weeks
nchi0727	LO2	2;3.0	M	Gestational age is 40 weeks
nchi0842	CHI	3;6.0	F	Gestational age is 40 weeks

Table 73: PC Controls

File	Code	Ages	Sex	Condition
nchi0942	CHI	3;6.0	M	Gestational age is 40 weeks
nchi1030	AUR	2;6	F	Gestational age is 40 weeks
nchi1139	ROS	3;3.0	F	Gestational age is 40 weeks
nchi1242	PRE	3;6.0	M	Gestational age is 40 weeks
nchi1336	HOP	3;0.0	F	Gestational age is 40 weeks
nchi1418	SC2	1;6.0	M	Gestational age is 40 weeks
nchi1539	SC1	3;3.0	M	Gestational age is 40 weeks
nchi1739	FRA	3;3.0	F	Gestational age is 40 weeks
nchi1821	CHI	2;0		Normal control from preschool
nchi1933	MUR	2;9.0	F	Gestational age is 40 weeks
nchi2121	STE	1;9.0	F	Gestational age is 40 weeks
nchi2239	GHA	3;3.0	M	Gestational age is 40 weeks
nchi2318	LAI	1;6.0	M	Gestational age is 40 weeks
nchi2421	FIN	1;9.0	F	Gestational age is 40 weeks
nchi2518	CA2	1;6.0	M	Gestational age is 40 weeks
nchi3130	CHI	2;6		Normal control from preschool
nma221	MA2	1;9		Normal twin of MAT
nma224	MA2	1;11.26	F	Normal twin of MAT
ma227	MA2	2;3.20	F	Normal twin of MAT
ma230	MA2	2;7.20	F	Normal twin of MAT
ma236	MA2	3;0.0	F	Normal twin of MAT
ma239	MA2	3;3.20	F	Normal twin of MAT
ma242e	MA2	3;6.20	F	Normal twin of MAT
ma324	MA3	2;0.0	F	Normal twin of MAT
ma327	MA3	2;3.20	F	Normal twin of MAT
ma330	MA3	2;6.27	F	Normal twin of MAT
ma336	MA3	3;0.0	F	Normal twin of MAT

Table 73: PC Controls

File	Code	Ages	Sex	Condition
ma339	MA3	3;3.20	F	Normal twin of MAT
ma342	MA3	3;6.20	F	Normal twin of MAT
	DAN	1;6.0–3–1.21	M	Preterm twin, control
	DEA	1;3–1;6	F	Preterm control
	GAS	1;6.0–1;9.0	M	Preterm twin, control
	JAC	1;9.0	F	Preterm twin, control
	KOR	2;11.6	F	Preterm control
	OTI	3;3	F	Preterm control
	REC1	1;6.18–1;9.28	M	Preterm control

The data for the twin study comes from two sets of twins in which one twin suffered early brain damage and the other did not.

Table 74: Twins

Code	Ages	Sex	Comments
NAM	2;6–7;0	F	focal lesion
TAK	2;6–7;0	F	normal twin of NAM
TYL	1;11–6:10	M	focal lesion
BRI	1;11	F	normal twin of TYL

Publications using these data should cite:

Feldman, H., Keefe, K., & Holland, A. (1989). Language abilities after left hemisphere brain injury: A case study of twins. *Topics in Special Education, 9,* 32–47.

Keefe, K., Feldman, H., & Holland, A. (1989). Lexical learning and language abilities in preschoolers with perinatal brain damage. *Journal of Speech and Hearing Disorders, 54,* 395–402.

Additional references include:

Ninio, A., Snow, C., Pan, B., & Rollins, P. (1994). Classifying communicative acts in children's interactions. *Journal of Communications Disorders, 27,* 157–188.

Flusberg

This directory contains files from children with autism and children with Down syndrome. The data were contributed by Helen Tager-Flusberg and reformatted into CHAT by Pam Rollins.

Publications using these data should cite:

Tager-Flusberg, H., Calkins, S., Nolin, T., Bamberger, T., Anderson, M., & Chandwick-Dias, A. (1990). A longitudinal study of language acquisition in autistic and Down syndrome children. *Journal of Autism and Developmental Disorders, 20*, 1–21.

Fujiki / Brinton

Bonnie Brinton
Department of Speech Communication
Brigham Young University
Provo, UT 84602
bonnie_brinton@byu.edu

Martin Fujiki
Department of Speech Communication
Brigham Young University
Provo, UT 84602
martin_fujiki@byu.edu

Forty of the 42 participants who participated in the following studies (samples from two participants were not transcribed in CLAN format) are included in this data base. Participant names, cities, states, and other identifying information (e.g., names of universities) have been randomly changed. Thus, those familiar with the geography of particular locations should not expect the names of cities and other institutions to make sense with regard to proximity. Anyone interested in using the morphological codes should recheck the codes themselves before using them.

Participants

All of the participants sampled were living in community residential settings, with the exception of two participants in the older group who were living in an extended care facility at the actual time of sampling. These participants were not excluded from the sample because they had lived in the community their entire lives and had only recently been placed in the extended-care setting. As will be described in more detail, each of the participants has a long (approximately 30 min.) and a short (approximately 10-15 min.) sample. There are two cases in which samples are shorter (see the two tables for specifics). For some participants (e.g., Sher) these samples were elicited in a single sitting. In four cases, only the longer sample was transcribed in CLAN and is included in the data base.

The two tables present descriptive information on gender, chronological age, full scale IQ score from the Wechsler Adult Intelligence Scale–Revised (WAIS–R from Wechsler, 1981), and sample length in minutes. In addition, the following information is provided from Fujiki, Brinton, Robinson, and Watson (1996).

Some individuals in the older group had little or no formal educational experience. Some had training experiences within institutional settings. Case history information for some participants indicated "special school" placement, however, the specific nature of these placements was difficult to determine. All of the individuals in the younger group had received special-education placements.

For both groups, auditory and visual status of the participants was unremarkable. Unremarkable visual status was defined as current binocular vision of 20/40 or better, with corrective lenses if needed. Unremarkable auditory status was indicated by passage of a pure tone screening test at 1000, 2000, and 4000 Hz at 45 dB/HL. General health status was also judged to be unremarkable. These judgments were made on the basis of facility records and interviews with each participant's case worker. All of the participants were ambulatory, as demonstrated by the ability to walk independently, and all of the participants had adequate verbal skills to participate in conversation. To ensure that participants demonstrated adequate linguistic structures to perform the experimental tasks, all participants were required to pass a brief screening, consisting of 10 minutes of conversation with a certified speech-language pathologist.

Procedures

Two conversational language samples were elicited from each participant by the same investigator. The first sample was 25 to 30 minutes long, and began with the investigator's asking the participant a series of product questions (e.g., what's your full name, where do you live, when is your birthday, and so forth). Following these questions, the investigator introduced five (and sometimes six) objects as topics of conversation. Following this the investigator asked the participant a series of questions requiring more extensive answers (e.g., What do you like about [city where participant lived]?).

A second-language sample that was approximately 10 to 15 minutes in length was also elicited from each participant. This sample, which was typically obtained on the same day as the longer sample, consisted of naturalistic conversation. Although the conversation was not structured, the investigator did insert several request for clarification sequences. These sequences make up the data base for Brinton and Fujiki (1996). For many participants an extra clarification sequence was elicited to ensure five usable sequences. In all cases, the first five sequences in the sample were used in the analysis.

For individuals in supported work settings, the samples were obtained at the participant's work setting. For those participants working in the community, testing was conducted at a supported work setting with which they had some association. For participants who were retired or were not employed, testing was conducted at a supported work setting near their homes. In all of these cases, the subject had some association with the setting, and was familiar with the facility and its personnel. All language samples were elicited by the same investigator.

Publications using these data should cite:

Brinton, B., & Fujiki, M. (1996). Responses to requests for clarification by older and young adults with retardation. *Research in Developmental Disabilities, 17,* 335–347.

Fujiki, M., Brinton, B., Watson, V., & Robinson, L. (1996). The production of complex sentences by young and older adults with mild to moderate retardation. *Applied Psycholinguistics, 17,* 41–57.

Hargrove

Patricia Hargrove
Department of Communication Disorders
Mankato State University
Mankato, MN 56001 USA
hargrove@vax1.mankato.msus.edu

This subdirectory contains a set of interviews in CHAT format between a speech therapist and six language-impaired children in the age range of 3 to 6. The files were contributed by Patricia Hargrove.

Publications using these data should cite:

Hargrove, P. M., Holmberg, C., & Zeigler, M. (1986). Changes in spontaneous speech associated with therapy hiatus: A retrospective study. *Children Language Teaching and Therapy, 2,* 266–280.

Holland

Holland, Audrey
Department of Speech and Hearing
University of Arizona
Tucson, AZ USA
alh@ccit.arizona.edu

The language transcripts were gathered under the direction of Audrey Holland and O.M. Reinmuth as part of research project funded by NINCDS entitled "Early Language Recovery Following Stroke." They were donated by Dr. Holland to the CHILDES in 1986 and reformatted from SALT to CHAT in 1988. Patients were seen for 15 minutes a day, 6 days per week throughout the course of their hospitalization, beginning at 24 to 72 hours post-stroke. The daily visits were conducted by two trained speech-language pathologists: one to converse with the patient and the other to observe, taperecord, and tally features of the interaction. For each patient there are three transcribed conversations, representing 5-minute segments from the first, middle, and last visits made during the patient's hospitalization. The file name includes a number that will indicate which visit it is. For example, there are files for the patient coded as Wilde: wilde1.cha, wilde9.cha, and wilde17.cha. In this case, the patient had 17 total visits: wilde1 is the first, wilde9 the ninth, and wilde17 the seventeenth and last.

Table 75: Holland Participants

Pseudonym	Onset Age	Side	Initial Type of Disorder
Athos	51	R	normal
Atkins	79	L	Wernicke
Barrie	19	B	uncertain + apraxia of speech
Basil	72	R	dysarthria + uncertain
Boris	38	B	unresponsive
Brown	59	L	global
Collin	75	L	global
Cyert	35	L	global/mixed
Davis	85	L	Wernicke
Getty	76	L	uncertain + dysarthria
Godot	77	R	R hem cog + L neglect + dysarthria
Gruman	45	L	Broca + apraxia of speech + dysarthria

Table 75: Holland Participants

Pseudonym	Onset Age	Side	Initial Type of Disorder
Hector	74	L	anomia + confusion
Henley	75	L	thalamic neglect + confusion
Holmes	64	L	conduction
Horace	60	L	uncertain
Jones	69	L	apraxia of speech + uncertain
Kirk	48	L	global
Malone	35	L	transcortical motor
Miles	76	L	Wernicke
Milan	61	L	global
Milton	74	R	normal
Murray	71	R	thalamic neglect + R hem cog
Neil	68	L	conduction
Norman	33	L	apraxia of speech + uncertain
Oliver	45	B	R hem cog
Parker	81	L	Wernicke
Robert	77	R	L neglect + R hem cog + dysarthria
Rudolf	69	L	conduction
Rupert	74	L	dysarthria
Scott	80	L	dysarthria + R neglect
Seller	61	L	Broca + dysarthria
Spade	93	L	Wernicke
Stone	40	L	uncertain + dysarthria
Stuart	61	L	uncertain
Taylor	55	B	unresponsive
White	73	L	uncertain + dysarthria
Wilde	82	L	global

Table 75: Holland Participants

Pseudonym	Onset Age	Side	Initial Type of Disorder
Wilson	64	R	R hem cog + L neglect + dysarthria
Young	65	L	dysarthria
Zenith	76	L	uncertain
Zipps	82	L	global

Publications using these data should cite:

Holland, A., Miller, J., Reinmuth, O., Bartlett, C., Fromm, D., Pashek, G., Stein, D., & Swindell, C. (1985). Rapid recovery from aphasia: A detailed language analysis. *Brain and Language, 24,* 156–173.

Hooshyar

Nahid Hooshyar
7818 La Verdura
Dallas, TX 75248 USA

This directory contains files from Down syndrome children and their mothers collected by Nahid Hooshyar in the context of a project entitled "Language Interactions between Mothers and Their Nonhandicapped Children, Mothers and Their Down syndrome Children, and Mothers and Their Language-Impaired Children." The data from the nonhandicapped and language-impaired children are not in CHILDES. The data were collected from 1984 to 1986 and contributed to the CHILDES system in 1988. They were originally formatted in SALT (Miller & Chapman, 1983), but were reformatted to CHAT by the SALTIN program. The project was supported by Grant No. 8402115 and CFDA 84.023D from the Department of Education.

The major goal of this study was to isolate and identify patterns occurring in language interactions between mothers and their nonhandicapped (NH), Down syndrome (DS), or language-impaired (LI) children. The study explored the nature of such language interactions and attempted to determine whether there were consistently recurring patterns within a group, and if so, whether these patterns were the same across groups. More specifically, this study was designed to investigate the following questions:

1. What kinds of language teaching strategies do mothers of nonhandicapped, Down syndrome, and language-impaired children utilize in language interactions with their children in "real life" situations?

2. What kinds of language learning strategies do nonhandicapped, Down syndrome, and language-impaired children bring into language learning situations?

3. Can contextual variables be identified that serve to evoke and/or control these strategies?

Participants

Three groups of mother–child dyads participated in this study: nonhandicapped children and their mothers, children with Down syndrome and their mothers, and children with language impairment and their mothers. Names of potential participants were obtained from a number of cooperating school systems and day-care centers in the Dallas/Fort Worth Metroplex, the Down syndrome Guild, and the Callier Center for Communication Disorders of the University of Texas at Dallas. Mothers were mailed an introductory letter explaining the nature of the study and a parental consent form. The introductory letter was followed by telephone contact during which mothers were given more detailed information about the tasks and time involved in this study. Mothers were asked to volunteer if their children could produce at least 10 words but were not yet regularly producing multiword utterances. The final criterion for inclusion of a child in the study was the child's level of linguistic development as measured by the mean length of utterance (MLU) as defined by

Brown (1973). Only children with MLU between 1 and 3 were included in this study.

Initial Interview

In order to ensure that children of the three groups were equal in their expressive and receptive language, the Vineland Adaptive Behavior Scales (VABS) (Sparrow, Balla, & Cichetti, 1984) was administered. Three to 5 days after the telephone contact, a member of the research team called each of the mothers to arrange an appointment for a home visit. During this visit, the same research assistant interviewed the mother using a family background and demographic characteristics questionnaire and the VABS. The purpose of this interview was to encourage communication, to allow the interviewer to study the attitudes of the mothers toward their child and to form other subjective observations useful in subsequent contacts with the mothers. The visit lasted between 3 to 4 hours. Although the purpose of the study was stated in the letter sent to the mothers, it was reiterated during the initial visit in the following format: "We are researchers at the University of Texas at Dallas and we would like to learn about the language development among three groups of children: nonhandicapped, Down syndrome, and language-impaired. We feel we will get a typical language sample if we observe children interacting with their mothers in their familiar environment. We would like you to carry on your daily activities as you ordinarily do."

Videotaping

Videotaping sessions were conducted in the participants' homes and were scheduled at the mothers' convenience. Participants were videotaped while engaged in each of the three activities (playtime, story time, and mealtime) for approximately 20 minutes. All sessions were completed during one home visit that lasted 2 to 3 hours. In most of the sessions only the child and the mother were present. However, in about 25% of the cases there was another child or adult present also. Two to 3 weeks after the videotaping session, each mother was mailed a questionnaire to assess the effects of the videotaping and the presence of the observer on the mother and child behavior.

Instruments

Mothers' rating of their children's social and adaptive behavior was assessed by the VABS survey form. This scale contains 297 items which measure adaptive behavior in four domains: (1) communication, (2) daily living skills, (3) socialization, and (4) motor skills. In interview form, it is designed to be used with parents of individuals aged zero to 18 years 11 months or of low-functioning adults. The scale was standardized on the performance of a representative national sample of handicapped and nonhandicapped individuals. Reported internal consistencies range from 0.89 to 0.98, and test–retest reliabilities range from 0.76 to 0.93.

For the purpose of this study, a detailed demographic characteristic and family background questionnaire was developed. The questionnaire consisted of 65 items grouped into eight categories: identifying information, demographic information, marital status, source of financial support, occupation, number of children, child-care, health of the child, reading, TV viewing, physical environment, and experience outside of the home. Questions included such areas as birth order, educational attainment, employment, and marital history of the parents. A second questionnaire was developed consisting of an open-ended question asking mothers to describe their feelings and thoughts about the videotaping session and the observer.

Participants

The final sample consisted of 40 NH (21 female, 19 male), 31 DS (14 female, 17 male), and 21 LI (7 female, 14 male) children and their mothers. Only the data from the Down syndrome group is in the CHILDES database. Of the children with Down syndrome, the karyotype of 30 were diagnosed as Trisomy 21 and one as Translocation. The LI children were of normal intelligence with language or speech production problems including articulation problems attributed primarily to middle ear infection, cleft palate (surgically corrected), and nonspecified causes.

All participants were white, English-speaking, and middle-class, as defined by Hollingshead Index of Social Status. The table that follows presents the birth order of the children. All mothers were currently married, living with a spouse, and primary caregivers of their children. The mean age for the mothers of the NH children was 30.0 years (SD = 0.80; Range = 20 to 45 years) and the mean age for the mothers of the two other groups was 36.0 years (SD = 1.34 and Range = 20 to 46 years for mothers of DS children; SD = 0.94 and Range 20 to 45 years for mothers of LI children). The educational level ranged from high school to postgraduate education for mothers of NH children and from partial college preparation to B.A. or B.S. degree for the other two groups. The mean parity, as defined by Ryder and Westhoff (1971), was 1.81 for families with NH children, 3.09 for families with DS children, and 2.05 for families with LI children. The mean age for NH children was 26.75 months (SD = 4.24; Range = 16 to 35 months), for DS children it was 64.48 months (SD = 17.87; Range = 38 to 138 months), and for LI children it was 44.84 months (SD = 9.23; Range = 32 to 69 months). The mean MLU for NH children was 1.85 (SD = 0.61; Range = 1.07 to 2.98), for DS children it was 1.64 (SD = 0.63; Range = 1.01 to 2.95), and for LI children it was 1.98 (SD = 0.66; Range = 1.04 to 3.00).

The mean Adaptive Behavior Composite (ABC) score on the VABS for NH children was 37.60 (SD = 46.53; Range = 17 to 32), for DS it was 44.35 (SD = 17.33; Range = 18 to 75), and for LI it was 41.33 (SD = 10.05; Range = 21 to 64). The mean Expressive Communication on the VABS for NH children was 29.05 (SD = 8.73; Range = 13 to 53), for DS it was 38.00 (SD = 21.36; Range = 12 to 89), and for LI it was 36.00 (SD = 12.12; Range = 17 to 62). The mean Receptive communication on the VABS for NH children was 39.82 (SD = 9.54; Range = 18 to 47), for DS it was 53.41 (SD = 27.88; Range = 14 to 94), and for LI it was 46.52 (SD = 17.66; Range = 30 to 94). The NH children were functioning significantly above their chronological age (CA) in expressive and receptive communication (t=

2.48 and $t = 9.2$ with $p = 0.02$ and 0.001, respectively). Children with DS were significantly delayed in their adaptive behavior, expressive and receptive communication functioning ($t = 8.06, 8.01, 4.53$ with $p < 0.001$ for the three scores). For LI children, the mean ABC and expressive communication scores were significantly delayed ($t = 2.22$ and $t = 3.67$ with $p = 0.04$ and 0.002, respectively).

Files

Each participant was videotaped during three different settings: playtime, story time, and mealtime. Only the playtime and story time transcripts are in the CHILDES database. The names of the files with playtime dialogs all begin with the letter "p" and the names of the files with storytime dialogs all begin with the letter "s." The participant numbers, pseudonyms, ages in months, ages in years, dates of recordings (for the story files), and dates of birth are as follows:

Table 76: Hooshyar Files

Code	Name	Months	Age	Date of Recording	Date of Birth
041	Shally	81	6;8.24	10-MAR-1985	16-JUN-1978
042	John	79(77)	6;7.0	4-APR-1985	
043	Alicia	86	7;6.0	30-MAR-1985	
044	Ruth	37(38)	3;1.0	18-APR-1985	
045	David	107	8;11.0	17-MAY-1985	
046	Beverly	55(46)	4;7.0		
047	Jerald	58	4;10.0	3-JUN-1985	
048	Robert	41	3;5.0	14-JUN-1985	
049	Cheryl	38	3;2.0		
050	Steve	56	4;8.0	29-MAY-1985	
051	Mary	95	7;10.0	4-JUN-1985	
052	Michael	42	3;6.0	17-JUN-1985	16-DEC-1981
053	Barton	95	7;10.25	14-JUN-1985	20-JUL-1977
054	Marilyn	40	3;5.9	19-JUL-1985	10-FEB-1982
055	Mark	40	3;4.18	8-AUG-1985	21-MAR-1982
056	Edward	65	5;5.0	20-AUG-1985	20-MAR-1980

Table 76: Hooshyar Files

Code	Name	Months	Age	Date of Recording	Date of Birth
057	Craig	45	3;9.0	22-AUG-1985	
058	Kim	102	9;4.0		
059	Taffie	47	3;10.3	2-OCT-1985	30-DEC-1981
060	Rick	52	4;5.9	3-JAN-1986	25-AUG-1981
061	Donald	47	3;11.16	7-FEB-1986	19-FEB-1982
062	Jack	38	3;2.0	18-FEB-1986	
063	James	138	11;6.0	14-APR-1986	
064	Barbara	99	8;3.0	8-AUG-1986	
065	Adam	108	9;5.0	7-AUG-1986	
066	Eileen	120	9;11.0	13-AUG-1986	
067	George	96	8;10.7	29-AUG-1986	22-OCT-1977
068	Sandra	108	9;7.10	23-OCT-1986	13-MAR-1977
069	Jody	108			
070	Ronald	96	7;11.13	20-AUG-1986	7-SEP-1978
071	Lynelle	84	7;0.5	23-AUG-1986	18-AUG-1979

All of the names given above are pseudonyms. The data from Participant 069 (Jody) were not provided to CHILDES.

Transcribing

Five research assistants participated in transcribing the videotaping. In order to have a uniform transcription, transcribers were trained to use SALT (Miller & Chapman, 1983) for preparing and marking the transcripts. Sample transcripts were jointly reviewed in conferences to clarify and answer questions about instructions. An utterance-by-utterance reliability of the transcription was estimated by having the transcribers independently transcribe 10 representative videotapes. Only after interrater agreement approached unity were the remaining videotapes transcribed. All transcriptions were made in ordinary English orthography with phonetic notation used in cases where an English word could not be identified. Normal English punctuation was used to denote intonation patterns, to make the meaning of a sentence clear, or to indicate the pauses and stops that the speaker made in speaking. The mood of each utterance was identified primarily on the basis of intonation and secondarily on the basis of structural features. For example, declarative sentences that ended in rising intonation were coded as interrogative mood. Seven assistants entered the transcribed records into the computer using WordStar. Finally, observers checked the transcripts of their own videotaping sessions to verify the accuracy and add necessary contextual information. The final product was a complete record of verbal and behavioral events and the context in which these occurred. In 1988, the SALT files were converted to CHAT format, using the SALTIN program.

Speech Act Codes

Every utterance was coded for its overall speech act function and specific value. The functions and their specific values were as follows:

1. Queries: leading, coaching, information request.
2. Declaratives: labeling, announcing, informing, explaining, idle chat.
3. Imperatives: request attention, request action, proposal for joint action.
4. Feedbacks: informative feedback, evaluative feedback, corrective feedback, verbal disapproval, granting permission.
5. Performatives: demonstrating, pointing, guiding, affect, joshing.
6. Imitations: exact, reduced, expanded, modified.
7. Self-repetition: exact, reduced, expanded, modified.
8. Syntactic well-formedness: sentence fragment, complete sentence, minor abbreviations.
9. Sentence types: yes–no question, wh-question, imperative, declarative.
10. Speech style: disfluent, run-on, unintelligible, stock expression.

Table 77: Hooshyar Test Means

Variable	NH Mean	NH *SD*	DS Mean	DS *SD*	LI Mean	LI *SD*
Age	26.75	4.24	64.48	17.87	44.84	9.23
MLU	1.85	0.61	1.64	0.63	1.98	0.66
ABC	37.60	46.53	44.35	17.33	41.33	10.05
Exp.Comm	29.05	8.73	38.00	21.36	36.00	12.12
Rec.Comm	39.82	9.54	53.41	27.88	46.52	17.66

NH (N = 40); DS (N = 31); LI (N = 21)

1. MLU — Mean Length of Utterance

2. ABC — Adaptive Behavior Composite
3. Exp. Comm — The Vineland Adaptive Behavior Scale (VABS)-Expressive
4. Rec. Comm — The Vineland Adaptive Behavior Scale (VABS)-Receptive

These data can only be used with the expressed permission of Dr. Hooshyar who requests that she be included as coauthor on any publications utilizing her data.

Publications using these data should cite:

Hooshyar, N. (1985). Language interaction between mothers and their nonhandicapped children, mothers and their Down children, and mothers and their language-impaired children. *International Journal of Rehabilitation Research, 4,* 475–477.
Hooshyar, N. (1987). The relationship between maternal language parameters and the child's language constancy and developmental condition. *International Journal of Rehabilitation Research, 10,* 321–324.

Other relevant publications include:

Brown, R. (1973). *A first language: The early stages.* Cambridge, MA: Harvard University Press.
Miller, J., & Chapman, R. (1983). *SALT: Systematic analysis of language transcripts, User's manual.* Madison, WI: University of Wisconsin Press.
Ryder, N. B., & Westhoff, C. F. (1971). *Reproduction in the United States in 1965.* Princeton, NJ: Princeton University Press.
Sparrow, S., Balla, D., & Cichetti, D. (1984). *Vineland Adaptive Behavior Scales: Interview edition.* Circle Pines, MN: American Guidance Service.

Leonard

Lawrence Leonard
Audiology and Speech Sciences
Purdue University
Heavilon Hall
West Lafayette, IN 47907 USA
xdxl@vm.cc.purdue.edu

The 11 children whose transcripts are provided here were diagnosed as specifically language-impaired (SLI). All scored above 85 on the Arthur Adaptation of the Leiter International Performance Scale and more than 1 standard deviation below their age on the composite (Picture Vocabulary, Oral Vocabulary, Grammatical Understanding, Sentence Imitation, Grammatical Completion) of the Test of Language Development-Primary. All children passed a hearing screening and a test of oral-motor function They showed no evidence of frank neurological impairment and displayed no signs of emotional disorder. Samples were obtained as the child played with an adult female research assistant. Common toys and picture books were the chief source of conversation. Only the utterances of the child appear in the transcripts. Transcripts were coded for Brown's 14 morphological categories. Word order was not preserved.

Ages are in years; months. IQ scores are from Leiter International Performance Scale, Arthur Adaptations. TOLD-P and TELD scores are composite z-scores:

Table 78: Leonard Test Scores

Child	Age	Sex	IQ	Test	Score
SLI-A	5;0	M	110	TOLD-P	2.20
SLI-B	4;3	F	120	TOLD-P	1.40
SLI-C	5;0	M	92	TOLD-P	1.86
SLI-D	4;4	M	100	TOLD-P	1.87
SLI-E	4;6	F	105	TOLD-P	1.87
SLI-F	4;6	M	98	TOLD-P	1.86
SLI-G	5;3	F	86	TOLD-P	1.60
SLI-H	3;8	M	134	TELD	1.00
SLI-I	5;7	M	99	TOLD-P	2.53
SLI-J	4;11	F	127	TOLD-P	1.40
SLI-K	3;9	M	125	TELD	1.47

Levy

Yonata Levy
Department of Psychology
Hebrew University
Mount Scopus
Jerusalem, Israel
msyonata@mscc.huji.ac.il

These data focus on children with neurological disorders. They were contributed by Yonata Levy of Hebrew University in Jerusalem. A comparable set of data from 10 control normal children contributed by Dr. Levy can be found in the Levy directory with the other normal Hebrew language samples.

These data were collected in naturalistic settings, mostly in the children's homes by the experimenter with sometimes one other member of the family present. The data were transcribed and coded by the experimenter who had collected the data. Here is the list of pseudonyms and syndromes:

Aviad — congenital LH infarct
Amit, Mike — Sotos syndrome
Avixai, Bat-El — fragile X
Cofit, Elior, Moriya, Netanel — hydrocephalus
Tamar — anatomical malformation
Teomin — twin brothers. Uri is normal and Shilo had an enlarged ventricle

For further information regarding these children, please contact Dr. Levy.

Malakoff / Mayes

Marguerite E. Malakoff
Department of Humanities and Social Sciences
Harvey Mudd College
301 E 12th St.
Claremont, CA 91711-5990
Office: (909) 607-3812
margo_malakoff@hmc.edu

Linda C. Mayes
Child Study Center
Yale University
230 S. Frontage Rd.
New Haven, CT

Participants

A sample of 74 infants (46 drug-exposed and 28 not drug-exposed) were randomly selected from a large longitudinal study of the effects of prenatal exposure to cocaine and other drugs on infant and child development. The mean age of the drug-exposed group was 24 months, 5 days (range from 22.9 to 26.1 months); the mean age of the not drug-exposed group was 24 months, 4 days (range from 22.9 to 26.8 months). There were 19 boys and 27 girls in the drug-exposed group and 10 boys and 18 girls in the not drug-exposed group. All children were accompanied by mothers.

Maternal cocaine exposure status was determined either by self-report of use during pregnancy or by a positive urine screen at a prenatal visit or at delivery. Nonexposed status was ascertained by maternal and infant urine toxicology and a negative maternal history of cocaine use during pregnancy and at the time of delivery. All infants in this sample remained in their mothers' care after delivery.

The sample was predominantly African American (85% drug-exposed and 82% not drug-exposed). Most women were in their twenties. However drug-using mothers were significantly older (mean age = 28.5) than non-drug-exposed mothers (mean age = 24.9, $F(1,71) = 12.74$, $p < .001$. The majority of the women in both groups were single mothers. There were no differences in the proportion of mothers in each group receiving prenatal care, and the majority of women in both groups had at least one prenatal visit.

Additional background information on children and mothers is available from Malakoff, Mayes, Schottenfeld, & Howell, (1999).

Procedures

Natural language data was transcribed from videotaped semistructured play at the 24-month follow-up visit. The sessions ranged from 4 to 8 minutes in length. The majority of the sessions (74%) were between 4.5 and 6.5 minutes long; only 8% were less than 4.5 minutes. The mean length of the play session was similar for both groups, with a mean of 5.6 minutes (*SD* = .94).

All play sessions took place in the same room and with the same set of toys. The caregiver and child were accompanied to a small room with a one-way mirror permitting observation and videotaping. A set of toys, which included a teddy-bear-like doll, a teaset, blocks, a blanket, a train, a doll, a set of stacking barrels, two picture-only books, a small ball, and a toy phone, were laid out visibly on the floor at one end of the room. Other furnishings in the room included a small chair and table and a quilted mat for the child to play on. Sessions were minimally 4 minutes in length and were at the end of the visit period. After a brief background survey administered by an investigator, the caregiver was asked to play normally with the child, and the two were left alone in the room until an investigator terminated the session.

Table 79: Malakoff/Mayes Children

Dyad	Sex	Session Length (minutes)	Premie (<36 mos)?	Cocaine in utero?	Other in utero A = alcohol C = cigarettes M = marijuana
1	female	6.00	No	No	C
2	female	4.97	No	No	C
3	male	5.50	No	No	A, C, M
4	male	5.23	No	No	
5	male	5.40	No	No	A
6	male	6.77	No	No	C
7	female	4.27	No	No	
8	male	4.10	No	No	
9	female	6.87	No	No	
10	male	4.47	No	No	
11	female	7.36	No	No	
12	female	4.70	No	No	
13	female	6.16	No	No	A, C

Table 79: Malakoff/Mayes Children

Dyad	Sex	Session Length (minutes)	Premie (<36 mos)?	Cocaine in utero?	Other in utero A = alcohol C = cigarettes M = marijuana
14	female	7.10	Yes	No	
15	female	5.30	No	No	C
16	female	7.20	No	No	
17	female	5.33	Yes	No	
18	male	4.80	No	No	
19	female	4.77	No	No	
20	male	4.00	No	No	
21	male	6.00	No	No	C, M
22	female	4.82	No	No	A, C
23	female	5.53	No	No	
24	female	6.00	No	No	
25	female	7.95	No	No	
26	female	6.47	No	No	A, M
27	female	5.70	No	No	
28	male	5.83	No	No	
29	male	5.63	No	Yes	
30	male	4.87	Yes	Yes	A, C
31	male	5.73	No	Yes	C
32	male	5.57	No	Yes	A, M
33	male	4.80	Yes	Yes	C
34	female	7.90	No	Yes	
35	female	5.00	Yes	Yes	A, C
36	male	8.07	No	Yes	A, C
37	female	6.00	No	Yes	A, C
38	female	5.23	No	Yes	C

Table 79: Malakoff/Mayes Children

Dyad	Sex	Session Length (minutes)	Premie (<36 mos)?	Cocaine in utero?	Other in utero A = alcohol C = cigarettes M = marijuana
39	female	5.23	No	Yes	A, C, M
40	female	4.91	Yes	Yes	C
41	male	4.83	No	Yes	C , M
42	female	5.26	No	Yes	A, C
43	female	4.88	No	Yes	A, C
44	male	7.40	No	Yes	C , M
45	female	5.90	No	Yes	A
46	female	4.90	No	Yes	A, C , M
47	male	4.40	No	Yes	C
48	female	5.00	No	Yes	A
49	male	4.33	Yes	Yes	C
50	female	5.60	No	Yes	A, C
51	male	6.83	No	Yes	A, C
52	female	7.60	Yes	Yes	C , M
53	female	4.77	No	Yes	A, M
54	female	5.37	No	Yes	A, C
55	female	4.93	No	Yes	A, C
56	female	5.27	No	Yes	A, C
57	female	4.60	No	Yes	A, C
58	male	5.00	No	Yes	C
59	male	5.27	Yes	Yes	A, C
60	female	5.97	No	Yes	C
61	female	6.28	No	Yes	C
62	male	5.07	No	Yes	A, C, M
63	female	5.63	No	Yes	A, C

Table 79: Malakoff/Mayes Children

Dyad	Sex	Session Length (minutes)	Premie (<36 mos)?	Cocaine in utero?	Other in utero A = alcohol C = cigarettes M = marijuana
64	male	6.30	No	Yes	C
65	male	5.90	No	Yes	A, C
66	female	5.07	Yes	Yes	A, C
67	male	5.50	No	Yes	C
68	male	5.27	No	Yes	A, C, M
69	female	4.53	No	Yes	C
70	female	7.00	Yes	Yes	A, C
71	female	5.40	Yes	Yes	A, C
72	female	5.40	Yes	Yes	C, M
73	female	5.23	No	Yes	A, C
74	female	5.27	No	Yes	C

Publication making use of these data should cite:

Malakoff, M. E., Mayes, L. C., Schottenfeld, R.S., & Howell, S. (1999). Language production of 24-month-old inner city children of cocaine-and-other-drug-using mothers. *Journal of Applied Developmental Psychology, 20.*

Oviedo

Eliseo Diez-Itza
Universidad de Oviedo
Dept. de Filosofía y Psicología
C/ Aniceto Sela
33005 Oviedo Spain
ditza@correo.uniovi.es

This directory contains two case studies. The first is a set of six transcripts from a short-term longitudinal study of a SLI child, conducted by Manuela Miranda, Verónica Martínez and Eliseo Diez-Itza at the University of Oviedo. The child's pseudonym is Edgar and his age was 7;10 at the beginning of the study. Dyadic verbal interaction between Edgar and Manuela Miranda was videotaped within monthly intervals during the speech therapy time in the school. The time duration of the sessions was approximately of 30 minutes. The activities included play and storytelling. The focus of the study was the phonological impairment.

This directory also contains two transcripts from a Williams Syndrome child. They are part of an ongoing research project on the linguistic and educational aspects of a Williams Syndrome (WS) population in Asturias (Spain) conducted by Eliseo Diez-Itza, Aránzazu Antón, Joaquín Fernández Toral and María Luisa García, at the University of Oviedo. Spontaneus verbal interaction between the child and the investigators was videotaped and transcribed in CHAT format. The child was recorded in two sessions at home with an interval of 8 months (at ages 9.3 and 10.0). The time duration of the two samples is approximately 90 and 60 minutes, respectively.

Phonological errors were coded in terms of the following categories of phonological processes:

ES (relativos a la estructura de la sílaba)
RD (reduplicación)
CF (supresión de consonantes finales)
SA (supresión de sílabas átonas)
AN (analogía)
DS (disimilación)
MT (metátesis): FO (fonémica), SI (silábica), CG (con grupo), SG (sin grupo)
RG (reducción de grupos)
CT (consonánticos): HM (homosilábicos), HT (heterosilábicos), EP (epéntesis), CL (coalescencia), GE (supresión del grupo entero),SP (supresión de un elemento), SU (sustitución de un elemento)
VO (vocálicos),DC (diptongos crecientes) /ie/, DD (diptongos decrecientes) /au/, DP (diptongos neutros) /ea/, HI (hiatos),TR (triptongos), SP (supresión de un elemento), SU (sustitución de un elemento), CL (coalescencia)
SM (asimilación): CN (contigua), NC (no contigua),PR (progresiva), RS (regresiva), DB (doble), CC (entre consonantes), VV (entre vocales), CV (de consonante a vocal), VC

(de vocal a consonante)

OM (omisión): LQ (líquidas), NS (nasales), ON (oclusivas sonoras), OR (oclusivas sordas), FC (fricativas), VL (vocales)

ST (sustitución): LQ (líquidas), SC (semiconsonantización),PV (posteriorización de vibrantes), OC (oclusivización), LV (lateralización de vibrantes), AM (ausencia de vibrante múltiple), AV (ausencia de vibrante simple), AL (ausencia de lateralización), LR (sustitución de l por vibrante), SV (simplificación de vibrante)

NS (nasales): DN (desnasalización),FT (frontalización), PT (posteriorización)

ON (oclusivas sonoras): SR (ensordecimiento),FT (frontalización), PT (posteriorización), FR (fricatización), DL (sustitución de d por líquida), NL (nasalización), LT (lateralización)

OR (oclusivas sordas): SN (sonorización), FT (frontalización), PT (posteriorización), DF (desafricación), FR (fricatización)

FC (fricativas): FT (frontalización),PT (posteriorización), OC (oclusivización), SN (sonorización), CE (ceceo), SE (seseo), PS (palatalización de s), AS (aspiración de s ante oclusiva)

NT (neutralización)

00 (procesos no analizables)

NI (no inteligible)

NG (no categorizable)

MP (proceso múltiple)

AD (adición)

Publications using these data should cite:

Diez-Itza, E., Anton, A., Fernandez Toral, J., & Garcia, M. L. (1998). Language development in Spanish children with Williams syndrome. In A. Koc, E. Taylan, A.S. Ozsoy, & A. Kuntay (Eds.), *Perspectives in language acquisition* (pp. 309–324). Istanbul: Bogazici University Press.

Miranda, M., Martínez, V., & Diez-Itza, E. (1998). Procesos fonológicos en la disfasia infantil. Paper presented at the Second Meeting on Language Acquisition, Barcelona.

Rollins

Pamela Rosenthal Rollins
University of Texas at Dallas
Callier Center for Communication Disorders
1966 Inwood Road
Dallas, TX 75214
214-905-3153
rollins@utdallas.edu

This corpus consists of transcripts of video recordings of 5 boys with autism who attended a preschool program for children on the autistic spectrum at the University of Texas at Dallas. To be included in this corpus, a child had to meet the following criteria: (a) have an initial diagnosis of autism by a psychologist or a neurologist; (b) have been preverbal at the time of intake; (c) have attended the preschool program for at least 1 year; and (d) have some conventional expressive vocabulary skills upon completion of the program. The preschool program routinely videotapes each participating child for the entire morning session several times during the school year. For each child, four videotapes were selected for later transcription and analysis (the first, last, and two intermediate tapes). The transcripts for each child are numbered 1 to 4 or 5 corresponding to the tape number. The header file indicates the date of the video recording as well as the child's age.

To capture each child's optimal level of on-task communicative functioning, only intervals where the child was interacting one-on-one with his clinician were transcribed and coded for analyses. Therefore, activities such as small group, music, and snack time were, by definition, excluded from the analyses. This criterion was used because the language skills of children on the autistic spectrum are influenced by both the setting and the participants. Furthermore, efforts to capture the child's optimal level of on-task communicative behaviors were made by excluding from the total number of usable minutes the following intervals: (a) when the clinician or child was out of the room, (b) when another child or teacher talked with the target child and clinician, (c) when the clinician attempted to engage the target child in an activity but where the target child refused to cooperate for longer than 30 seconds, (d) when the target child actively avoided an activity or interactions with the clinician for longer than 30 seconds, and (e) when the clinician and target child negotiated the next activity for longer than 60 seconds. This substantially reduced the total number of usable minutes available for transcription. Videotapes were viewed and cataloged. The catalog included a time record for each activity so that the total number of usable minutes for coding could be calculated. Activity header lines were used to mark each new activity on the transcript. Twenty minutes was the maximum number of usable minutes that was available for all children in the study at each time point. To ensure that the sample of 20 minutes was representative for each child the videotaped interactions were reviewed by persons familiar with each child.

Because the corpus was originally collected to describe pragmatic skills in children with autism from the prelinguistic to early one-word stage, a good deal of nonverbal information is transcribed. The transcripts include %spa codes using the Ninio, Snow, Pan, &

Rollins (1994) INCA system described in the CHAT manual. In order to be coded as communicative, each communicative act had to supported by behavioral evidence that the child had a plan/intention to achieve a goal with awareness that another person can be a means to that end. This behavioral evidence has been outlined by Prizant and Wetherby (1988) and includes the following: (a) alternating eye gaze between a goal and the listener, (b) persistent signaling until the goal has been met, (c) changing the quality of the signal until the goal has been met, (d) ritualizing or conventionalizing the form of signal within specific communicative contexts, (e) awaiting a response from the listener, (f) terminating the signal when the goal is met, (g) displaying satisfaction when the goal is attained or dissatisfaction when it is not. Communicative means is indicated on the third level of the speech act tier.

The gesture codes are adapted from McLean, McLean, Brady, and Etter(1991). The full set of codes is as follows:

Conventional gesture:

CT	conventional touch (i.e., contact point)
CP	conventional point proximal
CA	conventional point distal
CR	conventional reach proximal (toward object or person)
CB	conventional reach distal (toward object or person)
CO	conventional other (i.e., head nods)

Nonconventional gesture:

NT	nonconventional touch (i.e., CHI manipulates clinician's hand)
NP	nonconventional point proximal
NA	nonconventional point distal
NR	nonconventional reach proximal
NB	nonconventional reach distal
NO	nonconventional other (i.e. throws object, giving, showing)
NI	nonverbal imitation (clinician taps 2x on table, CHI imitates)

VC	vocalization
V+code from above	vocalization plus gesture
WD	words
W+code from above	words plus gestures
WDE	echolalia

Word-like vocalizations were transcribed on the main line and appended with @ap when there was sufficient contextual information to identify the target lexical item (e.g., saying "ba" when holding a ball was transcribed as ball@ap). Individual participant characteristics are presented in the table that follows. All of the children were relatively young at the start of the study (mean age of 2;7) and were severely delayed in language as measured by the SICD (mean receptive language age 1;2, and mean expressive language age 0;10). The delays in language skills were corroborated by the Vineland Adaptive Behavior Scales (Sparrow, Balla, & Cicchetti, 1984), as was the social impairment, as indicated in the following table. The mean of each Vineland subtest in this table is 100 and the standard

Table 80: Rollins Children

		SICD		Vineland			
Child	Age	Recept	Expr.	Commun	Daily Living	Social	Motor
Marshall	3;1	1;0-1;4	N/A	68	65	76	79
Roger	2;6	1;0	1;4	63	65	72	73
Sid	2;2	1;2	1;5	66	71	77	93
Josh	2;5	1;4	0;8	64	67	62	86
Carl	2;8	1;4	1;0-1;4	N/A	72	72	89

deviation is 15.

This research was supported by an American Speech and Hearing Foundation, First Investigators award.

Publications using these data should cite:

Rollins P. R. (1999). Pragmatic accomplishments and vocabulary development in preschool children with autism. *American Journal of Speech-Language Pathology: A Journal of Clinical Practice, 8,* 85–94.

Additional references are:

Bernard-Opitz, V. (1982). Pragmatic analysis of the communicative behavior of an autistic child. *Journal of Speech and Hearing Disorders, 47,* 99–109.
McHale, S. M., Simeonson, R. J., Marcus, L. M., & Olley, J. G. (1990). The social and symbolic quality of autistic children's communication. *Journal of Autism and Developmental Disorders, 10,* 229–310.
McLean, J., McLean, L., Brady, N., & Etter, R. (1991) Communication profiles of two types of gesture using nonverbal persons with severe to profound mental retardation. *Journal of Speech and Hearing Research, 34,* 294–308.
Ninio, A., Snow, C., Pan, B., & Rollins, P. (1994). Classifying communicative acts in children's interactions. *Journal of Communication Disorders, 27,* 157–188.
Prizant, B. M. & Wetherby, A. M. (1988). Providing services to children with autism (ages 0 to 2 years) and their families. *Topics in Language Disorders, 9,* 1–23.
Sigman, M., & Ungerer, J. A. (1984). Attachment behaviors in autistic children. *Journal of Autism and Developmental Disorders, 14,* 231–244.
Sparrow, S. S., Balla, D. A., & Cicchetti, D. V. (1984). *Vineland Adaptive Behavior Scales.* Circle Pines, MN: American Guidance Service.

Rondal

Jean Rondal
Laboratoire de Psychologie
Boulevarde du Rectorat, 5
Sart-Tilman
B-4000 Liège Belgium
jarondal@vm1.ulg.ac.be

This corpus contains files from 21 English-speaking Down syndrome children, along with a set of files from 21 children in the normal control group. The data from the control group are in the directory of English normal files and the data from the Down syndrome children are in the directory with the clinical subjects. The data were collected from children in Minnesota by Jean Rondal. A fairly full report on the project is given in Rondal (1978). The samples are matched for mean length of utterance. The original study was designed to examine differences in maternal speech directed to normal and Down syndrome children.

Participants

The participants of this study were 21 Down syndrome children and their natural mothers and 21 normal children and their natural mothers. As a condition for participating in the study it was required that none of the mothers in the two groups had been or were currently engaged in any early education curriculum for parents with special emphasis on promoting early language abilities in children. All of the normal children and their mothers and 14 of the identified Down syndrome children lived in the Minneapolis-St. Paul area. The seven remaining Down syndrome children and their mothers lived in other towns in Minnesota. Karyotypes were obtained for all the Down syndrome children and all were reported to be Trisomy 21s. There were 12 girls and 9 boys among the Down syndrome children, and 8 girls and 13 boys among the normal children. No effort was made to balance the two groups of children for gender, as it was thought not to be an important variable.

In order to participate in the study, the children could not have any debilitating heart condition, obvious sensory impairment, or more generally any medical condition (other than Down syndrome for the Down syndrome children) that might seriously limit their development, and their speech had to be reasonably intelligible. The normal and Down syndrome children were matched on linguistic development as measured by MLU. The children's MLU was computed using the criterion given in Brown (1973). The only exception to Brown's criterion was that MLU was based on the total sample (i.e., one–hour speech recording) rather than the first 100 utterances. On the basis of the children's MLU, the mother–child pairs were divided into three language-level categories for each population of normal and Down syndrome children. Specified MLU ranges for the three language levels were 1.00 to 1.50, 1.75 to 2.25, and 2.50 to 3.00. The following table lists child and mother MLU along with the child's age in months at the three language levels.

Table 81: Rondal Children

Level	No.	Group	Child	Sex	Age	Mother MLU	Child MLU
1	1	Down	Stella	f	47	3.69	1.41
1	2	Down	Jon	m	49	4.46	1.52
1	3	Down	Mel	m	36	3.36	1.04
1	4	Down	Baxter	m	38	3.90	1.04
1	5	Down	Selma	f	37	4.99	1.11
1	6	Down	Kevin	m	52	3.98	1.12
1	7	Down	Abby	f	54	3.30	1.55
		mean				3.95	1.25
1	1	Normal	Tansy	f	23	4.39	1.15
1	2	Normal	Shelly	f	20	5.07	1.54
1	3	Normal	Lana	f	22	4.38	1.43
1	4	Normal	Josh	m	22	4.16	1.05
1	5	Normal	Carla	f	26	3.55	1.52
1	6	Normal	Ken	m	22	3.56	1.06
1	7	Normal	Billy	m	25	4.53	1.10
		mean				4.23	1.26
2	8	Down	Bob	m	56	3.94	1.72
2	9	Down	Cheryl	f	57	3.52	1.79
2	10	Down	Sylvia	f	94	3.48	2.03
2	11	Down	Dan	m	56	4.90	1.96
2	12	Down	Janet	f	55	4.48	1.75
2	13	Down	Carrie	f	84	4.10	2.09
2	14	Down	Paul	m	62	6.27	2.22
		mean				4.38	1.94
2	8	Normal	Carl	m	24	4.89	1.76
2	9	Normal	Elbert	m	27	4.32	1.74

Table 81: Rondal Children

Level	No.	Group	Child	Sex	Age	Mother MLU	Child MLU
2	10	Normal	Dirk	m	28	4.40	1.94
2	11	Normal	Caleb	m	27	4.60	1.75
2	12	Normal	Vance	m	28	4.24	2.14
2	13	Normal	Marvin	m	25	5.21	2.24
2	14	Normal	Murray	m	27	4.81	2.07
		mean				4.64	1.95
3	15	Down	Mat	m	146	6.32	2.93
3	16	Down	Ava	f	121	5.39	3.06
3	17	Down	Kimmy	f	134	4.99	2.92
3	18	Down	Rhoda	f	100	4.88	2.70
3	19	Down	Missy	f	135	5.08	2.85
3	20	Down	Cassy	f	128	5.33	3.04
3	21	Down	Donald	m	74	5.53	2.59
		mean				5.36	2.87
3	15	Normal	Line	f	32	6.44	2.78
3	16	Normal	Jane	f	31	4.39	2.48
3	17	Normal	Andy	m	30	3.45	2.98
3	18	Normal	Martin	m	29	5.20	3.01
3	19	Normal	Jed	m	29	4.60	3.03
3	20	Normal	Kelly	f	29	5.65	2.87
3	21	Normal	Joel	m	28	4.14	2.97
		mean				4.84	2.88

There are two CHAT files from each child with the exception of Martin and Stella. The files for these two children were lost in 1976 and cannot be recovered. All of the names given are pseudonyms. Participants are identified by first names and with a three-digit code. In this code the first number is for the group level with "1" indicating Down syndrome and "2" indicating normal; the second number is for the language level, and the third number is for the participant number within the particular cell.

Matching

The mothers of normal children and the mothers of Down syndrome children were matched on the following criteria: ethnic group (white), familial monolingualism (English), familial structure (both husband and wife living at home), mother free of any major sensory handicap, maternal intelligence not obviously outside of the normal range (no intelligence test given), and socioeconomic status (the families selected for the study were predominantly drawn from the middle class). Perhaps more important than socioeconomic status (usually based on occupational and educational level of the head of the household) for research of this type, is the mother's educational level. The mothers selected for this study were matched on the Educational Scale supplied by Hollingshead in his two factor Index of Social Position. The overall means of the mothers of Down syndrome children on the Hollingshead's Educational Scale was 2.67 (SD = 1.02) versus 2.71 (SD = 0.90) for the mothers of normal children. This difference was found to be not significant.

No effort was made to match mothers of normal and retarded children for age, nor to match normal and retarded children for birth order, number of siblings, and age differences between the children in the family as it is known that in the cases of Trisomy 21, the mean age of the mother at the birth of the child is significantly older than in control populations. This, in turn affects birth order and family composition for Down syndrome children as they are more likely to be later-born children than are normal children. The average age of the mothers of Down syndrome children in this study was 514.86 months (SD 100.84 months) versus 338.29 months (SD 49.42 months for the mothers of normal children. The average birth order was 3.76 (SD 2.30) for the Down syndrome children and 1.76 (SD 0.89) for the normal children. From language level 1 to language level 3 respectively, approximately 12% to 40% of the siblings of the Down syndrome children were no longer living in the family home at the time of the study.

Data Collection

The verbal interaction between mother and child was tape recorded at home in a free-play situation. The investigator was present in the home during the tape recording and made every effort to keep his presence as discreet as possible. The mothers were told that the study was primarily about child language development in a plausible attempt to keep them as unconcerned as possible about their own speech. Moreover, the mothers were asked not to engage the investigator in conversation during actual recording.

It is possible that mother–child interactions in the presence of an observer are somewhat different from what they are "behind closed doors." Even if mothers modified their behavior toward the children in the observer's presence, it is improbable that they would be able to invent, at once, new and different mother–child interaction patterns (Moerk, 1972). Besides, there is no reason to expect the observer's presence to affect differentially the verbal behavior of mothers of normal and Down syndrome children.

In order to preserve as much spontaneity and naturalness in the mother–child interactions as possible, no specific instruction other than "do what you usually do when you play and talk with the child and use whatever kind of toys or material you want to use, only avoid recitations" was given to the mothers as to what they should do with the children during the free-play situation. It turned out the free-play situations and the material used by the mothers were surprisingly similar from home to home, particularly for those normal and Down syndrome children at language levels 1 and 2. The sessions alternated the use of Play-doh games; shape-matching or shape-folding games; play-action games such as the farm game, the airport, the village, the school, Sesame Street, McDonald's, or PlaySkool; and looking at picture and storybooks. The contents of the free-play situations were somewhat more heterogeneous for the two groups of children at the third language level, with several mothers of normal and Down syndrome children spending part or all of the two recording sessions in conversation with the child using toys and pictures as a support for conversation. There were two recording sessions each lasting half an hour for each mother and child pair. The two recording sessions took place on two different days at approximately a 1-week interval. They were preceded, on another day, by a 20-minute "get acquainted session" during which the investigator familiarized himself with the mother and the child, obtained first-hand information on the child's language level, and gave the child an opportunity to extinguish most of his or her orientation reactions to the tape recorder by having it displayed and functioning in the room, which additionally supplied information on the effects of the acoustics of the room on the tape recording.

Publications using these data should cite:

Rondal, J. (1978). Maternal speech to normal and Down's Syndrome children matched for mean length of utterance. In C. E. Meyers (Ed.), *Quality of life in severely and profoundly mentally retarded people: Research foundations for improvement.* Washington, DC: American Association on Mental Deficiency.

Additional relevant publications are:

Brown, R. (1973). *A first language: The early stages.* Cambridge, MA: Harvard University Press.
Moerk, E. (1972). Factors of style and personality. *Journal of Psycholinguistic Research, 1,* 257–268.

Ulm

Andrea Haege
Department of Phoniatrics and Pedaudiology
University of Ulm
Schillerstrasse 15, 89070 Ulm, Germany
phone: 0049-731-502-1701 fax: 0049-731-502-1702
andrea.haege@medizin.uni-ulm.de

These transcript data were contributed by Helge S. Johannsen, Hartmut Schulze, Dieter Rommel, and Andrea Haege from the phoniatric outpatients department of the University of Ulm in Germany. The data are a set of protocols taken from preschool and primary school children in the context of an experimental playing situation in which the children play half an hour with their mothers in the phoniatric clinic laboratory. The playing material is a farm building kit, a zoo kit, or a knight's castle. The transcribed language is not standard German but a Swabian dialect spoken in the region around Ulm. All assessed children came to the phoniatric clinic because of more or less severe stuttering and took part in a longitudinal study of the relations between different variables and the development of stuttering in childhood using CLAN. Transcripts of playing situations were taken in 6-months-intervals provided that the children's stuttering persisted. For example david1.cha is the transcript from the first contact, david2.cha is taken 6 months later, and so on. If the children recovered from their stuttering, they were withdrawn from further follow-ups. There are140 transcripts in the corpus, in which 94 protocols come from the first contact with the stuttering children and 46 from the fourth contact 18 months later. In order to protect privacy, all names were replaced with pseudonyms. Please inform the authors when using these data. In case of interest more details about the data and their context can be requested.

Publications using these data should cite one of these articles:

Haege, A. (1995). Cognitive abilities and interactional variables in young stutterers – first cross-sectional results of a five year longitudinal study. In C. W. Starkweather & H. F. M. Peters. *Stuttering: Proceedings of the first world congress on fluency disorders, Munich, Vol.1*. The International Fluency Association, Nijmegen, The Netherlands1995.

Haege, A., Rommel, D., Johannsen, H. S., & Schulze, H. (1997). Cognitive and linguistic abilities of stuttering children. In W. Hulstijn, H. F. M. Peters, & P. H. H. M. Van Lieshout (Eds.) *Speech production: Motor control, brain research and fluency disorders*. Elsevier, Amsterdam.

Haege, A., Rommel, D., Schulze, H., & Johannsen, H. S. (1994). Kindliches Stottern: Ätiologie und laufsbedingungen. Erste Ergebnisse einer fünfjährigen Längsschittstudie. *Folia Phoniatrica, 46,* 298–304.

Johannsen, H. S., Schulze, H., Rommel, D., & Haege, A. (1994). Stuttering in childhood: A five-year longitudinal study in progress. *Folia Phoniatrica, 46,* 241–249.

Rommel, D., Haege, A., Johannsen, H. S., & Schulze, H. (1997) Linguistic aspects of stuttering in childhood. In W. Hulstijn, H. F. M. Peters, & P. H. H. M. Van Lieshout (Eds.). *Speech production: Motor control, brain research and fluency disorders*. Elsevier, Amsterdam 1997.

5: Narrative Corpora

Table 82: Narrative Corpora

Corpus	Age Range	N	Comments
Frog Stories on page 244	3–adult	600	Narratives from 8 languages elicited using a picture book describing the adventures of a boy, a dog, and a frog
Gopnik on page 252	2–5 years	61	Cross-sectional study based on story book descriptions from a population of normal children
Hicks on page 254	1st grade 2nd grade 5th grade	20 18 5	Cross-sectional study of primary school childrens' narrative genre skills. Data focus on their ability to produce a range of narratives
MacWhinney / Bates 1 on page 258	3 years 4 years 5 years adult	30 30 30 30	Cross-sectional study using a picture description task in English, Italian, and Hungarian
MacWhinney / Bates 2 on page 259	3 years 6 years 10 years adult	76 53 44 103	Cross-sectional study using a film description task and a cartoon-description task with Hungarian and American children and adults

Frog Stories

Researchers in many countries have used Mercer Mayer's wordless "frog story" picture book entitled "Frog, where are you?" as a tool for eliciting narrative descriptions. The book tells a story without words in 24 pictures. The principle source for documentation of this work, its rationale, and the various data analysis procedures is the book by Berman and Slobin (1994). Because that book provides such complete documentation for this project, the current documentation will only cover the general issues in the research. Researchers can also consult that book for a complete listing of research in additional languages and with second-language learners using the Frog Story framework. CHILDES currently has data for seven languages. The following table summarizes the data available.

Table 83: Frog Story Corpora

Contributor	Languages	Ages	N
Aarssen, Jeroen & Bos, Petra	Dutch, Arabic, Turkish, and bilingual	4-10	175
Aksu-Koç, Ayhan	Turkish	3, 5, 9, 20	40
Bamberg, Michael	German	3, 5, 9, 20	43
Berman, Ruth	Hebrew	3, 4, 5, 7, 9, 11, 20	91
Cipriani, Paola	Italian	6, 8, 9	59
Hemphill, Lowry	English	6, 7, 8	30
Lopez-Ornat, Susana	Spanish	unknown	50
Marchman, Virginia	English	3, 4, 5, 9, 20	59
Orsolini, Margherita	Italian	-	-
Pearson, Barbara	Spanish, English	various	various
Sebastián, Eugenia	Spanish	3, 4, 5, 9, 20	59
Slobin, Dan I.	Russian	various	41
Strömqvist, Sven	Swedish	15	30

The addresses of the contributors of Frog Story data are:

Jeroen Aarssen
Tilburg University – BABYLON,
Center for Studies on Multilingualism in the Multicultural Society
P.O. Box 90153
5000 LE Tilburg
The Netherlands
J.Aarssen@kub.nl

Aksu-Koç, Ayhan
Department of Psychology
Bogaziçi University
80815 Bebek
Istanbul, Turkey
koc@boun.edu.tr

Bamberg, Michael
Department of Psychology
Clark University
Worcester, MA 01610
mbamberg@vax.clarku.edu

Berman, Ruth
Department of Linguistics
Tel-Aviv University
Ramat Aviv, Tel-Aviv 69978, Israel
rberman@ccsg.tau.ac.il

Petra Bos
Tilburg University – BABYLON,
Center for Studies on Multilingualism in the Multicultural Society
P.O. Box 90153
5000 LE Tilburg
The Netherlands
P.H.F.Bos@kub.nl

Cipriani, Paola
IRCCS "Stella Maris"
INPE-Universitá di Pisa
Viale del Tirreno, 331
Calambrone (Pisa), Italy

Hemphill, Lowry
Harvard Graduate School of Education
703 Larsen Hall

Cambridge, MA 02125 USA
hemphilo@hugse1.harvard.edu

Lopez-Ornat, Susana
Departamento de Procesos Cognitivos
Facultad de Psicología
Universidad Complutense de Madrid
Madrid 28223 Spain
pscog09@sis.ucm.es

Marchman, Virginia
School of Human Development
P.O. Box 830688
University of Texas at Dallas
Richardson, TX 75075-0688
vamarch@utdallas.edu

Orsolini, Margherita
Istituto di Pedagogia e Psicologia
Via Madonna degli Angeli 30
Chieti 66100 Italy

Pearson, Barbara Zuker
Department of English
University of Miami
Box 248145
Coral Gables, FL 33124
bpearson@miami.edu

Sebastian, Eugenia
Departamento de Psicologia Evolutiva
Univ. Autonoma de Madrid
Cantoblanco
Madrid, 34 Spain
eugenia.sebastian@uam.es

Slobin, Dan
Department of Psychology
University of California
Berkeley, CA 94720 USA
slobin@cogsci.berkeley.edu

Strömqvist, Sven
Department of Linguistics
University of Göteborg
Renstromsparken

Göteborg S-41298 Sweden
svens@hum.gu.se

The same procedures were followed across different age groups. Each participant was interviewed individually and was given the same instructions (with slight variations for adults, preschool children, and older children). A deliberate effort was made to minimize the burden on memory, and to make children aware in advance that they were being asked to tell a story. To this end, children were first asked to look through the entire booklet, and then to tell the story again, while looking at the pictures. They were explicitly oriented to the booklet as presenting a "story" in the initial instructions: "Here is a book. This book tells a story about a boy [point to picture on cover], a dog [point], and a frog [point]. First, I want you to look at all the pictures. Pay attention to each picture that you see and afterwards you will tell the story."

Because the goal was to leave the burden of narration on the child, without scaffolding by the adult, the various adult interviewers were instructed to minimize their verbal feedback to neutral comments that would not influence the form of expression chosen by the child. It was especially important that the interviewer avoid prompts that would lead to a particular choice of verb tense, aspectual marking, or perspective on the part of the child. The following prompt types were used, presented below in English, in order of preference (neutrality): (1) silence or nod of head, (2) "uh-huh," "okay," "yes," (3) "Anything else?" (4) "and...?"(5) "Go on."

For most of the languages, groups of 12 participants were recorded at several different age levels. The file names give the age level of the participant along with a letter. The files were originally transcribed in a format specified in the Berman and Slobin manual and then converted to CHAT in 1995. The conversion to CHAT was straightforward except for the English Berkeley data which will need some additional double-checking to eliminate inaccuracies. During the conversion, pictures were marked with @g headers. Researchers have used two different systems for marking picture or page numbers. One system uses 1a and 1b for left and right pages. The other system numbers pages without regard to left-right position. Here are the correspondences between the two systems:

1	1
2a	2
2b	3
3a	4
3b	5
4a	6
4b	7
5	8
6a	9
6b	10
7	11
8	12
9a	13

9b	14
10a	15
10b	16
11	17
12a	18
12b	19
13a	20
13b	21
14a	22
14b	23
15	24

The data from Berkeley, Israel, Germany, and Rome were collected in the context of a project directed by Dan I. Slobin and Ruth A. Berman with support from the United States-Israel Binational Science Foundation (Grant 2732/82), the Linguistics Program of the National Science Foundation (Grant BNS-8520008), the Sloan Foundation Program in Cognitive Science, the Institute of Human Development at UC Berkeley, the Committee on Research of the Academic Senate at UC Berkeley, and the Max-Planck Institute for Psycholinguistics. The Turkish data were gathered with support from the Bogazici University Research Fund (Project No. 86 B 0724). The Swedish project was supported by a Swedish Tercenary Foundation grant to Sven Strömqvist (Riksbankens Jubileumsfond, grant 91-231:01). The collection of the English corpus from Wolf and Hemphill was supported by a Program Project grant from NIH on the "Foundations of Language Assessment." The data from Miami were collected in conjunction with the Bilingualism Study Group Literacy Grant, supported by NIH Grant #1R01 HD 30762-01 to D. Kimbrough Oller and Rebecca Eilers.

For a full description of the data collection methods, codes, and analyses followed in most of these studies, please consult this basic work which should also be cited in publications using these data:

Berman, R. A., & Slobin, D. I. (1994). *Relating events in narrative: A crosslinguistic developmental study*. Hillsdale, NJ: Lawrence Erlbaum Associates.
Mayer, M. (1969). *Frog, where are you?* New York: Dial Press.

Additional details are available for a few of the corpora. These are given next.

Aarsen/Bos Corpus

In the description of the bilingual corpora for Aarssen / Bos on page 105, you can find a full description of this corpus.

Hemphill Corpus

This corpus, donated by Lowry Hemphill and Dennis Palmer Wolf, includes transcripts from 30 children whose discourse development was studied from ages 6 to 8. The work was funded by a larger project, "Foundations for Language Assessment in Spontaneous Speech," funded by the National Institutes of Health.

Participants were selected at age 1 from a larger sample of 100 children participating in the MacArthur Individual Differences Project. Information about participant recruitment and characteristics of the original sample can be found in Snow (1989) and Dale, Bates, Reznick, and Morisset (1989). The present sample of 30 children is 50% girls and 50% boys; all are white English-speakers. Fourteen of the children are from working class families; sixteen are from middle class families. All attained milestones for early language development (e.g., MLU) at appropriate ages. Children were videotaped in their home each year at ages 6, 7, and 8, participating in a range of narrative and other discourse tasks. This corpus includes data only for the wordless picture book narration task. Procedures for eliciting the narratives were to have the child look through Mercer Mayer's wordless "frog story" picture book entitled "A Boy, a Dog, A Frog" to develop a sense of the entire story depicted. This book is similar in format to the "Frog, Where are you?" book used in the other frog story research, but the actual events in the pictures are all different. Then the experimenter asked, "Can you tell me the story, looking through the book?" If the child seemed to have trouble producing narration at any point, the experimenter asked, "What happened next?"

Transcribers trained in CHAT conventions prepared the transcripts, using the videotaped frog story narrations. Utterance boundary decisions were based on intonation contours and pauses. Utterances are broken into grammatical clauses using [c] as a marker of clause boundaries. Each clause is coded for narrative function (e.g., event, reported speech, durative/descriptive), for verb forms, and for use of connectives.

Publications using these data should cite:

Miranda, E., Camp, L., Hemphill, L., & Wolf, D. (1992). *Developmental changes in children's use of tense in narrative.* Paper presented at the Boston University Conference on Language Development, Boston.

Additional relevant references include:

Dale, P., Bates, E., Reznick, S., & Morisset, C. (1989). The validity of a parent report instrument. *Journal of Child Language, 16,* 239–249.
Mayer, M. (1972). *A boy, a dog, a frog.* New York: Dial Press.
Snow, C. E. (1989). Imitativeness: Atrait or a skill? In G. Speidel & K. Nelson (Eds.), *The many faces of imitation.* New York: Reidel.

Pearson Corpus

This directory contains frog story narratives collected in Miami, Florida by Barbara Zuker Pearson with the help of Ana Maria Ferrer, Patricia Ortega, Mayrela Palau, Samantha Pearson, Esperanza Rodriguez, and Yael Wiesner. This is the second set of frog stories collected in conjunction with the Bilingualism Study Group Literacy Grant, supported by NIH Grant #IR01 HD 30762-01 to D. Kimbrough Oller and Rebecca Eilers, with Barbara Pearson and Vivian Umbel.

There are 447 files: 269 in English and 178 in Spanish. They complete the 20 cells of a nested factorial with the factors explained later in the description of the ID numbers. There are 16 cells of 10 Spanish-English bilinguals, with two stories each (for the most part), and 4 cells of monolinguals, 20 children in each with only one story per child. All of the children were born in the United States; they were enrolled in three different instructional programs in Dade County Public Schools in Miami: 1) English immersion for Hispanic students, 2) so-called "two-way" bilingual programs for Hispanic students with 50% Spanish and 50% English instruction, 3) regular monolingual English classrooms for non-Hispanic students, and 4) monolingual English children in schools with primarily Hispanic populations. (Groups 1, 3, and 4 have essentially the same instructional program, but the relation between the student's own language and the language of the peer population is different.) The stories are on audiotape and 15% of the tapes have been independently transcribed twice for reliability; another 60% have had "second listenings" (where the second transcriber worked from the first listener's transcription). There are six directories of files:

BLENG2:	Bilingual 2nd graders speaking English
BLENG5:	Bilingual 5th graders speaking English
BLSPAN2:	Bilingual 2nd graders speaking Spanish
BLSPAN5:	Bilingual 5th graders speaking Spanish
MLENG2:	Monolingual English children 2nd graders
MLENG5:	Monolingual English 5th graders.

Most, but not all, of the bilingual children have both an English and a Spanish story, which can be located by matching the ID number and file names in the English and Spanish directories. Those who wish to work with the matching files would be advised to modify the file names to indicate the language of the story, but should be aware that the @ID line matches the current file name and does not distinguish language. Whether the Spanish or English was told first (on different days) is indicated in the header.

ID Numbers: Files are arranged in English and Spanish directories by ID number, which gives information about group status: digit 1 is school type (above), digit 2 is SES (1=mid, 2=low), digit 3 is language of the home (1 = mostly Spanish, 2 = English and Spanish equally, 3 = only English), and digit 4 is grade (2 = 2nd, 3 = 5th), followed by a 4-digit unique identifier. (For example, 21131489.cha are the stories from participant #1489: she is a bilingual in a two-way school, mid-SES, with mostly Spanish in the home, in fifth grade at the time of the story.) Within the header, gender is indicated as M or F; the approximate age is in parentheses alongside the grade, 7 or 8 years old for second grade, 10 or 11 for fifth grade. The project records also have birthdays for each child and information about the country of the parents' origin.

The transcribing conventions were derived loosely from the guidelines found in Berman and Slobin (1994) and then converted to CHAT with extensions as noted in the 00depadd file. Comments in the text marked by %exc indicate nonnarrative comments and %pro indicates a pronunciation that is not predictable from the standard orthography. Each verbed clause is marked by a [c]. Verbed clauses need not have a finite verb and in some cases the verb will be absent, as in ellipsis. Modals and aspectual serial verbs are considered as a single verb, as long as the subject does not change. Morphological errors or omissions are marked with %err coding, although users should be aware that this coding has not been found reliable and is used only as a guide by the original researchers.

Strömqvist corpus

Pairs of spoken and written frog stories were elicited as part of the Swedish project "Speaking and writing from a linguistic and didactic perspective." The central research questions were "What is the interaction between the flow of thought and the flow of language when you are speaking versus when you are writing?" and "How does this interplay change during the course of language development?"

In this particular experiment the participants were presented with a monologically oriented task of narrating the frog story picture by picture under two conditions: speech and writing. Before asked to produce their first narrative, the participants were invited to look through the picture book. The spoken narrations were videotaped and the written ones were computer-logged. When using Textlogger, the participant activates a picture in the left half of the screen by clicking the mouse, and proceeds by writing in a text window (the right half of the screen).

In June 1995, the project archive had videotaped oral frog stories and computer-logged written frog stories from 30 ninth-graders. The participants, 15 girls and 15 boys, were 15 years old and had used word processing for more than 2 years by the time of the experiment. The order of the two conditions (speech and writing) was controlled; half of the participants started with writing and continued with speaking, whereas the other half proceeded in the opposite order. In order to facilitate comparison of the spoken and written stories, the transcripts are structured as a "dialogue" between *WRI and *SPO, where each adjacency pair of utterances <WRI,SPO> corresponds to the written and spoken description of a given picture by the participant in question. There are, thus, 30 files, where each file contains, in the pair-wise fashion described, the written and spoken versions from the subject in question. The files are named with the pseudonyms of the participants. The 30 files from the 15-year-olds are contained in the directory 15s2w (the 15 participants who started the narration experiment in the spoken condition and continued in the written one) and 15w2s (the 15 participants who started in the spoken condition and continued in the written). In addition, there are spoken and written frog stories from fourteen 9-year-olds.

Gopnik

Myrna Gopnik
Department of Linguistics
McGill University
1001 Sherbrooke W.
Montréal, PQ H3A 1G5 Canada

This directory contains data that were contributed by Myrna Gopnik of McGill University to the CHILDES in August of 1988. They include story book descriptions from normal children between the ages of 2 and 5.

The file names use this syntax:

Storytype	f (free) or p (prompted) or q (questionnaire) or g (game)
StudentID	3-digit number
Booktype	1 (free) 2-5 (one of four books)
Session	1, 2, or 3 (which test session)

Table 84: Gopnik Children

ID	Sex	Birthdate	Teacher	Verified
01	F	27-10-78	LS	Y
02	F	12-08-78	LS	Y
03	F	01-07-79	LS	Y
04	F	10-02-79	LS	Y
05	M	29-11-78	LS	Y
06	M	23-10-78	LS	Y
07	M	31-08-78	LS	Y
08	F	17-08-79	LS	Y
09	M	06-12-79	BL	Y
10	M	13-12-79	BL	N
11	M	14-11-80	LD	N
12	M	19-01-81	LD	N
13	M	26-05-81	BL	N
14	M	25-07-80	BL	Y

Table 84: Gopnik Children

ID	Sex	Birthdate	Teacher	Verified
15	M	05-01-80	BL	Y
16	F	20-08-79	LS	Y
17	F	29-03-79	LS	N
18	F	19-02-80	BL	Y
46	F	21-01-81	LD	Y
47	M	02-04-80	HD	N
48	M	01-03-81	LD	N
49	F	17-02-82	LG	N
50	F	01-06-80	XY	N
51	F	09-10-79	BL	N
52	M	18-02-82	SG	N
53	F	20-04-82	SG	N
54	M	28-01-80	BL	N
55	F	01-01-80	XY	N
56	M	12-10-80	BL	N
57	F	19-03-82	LG	N
58	M	28-05-80	BL	N
59	F	06-03-81	LD	N
60	M	31-08-82	LG	Y
61	F	11-03-82	XY	N

Publications using these data should cite:

Gopnik, M. (1989). Reflections on challenges raised and questions asked. In P. R. Zelazo & R. G. Barr (Eds.), *Challenges to developmental paradigms*. Hillsdale, NJ: Lawrence Erlbaum Associates.

Hicks

Deborah Hicks
Department of Educational Development
College of Education
University of Delaware
Newark, DE 19716 USA
hicks@brahms.udel.edu

The narratives in this directory were collected by Deborah Hicks in the context of a study of primary school children's narrative genre skills, focusing on their ability to produce a range of kinds of narratives. In the study, children from three primary grade levels — first, second, and fifth —were shown a shortened version of the silent film, "The Red Balloon." After viewing the film, children were asked to tell the film's events in three different ways: as a factual news report, an ongoing event case, and as a more embellished story. These three narrative genres are representative of what Heath (1983) terms "key" narratives, or narratives that are found crossculturally in children's language learning environments. The narrative data were coded by utterances for linguistic forms that might mark genre differences.

This directory contains four subdirectories: 1st, 2nd, 5th, and del. The first three are taken from first, second, and fifth graders in Cambridge, Massachusetts. The fourth is taken from a lower-class SES group in Delaware. For comparison with the Delaware children, these 12 files in the 1st grade directory were used: 4, 5, 12, 16, 27, 29, 30, 35, 38, 39, 40, and 42.

The children with files in the subdirectories called 1st, 2nd, and 5th were first grade, second grade, and fifth grade students in a private elementary school in Cambridge, Massachusetts. The majority of students attending this school were members of middle class families in which one or both parents were working professionals, so that these children could be considered members of mainstream culture. The classrooms were somewhat progressive in nature, so that children were free to choose from a range of activities those that they would work on. Many of the activities that children performed regularly were language activities, such as recounting on tape a story of how the world was created, writing about "what we did in science class," and recounting personal experiences during sharing time episodes. The narrative genre tasks were thus presented to the children as one of the many options available, and in all but a few cases, children were willing and eager to leave the room for the tasks.

Before performing any of the narrative tasks, children were told that they would watch a film and would then tell what happened in the film in three different ways. In the case of the online narration task, children listened to the experimenter saying "This is [child's name] and Deborah, sportscasters, and we're gonna say everything we see happening in the film. I'm gonna start off and then [child's name] is gonna take over." The child then watched the 3-minute segment of the film and then the experimenter started the narration by saying "The little boy and the red balloon are going past a church steeple. And they're coming to a bakery shop. The little boy is looking inside the bakery shop. Now he's check-ing in his pocket to see if he has enough money to buy something to eat. Looks good. Now he's walking into the bakery shop." Then the experimenter turned to the child and asked, "Can you take over now and be the sportscaster?" The order of the report and event cast tasks was randomly selected within grade levels.

The storytelling task was performed separately from the report and event cast, in a ses-sion that took place approximately 1 hour after the completion of the first two tasks. This particular research design was chosen on the grounds that performance of three consecutive tasks would be too demanding for many of the children in the study, particularly the 5-year-old children. For the storytelling task, the leading given by the experimenter was "This is [child's name] and Deborah, and we're gonna be storytellers and tell the story of The Red Balloon. I'm gonna start off and then [child's name] is gonna take over." During this, the experimenter holds a "storybook" which has on the front cover a picture from the film but which has neither words nor pictures inside. The experimenter then says "The Red Balloon. Once upon a time there was a little boy who lived in Paris, France. One day, on his way to the bus stop, he found this big beautiful red balloon. He wanted the balloon to be his friend." Then the experimenter turns to the child and says, "Can you take over now and be the storyteller?" At this point, the experimenter passes the storybook to the child.

In an attempt to create some degree of homogeneity in the data, in addition to providing an interaction with the highest possible degree of ecological validity, children were provid-ed with a great deal of contextual support for the tasks. As was noted in the introductory section to this chapter, children were reminded before each task of the particular narrative "voice" they were to assume: that of a news reporter, a sportscaster, or a storyteller. For the storytelling task, children were also given a storybook containing only a single picture on the outside cover, which they were encouraged to hold during the story narration.

The data obtained from the study were transcribed in CHAT and analyzed using the CLAN programs for child language analysis. The entire narration was divided into clauses with one clause on each line of the CHAT transcript. The segmentation of the narrative data was done on the basis of clause units of analysis, following Berman and Slobin (1994). Clause units were defined as any linguistic utterance containing a predicate, so that the fol-lowing would all be considered separate units of analysis: "he climbed up the stairs", "when the boy was inside the bakery shop," and "the boys who stole the balloon." Segmentation of complement clauses was done so that the utterance "he saw the balloon floating by the door" was segmented into "he saw" and "the balloon floating by the door." Utterances con-taining verbs with three arguments such as "he told the balloon to stay by the door" were segmented as "he told the balloon" and "to stay by the door."

The narrative data were examined in terms of children's use of specific linguistic forms representing three basic subsystems: a) syntactic constructions, b) temporal and event ex-pressions, and c) indexical clauses. The analysis of syntactic constructions was designed to assess possible genre differences in the syntactic complexity of event casting, reportative, and story narratives. The analysis of expressions of temporality and event relations was de-signed to examine genre differences in how temporal and logical relations between events were expressed in the discourse. Finally, the analysis of indexical clauses was an attempt to assess genre differences in how children went beyond the basic narration tasks to provide evaluative or descriptive information about events in the narrative.

Coding

The codes for assessing genre differences in children's narratives consists of three basic sections representing different linguistic subsystems. The codes for syntax are drawn from Berman and Slobin (1994) and Quirk and Greenbaum (1972). The codes are designed to assess differences in syntactic complexity among the three narrative genres. The codes for temporality and event relationships are drawn primarily from Berman and Slobin (1994) and are designed to assess genre differences in the use of verb forms, aspectual markers, timemarkers and logical connectors. Finally, the measures for indices and intensifiers are designed to assess differences in the marking of nonmainline event clauses or in the embellishment of narrative clauses through the use of highlighters and intensifiers.

Syntactic Codes

IND	independent clause
SADV	subordinate adverbial clause "holding his balloon"
CMP	complement clause
REL	relative clause
QES	questions
DIA	direct dialogue, quoted from characters
NEG	negation

Event Codes

T:SQ	temporal sequential marker
T:CN	temporal connective
T:ADV	temporal adverb
MOD	modals
MODV	modal verbs
HYP	hypothetical statement
FUT	future constructions
L:CONT	one event is contingent on another, as in "when X, they Y"
L:TR	one event is contrasted with another
CES	concessive
PUR	purpose
REA	reason
RES	result

C:TEM	clauses in temporal sequence
C:AD	clauses in adversive relationship
C:C:REA	clauses in reason relationship

Indexical Codes

I:DES	indicator of description
I:COM	indicator of comparison
I:S	indicator of internal state
I:S:EMO	indicator of emotional state
I:S:PHY	indicator of physical state
I:S:MEN	indicator of mental state verb
I:E	indicator of evaluation
I:O	indicator of orientation
I:MET	indicator of metaphor or simile
I:META	indicator of metacomments
I:TNG	indicator of tangential remarks

E:DES	event descriptions
E:HAB	habitual events
E:I:EMO	internal state events
E:I:MEN	internal mental states
E:I:PHY	internal physical states
C:MET	commentary involving metaphors or similes
C:COM	commentary on narration

EX:ADJ	adjectival expansions
EX:ADV	adverbial expansions
INTN	intensifiers
STR	stress
P	pitch marking

Publications using these data should cite:

Hicks, D. (1990). Kinds of texts: Narrative genre skills among children from two communities. In A. McCabe (Ed.), *Developing narrative structure*. Hillsdale, NJ: Erlbaum.

Additional references include:

Berman, R. A. and D. I. Slobin (1994). *Relating events in narrative: A crosslinguistic developmental study.* Hillsdale, NJ, Lawrence Erlbaum Associates.

Heath, S. (1983). *Ways with words: Language, life and work in communities and classrooms.* Cambridge, Cambridge University Press.

Quirk, R., S. Greenbaum, et al. (1972). *A grammar of contemporary English.* London, Longman.

MacWhinney / Bates 1

Brian MacWhinney
Department of Psychology
Carnegie Mellon University
Pittsburgh, PA 15213
macw@cmu.edu

Elizabeth Bates
Cognitive Science Department
University of California
La Jolla, CA 92093
bates@crl.ucsd.edu

These data were gathered in English, Italian, and Hungarian with adults and children aged 3, 4, and 5 years using the picture description task of MacWhinney and Bates (1978) that was described in Table 60 on page 188. In the 1978 experiment, there were 120 participants: 40 Americans, 40 Hungarians, and 40 Italians. Within each language community, there were ten 3-year-olds, ten 4-year-olds, ten 5-year-olds, and ten adults. The chief focus of attention was on the development in the 3–6 year period. The adult participants were included as controls to see if any further developmental changes might be present after age 6 in use of these devices. Each group of 10 participants included five females and five males. The children were enrolled in nursery schools in Denver, Budapest, and Rome. There is every reason to believe that the children at each age were generally equal in terms of overall linguistic ability, because they were all normal, middle-class members of the majority culture and all resided in large metropolitan areas within what is commonly known as Western culture. Unfortunately, no cross-culturally valid measure of general linguistic ability is yet available.

Before a participant was tested, the pictures were placed into the order in which they were to be administered. The order of the nine series of pictures within each series was also randomized. Following each series, a picture of a common object such as a bottle or a sailboat was inserted. This was done to break up any set (*Einstellung*) effects. Participants were examined individually. Each participant was first seated next to the experimenter at a table. The participant was told that he or she would be asked to describe some pictures. Adults were told to describe the pictures in a simple direct fashion. The experimenter showed the pictures to each participant one at a time in the sequence determined by the randomization procedure. Two probes were used: "Tell me about this picture" and "What's happening in this picture?" Use of the two probes was also randomized. Each session was taperecorded in its entirety.

Publications using these data should cite:
MacWhinney, B., & Bates, E. (1978). Sentential devices for conveying givenness and newness: A cross-cultural developmental study. *Journal of Verbal Learning and Verbal Behavior, 17,* 539–558.

MacWhinney / Bates 2

This directory contains the Hungarian and English data from the film description study that Brian MacWhinney and Elizabeth Bates conducted during 1980 to 1982. The results of this work were never published in full. The Italian data from the study are not yet included. There were two orderings of the film — order A and order B. There was also a single version of a cartoon film. Participants came from four age groups: 3, 6, 10, and adult. The file names give the age of the participant, which version of the film they saw, and their participant number.

Script for Pixolation Film

* = line for coding summary data

Scene	Seg	Script A	Script B
1a	1	Hippo turns. (zoom and cut)	Kangaroo turns. (zoom and cut)
	2*	Hippo, ladder, and lock on stage.	Kangaroo, orange, and pencil on stage.
	3	Hippo moves.	Orange moves.
	4	Hippo hits ladder.	Orange hits kangaroo.
	5	Ladder moves.	Kangaroo moves.
	6	Ladder hits lock.	Kangaroo hits pencil.
	7	Lock moves.	Pencil moves.
1b	1	Lion turns.(zoom and cut)	same as A
	2*	Lion, spool, and ball on stage.	same as A
	3	Lion moves.	same as A
	4	Lion hits spool.	same as A
	5	Spool moves.	same as A
	6	Spool hits ball.	same as A
	7	Ball moves.	same as A
1c	1	Kangaroo turns. (zoom and cut)	Hippo turns.(zoom and cut)
	2*	Kangaroo, orange, pencil on stage.	Hippo, ladder, and lock on stage.
	3	Orange moves.	Hippo moves.
	4	Orange hits kangaroo.	Hippo hits ladder.
	5	Kangaroo moves.	Ladder moves.
	6	Kangaroo hits pencil.	Ladder hits lock.
	7	Pencil moves.	Lock moves.
2a	1*	Bottle, goat, and lock on stage.	Block, pipe, and dog on stage.
	2	Bottle moves.	Block moves.
	3	Bottle hits goat.	Block hits pipe.
	4	Goat moves.	Pipe moves.
	5	Goat hits lock.	Pipe hits dog.
	6	Lock moves.	Dog moves.
2b	1*	Block, pipe, and dog on stage.	Bottle, goat and lock on stage.
	2	Block moves.	Bottle moves.

	3	Block hits pipe.	Bottle hits goat.
	4	Pipe moves.	Goat moves.
	5	Pipe hits dog.	Goat hits lock.
	6	Dog moves.	Lock moves.
2c	1*	Giraffe, stool, and tree on stage.	same as A
	2	Giraffe moves.	same as A
	3	Giraffe hits stool.	same as A
	4	Stool moves.	same as A
	5	Stool hits tree.	same as A
	6	Tree moves.	same as A
3a	1*	Cow, basket, and table on stage.	Chair, fish, and TV on stage.
	2	Cow moves.	Chair moves.
	3	Cow hits basket.	Chair hits fish
	4	Basket moves.	Fish moves.
	5	Cow moves.	Chair moves.
	6	Cow hits (pushes) table.	Chair hits TV.
	7	Table moves.	TV moves.
3b	1*	Chair, fish, and TV on stage.	Flowerpot, ball, and pig on stage.
	2	Chair moves.	Flowerpot moves.
	3	Chair hits fish.	Flowerpot hits ball.
	4	Fish moves.	Ball moves.
	5	Chair moves.	Flowerpot moves.
	6	Chair hits TV.	Flowerpot hits pig.
	7	TV moves.	Pig moves.
3c	1*	Flowerpot, ball, pig on stage.	Cow, basket, and table on stage.
	2	Flowerpot moves.	Cow moves.
	3	Flowerpot hits ball.	Cow hits basket.
	4	Ball moves.	Basket moves.
	5	Flowerpot moves.	Cow moves.
	6	Flowerpot hits pig.	Cow hits table.
	7	Pig moves.	Table moves.
4a	1	Cylinder on stage.	scene only appears in A
	2	Ball moves.	
	3	Ball hits cylinder.	
	4	Cylinder falls.	
4b	1	Cylinder on stage.	same as A
	2	Ball moves.	
	3	Ball hits cylinder.	
	4	(Cylinder falls.)	
4c	1	Cylinder on stage.	same as A
	2	Ball enters.	
	3	Ball misses cylinder.	
	4	Cylinder doesn't fall.	
	5	Ball exits.	
4d	1	(Ball enters.)	same as A
	2	(Ball hits cylinder.)	

	3	(Cylinder falls.)	
	4	Cylinder lying down.	
	5	Ball exits.	
4e	1	(Ball misses cylinder.)	same as A
	2	(Cylinder doesn't fall.)	
	3	Cylinder stands.	
	4	Ball moves.	
5	1*	Man, stick, and ball on stage.	same as A
	2	Man looks at stick and ball.	
	3	Ball moves.	
	4	Ball hits stick.	
	5	Stick falls over.	
	6	Man looks (during action).	
7a	1*	Gorilla and camel on stage.	Camel and elephant on stage.
	2	Gorilla chases camel. (cut)	Camel chases elephant. (cut)
7b	1*	Gorilla and stag on stage.	Deer and elephant on stage.
	2	Gorilla chases stag. (cut)	Deer chases elephant. (cut)
7c	1*	Gorilla and elephant on stage.	Gorilla and elephant on stage.
	2	Gorilla chases elephant.	Gorilla chases elephant.
8a	1*	Apple and stool on stage.	Apple and stool on stage.
	2	Apple chases stool. (cut)	Apple chases stool. (cut)
8b	1*	Apple and dog on stage.	Stool and dog on stage.
	2	Apple chases dog.	Stool chases dog.
8c	1*	Cow and zebra on stage.	Cow and zebra on stage.
	2	Cow chases zebra. (cut)	Cow chases zebra. (cut)
8d	1*	Zebra and seal on stage.	Cow and seal on stage.
	2	Zebra chases seal.	Cow chases seal.
8e	1*	Camel and giraffe on stage.	Camel and giraffe on stage.
	2	Camel chases giraffe. (cut)	Camel chases giraffe. (cut)
8f	1*	Bottle and camel on stage.	Bottle and giraffe on stage.
	2	Bottle chases camel.	Bottle chases giraffe.
8g	1*	Chair and table on stage.	Chair and table on stage.
	2	Chair chases table. (cut)	Chair chases table. (cut)
8h	1*	Hippo and chair on stage.	Hippo and table on stage.
	2	Hippo chases chair.	Hippo chases table.
8i	1*	Cow and apple on stage.	Cow and apple on stage.
	2	Apple chases cow.	Cow chases apple.
9a	1	(Big) orange on plate.	(Big) orange on plate.
	2	(Big) orange moves. (cut)	(Big) orange moves. (cut)
9b	1	(Big) oranges on stage.	Big and small orange on stage.
	2	One (big) orange moves.	(Big) orange moves.
	3	(Big) orange hits (big) orange.	(Big) orange hits (small) orange.
	4	(Big) orange moves.	(Small) orange moves.
	5	(Big) orange stays. (cut)	(Big) orange stays. (cut)
9c	1	(Big) orange on plate.	(Big)orange on plate.
10a	1	Man and woman face each other.	Man and woman face each other.

		A	B
	2	Man has ball.	Woman has ball.
	3	Man walks to woman.	Man walks to woman.
	4	Man hands woman a ball.	Man grabs ball from woman.
10b1	1	Woman sits down. (cut)	Woman sits down. (cut)
10b2	1	Woman and man stand facing. (cut)	Woman sitting; man facing. (cut)
	2	Woman moves to man (cut).	Man moves to woman. (cut)
10b3	1	Camera behind woman.	Camera behind man.
	2	Woman grabs ball.	Man gives ball to woman.
10c1	1	Woman skips. (cut)	scene omitted
10c2	1	Woman and man stand facing.	scene omitted
	2	Woman moves to man.	scene omitted
10c3	1	Camera behind woman.	scene omitted
	2	Woman gives ball to man.	scene omitted
10d1	1	Woman reads a book. (cut)	Woman reads a book. (cut)
10d2	1	Woman stands alone.	Woman stands alone (cut).
	2	Camera zooms in.	omitted
	3	Woman walks, raises hand, (cut)	omitted
10d3	1	Man and woman standing close.	same as A
	2	Man drops orange in her hand.	same as A
11a	1	Man 1 and man 2 standing.	same as A
	2	Man 1 paints himself.	Man 2 bounces a ball.
	3	Man 2 bounces a ball.	Man 1 paints himself.
	4	Man 1 climbs a ladder.	same as A
11b	1	Woman 1 and 2 are standing.	same as A
	2	Woman 1 turns around.	Woman 2 bounces a ball.
	3	Woman 2 bounces a ball.	Woman 1 turns around.
	4	Woman 1 sits down.	same as A
12a	1	Tree pulls active walrus.	Tree chases panther.
12b	1	Tree circles alligator.	Tree pulls camel. (cut)
12c	1	Tree pushes active penguin.	Tree circles alligator.
12d	1	Tree chases panther.	Tree pushes sheep.
12e	1	Tree falls on bear.	Tree pulls active walrus. (cut)
12f	1	Tree pushes neutral sheep.	Tree falls on bear.
12g	1	Tree hits gorilla.	Tree pushes active penguin.
12h	1	Tree pulls neutral camel.	Tree hits gorilla.
12i	1	Buffalo pushes active tree.	Buffalo pushes passive tree.
12j	1	Buffalo pushes neutral tree.	Buffalo pushes active tree.
13a	1*	(Lemon, apple, orange on stage.)	same as A
	2	Lemon moves.	
	3	Lemon hits apple.	
	4	Apple moves.	
	5	Apple hits orange.	
	6	Orange moves.	
13b	1*	(Lemon, apple, orange on stage.)	same as A
	2	Lemon moves.	
	3	Apple and orange on stage.	

	4	Lemon moves.	
	5	Lemon hits apple.	
	6	Apple moves.	
	7	Apple hits orange.	
	8	Orange moves.	
13c	1*	Apple and orange on stage.	same as A
	2	Lemon moves.	
	3	Lemon hits apple.	
	4	Apple moves.	
	5	Apple hits orange.	
	6	Orange moves.	
13d	1*	Apple and orange on stage.	same as A
	2	Lemon moves.	
	3	Orange, lemon, apple on stage.	
	4	Lemon moves.	
	5	Lemon hits apple.	
	6	Apple moves.	
	7	Apple hits orange.	
	8	Orange moves.	
13e	1*	Lemon, apple, orange on stage.	same as A
	2	Lemon moves.	
	3	Lemon hits apple.	
	4	Apple moves.	
	5	Apple hits orange.	
	6	Orange moves.	

Film A order was 8a–d, 11a, 8e–f, 13c, 8g–h, 10a, 8i, 4a-e, 10c, 12, 11b, 2, 13e, 7, 13b, 1, 10d, 9, 13d, 5, 10b, 3, 13a.

Film B order was 8a–d, 13a, 8e–f, 11b, 8g–h, 4b–e, 8i, 10a, 3, 13e, 10b, 5, 13c, 10d, 9, 1, 13d, 7, 13b, 2, 11a, 12.

Reasons for Stimuli

1. The treatment of the orange as an animate should be strongest in Film A where focus is achieved cinematographically. Focus on the kangaroo should induce more backgrounding of the hitting by the orange.

2. It is interesting to compare "bottle" with "orange" in (1) and to compare across versions for effects of the previous priming scene. Perhaps "dog" will be passivized?

3. Here we might expect conjunctions instead of relatives and fewer passives than in (1) and (2). Do children have a hard time "letting go" of the fish when it is already the perspective?

4. These should ellicit forms such as "will hit," "will miss," "hit," and "missed."

5.   Backgrounding of "man," cause inferred in (3), multiple setting in ASL.

6.   Omitted.

7.   This should ellicit devices that mark anaphoric givenness and singularity of newness.

8.   These should be marked by coordination in compound presentation, givenness of distant items, with possible referent confusion.

9.   Set operation, confusability.

10A. Segment a should ellicit "gives", whereas segment b should ellicit less "gives" than 10B. Segments a, c, and d should ellicit "gets."

10B. Segment a should ellicit "takes" and "grabs." In segment b "gives" should be stronger than in 10A. Segments a and d should ellicit "gets."

11. Relative clauses, and so forth.

12. Perspective, givenness.

13. Stage setting, ASL marking, shifts.

Devices Used Across Segments

1.   Scene contrast: Contrast with a whole previous scene. Examples: *in this scene, however*; *and now in this scene.* Code on each segment of the entire scene.

2.   Scene parallelism: Parallel to a previous scene. Examples: *exact same thing as before, but with a goat; the same black ball hit the orange stick again.* Code on each segment of the entire scene.

3.   Movie scene specification: May apply to either a segment or a whole scene. Code on segment on which occurs. Examples: *in this episode, scene, shot, in the picture, in this one, here in the second one.*

4.   Global description: Example: *fruit rolling around.*

Devices Used in Particular Segments

1.   Segment ellipsis: No material in the segment at all.

2.   Interactionals. Examples: *OK, allright, well, um,* and so forth. Code on segment if occurs anywhere within the segment.

3.   Evidentials: References to the perceiver. Examples: *we see that, it appears, we can see, you see a,* and so forth.

4.   Location specification: Physical location within the "room" or frame depicted. Examples: *in the room, on the table, it left the screen, off stage, came on stage,* and so forth. Do not code plain *off, in,* or *away* as in *then the cow went in/off/away.* Although the latter may imply location, they are not very specific and are already captured as the main function of the directional adverb category. Also, do not code the presentative (e.g., *there is a dog*), because it may imply existence rather than loca-

tion; however, do code utterances such as *the dog was there*, because these are locative and not captured by any other category. Note that this category should not be confused with pansegmental #3, which refers to the contents of a segment or scene as a whole. For instance, *in this scene, a dog chased a cow* would be coded #3 pansegmental, because elements of the scene are not assigned locations.

5. Segment parallelism: Like #2 pansegmental, but referring only to segment rather than scene similarity. The referents involved will determine which coding is applicable. Examples: *in both of these, the same as, the exact same thing, in the same sequence*. More specifically, an example would be *the hippo hit the ladder and then did the same to a lock* — the referents being parallel within multiple segments of a single scene. Code parallelism on the latter segment (e.g., *hippo hit lock*).

6. Segment contrast: Analogous to #1 of pansegmental, but referring to segment rather than scene contrast. The referents involved will determine which coding is applicable. Examples: *here, however, in this case, in turn, and now*. (The very common phrase *and then* has been double-coded as #7 and #8. Although such a combination might conceivably be considered a method of segment contrast, it was not so regarded here. Instead it was considered to be primarily a mode of coordination and ordering.)

7. Segment order: Examples: *then, first*, and so forth. May be double-coded #3 pansegmental, but only when order also suggests a movie scene, e.g., *in the first one/in the second scene*. In these cases a noun or pronoun must indicate reference to the scene.

8. Coordination: Example: *and*. Code when occurs within a segment (e.g., *a cow and an apple were there*. An exception would be for adjectival coordinations because they are script-external (e.g., *a brown and white cow hit the ladder*. When coordination occurs between segments code on the following segment. In the case of *acow ran and it hit an apple*, the *cow hit apple* segment would be coded as #8).

9. Cotemporality: Examples: *while, during*.

10. Restrictive relativization relevant to script: Relativizations that must discriminate among two similar scripted objects. Example: *the man who painted his face* when one man did and one man did not.

11. Nonrestrictive relativization relevant to script: Example: *the apple hit the lock which went off stage*. Code under the segment *lock moves*. Causatives such as *the apple hit the lock which made the lock go off stage* were not coded here because the relativizer"which" refers to the contents of the entire previous phrase, rather than a single noun. These causatives are captured by #9 of Verbal Specification.

12. Segment negation: Examples: *it didn't hit the cylinder; you don't see if it falls or not*. Do not code nominal negation here.

13. Backward conflator: Transitive action conflating previous intransitive motion. Example: *the apple rolled into the orange* implies previous movement of the apple. Code the segment *apple hits orange* as a backward conflator even if the previous segment is not ellipsed. Other likely backward conflators are *runs into* and *bumps (into)*.

14. Backward conflatee: Segment ellipsed as indicated in #13. Also code as #1 (ellipsed). Do not code as a conflatee unless actually ellipsed.

15. Forward conflator: A transitive that conflates a following intransitive motion. Example: *the goat knocked over the bottle* on the segment *goat hits bottle* implies movement in the following *bottle moves* segment. Other likely forward conflators include *pushed over, push*, and *nudge.* Code as a conflator even if the following segment is not ellipsed. For some speakers, *bump* seems to have the potential to be considered as both a backward and forward conflator. It was coded only as a backward conflator because it necessarily implies some movement on the part of the one who bumps. It may or may not imply a substantial degree of movement (although it may tend to imply recoil or surprise) on the part of the bumpee. Other somewhat ambiguous cases include *the goat knocked into the bottle, the apple pushed into the orange.* The unusual pronouns may tend to move these in the direction of backward conflation: they were nonetheless treated as forward conflators, that is, as if they were more typical usages of these verbs.

16. Forward conflatee: Segment actually ellipsed by #15. Code only if ellipsed and double code for ellipsis (#1).

17. Double forward conflation: Examples: *the giraffe pushes the chair into the lock.* Three segments are involved: "giraffe hits chair", "chair moves", "chair hits lock". Code #17 on "chair hits lock." Code #15 and #16/#1 on "giraffe hits chair" and "chair moves," respectively.

18. Error: The purpose of this code is to identify those segments that seem to be difficult to perceive. Examples: Role errors (example, *the dog pushes the cow* when the cow has pushed the dog) and errors that make it impossible to tell what roles are assigned. Also apply this code to major nominal errors that are not role errors (example, *the dog pushes the cow* when there is no dog in the scene, and a giraffe has pushed the cow). Do not use this code for minor nominal errors with no impact (e.g., calling a horse a donkey). Also use this code for errors requiring prompting (indicated on transcripts as empty parentheses).

19. Self-correction: Retraced false starts (not hesitations, interactionals, or simple repeats). Use the corrected production for all other coding.

20. Out of script order: Whole segments are out of order. This is indicated in the transcripts by segment numbers that are out of sequence.

Nominal Specification Devices

1. Ellipsis: Any reference to the nominal (via noun, pronoun, and so forth) is missing. This is also used when the nominal is incorrect and additional coding would be misleading.

2. Definite article: *the.*

3. Indefinite article: *a, an.*

4. Definite pronoun: *he, she, it, they, we, this, that, those* (Note that the use of relative

pronouns is indicated by #13, #14, or #15.)

5. Indefinite pronoun: *one, some, something, another.*

6. Deictic adjective: *that dog, this cow.*

7. Indefinite adjective: *another* animal, *some* fruit, *one* cow, the *other* cow, *all* the objects.

8. Deverbal adjective: the *moving* goat, the *fallen* cylinder. Such adjectives lead to the ellipsis of a scripted segment. For example, *the moving goat hit the bottle* ellipses the segment "the goat moves."

9. Negated nominal: *nobody, none, nothing, none of the, not the ball* etc.

10. Possessive adjective: *his, its.*

11. Other Adjective: *big, fat.*

12. Prepositional phrase used to modify scripted noun. Example: *with the stripe.* Sometimes, within the prepositional phrase, possessives or other adjectives appear that refer indirectly to the scripted noun or its parts (e.g., the hippopotamus *with his big mouth*). These are given the codings appropriate to their respective types of adjective (#10 for the possessive and #11 for other adjectives) in addition to the preposition code, because they refer indirectly or in part to the scripted noun. Prepositional phrases used as adverbs are not coded here. For example, in *pushed with his nose* the prepositional phrase is treated as an adverb and thus does not receive either a #10 coding for *his* or a #12 coding.

13. Nominal specified by restrictive relative clause.

14. Nominal specified by nonrestrictive relative clause: in, *the apple was hit by a lock which went off stage*, the lock is nonrestrictively specified by the relative *which went off stage*. The relative is coded on the segment "lock moves." Note: Do not code "lock" as ellipsed because it is substituted for by the relative pronoun in this segment.

15. Nominal specified by script-external relative clause or script-external adverbial: *the goat that had the red collar hit the table; there is an orange sitting on the plate.* (In the latter example, where the script has "the orange" simply "on stage," then the specification of it as "sitting" is taken as a script-external adverbial that is auxiliary to the scripted presentative. Where the script actually has the stative scripted, as in "cylinder lying down," the coding is #23 rather than #15. Unfortunately, there is some inconsistency in the scripting. In the cylinder sequences, the distinction between "on stage" and "lying down" or "standing up" does not seem to be entirely principled. That is, it does not seem to relate to whether the object is to undergo a change of state or to any other discernable principle. Unfortunately, such differences in the script must make other differences in the coding, as noted below. Since the decision had been made not to alter the script, the only reasonable response was to acknowledge it in a consistent manner, which has been done.) When #15 is coded for unscripted relative clauses, also indicate via #13 or #14 whether the relative is restrictive or nonrestrictive. Do not code at the level of segmental device.

16. Stress: (Note that this device is not yet marked on the transcripts and thus cannot be coded.)

17. Noun phrase coordination: *the lemon and the orange*. Mark each noun coordinated, for example, code both the lemon and the orange with a #17.

18. Left dislocation: Initialization in clause with a pronoun copy in standard position, as in *the table, it hit the lock*.

19. Preverbal positioning: Immediately preceding the *scripted* noun: not separated by another noun. In "the dog chased the stool," the dog is obviously the preverbal nominal element. In *we saw the dog chasing the stool*, the dog is still considered to be preverbal because "chase" is the scripted verb. There are a few cases in which a noun is coded as immediately preverbal although it may not be in the strictest sense. For instance, in *the spool of thread bumped the lock*, "spool" is the scripted noun. Although spool does not immediately precede the verb, *spool of thread* functionally refers to the same entity. Indeed, *thread* alone may often be used to make the same reference. In the few cases like this, the presence of the prepositional modifier did not seem to justify disqualifying its noun as preverbal. A final note: again, there is some confusion in the sequences scripted "on stage." The coding of *there is a cylinder standing up* therefore depends on whether the script reads "cylinder on stage" or "cylinder standing up." In the former, the scripted verb is taken to be the presentative, which *cylinder* follows postverbally. In the latter the scripted verb is taken to be the stative, which *cylinder* precedes. (Responses vary from *a cylinder is there* to *there is a cylinder* to *a cylinder is standing there* to *there is a cylinder standing there*. Perhaps one should rethink the position of the "on stage" vs. its stative alternatives in the script, although this was not originally seen as viable.)

20. Postverbal positioning: Immediately following the scripted verb; not separated by another noun. In *the dog chased the stool*, the stool is the postverbal nominal element. In simple, scripted presentatives (e.g., *there was/we had an orange, a lemon, and an apple*) in the scripted "lemon, apple, orange on stage"), code the noun that follows the presentative verb as immediately postverbal. (Here that would be the orange.) In the case of a presentative that is not scripted and an adverbial that is, (e.g., *there is a dog chasing a cow* for the scripted "dog chases cow," dog is considered to be immediately preverbal vis-a-vis the scripted verb and cow is considered to be immediately postverbal.

21. Placement in a by-clause: Indexes the use of the passive. Mark only the noun that actually occurs in the clause, (e.g., in *the dog was chased by the stool* mark only the stool.)

22. Presentative nominal: Any presentative, whether scripted or not. Examples: *There's a dog, We had a dog, They showed an apple chasing an orange*.

23. Nominal specified by a scripted adverbial: *There's a dog chasing a cow: We see a kangaroo turn.*

Verb Specification Devices

1. Ellipsis: Include all types of gapping as well as complete ellipsis of scripted verb. Examples: NP + NP VP (*the dog and ball ran*); VP NP + NP (*there was an orange*

and an apple); presentative without any form of the scripted verb.

2. Presentative: Any form that introduces a referent. Examples: *there is, they show, we have.* Most frequently these will appear when there is a new "on stage" element. When a presentative is not scripted in this way but used to introduce scripted action, code on the scripted action verb, in addition to other applicable codings (e.g., in *we see an apple chasing a stool*, code a presentative on *chasing*.

3. Deleted presentative: A sentence in which the main verb is missing. Example: *an apple which gets hit by a dog* (where *there is* should occur). Only coded on the first segment of each coordinated sequence, such as *apple moves* for *an apple running and hitting a stool.*) Where sequences are not coordinated with *and*, each is coded for a deleted presentative. Example: Code #3 on both *apple hits stool* and *apple hits cow* for a noncoordinated response such as *Apple hitting stool. Apple hitting cow.*

4. Stative: Examples: *an orange is sitting on a plate, standing, resting.* Code even when statives are not specifically scripted.

5. Directional adverb: *after, around, on, into.*

6. Exit directional: A subset of directionals which indicate something has left. Even though a subset, do not double-code a #5. In the interests of objectivity and uniformity, code *all* instances of the following: *off, away, off stage.* The "exit" component of these may be vague, because *off* may mean "off the plate" or "off stage" and *away* may simply mean "away from another animal or object." All "exists", including those simply relative to another object or position should be coded.

7. Manner adverb: Put any nondirectional adverbs in this category. Examples: *slowly, in a circle, twisting, sort of, just* etc. However, adverbs of time or order such as *then* were not included, because they already make up pansegmental category #7.

8. Causative replacing action: Examples: *the lemon made the apple roll into the orange.*

9. Causative coded on resultant: Examples: *the orange hit the lemon, making it roll into the apple*; *the orange hit the kangaroo, which made it hit the pencil.* Code causative on the segment with "roll into" or "hit," respectively, because the causative does not replace the action as in #8 .

10. First member(s) of coordinate verb phrase: All verbs in script (in different segments). To be assigned the #10/11 coding an explicit *and* must occur at the end of the sequence. Examples: "moved" in *moved and hit*; both "turned" and "moved" in *the hippo turned, moved over, and hit the ladder.*

11. Last member of coordinate verb phrase: All verbs must be in the script (in different segments); an explicit *and* must occur at the end of the sequence. Examples: "hit" in *moved and hit.*

12. Double transitive: Two transitive verbs in one segment where script has only one verb. Example: *hit it and knocked it over.*

13. Double coding of motion: Two intransitive verbs where script has only one. Example: *the ball rolls and then it goes and hits.* This is coded on "hits".

14. Passive.

15. Reciprocal: Example: *touched each other.*

16. Reflexive: Examples: *himself, herself, themselves.* Code only for scripted verbs. Some scripted verbs cannot be coded according to this scheme, (e.g., if the scripted verb occurs as an adverbial, in the infinitive).

17. Past imperfect: Examples: *was chasing, was being chased by, there was.*

18. Past perfect: Examples: *chased, was chased by, we saw.*

19. Present imperfect: Examples: *is chasing, is being chased by, there is, we have.*

20. Present perfect: Examples: *chases, is chased by.* In segments like "apple moves," a description such as *goes rolling* was classified as present perfect (for *goes* as an indicator of movement) plus an adverb indicating the manner of movement (rolling).

21. Retrospective: Example: *has chased.*

22. Inchoative: Example: *is about to.*

23. Inceptive: Examples: *starts to, started to.* (Also code for tense, when possible.) Examples: *started spinning* would be coded as the imperfect past as well as inceptive. There is no tense coding for the infinitive plus inceptive, as in *started to spin.*

24. Generalized verb: Verb that does not specify who does what. Example: *the orange and the apple chased around.*

25. Adverbial: Scripted verb is in adverbial form. Example: "chasing" in *there was an apple chasing a stool.*

26. Continuation: Emphasizes ongoing aspect of activity. Example: *keeps rolling, continues to move.*

Stimulus Properties

Segmental

1. Is there a preceding segment?   PSEG
2. Is there a following segment?   FSEG
3. Is the preceding segment dynamic (i.e. movement)?   PDYN
4. Is the following segment dynamic?   FDYN
5. Is the preceding segment transitive?   PTRAN
6. Is the following segment transitive?   FTRAN
7. Is there a preceding cut?   PCUT
8. Is there a following cut?   FCUT
9. Is there an observer present?   OBS
10. Is there an inferred action (i.e. not actually seen)?   INF
11. Does the previous scene have parallel structure?   PAR

Nominal

1.	Is the word a noun or a pronoun?	N
2.	Is it exophorically given (achieved by leaving projector on)?	EXO
3.	Is it anaphorically given (achieved by presence in current scene)?	ANA
4.	Was it nominated as topic (in constrained production task)?	NOM
5.	Is it the only element that is given or only that is new?	SANA
6.	Is the referent confusable?	CONF
7.	Is the element cinematographically salient?	CSAL
8.	Was it previously salient (in current scene)?	PSAL
9.	Is it potent?	POT
10.	Is it animate?	ANI
11.	Is it human?	HUM
12.	Singularity of animacy?	SANI
13.	Is it currently the perspective (based on verb markedness)?	CPER
14.	Was it previously a perspective?	PPER
15.	Is it moving?	MOV
16.	Singularity of motion?	SMOV
17.	Was it the first mover?	FMOV
18.	Was it used as reference location?	LOC
19.	Was there an earlier segment within this scene with same verb?	PARS
20.	Did the item appear in the same role in an earlier segment?	SAME
21.	Different animacy in the parallel segment in the previous scene?	ADIF

Verbal

1.	Action?	ACT
2.	Transitive?	TRAN
3.	Static?	STAT
4.	Collision?	COL
5.	Percussive?	PERC
6.	Result of previous action?	RES
7.	Negation of expectation?	NEG

Participant-Generated

1. Was the first segment ellipsed?   FELL
2. Was the last segment ellipsed?   LELL
3. Was the previous segment ellipsed?   PELL
4. Was the following segment ellipsed?   FSELL
5. Was the item previously mentioned?   PMEN
6. Was there a preceding presentative?   PPRE

Script of Cartoon

1.   Woodpecker is pecking in a tree.
2.   Dog runs in from off stage and runs up to the tree.
3.   Bird stops pecking and dog barks at bird.
4.   Bird looks at dog.
5.   Bird pecks at tree again (pecks until has almost pecked through tree branch).
6.   Bird stops pecking and tree top falls to the ground.
7.   Dog and bird run off stage.
8.   Tree top follows (chases) dog and bird.
9.   Bird and dog and tree top come back on stage and tree top chases dog which chases bird.
10. Bear walks into cave.
11. Bird and dog go into cave.
12. Bird and dog come out of cave then bear follows (chases) them.
13. Bird and dog run up an evergreen tree together.
14. Tree runs away with bird and dog in it.
15. Bear picks up a stick.
16. Bear walks along and encounters a banana tree and hits the tree with the stick.
17. Banana falls on bear.
18. Bear picks up banana and eats it.
19. Bear walks along and encounters an apple tree, picks up another (duplicate) stick and hits the tree.
20. An apple falls on the bear.
21. Bear drops stick and then picks up the apple and eats it.
22. Bear picks up the same stick and walks to a banana tree and hits the tree with the stick. (Note: the banana tree now has a monkey in it.)
23. Monkey falls on bear.

24. Monkey gets up and growls at bear.
25. Monkey grabs stick from bear.
26. Bear points at banana tree.
27. Monkey hits banana tree with stick.
28. Bananas fall on bear and monkey.
29. Bear and monkey shake hands and then they each pick up a banana and eat it.

6:   Germanic Languages

Table 85: Germanic Languages

Corpus	Age Range	N	Comments
Danish – Plunkett on page 276	Anne 0;8.12– 2;3.9 Jen 0;11.15– 2;5.12	2	Longitudinal study of two Danish children
Dutch – Levelt / Fikkert on page 280	1;0–2;11	12	Longitudinal study with 20,000 utterances from 12 monolingual children acquiring Dutch as their first language
Dutch – Gillis on page 282	0;11.15–1;11.28	1	Longitudinal corpus of bi-weekly recording sessions of a boy learning Dutch
Dutch – Groningen on page 284	1;05–3;07	7	Longitudinal study of the spontaneous speech of seven Dutch children in an unstructured home setting
Dutch – Schaerlaekens on page 293	1;8.19–2;10.23, 1;10.18–3;1.8	6	Longitudinal study of the spontaneous dialogues of two sets of triplets
Dutch – Utrecht on page 296	2;2–3;1	2	Longitudinal study of two children with disfluencies using recording sessions made in the children's home
Dutch – van Kampen on page 310	Laura 1;9.18– 5;10.9 sarah 1;6.16–6;0	2	Longitudinal corpus of mother–child interactions with monthly taperecorded sessions in an unstructured home setting
Dutch – Wijnen on page 311	2;7–3;10	1	Longitudinal study of unstructured child–father interactions in a child who was a slow starter in both grammar and phonology
German – Clahsen on page 312	2;9–3;6 1;11– 2;5 2;9–3;6	3	Longitudinal German study of the twins Daniel and Mathias and their younger sister Julia with recordings made in the home
German – Wagner on page 314	1;5–14;10	13	Set of 13 mini-corpora in German in which participants wore a transmitter microphone in situations based on individual daily routine

Table 85: Germanic Languages

Corpus	Age Range	N	Comments
German – Weissen-born on page 317	7–11 14 adult	14	Cross sectional study using a laboratory route description task with pairs of participants in German at three ages.
German – Wode on page 319	2–8	3	Longitudinal study of the day to day routine from three German siblings
Swedish – Göteborg on page 321	Markus 1;3.19–6;0.09 Eva 1;0.21–3;9.23	2	Longitudinal study of two monolingual Swedish children

Danish – Plunkett

Kim Plunkett
Department of Psychology
University of Oxford
Oxford, England
kim.plunkett@psy.oxford.ac.uk

This directory contains longitudinal corpora from two Danish children — Anne and Jens — studied by Kim Plunkett of Århus University from 1982 to 1987. The data were contributed to CHILDES in 1989. The children's ages during the study were 8 months to 6 years for Anne and 11 months to 6 years for Jens. In addition to the CHAT transcripts, results from the Uzgiris-Hunt Infant Assessment Scales are available for both children during the first year of the study, as are results of various comprehension tests. Copies of the original videotapes can be made available.

The data were collected in the context of a project entitled "Projekt B," which is a longitudinal investigation of Danish children's linguistic, cognitive, and social development. The main purpose of the study is to establish a profile of young Danish children's language development in relationship to their developing cognitive and social skills using the techniques of developmental psycholinguistic analysis. Even with a sample of only four children, individual differences in development demand a more refined account than the generalist approaches prevalent during the 1970s.

The study began when the boy and girl were 0;11.15 and 0;8.1 respectively. Data collection continued until both children were 6;0. The girl had a sister who was 2 years older. Both parents had completed a university education. The boy is a single child. The father was a skilled worker and the mother had just started on a university education. Both children spent a good deal of time in nursery school. The children were visited in their homes fortnightly. Each visit consisted of an interview, testing procedures, and a free play session. The interview focused on the parents' observations of their child's language behavior since the previous visit; whether any new words had emerged; whether the child had begun using old words in new ways; whether the child's social and communicative skills had developed in any way; finally, any other noteworthy developments the parents may have observed. To this end, the parents were asked to keep a diary of the various aspects of their child's development on a week-to-week basis. The contents of the diary formed the basis of much of the discussion in the interview session. The testing procedures were taken from the Uzgiris-Hunt Infant Assessment Scales (Uzgiris & Hunt, 1975). The rationale for these scales is based on Piaget's (1952) theory of the sensorimotor period. The object permanence and means–ends subscales were administered on each visit. The remaining sub-scales were administered less frequently. In the final free play session, parent and child were encouraged to engage in a variety of social situations. An attempt was made to establish some regularity in the kind of situations observed across visits (feeding time, solving a problem together, story-telling). However, importance was attached to collecting naturalistic data and so coercion was avoided. The entirety of each visit, which lasted approximately 90 minutes, was recorded on videotape. Transmitting microphones were used to collect the vocal data from child and parent.

After the visit, a transcription was made of the videotape. A standard orthographic transcription was made of all the verbal behavior during the session together with a transcription of any nonverbal activity that might aid in the interpretation of the verbal behavior. The speech of all participants was analyzed into utterances after Snow's (1972) guidelines. On this view, utterances are not defined in terms of adult grammatical structures like the sentence but according to the pauses and intonational patterns in the dialogue. Utterances were then analyzed into morphemes. For children, this can be a problematic process. For example, "What is that" may be uttered by the child as a single undifferentiated formula. In such cases, utterances are coded as containing only a single morpheme. The criteria used for deciding the morphemic breakdown of an utterance are based on articulatory and fluency criteria (Peters, 1983). A distinction between idiosyncratic expressions, lexicalized morphemes, and formulaic expressions is made explicit in the coding of the transcription such that a variety of different analyses can be performed on the same database. For example, it is an easy matter using the CLAN programs to observe the effect of including or excluding a child's idiosyncratic expressions in an MLU count.

Table 86: Danish Files

File	Date	Age	File	Date	Age
anne01.cha	04-NOV-82	0;8.12	jens01.cha	29-OCT-82	0;11.15
anne02.cha	19-NOV-82	0;8.27	jens02.cha	12-NOV-82	0;11.28
anne03.cha	03-DEC-82	0;9.11	jens03.cha	25-NOV-82	1;0.11
anne04.cha	08-JAN-83	0;10.16	jens04.cha	10-DEC-82	1;0.26
anne05.cha	22-JAN-83	0;11.2	jens05.cha	07-JAN-83	1;1.23
anne06.cha	?-FEB-83	1;0	jens06.cha	20-JAN-83	1;2.6
anne07.cha	21-FEB-83	1;0.1	jens07.cha	04-FEB-83	1;2.20
anne08.cha	07-MAR-83	1;0.15	jens08.cha	04-MAR-83	1;3.20
anne09.cha	21-MAR-83	1;1.1	jens09.cha	25-MAR-83	1;4.11
anne10.cha	11-APR-83	1;1.19	jens10.cha	08-APR-83	1;4.24
anne11.cha	25-APR-83	1;2.5	jens11.cha	20-APR-83	1;5.6
anne12.cha	16-MAY-83	1;2.24	jens12.cha	06-MAY-83	1;5.22
anne13.cha	06-JUN-83	1;3.14	jens13.cha	27-MAY-83	1;6.13
anne14.cha	20;JUN-83	1;4-0	jens14.cha	10-JUN-83	1;6.26
anne15.cha	06-JUL-83	1;4.14	jens15.cha	28-JUN-83	1;7.14
anne16.cha	21;JUL-83	1;5.1	jens16.cha	15-JUL-83	1;8.1

Table 86: Danish Files

File	Date	Age	File	Date	Age
anne17.cha	16-AUG-83	1;5.24	jens17.cha	02-AUG-83	1;8.18
anne18.cha	29-AUG-83	1;6.9	jens18.cha	18-AUG-83	1;9.4
anne19.cha	10-SEP-83	1;6.18	jens19.cha	30-AUG-83	1;9.16
anne20.cha	24-SEP-83	1;7.4	jens20.cha	16-SEP-83	1;10.2
anne21.cha	08-OCT-83	1;7.16	jens21.cha	28-SEP-83	1;10.14
anne22.cha	29-OCT-83	1;8.9	jens22.cha	12-OCT-83	1;10.28
anne23.cha	12-NOV-83	1;8.20	jens23.cha	29-OCT-83	1;11.15
anne24.cha	29-NOV-83	1;9.9	jens24.cha	16-NOV-83	2;0.2
anne25.cha	17-DEC-83	1;9.25	jens25.cha	07-DEC-83	2;0.23
anne26.cha	07-JAN-84	1;10.15	jens26.cha	20-DEC-83	2;1.6
anne27.cha	08-FEB-84	1;11.16	jens27.cha	05-JAN-84	2;1.21
anne28.cha	16-DEC-84	2;9.24	jens28.cha	25-JAN-84	2;2.11
anne29.cha	01-MAR-84	2;0.9	jens29.cha	09-FEB-84	2;2.25
anne30.cha	15-MAR-84	2;0.23	jens30.cha	28-FEB-84	2;3.14
anne31.cha	29-MAR-84	2;1.9	jens31.cha	13-MAR-84	2;3.29
anne32.cha	05-APR-84	2;1.13	jens32.cha	29-MAR-84	2;4.15
anne33.cha	26-APR-84	2;2.6	jens33.cha	05-APR-84	2;4.21
anne34.cha	10-MAY-84	2;2.20	jens34.cha	17-APR-84	2;5.3
anne35.cha	29-MAY-84	2;3.9	jens35.cha	26-APR-84	2;5.12
anne36.cha	missing		jens36.cha	10-MAY-84	2;5.26
anne37.cha	missing		jens37.cha	24-MAY-84	2;6.10
anne38.cha	05-JUL-84	2;4.13	jens38.cha	07-JUN-84	2;6.21
anne39.cha	07-AUG-84	2;5.15	jens39.cha	25-JUN-84	2;7.11
			jens40.cha	missing	
			jens41.cha	19-JUL-84	2;7.5
			jens42.cha	14-AUG-84	2;8.0

Every file comes with a list of warnings regarding certain inherent limitations in the quality or potential use of the data. The list of warnings is as follows:

1. These data are not useful for the analysis of overlaps, because overlapping was not accurately transcribed.

2. Retracings and hesitation phenomena have not been accurately transcribed in these data.

3. Sections of the session that repeat previous episodes were not transcribed, i.e. repetitions of identical utterances in similar situations are excluded.

4. Productive units within an utterance are identified on the basis of articulation and fluency criteria.

5. The phonetic tier is used to describe the child's pronunciation of a given sound. However, it does not provide a precise phonetic analysis.

6. Immediate imitations are excluded.

7. Note that a timing irregularity occurs in this session.

8. Note blank lines indicate shorter gaps in the transcription.

9. Note that gaps in the timing indicate untranscribed material.

10. Modifications of verb and noun stems by regular inflections are marked on the main text line. However, when the stem itself is notified this change is not marked on the main text line. Instead the basic stem is used and the correct modified form is noted on the %cor tier.

11. The present tense inflections are marked by @n; the plural inflections by @f; the definite plural by @fd; the infinitive by @i; the definite inflections by @d; past participle by @pp; past tense by @pt; comparative by @cp; superlative by @sp3; tillægsord ubestemte forms by @ki (intetkœn), @kf (fælleskœn), @kif (flertal intetkœn), @kff (fælleskœn, flertal), @kd (intetkœn, fælleskœn, ental, flertal, bestemte former); passive of verbs by @p; and genitive of nouns by @g.

12. Irregular forms are marked on the main text line.

Publications using these data should cite:

Plunkett, K. (1985). *Preliminary approaches to language development*. Århus: Århus University Press.

Plunkett, K. (1986). Learning strategies in two Danish children's language development. *Scandinavian Journal of Psychology, 27,* 64–73.

Other relevant references include:

Peters, A. (1983). *The units of language acquisition*. New York: Cambridge University Press.

Piaget, J. (1952). *The origins of intelligence in children*. New York: International Universities Press.

Snow, C. E. (1972). Mothers' speech to children learning language. *Child Development, 43,* 549–565

Uzgiris, I., & Hunt, J. (1975). *Toward ordinal scales of psychological development in infancy*. Champaign: University of Illinois Press.

Dutch – Levelt / Fikkert

Claartje Levelt
Department of Linguistics
De Boelelaan 1105
Amsterdam, The Netherlands 1081-HV
levelt_cc@let.vu.nl

Paula Fikkert
Fachgruppe Sprachwissenschaft
Universität Konstanz
D-78434 Konstanz, Germany
paula.fikkert@uni-konstanz.de

The CLPF (Claartje Levelt, Paula Fikkert) corpus contains 20,000 utterances from 12 monolingual children acquiring Dutch as their first language. The children were between 1;0 and 1;11 at the beginning of an approximately 1-year period of data collection. All children came from middle- to upper-middle-class homes. Recordings were made on a two-weekly basis on a DAT recorder in a natural setting in the children's homes. The tapes were transcribed by two separate transcribers, using the International Phonetic Alphabet, and transcriptions were compared. Only when complete agreement on the transcription was reached it was entered in a computerized database, WordBase, developed at the Max Planck Institute for Psycholinguistics. The phonetic transcriptions use the IPARoman font.

The pseudonyms for the participants in this study are CH1 = Enzo (M, first child), CH2 = Robin (M, first child), CH3 = Tirza (F, third child), CH4 = Eva (F, second child), CH5 = Catootje (F, first child), CH6 = Leonie (F, second child), CH7 = Tom (M, second child), CH8 = Jarmo (M, second child), CH9 = Elke (F, first child), CH10 = Noortje (F, second child), CH11 = Leon (M, second child), CH12 = David (M, first child).

This corpus contains several additional coding tiers. Apart from the standard %eng, %pho, and %mor lines, there are also these three tiers:

%sad:	the CV-structure of the utterance as produced by an adult
%sch:	the CV-structure of the child's utterance
%phm:	phonological markings

Every %phm line starts with $s (spontaneous) or $i (imitation). This is followed by codes that capture phonological phenomena observed in the child's utterance. An almost complete list of these codes follows. Not all the utterances in the files have been coded exhaustively, nor have all the phonological processes been captured by a code.
%phm codes:

1	consonant substitution
1I	initial consonant,
1m	medial consonant
1f	final consonant
1:voc	consonant is vocalized

2	vowel substitution
2s	stressed vowel
2us	unstressed vowel
2d	diphthong
3	assimilation
3R	assimilation from right to left
3L	assimilation from left to right
4	vowel harmony
4s	stressed vowel is trigger
4u	unstressed vowel is trigger
5	cluster phenomena
5I	cluster in initial position
5m	cluster in medial position
5f	cluster in final position
5:r	cluster reduction
5:f	consonant fusion
5:sub	cluster substitution
5:syll	cluster syllabification
5:ok	cluster is intact
5:del	cluster is deleted
6	metathesis
7	deletion of consonant, i, m, or f
8	reduplication
9	additional consonant, i, m or f
10	deletion of vowel
A	less syllables than in target
B	extra syllable
C	stress error
D	change in CV structure
E	syllable weakening
F	syllable strengthening
VC	vowel-consonant assimilation

Publications using these data should cite:

Fikkert, P. (1994), *On the acquisition of prosodic structure*. The Hague: Holland Academic Graphics.
Levelt, C. (1994), *On the acquisition of place*. The Hague: Holland Academic Graphics.

Dutch – Gillis

Steven Gillis
University of Antwerp
Germaanse – Linguistiek
Universiteitsplein 1
B-2610 Wilrijk Belgium
gillis@uia.ac.be

This directory contains a longitudinal corpus from a boy learning Dutch. The corpus was donated to the CHILDES by Steven Gillis, Department of Germanic Linguistics, University of Antwerp, Belgium. The data are in CHAT format without English glosses.

The child, Maarten, was a Flemish boy learning Dutch. Biweekly videotapings were taken at the child's home between the ages of 0;11.15 and 1;11.28. Recordings began when the child's vocalizations exhibited what Dore, Franklin, Miller, and Ramer (1976) called phonetically consistent forms. They lasted until the child's MLU exceeded 1.5 for three consecutive sessions. The entire corpus consists of 29,324 intelligible child utterances. The child was recorded for an average of 3 hours a week for a total of 104 hours of recording (average: 1:18 hours per recording, with a range of 0:15:18 hours to 3:44:52 hours). The sessions included interactions between the child and an adult (usually his mother) as well as solitary play. All recordings were made in an unstructured regular home setting.

Table 87: Gillis Files

File	Age	Length	# utts	File	Age	Length	# utts
66	1;09.21	2:30:48	515	73	1;10.19	3:29:23	1377
67	1;09.23	1:48:49	302	74	1;10.25	2:53:33	982
68	1;09.27	1:58:40	430	75	1;11.01	2:57:02	1037
69	1;10.01	3:44:52	1061	76	1;11.04	3:05:18	1085
70	1;10.03	1:52:12	803	77	1;11.08	3:05:18	1176
71	1;10.10	2:29:46	624	78	1;11.15	1:53:51	661
72	1;10.14	3:29:51	1369	79	1;11.27	3:05:18	n.t.

The video recordings were transcribed according to the CHAT conventions and include the child's vocalizations in Dutch UNIBET transcription on the %pho tier. There are no adult glosses of the child's utterances. The transcripts also include the adults' utterances in normal graphemic transcription on the main tier and the child's and the adults' nonverbal behavior (gestures, gaze direction, object manipulation), notes on the synchronization of the verbal and the nonverbal behaviors, and description of the context. All this information can be found on the %sit tier, which is at the present written in Dutch.

In the %sit line, dashes separate actions. The match of actions to the phonology is sometimes indicated. Three-letter codes indicate the actor and the addressee. For example, MXA means that M did X to A. MXA &1 MYB means that M did X to A and while this is going on M does Y to B.

Publications using these data should cite:

Schaerlaekens, A., & Gillis, S. (1987). *De taalverwerving van het kind: een hernieuwde orientatie in het Nederlandstalig onderzoeks*. Groningen: Wolters-Noordhoff.

Dutch – Groningen

Gerard Bol
bol@let.rug.nl

Evelien Krikhaar

Frank Wijnen
Department of Linguistics
University of Groningen
Oude Kijk in 't Jatstraat 26
Groningen 9712 EK Netherland
frank.wijnen@let.rug.nl

This corpus contains longitudinal data from seven Dutch children (six boys and one girl) between 1;05 and 3;07. The data (208 audio recordings totaling more than 170 hours) have been gathered in a research project supported by the Dutch Organisation for Scientific Research (NWO) grants to Gerard Bol (300-174-005), Evelien Krikhaar (560-256-065), and Frank Wijnen (300-174-006). In this research there has been assistance from Marjan Bosje, Caroline Elskamp, Puck Goossens, Wenckje Jongstra, and Paulien Rijkhoek. All recordings contain spontaneous speech of the children in an unstructured regular home setting, talking with their father or mother and an investigator.

The tables present data for Abel, Daan, Iris, Josse, Matthijs, Peter, and Tomas, preceded by information concerning the compiler and the independent coder, the recording time and the biographical data of the child. Some audio recordings are not transcribed as a result of poor recording quality or other technical problems. This is indicated by nwo (= not written out). The file names give the children's ages in years, months, and days.

The Abel Files

These files were compiled by Gerard Bol and checked by Paulien Rijkhoek and Marjan Bosje. Each transcription is based on a 45-minute audio recording. Abel, born 31-OCT-1990, was the first male child of Jeanet (mother) and Arjen (father). Both parents were university educated. Their place of residence was Amsterdam. The mother was the primary caretaker, the father worked full-time. Abel attended a toddler's play group three days a week. On 23-MAY-1993 a second child (Marijn, boy) was born.

Table 88: Abel Files

No	Age	File	No	Age	File
01	1;10.30	abe11030.cha	15	2;07.15	abe20715.cha
02	1;11.12	abe11112.cha	16	2;07.29	abe20729.cha
03	1;11.26	abe11126.cha	17	2;08.13	abe20813.cha
04	2;00.11	abe20011.cha	18	2;10.00	abe21000.cha
05	2;01.02	abe20102.cha	19	2;10.14	abe21014.cha
06	2;01.16	abe20116.cha	20	2;10.28	abe21028.cha
07	2;02.19	abe20219.cha	21	2;11.10	abe21110.cha
08	2;03.02	abe20302.cha	22	3;00.02	abe30002.cha
09	2;03.23	abe20323.cha	23	3;00.23	abe30023.cha
10	2;04.09	abe20409.cha	24	3;01.07	abe30107.cha
11	2;04.23	abe20423.cha	25	3;01.21	abe30121.cha
12	2;05.06	abe20506.cha	26	3;02.11	abe30211.cha
13	2;05.27	abe20527.cha	27	3;03.08	abe30308.cha
14	2;06.11	abe20611.cha	28	3;04.01	abe30401.cha

The Daan Files

The Daan files were compiled by Paulien Rijkhoek and checked by Puck Goossens. Each transcription is based on a 45 to 60 minutes audio recording. Daan (6-SEP-1991, boy) was the first child of Josje (mother) and Rob (father). Both parents were university students (Dutch literature and Law, respectively). In addition, Daan's mother had a part-time administration job at home. His father worked mornings but was at home in the afternoon. Strictly speaking, there was no primary caretaker. The family lived in Groningen. In September 1993, the family moved to another house. On 18-DEC-1993, a baby sister (Rosa) was born. Beginning in January 1994 (after transcription 32), Daan visited a play group (for 2- to 4-year olds) on two weekday mornings. Daan's mother was almost always present during the recordings, because they usually took place in the morning.

Table 89: Daan Files

No	Age	File	No	Age	File
01	1;07.23	nwo	19	2;05.25	daa20525.cha
02	1;08.13	nwo	20	2;06.11	daa20611.cha
03	1;08.21	daa10821.cha	21	2;06.25	daa20625.cha
04	1;09.09	daa10909.cha	22	2;07.15	daa20715.cha
05	1;10.01	daa11001.cha	23	2;07.24	daa20724.cha
06	1;10.16	daa11016.cha	24	2;08.13	daa20813.cha
07	1;11.21	daa11121.cha	25	2;08.27	daa20827.cha
08	2;00.04	daa20004.cha	26	2;09.10	daa20910.cha
09	2;00.22	daa20022.cha	27	2;10.14	daa21014.cha
10	2;00.29	daa20029.cha	28	2;10.28	daa21028.cha
11	2;01.21	daa20121.cha	29	2;11.19	daa21119.cha
12	2;02.02	daa20202.cha	30	3;00.01	daa30001.cha
13	2;02.16	daa20216.cha	31	3;00.15	daa30015.cha
14	2;03.04	daa20304.cha	32	3;01.00	daa30100.cha
15	2;04.00	daa20400.cha	33	3;01.14	daa30114.cha
16	2;04.14	daa20414.cha	34	3;01.28	daa30128.cha
17	2;04.28	daa20428.cha	35	3;02.25	daa30225.cha
18	2;05.11	daa20511.cha	36	3;03.30	daa30330.cha

The Iris Files

These files were compiled by Evelien Krikhaar and Frank Wijnen. Transcriptions are based on 30 to 75 minutes of audio recording. These data have not been checked by an independent coder. Iris, born 16-JUL-1990, was the eldest female child of Hennie (father) and Floortje (mother). Hennie was a system manager at the university computer center, Floortje was an artist. Hennie and Floortje had one other child, Matthijs (a boy), born 13-FEB-1992. They lived in Utrecht. Floortje was the primary caretaker. Hennie worked full-time. Three days a week, Floortje worked in her workshop. On those days, the children stay at a daycare center.

Not long after the first taping session, Iris developed middle ear problems, which turned out to be rather persistent. She suffered from several bouts of otitis media. Verbal communication appeared to be hindered. On 13-OCT-1992 she had her tonsils out. On 15-APR-1993 tympanic tubes were placed on both sides. Since then, speech communication appeared to have significantly improved. Nonetheless, her linguistic development appeared to be somewhat retarded.

Table 90: Iris Files

No	Age	File	No	Age	File
01	2;01.01	iri20101.cha	18	2;10.08	iri21008.cha
02	2;01.22	nwo	19	2;10.22	iri21022.cha
03	2;02.06	nwo	20	2;11.05	iri21105.cha
04	2;02.21	nwo	21	2;11.12	iri21112.cha
05	2;03.05	nwo	22	3;00.17	iri30017.cha
06	2;03.19	nwo	23	3;01.00	iri30100.cha
07	2;04.02	nwo	24	3;01.14	iri30114.cha
08	2;04.22	nwo	25	3;01.28	iri30128.cha
09	2;05.12	iri20512.cha	26	3;02.11	iri30211.cha
10	2;05.26	nwo	27	3;03.09	iri30309.cha
11	2;06.09	nwo	28	3;03.23	iri30323.cha
12	2;07.06	nwo	29	3;04.06	iri30406.cha
13	2;08.13	iri20813.cha	30	3;04.20	iri30420.cha
14	2;08.29	nwo	31	3;05.04	iri30504.cha
15	2;09.10	iri20910.cha	32	3;05.18	iri30518.cha
16	2;09.26	iri20926.cha	33	3;06.15	iri30615.cha
17	2;10.01	iri21001.cha			

The Josse files

These files were compiled by Gerard Bol and checked by Caroline Elskamp. Each transcription is based on a 45 minute audio recording. Josse, born 22-SEP-1990, the first male child of Hanneke (mother) and Ab (father). Both parents were university educated. Their place of residence was Amsterdam. The mother and the father both worked part-time and took care of Josse one day a week (plus week-ends). Josse visited daycare center three days a week. On 16-JUL-1993 a second child (Ruben, a boy) was born.

Table 91: Josse Files

No	Age	File	No	Age	File
01	2;00.07	jos20007.cha	15	2;08.04	jos20804.cha
02	2;00.21	jos20021.cha	16	2;08.18	jos20818.cha
03	2;01.12	jos20112.cha	17	2;09.02	jos20902.cha
04	2;01.26	jos20126.cha	18	2;09.16	jos20916.cha
05	2;02.08	jos20208.cha	19	2;11.09	jos21109.cha
06	2;02.22	jos20222.cha	20	2;11.23	jos21123.cha
07	2;03.28	jos20328.cha	21	3;00.06	jos30006.cha
08	2;04.11	jos20411.cha	22	3;00.20	jos30020.cha
09	2;04.25	jos20425.cha	23	3;01.10	jos30110.cha
10	2;05.11	jos20511.cha	24	3;01.24	jos30124.cha
11	2;06.01	jos20601.cha	25	3;02.15	jos30215.cha
12	2;06.22	jos20622.cha	26	3;02.29	jos30229.cha
13	2;07.06	jos20706.cha	27	3;03.27	jos30327.cha
14	2;07.20	jos20720.cha	28	3;04.17	jos30417.cha

The Matthijs files

These files were compiled by Evelien Krikhaar and checked by Marjan Bosje. Each transcription is based on a 45 to 60 minutes audio recording. Matthijs, born 27-MAR-1991, was the eldest male child of Marlies and Boudewijn. Marlies had a part-time job as an or-thopedagogical therapist. Boudewijn was a musician (conductor and pianist) and worked at home when Marlies was working. Marlies was the primary caretaker. From the age of 2;0 Matthijs went to a daycare center for two mornings a week. Marlies and Boudewijn had one other child, Frederike (girl), who was born 5-DEC-1992. The family lived in Utrecht.

The Peter files

These files were compiled by Frank Wijnen and checked by Paulien Rijkhoek. Each

Table 92: Matthijs Files

No	Age	File	No	Age	File
01	1;05.22	nwo	27	2;06.11	mat20611.cha
02	1;06.03	nwo	28	2;06.19	mat20619.cha
03	1;06.22		29	2;07.02	mat20702.cha
04	1;07.07	nwo	30	2;07.09	mat20709.cha
05	1;07.21	nwo	31	2;07.23	mat20723.cha
06	1;08.03	nwo	32	2;08.05	mat20805.cha
07	1;09.02	nwo	33	2;08.20	mat20820.cha
08	1;09.15	nwo	34	2;09.15	mat20915.cha
09	1;09.30	nwo	35	2;09.26	mat20926.cha
10	1;10.13	mat11013.cha	36	2;10.08	mat21008.cha
11	1;10.27	nwo	37	2;10.22	mat21022.cha
12	1;11.10	mat11110.cha	38	2;11.03	mat21103.cha
13	1;11.24	mat11124.cha	39	2;11.19	mat21119.cha
14	2;00.09	mat20009.cha	40	3;00.09	mat30009.cha
15	2;00.24	mat20024.cha	41	3;00.20	mat30020.cha
16	2;01.07	mat20107.cha	42	3;01.04	mat30104.cha
17	2;01.21	mat20121.cha	43	3;01.13	mat30113.cha
18	2;02.09	mat20209.cha	44	3;01.24	mat30124.cha
19	2;02.20	mat20220.cha	45	3;02.12	mat30212.cha
20	2;03.01	mat20301.cha	46	3;02.29	mat30229.cha
21	2;03.19	mat20319.cha	47	3;03.05	mat30305.cha
22	2;04.24	mat20424.cha	48	3;04.09	mat30409.cha
23	2;05.01	mat20501.cha	49	3;04.26	mat30426.cha
24	2;05.13	mat20513.cha	50	3;05.13	mat30513.cha
25	2;05.26	mat20526.cha	51	3;06.03	mat30603.cha
26	2;06.03	mat20603.cha	52	3;07.02	mat30702.cha

transcription is based on a 45 to 60 minute audio recording. Peter, born 19-APR-1991, the only male child of Jeroen and Leida, both university educated (lawyer and veterinarian, respectively). They lived in Bunnik, a small town some 5 km. from Utrecht. Leida was the primary caretaker. Jeroen worked full-time.

Table 93: Peter Files

No	Age	File	No	Age	File
01	1;05.02	nwo	16	2;00.28	pet20028.cha
02	1;05.09	pet10509.cha	17	2;01.13	pet20113.cha
03	1;06.00	pet10600.cha	18	2;01.26	pet20126.cha
04	1;06.28	pet10628.cha	19	2;02.03	pet20203.cha
05	1;07.18	pet10718.cha	20	2;03.07	pet20307.cha
06	1;08.02	pet10802.cha	21	2;03.21	pet20321.cha
07	1;08.16	pet10816.cha	22	2;04.12	pet20412.cha
08	1;09.06	pet10906.cha	23	2;04.19	pet20419.cha
09	1;09.20	pet10920.cha	24	2;05.03	pet20503.cha
10	1;10.03	pet11003.cha	25	2;05.15	pet20515.cha
11	1;10.17	pet11017.cha	26	2;05.29	pet20529.cha
12	1;11.03	pet11103.cha	27	2;07.14	pet20714.cha
13	1;11.10	pet11110.cha	28	2;08.22	pet20822.cha
14	1;11.25	pet11125.cha	29	2;09.26	nwo
15	2;00.07	pet20007.cha			

The Tomas files

These files were compiled by Caroline Elskamp and checked by Paulien Rijkhoek. Tomas, born 3-SEP-1991, was the first male child of Nienke (mother) and Be (father). Both parents were university educated. They lived in Groningen. The mother and the father both worked part-time and took care of Tomas one or two days a week (plus weekends). On 5-OCT-1994 a second child, Sam (boy), was born.

Table 94: Tomas Files

No	Age	File	No	Age	File
01	1;07.05	tom10705.cha	15	2;03.20	tom20320.cha
02	1;07.14	tom10714.cha	16	2;04.17	tom20417.cha
03	1;08.03	tom10803.cha	17	2;05.07	tom20507.cha
04	1;08.16	tom10816.cha	18	2;06.00	tom20600.cha
05	1;09.00	tom10900.cha	19	2;06.14	tom20614.cha
06	1;09.14	tom10914.cha	20	2;07.10	tom20710.cha
07	1;09.27	tom10927.cha	21	2;08.01	tom20801.cha
08	1;10.11	tom11011.cha	22	2;08.27	tom20827.cha
09	2;00.13	tom20013.cha	23	2;09.12	tom20912.cha
10	2;00.27	tom20027.cha	24	2;09.26	tom20926.cha
11	2;01.12	nwo	25	2;10.10	tom21010.cha
12	2;02.01	tom20201.cha	26	2;10.24	tom21024.cha
13	2;02.15	tom20215.cha	27	3;01.02	tom30102.cha
14	2;03.06	tom20306.cha			

Publication using these data should cite one of these studies:

Bol, G. W. (1995), Implicational scaling in child language acquisition: the order of production of Dutch verb constructions, In M. Verrips & F. Wijnen (Eds.), *Papers from The Dutch-German Colloquium on Language Acquisition*, Amsterdam Series in Child Language Development, 3, Amsterdam: Institute for General Linguistics.

Bol, G. W. (1996), Optional subjects in Dutch child language, In C. Koster & F. Wijnen (Eds.), *Proceedings of the Groningen Assembly on Language Acquisition*, 125–135.

Ruhland, R., Wijnen, F. & van Geert, P.(1995), An exploration into the application of dynamic systems modeling to language acquisition. In M. Verrips & F. Wijnen (Eds.), *Approaches to parameter setting*.

Wijnen, F. (1993a), Verb placement and morphology in child Dutch: do lexical errors flag grammatical development? *Antwerp Papers in Linguistics, 74,* 79–92.

Wijnen, F. (1995a), Clause structure develops, In M. Verrips & F. Wijnen (Eds.). *Papers from the Dutch-German Colloquium on Language Acquisition* Amsterdam Series in Child Language Development, 3, Amsterdam: Institute for General Linguistics.

Wijnen, F. (1995b). Incremental acquisition of phrase structure. In J. N. Beckman (Ed.), *Proceedings of the North East Linguistic Society 25.* Amherst, MA: GLSA Publications, vol. 2, p. 105–118.

Wijnen, F. & G. Bol (1993). The escape from the optional infinitive stage. In A. de Boer,

J. de Jong & R. Landeweerd (Eds.) *Language and Cognition 3*, University of Groningen, Dept. of Linguistics.

Wijnen, F. The temporal interpretation of Dutch children's root infinitivals. *Proceedings of CLS 1996.*

Wijnen, F. Temporal reference and eventivity in root infinitivals. MIT Working Papers in Linguistics.

Wijnen, F. & M. Verrips, The Acquisition of Dutch Syntax, In S. Gillis & A. De Houwer (Eds.), *The Acquisition of Dutch*. Amsterdam/Baltimore: Benjamins.

Dutch – Schaerlaekens

A. M. Schaerlaekens
Centrum voor Taalverwervingonderzoek
Kapucignenvoor 33
Leuven, 3000 Belgium

These data were originally collected by A. M. Schaerlaekens in 1969 and 1970. The data were collected by recording the spontaneous dialogues of two sets of triplets. For this purpose, the children were wearing small, wireless transmitters which were sewn into their aprons. Further details of the procedure can be found in Schaerlaekens (1973).

Participants

The original database consists of the spontaneous language of two triplets between the ages of 1;10.18 and 3;1.7 for the first set and 1;6.17 and 2;10.23 for the second set. Gijs, Joost, and Katelijne are nonidentical triplets, two boys and one girl. They were born in the following order: Joost, Katelijne, and Gijs. At 1;6, they were administered the Gesell Developmental Scales, showing no perceptible differences as to psychomotor development. At 4;2 they participated in a nonverbal intelligence test (Snijders-Oomen), which yielded an above average IQ. The children were recorded at monthly intervals. Due to problems with the equipment, however, there are no data available for particular months.

Arnold, Diederik and Maria are also nonidentical triplets, two boys and a girl. They were born in the following order: Diederik, Arnold, Maria. When they were 1;6, the Gesell Developmental Scales were administered, showing no perceptible differences as to psychomotor development. At the age of 4;2 they participated in a nonverbal intelligence test (Snijders-Oomen), which yielded an above average IQ.

Table 95: Data For Gijs, Joost, and Katelijne

Session	Date	Age
1	1-MAR-1969	1;8.29
2	29-APR-1969	1;9.24
3	29-MAY-1969	1;10.24
4	10-JUN-1969	1;11.5
5	2-JUL-1969	1;11.27
6	17-JUL-1969	2;0.12
7	23-SEP-1969	2;2.18
8	29-DEC-1969	2;5.24

Table 95: Data For Gijs, Joost, and Katelijne

Session	Date	Age
9	28-JAN-1970	2;6.23
10	24-FEB-1970	2;7.19
11	24-MAR-1970	2;8.19
12	28-MAY-1970	2;10.23

Table 96: Data For Arnold, Diederik, and Maria

Session	Date	Age
1	11-JUL-1969	1;10.18
2	11-SEP-1969	2;0.19
3	25-SEP-1969	2;1.2
4	16-OCT-1969	2;1.23
5	25-NOV-1969	2;3.2
6	6-JAN-1970	2;4.14
7	10-FEB-1970	2;5.18
8	17-MAR-1970	2;6.22
9	23-APR-1970	2;8.1
10	21-MAY-1970	2;8.28
11	11-JUN-1970	2;9.19
12	21-JUL-1970	2;10.28
13	30-SEP-1970	3;1.7

Transcription and Coding

The speech of the children was graphemically transcribed. The original transcription can be found on the %tra tier in the files. The main tiers contain a conventionalized transcription. Unfortunately the language of the children's parents was not transcribed and the audiotapes could not be used anymore for transcription in 1992.

The data were reformatted into CHAT in 1993. On the %mor-tier, words are coded for their part-of-speech and for their morphosyntactic properties. The coding was done with a Dutch version of the MOR program. A preliminary syntactic coding was performed using the following categories and abbreviations:

S	Subject
D	Direct Object
I	Indirect Object
P	Prepositional Phrase
C	Complement
B	Adverbial Complement
Neg	Negation
X	Other
V	Main (lexical) verb
Aux	Auxiliary
Cop	Copula

For each of the verbal categories the markers ""f" for "finite verbform" and "nf" for "non-finite verbform" were added.

Agreement was coded on the %agr tier. The following categories (and numeric codes) were used:

1	correct agreement
2	incorrect agreement
3	no agreement: subjectless sentence
4	other (a.o. verbless sentences)

Publications using these data should cite:

Schaerlaekens, A. M. (1973). *The two-word sentence in child language.* The Hague: Mouton.

Additional relevant publications include:

Gillis, S., & Verhoeven, J. (1992). Developmental aspects of syntactic complexity in two triplets. *Antwerp Papers in Linguistics, 69.*

Schaerlaekens, A., & Gillis, S. (1987). *De taalverwerving van het kind: een hernieuwde orientatie in het Nederlandstalig onderzoeks.* Groningen: Wolters-Noordhoff.

Schaerlaekens, A. M. (1972). A generative transformational model of language acquisition. *Cognition, 2,* 371–376.

Dutch – Utrecht

Loekie Elbers
Department of Psychology
University of Utrecht
Heidelberglaan 1
3584 CS Utrecht Netherlands
elbers@fsw.ruu.nl

Wijnen, Frank
Department of Linguistics
University of Groningen
Oude Kijk in 't Jatstraat 26
Groningen 9712 EK Netherland
frank.wijnen@let.rug.nl

The Utrecht corpus is based on weekly home tapings of two Dutch boys, Thomas and Hein, between the ages of roughly 2;3 and 3;1. The corpus was compiled by Loekie Elbers and Frank Wijnen (University of Utrecht) with assistance from Joke van Marle, Trudy van der Horst, Herma Veenhof-Haan, and Inge Boers. The recordings were made by the children's mothers. The data were used in two projects focusing on the relation between language acquisition and developmental disfluency. Both Hein and Thomas showed an increase of disfluency around age 2;7-2;8. In Thomas, the disfluency was mild, in Hein it was severe. In both children, the frequency of disfluencies dropped subsequently, until it reached a level comparable to that in the initial samples.

The recordings were generally made in unstructured settings. Usually, the target child and an adult interlocutor (mostly the mother) were engaged in some everyday routine, such as having breakfast, playing, getting dressed, or looking through picture books. Both children were regularly presented with a particular picture book, entitled "The little giantess", in order to attain some standardization of the recording conditions in some sessions. The use of this book is indicated in the @Situation or @Activities header. In most instances where the book is used, the transcriptions contain explicit references to the picture book pictures by means of @Stim headers. In some of the recordings of Thomas, his mother uses a puppet (Kermit the Frog) to stimulate (or motivate) the conversation.

An overview of the available material and some indications of progress in processing the data follows. Some 71 hours of recordings were collected. All usable samples of Thomas and Hein are transcribed. Generally, samples involving other children in addition to the target child were not transcribed.

The number and character of reliability checks on the transcriptions are indicated by the number after "lit" [= "literal transcription"] in the "Progress" column. A zero (0) indicates that the file contains an initial transcription that has not been checked. One (1) means that the initial transcription is checked, either by the person who made the initial transcription, or by somebody else. A two (2) indicates that the session was transcribed by two independent coders, and that the final version was constructed by means of a consensus procedure. In the "lit2" files, data on which the first and second transcriber could not reach an agreement are represented with "xxx." The presence of "hes" or "mor" in the "Progress" column indicates that a full %hes line was coded for hesitations or that a %mor line was coded for morphology. The presence of other participants, as well as other salient or exceptional characteristics of the tapings are mentioned in the "Remarks" column.

Table 97: Thomas Files

Tape	Dur	Date	Age	Progress	Remarks
T01	60	800716	2;3.22	lit2	mor hes
		800717	2;3.23	lit2	mor hes
		800719	2;3.25	lit2	mor hes
T02	90	800722	2;3.28	lit2	mor hes
		800724	2;4.0	lit2	mor hes
		800727	2;4.3	lit2	mor hes
T03	60	800730	2;4.6	lit2	mor hes
		800801	2;4.8	lit2	mor hes
T04	90	800801	contin	lit2	mor hes
		800803	2;4.10	lit2	mor hes
		800804	2;4.11	lit2	mor hes
		800807	2;4.14	lit2	mor hes
		800809	2;4.16	lit2	mor hes
T05	60	800819	2;4.26	lit0	+Doortje
		800820	2;4.27	lit0	
		800823	2;4.30	lit0	
T06	60	800827	2;5.3	lit2	mor hes
		800828	2;5.4	lit2	mor hes
		800830	2;5.6	lit2	mor hes
T07	60	800903	2;5.10	lit0	
		800904	2;5.11	lit0	
		800907	2;5.14	lit0	

Table 97: Thomas Files

Tape	Dur	Date	Age	Progress	Remarks
		800908	2;5.15	lit0	
T08a	45	800909	2;5.16		not transcribed+Hella
T09	60	800910	2;5.17	lit2	mor hes
		800912	2;5.19	lit2	mor hes
		800914	2;5.21	lit2	mor hes
T10	60	800918	2;5.25	lit2	mor hes
		800920	2;5.27	lit2	mor hes
T08b	45	801019	2;6.25	lit0	
		801022	2;6.28	lit0	
T11	60	801025	2;7.1	lit2	mor hes
		801026	2;7.2	lit2	mor hes
T12	60	801101	2;7.7	lit2	mor hes
		801102	2;7.8	lit2	mor hes
T13	60	801102	contin	lit1	mor hes
		801106	2;7.12	lit1	mor hes
		801108	2;7.14	lit1	mor hes
T14	60	801114	2;7.20	lit1	mor hes
		801116	2;7.22	lit1	mor hes
T15	60	801121	2;7.27	lit1	mor hes
		801122	2;7.28	lit1	mor hes
T16	60	801126	2;8.2	lit2	mor hes
		801129	2;8.5	lit2	mor hes
T17	60	801130	2;8.6	lit2	mor hes
		801202	2;8.8	lit2	mor hes +Doortje
		801204	2;8.10	lit2	mor hes
		801205	2;8.11		not transcribed
		801209	2;8.15	lit2	mor hes

Table 97: Thomas Files

Tape	Dur	Date	Age	Progress	Remarks
T18	60	801210	2;8.16	lit2	mor hes
		801211	2;8.17	lit2	mor hes
		801213	2;8.19	lit2	mor hes
		801214	2;8.20	lit2	mor hes
		801217	2;8.22	lit2	mor hes
T19	30	801218	2;8.24	lit2	mor hes
		801220	2;8.26	lit2	mor hes
T20	60	801226	2;9.2	lit2	mor hes
		801228	2;9.4	lit2	mor hes
		801229	2;9.5	lit2	mor hes
T21	60	810101	2;9.8	lit1	mor hes
		810103	2;9.10	lit1	mor hes
		810105	2;9.12	lit0	
		810108	2;9.15	lit0	
T21A	60	810117	2;9.24		not transcribed +Kim
		810119	2;9.26	lit0	T-O-T
T22	60	810126	2;10.2	lit1	mor hes
		810128	2;10.4	lit1	mor hes
		810130	2;10.6	lit0	
		810201	2;10.8	lit0	
T23	60	810207	2;10.14	lit0	
		810208	2;10.15	lit0	
		810212	2;10.19	lit0	
T24	60	810216	2;10.23	lit2	mor hes
		810219	2;10.26	lit2	mor hes +Opa
T25	60	810222	2;10.29	lit2	mor hes
		810223	2;10.30	lit2	mor hes

Table 97: Thomas Files

Tape	Dur	Date	Age	Progress	Remarks
		810225	2;11.1	lit2	mor hes
		810226	2;11.2	lit2	mor hes
		810304	2;11.8	lit2	mor hes
T26	60	810314	2;11.18	lit2	mor hes
		810315	2;11.19	lit2	mor hes

Table 98: Hein Files

Tape	Dur	Date	Age	Progress	Remarks
H01	60	800725	2;4.11	lit1	mor hes
		800728	2;4.14	lit1	mor hes
		800730	2;4.16	lit1	mor hes
		800801	2;4.18	lit1	mor hes
		800804	2;4.21	lit1	mor hes
H02	60	800804	contin	lit1	mor hes
		800806	2;4.23	lit1	mor hes
		800808	2;4.25	lit1	mor hes
H03	60	800825	2;5.11	lit1	
		800828	2;5.14	lit1	mor hes
		800831	2;5.17	lit1	
H04	60	800902	2;5.19	lit1	mor hes
		800904	2;5.21	lit1	
		800907	2;5.24	lit0	
H05	60	800916	2;6.2	lit1	mor hes
		800919	2;6.5	lit0	
		800921	2;6.7	lit0	
H06	60	800922	2;6.8	lit1	mor hes

Table 98: Hein Files

Tape	Dur	Date	Age	Progress	Remarks
		800924	2;6.10	lit0	
		800928	2;6.14	lit0	
H07	60	800930	2;6.16	lit1	mor hes
		801003	2;6.19	lit0	
		801007	2;6.23	lit0	
H08	60	801011	2;6.27	lit1	mor hes
		801012	2;6.28	lit0	
		801015	2;7.1	lit1	mor hes
H09	60	801019	2;7.5	lit1	mor hes
		801021	2;7.7	lit1	mor hes
		801026	2;7.12		not transcribed +Susan
H10	60	801028	2;7.14	lit1	mor hes
		801031	2;7.17	lit1	mor hes
		801103	2;7.20	lit1	mor hes
		801105	2;7.22	lit1	mor hes
H11	60	801110	2;7.27	lit1	mor hes
		801113	2;7.30	lit1	mor hes
		801116	2;8.2	lit1	mor hes
H12	60	801118	2;8.4	lit1	mor hes
		801121	2;8.7	lit0	
		801124	2;8.10	lit0	
H13	60	801128?	2;8.14	lit1	mor hes
		801130	2;8.16	lit1	mor hes
		801202	2;8.18	lit0	
H14	60	801204	2;8.20	lit1	mor hes
		801207	2;8.23	lit0	
		801209	2;8.25	lit0	

Table 98: Hein Files

Tape	Dur	Date	Age	Progress	Remarks
		801212	2;8.28	lit0	
H15	60	801215	2;9.1	lit1	mor hes
		801221	2;9.7	lit0	
		801225	2;9.11	lit0	
H16	60	801228	2;9.14	lit1	mor hes
		801230	2;9.16	lit0	
		810108	2;9.25	lit0	
H17	60	810111	2;9.28	lit1	mor hes
		810114	2;10.0	lit0	
		810119	2;10.5	lit0	
H18	60	810121?	2;10.7	lit1	mor hes
		810124?	2;10.10	lit0	
		810126	2;10.12	lit0	
H19	60	810202	2;10.19	lit1	mor hes
		810207	2;10.24	lit1	mor hes
		810209	2;10.26	lit1	mor hes
		810213	2;10.30	lit0	
H20	60	810215	2;11.1	lit1	mor hes
		810216	2;11.2	lit0	
		810217	2;11.3	lit0	
		810221	2;11.7	lit0	
		810222	2;11.8	lit0	
H21	60	810226	2;11.12	lit1	mor hes
		810302	2;11.16	lit0	
		810304	2;11.18	lit0	
H22	60	810312	2;11.26	lit1	mor hes
H23	60	810321	3;0.7	lit1	mor hes

Table 98: Hein Files

Tape	Dur	Date	Age	Progress	Remarks
		810325	3;0.11	lit1	mor hes
		810403	3;0.20	lit1	mor hes
H24	60	810409	3;0.26	lit1	mor hes
		810413	3;0.30	lit1	mor hes
		810417	3;1.3	lit1	mor hes
		810423	3;1.9	lit1	mor hes
H25	60	810423	contin	lit1	mor hes
		810430	3;1.16	lit1	mor hes
		810508	3;1.24	lit1	mor hes

The files are labeled in accordance with the date of recording. For instance, t800716.cha represents the recording of Thomas made on July 16, 1980.

Hesitation Coding

The main lines of both the children and adult speakers contain various codes for non-fluencies and hesitations. Usually, the standard CHAT diacritics are used. You may however also find some nonstandard codes, such as [$I] (interrupted word) or [$B] (block). Additionally, these square-bracketed entries indicating aspects of prosody are provided:

[=! rising]	rising contour
[=! falling]	falling contour
[=! contin]	continuation contour
[=! f]	loud
[=! ff]	very loud
[=! p]	soft
[=! pp]	very soft (whispered)

The codes included on the %hes line and their meanings are as follows:

$REP	repetitions
$rep|wrd	word repetition
$rep|wst	word string repetition
$rep|isg	initial segment(s) repetition
$rep|isy	initial syllable repetition

$rep|cpx	a composite of several of the above
$COR	self-corrections
$cor|dx_ry	a self-correction with delay of x words and retracing of y words
$WBR	word break
$BLK	block
$UPS	unfilled (silent) pause
$FPS	filled pause (uh)
$SSI	senseless sound insertion

For $UPS, $FPS, and $SSI, scoping numbers indicate the position of the word following the disfluency. For $WBR and $BLK, the scoping number indicates the position of the affected word. For $COR and $REP, the scoping number indicates the beginning of the repetition or retracing.

If needed for the disambiguation and interpretation of the text or the nonfluencies and errors, phonetic UNIBET-transcriptions are supplied on the %pho tier. The UNIBET used in this corpus conforms by and large to the table for Dutch in the manual. Please note that not all speech errors have yet been explicitly coded on %err tiers, particularly in the corpus of Thomas.

Morphological Coding

In the corrected transcriptions (lit1 and lit2), word classes of the words produced by the children are coded on %mor tiers in a one-to-one fashion. This is indicated by the entry "mor" in the "Progress" column. The morphological codes have the general format:

<i>$AAA=BBB|CCC_DDD_etc

<i>	scoping
AAA	syntactic class, such as DET.
	Also "zero derivations" may be marked by this part of the code, e.g., "N=V" = nominalized verb.
BBB	lexical class, such as N, V or PREP.
CCC	subclassifications for tense, person

The code COMM stands for Dutch "common" gender. The article "een" (a) is usually transcribed as "'n," in order to distinguish it from "een" (one). The transcription of "het" may be "'t," depending on the pronunciation.

Phonetics

In principle, phonetic transcription in the Utrecht corpus follows the IPA to ASCII conversion table in the CHILDES manual. However, some adaptations were necessary, because we wanted to be able to transcribe some regularly used sounds that are not phonemic in Dutch. The additional sounds used were:

Table 99: Sounds

Sound	Definition
F	bilabial, unv.
T	dental, unvoiced
D	dental, voiced
C	velar, unvoiced
W	bilabial, voiced
R	uvular, unvoiced, trill
9	uvular, glide
J (old: jn)	palatal, voiced
8 (old: oe)	half low, middle, rounded bUs
au	pAUw
ei	gEIt

The Book

The book is *De kleine reuzin* by Philippe Dumas ["The little giantess," translated from the French "La petite geánte" by Thea Schierbeek-Tulleken. Published by Uitgeverij Lotus, Leopoldstraat 43 Antwerpen (Belgium); ISBN 90 6290 572 2].

The story is about two dolls, a girl and a boy, who — together with the little girl that takes care of them — embark on an adventurous trip during the night. The story takes the perspective of the dolls, who are described as children. The little girl is seen as a giantess, hence the title of the book. During the nocturnal adventure, however, the little girl shrinks to the size of the dolls. The three figures ride out on the back of the family dog and play games, swim, make a bonfire and have a cup of tea with a rabbit family, who happens to be bored to sleep by the sandman telling stories. They return at the crack of dawn. The little girl grows to her usual size again and the three of them are safely in bed when the little girl's mother enters the bedroom with the morning tea.

The book contains 27 pictures, most of which are printed on single pages, so that usually two pictures can be seen simultaneously. In the ensuing descriptions, the boy doll will be referred to as B, the girl doll as G, and the little girl as M. The pictures were assigned numbers according to their order in the book. Each picture in the book is accompanied by a few lines of text of which virtually literal English translations are included in the present file under the TEXT headings.

Frontispiece: A large, wide-open window facing hill slopes with bushes and trees. A large, cratery full moon is in the sky. A little girl, seen from the back, looks out of the window, holding a burning candle in her right hand, the arm stretched. There is a picture on the wall next to the window. Below the picture walks a cat. In the foreground is a pile of books topped by a fish bowl, in which a goldfish swims. A large yellow book leaning against the fish bowl is entitled *De kleine reuzin*. Two dolls are sitting on the floor, halfway between the book pile and the window.

Table 100: Text of *De kleine reuzin*

No.	Picture	Text
1	B and G stand in front of some indoor plants. G has long black hair, B short blond.	Once upon a time, there were two little children who, unbelievably, were so sweet that they never ever broke something or said an ugly word.
2	B and G are sitting on a wooden doll's bed, facing each other.	The girl had black hair and the boy was blond. They had eyes of glass and plastic bellies.
3	M holds B and G in her arms, B on the left side, G on the right. M stands in a nursery room with some toys on the floor and various items on the wall.	In the same house also lived a giantess, who loved them very much...
4	M is seen from the back, she is barefoot and is holding the dolls in an awkward manner: G by the left arm and B by the leg.	...but who sometimes treated them very roughly.
5	B, G, and M are seated at a doll-scaled table on which there are some little saucers and cups. The dolls wear napkins around their necks. M holds a plate on her lap and a spoon in her hand. In the background is a doll's house.	But the worst thing was that she never gave them anything to eat, she only pretended.
6	M is being undressed by her mother. Her mother pulls a dress over her head; she is naked up to the waist. B and G sit on the floor and watch.	Every night other giants came and washed the little giantess and took her to bed.
7	M, B, and G are in M's bed, asleep. The dolls lie next to M, one on each side.	The children slept next to her, each at another side. One left, the other right, just as they felt like.

Table 100: Text of *De kleine reuzin*

No.	Picture	Text
8	A large French style country house with an annex in the middle of a meadow at night. The sky is star-spangled, the moon is up.	But precisely at midnight something miraculous happened: it was very still and very dark and... suddenly the giantess became smaller and smaller, until she was as small as her little friends.
9	[two pages]: An attic. At the left side some paintings or picture frames lean against a wall. The family dog is asleep on the floor in front of the paintings. In the middle stands a large wicker chair. To the right of this, a wooden stair case. M, now doll-sized, B and G pass in front of the banisters, walking toward the downward stairs.	She woke them up and the three of them tip-toe-ed down the stairs.
10	A large refrigerator with an open door, lit on the inside, and filled with various food. G is sitting on B's neck, reaching for a large piece of cake, while M is keeping the door open.	They went to the kitchen to have a bite, they woke up the dog, and then...!
11	M, B, and are G are sitting on the dog's back. They are at a cobble-stoned beach. In the background are some green-topped cliffs.	Then they went outside to begin an exciting adventure.
12	The dog, M, B and are running through a flower-littered meadow.	What fun it is to run through the night with the wind in your hair.
13	M, B, and G are standing among some huge flowers, watching the moon and the stars.	And to watch the stars and catch your breath again.
14	M, B, and G are playing at leap frog with a rabbit in front of the rabbit's hole. The rabbit is in the foreground. M bends while B jumps over her.	Their games were not very silent.
15	An owl flying spreaded-wingedly in front of some shady trees.	To the horror of an old, lonesome owl.
16	M, B, and G are swimming in a lake, their heads and hands protruding from the water.	Luckily, it was a warm night and they could go for a swim in the lake...

Table 100: Text of *De kleine reuzin*

No.	Picture	Text
17	M, B, and G are swimming among a flock of ducks, near the waterside. One duck is seen in the behind, while diving.	...where there were a lot of animals, ducks, and musical frogs.
18	The children are rowing in old shoes, M and B in a large brown one, G in a smaller blue one, past a spoonbill, which is standing on one leg, grooming his feathers.	After that, they rowed to an island in a little boat made from an old shoe.
19	The three are standing around a bonfire on a little island in the middle of the lake. The fire is bright and smoking. Insects are swarming around it. In the background are the silhouettes of four willows against the night sky. In the foreground, a fox, seen on the back, is squatting on the near shore, watching the children.	Where they also made a bonfire, to point the way to lost butterflies.
20	The interior of a rabbit's hole. The three are seen on the face, kneeling on the floor. A tea trolley is in front left. Mother rabbit, wearing a long green dress and an flowery apron, is seen on the back. She carries a tray with a tea pot. There is a brightly colored rug on the floor in front of the children. Behind them, at the far end, is the hole's entrance. The night sky is visible.	At the end of the night they visited the rabbits. They were very nice and asked them whether they would like a cup of tea or perhaps a bowl of onion soup.
21	A brightly lit room in the rabbit's hole. The fire is burning. Five rabbits as well as B, G, and M are gathered around it. The sandman (Klaas Vaak) is leaning against the mantelpiece. Most rabbits have their eyes closed.	What a pity that the sandman was there as well, who was even more boring than the rain. His stories made you fall asleep.
22	The three sit on the branches of a leafless tree. Around them, on other branches, are several crows. Also, there are some nests. The sky is turning lighter..	But at that time the sun almost rose and they had to go back home.
23	The three walk through a green meadow past a huge cow, which is seen from the behind. Her large udder almost touches the ground.	On their way back they saw all kinds of monsters from a long time ago that were waking up.

Table 100: Text of *De kleine reuzin*

No.	Picture	Text
24	(two pages): M, B, and G and the dog walk down a hollow country road. They are seen from the back, having their arms around one another's shoulders. At the left side, a horse and a foal look over a fence. There are three milk containers near the fence. Some rooftops protrude from behind the road banks. In the distance are meadows. The stars are still discernible in a brightening sky.	Hurry, hurry! Make haste! The chickens are already up and about. And the rooster will soon start to crow and wake everybody up.
25	The three are seen en silhouette against a now light blue sky with some purplish clouds half covering the moon sickle. M is now evidently taller than B and G.	And even worse, the little giantess would soon start to grow again and become as big as she was before.
26	M, B and G are back in M's room. M has regained her normal size. She is lying on the canopied bed, uncovered. B is seen climbing into the bed.	As fast as possible they climb back into their bed.
27	M's mother, dressed in a green morning robe, is standing near M's bed, holding a tray with a teapot and several other steaming containers. M is looking up to her mother, the two dolls on her lap.	Just in time! In came the big giantess and said: "Good morning!"

Publications using these data should cite:

Elbers, L. (1985). A tip-of-the-tongue experience at age two? *Journal of Child Language, 12*, 353–365.

Elbers, L., & Wijnen, F. (1992). Effort, production skill, and language learning. In C. Ferguson, L. Menn, & C. Stoel-Gammon (Eds.), *Phonological development: Models, research, implications*, Parkton, MD: York.

Wijnen, F. (1988). Spontaneous word fragmentations in children: Evidence for the syllable as a unit in speech production. *Journal of Phonetics, 16*, 187–202.

Wijnen, F. (1990). The development of sentence planning. *Journal of Child Language, 17*, 550–562.

Wijnen, F. (1992). Incidental word and sound errors in young speakers. *Journal of Memory and Language, 31*, 734–755.

Dutch – van Kampen

Jacqueline van Kampen
OTS, Trans 10
3512 JK Utrecht
The Netherlands
jacqueline.vankampen@let.ruu.nl

The van Kampen corpus is based on tapings of two Dutch girls. Laura was studied from the age of 1;9.18 to 5;10.9 and Sarah from 1;6.16 to 6;0. The child's age at each session is given inside each file. The recordings were made roughly once or twice every month by the mother of the children (Jacqueline van Kampen). The Laura corpus exists of eighty 45-minute recordings. The collection of the data is funded by the Netherlands Organization of Scientific Research (NWO), project 300-171-027 "The acquisition of WH-questions." Assistance was provided by Christel de Heus, Evelien Krikhaar, Jacky Vernimmen and Simone Boezewinkel.

The recordings were made using a Prefer OCC/1121 microphone and a Nakamichi 350 recorder. The transcribers used a Sanyo TRC 9010 with foot pedal. The recordings were made in unstructured, regular home settings between the target child and the mother. The initial transcription is done by one of the assistants. The final version is always checked by Van Kampen. There has been no explicit use of %mor or %syn tiers. Only in the cases when the child used nonadult words or incomprehensible utterances, was the %pho tier was used. Utterances containing the tag-question marker "he" at the end have not been given a question mark. This is done to distinguish them from real questions with inversion.

Please discuss use of these data with Dr. van Kampen. Additional diary notes on the children's development are also available from Dr. van Kampen.

Publications using these data should cite:

Van Kampen, N. J. (1994). The learnability of the left branch condition, *Linguistics in the Netherlands*.

Dutch – Wijnen

Frank Wijnen
Department of Linguistics
University of Groningen
Oude Kijk in 't Jatstraat 26
Groningen 9712 EK Netherland
frank.wijnen@let.rug.nl

The Wijnen Corpus was compiled by Frank Wijnen and Herma Veenhof-Haan. The corpus is based on home tapings of one Dutch boy, Niek, between the ages of 2;7 and 3;10. The recordings were made by Niek's father (Frank Wijnen). The data were mainly used in a project focusing on the relation between language acquisition and developmental disfluency.

Niek was a slow starter in language, both with respect to grammar and to phonology. The first sample in the corpus, at age 2;7, yields an MLU (in words) of 1.72. Some details of Niek's grammatical development are given in Wijnen and Elbers (1993). Further information is available on request. Niek's phonological development was also slow. Particularly, he persisted in various substitution processes, most notably "fronting," that is, substituting alveolar consonants for back obstruents and clusters. This behavior gradually disappeared during the period of observation. At approximately age 4;6, he had developed into a fluent and competent speaker, intelligible for adults other than his parents.

The recordings were generally made in unstructured settings. Usually, the target child and an adult interlocutor (mostly the father) were engaged in some normal everyday routine: playing (often with Legos), looking through picture books, and so forth.

An overview of the available material and some indications of progress in processing the data is given below. Some 31 hours of recordings were collected. A subset of these, amounting to 23 hours, were transcribed. The presence of participants other than one of the parents, as well as other salient or exceptional characteristics of the tapings are mentioned in the "Remarks" column. Additional aspects of the coding and transcription techniques can be found in the description of the "Utrecht" corpora.

The data files are labeled in accordance with the participant's age at the date of recording. For instance, "nie31017.cha" represents the recording made at age 3;10.17.

Publications using these data should cite:

Wijnen, F. (1988). Spontaneous word fragmentations in children: Evidence for the syllable as a unit in speech production. *Journal of Phonetics, 16,* 187–202.

Wijnen, F. (1992). Incidental word and sound errors in young speakers. *Journal of Memory and Language, 31,* 734–755.

Wijnen, F., & Elbers, L. (1993). Effort, production skill, and language learning. In C. Ferguson, L. Menn, & C. Stoel-Gammon (Eds.), *Phonological development.* Timonium, MD: York.

German – Clahsen

Harald Clahsen
Department of Linguistics
University of Essex
Colchester C04 3SQ England
harald@essex.ac.uk

This corpus was contributed by Harald Clahsen. Please inform Dr. Clahsen when using these data. Details about data collection techniques and sociobiographical status of the informants are given in the attached excerpt from Clahsen (1982).

Please note that the data in this subdirectory are only a subset of the total amount of data collected for the three informants. The remaining data have not yet been entered into the computer. File names and the corresponding ages of informants are:

Table 101: Clahsen Files

Daniel	Age	Julia	Age	Mathias	Age
dan17.cha	2;9.28	jul21.cha	1;11.21	mat17.cha	2;9.7
dan18.cha	2;10;14	jul22.cha	2;0.21	mat18.cha	2;10.14
dan19.cha	2;11.14	jul23.cha	2;1.14	mat19.cha	2;11.14
dan21.cha	3;0.21	jul24.cha	2;2.21	mat21.cha	3;0.21
dan22.cha	3;1.21	jul25.cha	2;3.21	mat22.cha	3;1.21
dan23.cha	3;2.14	jul26.cha	2;4.21	mat23.cha	3;2.14
dan24.cha	3;3.21	jul27.cha	2;5.21	mat24.cha	3;3.21
dan25.cha	3;4.21			mat25.cha	3;4.21
dan26.cha	3;5.21			mat26.cha	3;5.21
dan27.cha	3;6.28			mat27.cha	3;6.28

The three children in this study came from a family that lived in the neighborhood of the investigator. Daniel and Mathias were twins and Julia was their younger sister. The family was upper-middle-class. The father was born in 1942. The mother was born in 1944. He was a well-paid lawyer and she was a doctor.

The twins had perinatal anoxia that led to a mild paresis that was successfully treated with gymnastics exercises. In their second year, the twins also had diarrhea for several weeks. Julia was always healthy. A Kramer IQ test yielded scores of 128 for Matthias, 123 for Daniel, and 121 for Julia. Matthias was demanding and sometimes aggressive. Daniel was more introverted. Julia was more normal in her temperament.

Following Brown (1973), video recordings of 45 to 60 minutes length were made at regular intervals of 2 or 3 week periods. Recordings were made in the home with the mother present. A small portable video camera with an attached microphone was used to minimize interference with the natural situation. Recordings were transcribed and double-checked within a week.

Publications making use of these data should cite:

Clahsen, H. (1982). *Spracherwerb in der Kindheit: Eine Untersuchung zur Entwicklung der Syntax bei Kleinkindern.* Tübingen, Germany: Gunter Narr.

German – Wagner

Klaus Wagner
Universitat Dortmund
Fachbereich 15 – Kindersprache
Postfach 500500
Dortmund 4600 Germany

This directory contains a set of 13 mini-corpora collected by Klaus R. Wagner of the University of Dortmund and his students and coworkers. As indicated in the following table, the ages of the participants ranged from 1;5 to 14;10.

Table 102: Wagner Children

No.	Participant	Age	Researcher	Length in Minutes
1	Katrin	1;5	Schwarze	202
2	Nicole	1;8	Kadatz	241
3	Andreas	2;1	Wahner	213
4	Carsten	3;6	Hoffmann-Kirsch	189
5	Gabi	5;4	Brinkmann	152
6	Frederick	8;7	H	
7	Roman	9;2	Otto	311
8	Kai	9;6	Corzillius/Landskr	
9	Teresa	9;7	Wagner	804 (one day)
10	Regina	10;7	Giljohann	1430 (6 days)
11	Markus	11;4	Brönner	188
12	Christiane	12;2	Pagels/Gasse	430
13	Axel	14;10	Vette	254

The participants wore a transmitting microphone and were therefore free to move about as they wished. This is of immense importance for studies aiming at eliciting and describing the spontaneous speech of children. Within a radius of 300 meters around the recording apparatus, the child can move freely, play, skip, climb trees, drive a go-cart, and so forth. The transcription system is that used in the pilot study (Wagner, 1974) with certain improvements after Ehlich & Rehbein (1976). The transcripts include all the participants' utterances verbatim, including paralanguage; all interlocutor utterances in full as far as they concern the subject, otherwise abbreviated; and detailed information on the communicative setting (place, action, particular circumstances).

The following list gives two further types of information about the corpora: the communication situations in which participants found themselves during recording and parental social status.

(1) *Schwarze corpus: Katrin (1;5)*. The situations included: breakfast, playing (tap, milk lorry, dolls), helping to sort crockery, playing with bricks and dolls, nappy change, looking at guinea pigs, lunch, and monologues in bed. Social status: mother (researcher) was qualified in child care; father was a parson; upper-middle-class.

(2) *Kadatz corpus: Nicole (1;8)*. The situations included: waking up, playing and jumping about in parents' bed, on her potty and getting dressed, breakfast and playing in her high-chair, at the kitchen window, painting, clearing the table, painting and playing with a toy clock, playing with a big doll, playing a board game, on her potty, playing a board game, eating, getting undressed, and monologues in bed. Social status: mother was a saleswoman; father (researcher) was a trainee teacher; upper-working-class.

(3) *Wahner corpus: Andreas (2;1)*. The situations included: eating a sandwich, playing (metal foil, animals, helicopter, toothbrushes, spinning top), playing with grandfather and Caesar the rabbit (doll), playing with grandfather and a Santa Claus doll, reciting a poem, looking at a picture book with brother and aunt (researcher), playing with a Lego tank, a candle, matches, drinking juice, and playing football with a beachball. Social status: mother stopped working after the birth of her first child (participant's elder brother); father was a supervisor of apprentices in an electrical workshop and was studying electrical engineering to become an electrical technician; upper working-class or lower-middle-class.

(4) *Hoffmann-Kirsch corpus: Carsten (5;4)*. The situations included: playing (role-playing, driving a car, "writing" = drawing), cutting up a birthday card, eating chocolate and looking at pictures with grandma, going into the cellar, playing at being a dog, going to the milkman, buying yogurt, eating yogurt, looking at and talking about pictures, having lunch, cuddling and talking to grandma, playing with cars (role-playing), cuddling and talking to his mother (researcher), crying (after being bumped), and being comforted by grandma. Social status: mother (researcher) was a trainee teacher; father was a car salesman; middle-class.

(5) *Brinkmann corpus: Gabi (5;4)*. The situations included: talking about her brother's birthday, breakfast, playing dominoes, eating Nutella (chocolate spread), playing dominoes again, and drawing. Social status: mother was a housewife; father was a lawyer; upper-middle-class.

(6) *H* The situations included: waiting for the end of break; lessons: understanding things, mathematics, German, understanding things, German composition; break; lesson: braille; end of school, being driven home, arriving at home, collecting Andreas (playmate), and playing with a racing car set. Social status: mother (researcher) was a trainee teacher, entrance qualifications gained through further education, upper working-class or lower middle-class.

(7) *Otto corpus: Roman (9;2)*. The situations included: playing monopoly with Georg (younger brother), getting ready to go out, at the sports ground, relaxed conversation, playing with little cars, drive to the camp site, at the camp site, going home, going on with the game of monopoly with Georg, watching television (sports program), and playing with rac-

ing car set. Social status: mother was a gymnastics teacher; father (researcher) had 12 years in the armed forces as a sergeant and was a trainee teacher; middle-class.

(8) *Corzillus/Landskru* The situations included: getting up, putting on the microphone transmitter, breakfast, going to school in the car, lessons (drawing, understanding things, mathematics (test), language, reading, singing) with breaks, going home, lunch, playing monopoly, driving a go-cart, playing in a Citroen 2CV, soldering, drawing, making a tassel, collecting food, watching television, and memory game. Social status: mother was a landlady; father (researcher) was a draughtsman who died when participant was 3 years old, upper-working-class.

(9) *Wagner corpus: Teresa (9;7)*. The situations included: waking up, getting dressed, sewing on the microphone transmitter, breakfast, packing her bag, drive to school, before lessons, lessons (arithmetic, language), 10 o'clock break, prizegiving, drive home, clearing things away, reading the mail, Teresa's file, picking gooseberries, playing with girl-friends (catching the cat, dressing up, clowns, ballet kidnappers), lunch, picking and cleaning gooseberries, homework, having coffee, clearing away toys, playing with Anke (coffee table, climbing a tree, playing on the grass, hopping on the patio, gold investigators, eating, ducat gold thieves), watching television, skipping, having dinner, watching television news, and going to bed. (For a more detailed discussion of speech situations see Wagner (1974: 203-38).) Social status: mother was a teacher for eight years, then housewife; father (researcher) was a secondary school teacher in various school types, later university lecturer; middle-class.

(10) *Brunner corpus: Markus (11;4)*. The situations included: making a veteran car (toy car made by cutting out and pasting cardboard), and using a microscope. Social status: mother (researcher) was a trainee teacher; father was a certified engineer, architect, professor; upper-middle-class.

(11) *Pagels/Gasse corpus: Christiane (12;2)*. The situations included: saying hello, making a crib, lunch, continuing work on the crib, skating, playing a word game, doing crochet, having coffee, singing Advent songs, reading aloud, conversation, watching television, drawing, having dinner, and doing schoolwork. Social status: mother spent 10 years working in business, then housewife; father was a skilled art metal worker, retrained as a teacher of art and vocational preparation at a school for mentally handicapped children; upper working-class or lower-middle-class.

(12) *Vette corpus: Axel (14;10)*. The situations included: talking about cassette recorders, solving arithmetical problems, playing table tennis, having coffee, playing cards, recording music, and playing table tennis. Social status: mother is a housewife; father is a moulder in an iron-foundry; working-class.

Ehlich, K., & Rehbein, J. (1976). Halbinterpretative Arbeitstranskription (HIAT). *Linguistische Berichte, 45,* 24–41.

Wagner, K. R. (1974). *Die Sprechsprache des Kindes. Teil 1: Theorie und Analyse.* Dösseldorf: Präger.

Publications using these data should cite:

Wagner, K. R. (1985). How much do children say in a day? *Journal of Child Language, 12,* 475–487.

German – Weissenborn

Jürgen Weissenborn
Department of Linguistics
University of Potsdam
Potsdam, German
weissenb@rz.uni-potsdam.de

This corpus is a set of protocols taken from older children by Jürgen Weissenborn of the Max-Planck-Institut in the context of experimental elicitations of route descriptions. This corpus contains verbal protocols taken from a route-description task administered to German children and adults. The experiment carried out consisted of a route description task with pairs of German children of the same age — 7, 8, 9, 10, 11, and 14 years. In each group, 6 to 10 pairs of participants were tested.

The participants could not see each other. Each had an identical model of a small town in front of him and the direction giver had to specify for the other participant the route of a toy car through the town. The task material consisted of two identical three-dimensional wooden models of towns (0.60m by 0.70m). The houses, with red or blue roofs and two different sizes, were organized symmetrically (mirror-image) around a central axis. Four different paths (A, B, C, and D) of equal difficulty (same number of subpaths and turning points) were defined and each was then successively described by one child to another under three different conditions.

1. with supplementary landmarks (trees, animals, cars) destroying the symmetry of the display and with gestures (the children were allowed to use their hands freely during the description);

2. without landmarks and with gestures; and

3. without landmarks and without gestures (the children were sitting on their hands).

These conditions were combined with paths A to C as follows: 1A-2B-3C; 2B-1C-3A; and so forth. Path D was always described by the child to the experimenter under condition 2. The descriptions were videotaped.

The symmetrical design of the model was chosen because the referential determinacy of any path description that refers to it is only guaranteed if these descriptions are embedded in a verbal reference frame that has jointly been defined by the participants. For example, a description like "You pass under the bridge" would not suffice given that there are two bridges. The same holds for every other building. In order to resolve this indeterminacy the use of relational expressions like "left," "right," "in front of," and "behind" is required. But, the reference of these terms is itself indeterminate between the deictic and the intrinsic perspective when applied to oriented objects. Thus, when applied to the toy car that the child drives along the path, "left" and "right" coincide with the describer's perspective as long as the car moves away from him; when the car moves towards him this is no longer the case so that, at least for this instance, the describer has to specify explicitly which perspective he has chosen if he wants to avoid misunderstandings.

This is only possible if these alternative perspectives are discriminated and if the ensuing necessity to coordinate the speaker's and listener's perspective is recognized. Notice that the two perspectives or reference frames are not equivalent in terms of cognitive complexity. The deictic perspective is based on the projection of the body schema of the speaker onto the experimental display whereas in the intrinsic perspective it is first mentally transposed onto the oriented object (i.e., the toy car) and then projected onto the display thus necessitating the constant coordination between the original deictic and the transposed intrinsic use. Thus the structure of the experimental display asking for the use of these spatial terms has necessary conversational implications in that it requires the negotiation of the rules of use of these terms in order to establish a shared frame of reference and action.

What has been said so far about the consequences of the experimental design for the task solution applies in particular to condition 2. The task requirements are obviously quite different in condition 1 where the symmetrical design is destroyed by the introduction of additional landmarks. In this condition an unambiguous description of the path could be achieved by relying mainly on the information provided by these elements without necessarily using relational terms like "left" and "right." That is, these landmarks furnish a concrete and fixed frame of reference, external to the describer. Condition 3 was designed to study the influence of the absence of gestures on the child's descriptive abilities.

In order to evaluate the describer's ability to establish a coherent frame of reference a certain number of parameters have been defined that are considered to characterize each individual describer's performance, that is completeness of the path description defined in terms of adequate characterization of the turning points and the connections between them, prevailing perspective, perspective awareness, and so forth.

Publications using these data should cite:

Weissenborn, J. (1985). Ich weiss ja nicht von hier aus, wie weit es von da hinten ist: Makroräume in der kognitiven und sprachlichen Entwicklung des Kindes. In H. Schweizer (Ed.), *Sprache und Raum*. Stuttgart: Metzlersche.

Weissenborn, J. (1986). Learning how to become an interlocutor: The verbal negotiation of common frames of reference and actions in dyads of 7- to 14-year-old children. In J. Cook-Gumperz (Ed.), *Children's worlds and children's language*. The Hague: Mouton.

German – Wode

Henning Wode
Englishes Seminar
Christian-Albrechts-Universität
Olshausenstraße 40
D-2300 Kiel 1 Germany

This corpus is a set of transcripts of interactions collected by Henning Wode of the University of Kiel with a chief focus on the language development of his son Lars and daughter Inga. Both were acquiring German as their first language.

The material was gathered in a longitudinal day-by-day routine involving both notes taken spontanteously and tape recordings using a portable Uher tape recorder. Data were collected while the children were engaged in all kinds of activities, including meals, games, walks, and sports. The written notes contain phonetic details of the utterances and comments about the situational context. A rigid data collection procedure, involving fixed intervals or time limits for recording sessions, was not maintained.

The participants in these interactions are:

BAR   Barbara Wode, wife of Henning and mother of Heiko, Birgit, Lars, and Inga. She was born in 1945.
HEN   Henning Wode, husband of Barbara and father of the four children. Born in 1937.
HEI   Heiko Wode, the oldest child (son), born in May 1966.
BIR   Birgit Wode, second child (daughter), born in May 1967.
LAR   Lars Wode, third child (son), born in May 1969.
ING   Inga Wode, fourth child (daughter), born in May 1971.
BEL   Belinda, an American visitor with the family, born 1960.

Some of the special codings in the original version include "korrigiert" for corrected and "erneut" for a new start. These have not yet been changed to [//]. Comments were originally marked with @@ and overlaps with @*@.

Papers using these data should cite one or two of these articles.

Wode, H. (1974). Natürliche Zweitsprachigkeit: Probleme, Aufgaben, Perspektiven. *Linguistische Berichte, 32,* 15–36.
Wode, H. (1977). Four early stages in the development of LI negation. *Journal of Child Language, 4,* 87–102.
Wode, H. (1978). The L1 vs L2 acquisition of English interrogation. *Indian Journal of Applied Linguistics, 4,* 31–46.
Wode, H. (1979). Operating principles and "universals" in L1, L2, and FLT. *International Review of Applied Linguistics, 17,* 217–231.
Wode, H. (1980). Grammatical intonation in child language. In L. R. Waugh & C. Schooneveld (Eds.), *The melody of language*, (pp. 291–345). Baltimore, MD: University Park Press.

Wode, H. (1981). Language-acquisitional universals: A unified view of language acquisition. In H. Winitz (Ed.), *Native language and foreign language acquisition.*, (Vol. 379). New York: New York Academy of Sciences.

Wode, H. (1987). The rise of phonological coding abilities for the mental representation of lexical items. In H. Bluhme & G. Hammarström (Eds.), Descriptio linguistica. Tübingen: Narr.

Wode, H., & Allendorff, S. (1981). Some overgeneralizations in the L1 acquisition of interrogative pronouns. *International Review of Applied Linguistics, 19,* 31–44.

Swedish – Göteborg

Sven Strömqvist
Department of Linguistics
University of Göteborg
Renstromsparken
Göteborg S-41298 Sweden
svens@hum.gu.se

The 74 computerized transcription files contained in this second release of the Swedish corpus relate to the project "Databasorienterade studier i svensk barnspraaksutveckling" (Database oriented studies of Swedish child language development), in which the language development in five monolingual Swedish children is analyzed. The project is supported by the Swedish Research Council for the Humanities and Social Sciences (HSFR), grant F 783/91 and F 517/92 to the Department of Linguistics, University of Göteborg, Sweden. A comprehensive guide to the Swedish corpus is presented in Strömqvist, Richtoff, and Anderson (1993).

The five children under study grew up in middle-class families on the west coast of Sweden. The families speak standard Swedish with a modest touch of the regional variant. The recorded material relates to a wide range of activity types: everyday activities in the home (such as meals, bedtime procedures, cooking, washing, etc); freeplay; story telling; as well as adult–child interaction; child–child interaction; and soliloquy.

Data collection for two of the children — a boy Markus from 1;3.19 to 6;0.09, and a girl Eva from 1;0.21 to 3;9.23 —is already completed. The data from Markus and Eva, who are siblings, constitute one component of the larger Swedish corpus. The second component includes data from Harry and Thea, who are siblings, and from Anton. These files constitute "Richthoff's corpus." Data collection started at 1;11.08 for Anton, at 1;5.26 for Harry, and at 1;0.02 for Thea.

Index

The name of each of the computerized transcription files reflects the name of the child and his or her age (in months and days) at the time of the recording. The present release of the corpus contains 74 transcription files: 28 from Markus (ma15_19.cha to ma33_29.cha), 20 from Anton (ant23_08.cha to ant34_04.cha) and 26 from Harry (har18_20.cha to har35_07.cha).

Transcription Conventions

All main tiers (both child and adult) have been morphologically segmented by means of the symbols # (prefix), + (lexical compound) and - (suffix). The utterance delimiters ! and ? indicate exclamation and question, respectively. A full stop is used as a default utterance delimiter but has no specific linguistic meaning. It should be read as ambiguous with respect to functions like statement, request, and so forth. Utterances have been identified on intonational criteria. In the present release, only the 28 Markus files are checked for reliability. The reliability check indicates a breaking point at 18;10. In the transcripts before ma18_10.cha the two project transcribers agreed on utterance segmentation in 80-85% of the cases, whereas after 18_10 they agreed in 96-99% of the cases.

Lexicon Files

The transcripts are morphologically oriented and take Swedish orthography as a point of departure but allow for deviations from the orthographic norm in order to capture qualities of spoken Swedish. In particular, we have tried to avoid the fallacy of overrepresenting or underrepresenting the child's knowledge of morphology in terms of the adult norm. The three children so far transcribed vary considerably in acquisition structure and way of speaking and this is reflected in the transcripts. The word forms in the transcripts of Markus are, as a rule, sufficiently transparent to be successfully interpreted by a speaker of Swedish. In contrast, several of the early transcripts of Harry are less transparent and majority of the transcripts of Anton are rather opaque. As a guide to these opaque word forms we have constructed a set of lexicon files for Harry and Anton. Each of Harry's 26 and Anton's 20 transcript files is matched with a lexicon file containing a list of the opaque word forms in the transcript file, the transcriber's interpretation of the opaque word form in terms of the closest adult/target word form (the child's form is often ambiguous and several interpretations/target forms are rendered) and the token frequency of the opaque word form. There is a strong tendency for ambiguous forms to be among the most frequent forms, generally. The file har32_25.cha has a matching lexicon file har32_25.lex, which, among many other entries and lines, contains the line "27 e aer/en/ett" which means: 27 tokens of the transcribed form "e" which is used by the child as sometimes "aer" (copula:PRES), sometimes "en" (indefinite article:common gender), and sometimes "ett" (indefinite article:neuter gender).

Coding

In the present version of the text files, three things are coded: time, word accents, and feedback. First, a %tim tier is used to indicate the temporal location of an utterance in minutes and seconds from the start of the recording (e.g., "32:12" means 32 minutes and 12 seconds). Second, a %wac: word accent tier is used to code word accents. So far, the marked word accent, "accent 2" (grave), is coded only when it occurs in utterance focus position. The code used for marking accent 2 in focus position is WAC2:FOC. Unclear cases are marked WAC2:FOC? (The auditive identification of accent 2 contours is far from unproblematic. The presence of only a %wac tier indicates an instance of accent 2 on which the two transcribers agreed. For cases where there was a disagreement between the two transcribers, an additional %wan tier is used to indicate a conflicting judgment.) Third, a %nfb tier is used to code so-called narrow feedback morphemes. Only feedback giving morphemes (such as hm, naehae) have been coded so far. The code used for marking feedback givers is "FBG." Unclear cases are marked "FBG?" In addition to the three coding tiers mentioned, a fourth %aaf tier is used to indicate that one or several word forms on the main tier have been subjected to acoustic analysis and are stored in an acoustic analysis file. The acoustic analysis tier provides information necessary for the identification of the matching aaf file(s). Whereas %tim: is a standard option from the CHILDES manual, %wac:, %nfb:, and %aaf: are not. The three latter codes have only been used for project internal purposes.

An Acoustic Archive

In addition to the computerized transcription files, we have created a computerized acoustic archive containing a sample of a little more than 500 disyllabic word forms from Markus 18;10 to 26;10. The archive is created in MacSpeech Lab environment. The sample contains both monomorphemic and dimorphemic word forms, the latter being either lexical compounds or stems plus an inflectional suffix. Further, the sample contains word forms that make up one-word utterances as well as word forms from the initial, medial or final position in multi-word utterances. Copies of the acoustic archive can be obtained from Sven Strömqvist who welcomes comments and questions relating to the Swedish corpus.

Publications using these data should cite:

Plunkett, K., & Strömqvist, S. The acquisition of Scandinavian languages. In D. I. Slobin (Ed.), *The crosslinguistic study of language acquisition: Volume 3*, pp. 457-556. Hillsdale, NJ: Lawrence Erlbaum Associates.

Strömqvist, S., Richthoff, U., & Andersson, A.-B. (1993). Strömqvist's and Richthoff's corpora: A guide to longitudinal data from four Swedish children. *Gothenburg Papers in Theoretical Linguistics, 66.*

7:   Romance Languages

Table 103: Romance Languages

Corpus	Age Range	N	Comments
Catalan – Serra / Sole on page 326	1–4	10	Longitudinal study of language acquisition in Catalan and Spanish children
French – Champaud on page 327	1;9.18–2;5.27	1	Longitudinal study of language development in French with recordings made over a 28-month period
French – Leveillé on page 329	2;1.19–3;3.12	1	Longitudinal study with weekly recording sessions
French – Montréal on page 331	5;6–11;6	36 s	Cross sectional study focusing on speech acts in Kindergarten, third- and fourth-grade children playing "veterinarian" and "assistant"
French – Rondal on page 336	2;3–4;9	1	Large longitudinal corpus of mother–child interactions in French with some English
Italian – Calambrone on page 338	large age range	17	Contains both longitudinal and crosssectional data from six normal and 11 language disordered Italian-speaking children
Italian – Roma on page 341	1;4–4;0	1	Longitudinal study of a single child
Portuguese – Batoreo on page 343	5, 7, 10, adult	120	Elicited narratives describing two picture book stories
Portuguese – Porto Alegre on page 345	5;0–9;6	161	Cross sectional study with 9 age groups that focuses on language development in the period of the acquisition of literacy
Portuguese – Florianópolis on page 347	1;8.21 1;10.20 2;2.8	1	Longitudinal study of one Brazilian Portuguese child's 5530 utterances in broad phonetic transcription (including intonational patterns) collected in three sessions

Table 103: Romance Languages

Corpus	Age Range	N	Comments
Spanish-ColMex on page 348	6–8	90	School-aged children
Spanish – Diez-Itza on page 349	3;0–3;11	20	First 10 boys and 10 girls from a larger corpus under preparation
Spanish – Linaza on page 350	2–4 years	1	Longitudinal study of a child learning Spanish
Spanish – López Ornat on page 351	1;7–3;11	1	Longitudinal study of a child learning Spanish
Spanish – Marrero / Albalá on page 352	1;6–8;0	6	Longitudinal study of Spanish children from the Canaries with12 data files
Spanish – Montes on page 353	1;7.20–2;11.14	1	Longitudinal study of parent–child interactions
Spanish – Romero on page 356	2;0	1	Cross sectional study of one child at age 2
Spanish – Serra / Sole on page 358	1;4.8–3;10.20	1	Longitudinal study of a monolingual Spanish-speaking child in Cataluña
Spanish – Vila on page 359	0;11–4;8	1	Longitudinal corpus with 35 recordings

Catalan – Serra / Sole

Miquel Serra
Departament de Psicologia Basica
Universitat de Barcelona
Adolf Florensa s/n
Barcelona, 08028 Spain
mserra@psi.ub.es

The Serra–Sole longitudinal study includes 10 children. Five are monolingual Catalan, four are bilingual Catalan-Spanish, and one is monolingual Spanish. The Spanish-speaking child (#10) is included in the Spanish directory. The other children are in the Catalan directory. The children were videotaped monthly from 1 to 4 years of age from 1986 to 1989. They were videotaped at their homes in spontaneous interaction with a familiar adult, usually the mother, in sessions of 30 to 45 minutes. All the children belong to middle-class families. The research project is entitled "Language acquisition in Catalan and Spanish children" and is directed by Miquel Serra (Universitat de Barcelona) and Rosa Sole (Universitat Autonoma de Barcelona). It has received support from the Spanish research council (Grants DGICYT PB84/0455; PB89/0317; PB91/0851; PB94/0886). The research assistants of the project have been: Montserrat Cortes, Connie Schultz, Elisabet Serrat, Vicens Torrents, and Melina Aparici. Cristina Vila and Montse Capdevila have collaborated in different stages of it. The authors would appreciate receiving a copy, or a summary, of any work using the corpus.

Table 104: Monolingual Catalan Children

Number	Name	# Files	Age Range	Sex
01	Pep	31	1;0.27–3;6.21	M
03	Alvar	20	1;2.28–3;1.13	M
05	Guillem	-	1;0.0–4;0.0	M
08	Gisela	-	1;7.14–4;2.3	M
09	Laura	-	1;7,20–4;0.10	F

Table 105: Bilingual Catalan–Spanish Children

Number	Name	# Files	Age Range	Sex
02	Antoni	23	1;4.1–3;0.24	M
06	Marti	24	0;10.14–4;0.13	M
07	Josep Andreu	24	0;10,1–4;0.3	M
12	Caterina	18	1;1.17–4;3.21	F

French – Champaud

Christian Champaud
Laboratoire de Psych. CNRS
28, Rue Serpente
Paris 75006 France
kail@ext.jussieu.fr

This subdirectory contains data that were videotaped, transcribed, and coded in CHAT by Christian Champaud, Chargé de Recherches at the C.N.R.S. (UA 316). The participant of the study is Grégoire. The work was done in collaboration with Grégoire's family with particular assistance from his mother Dominique. Thanks are due to Catherine Marlot, Danièle Boussin, and Françoise Roland for transcription, rechecking, and typing. This work is still in progress and new data are still being added to the corpus.

Grégoire was the third child of Dominique (mother, born on 3-AUG-46) and Michel (father, born on 5-APR-48, whose usual name is Kôfy). Grégoire was born on 28-APR-86. His elder brother, Adrien, was born on 21-APR-80. The other brother, Victor, was born on 16-JUN-83. Grégoire's parents lived in Paris, France, and the only spoken language in the family was French. Both parents had college degrees. Dominique was a professor of French, who left her job in order to take care of her family. She had experience in developmental psycholinguistics (investigations conducted with Laurence Lentin) and in linguistics. Michel was a professor of German at the University of Paris III. The socioeconomic status of Grégoire's family can be characterized as upper-middle-class.

Space Insertion

In French, when a word begins with a vowel, this leads in some cases to the disappearance of the final vowel of the preceding word: "l'ami" and not "le ami." The vowel -e is elided, and in the spelling, the two words are linked together by an apostrophe. This is the case for a determiner preceding a noun, or for a clitic pronoun preceding a verb, and so forth. It is important to add a space after the apostrophe in these cases. It allows to make searches for some determiners or articles, for pronouns, and for the words that follow, as whole words. It allows also to include them in frequency counts, or to take them into account for computing the MLU in words. This decision implies that, in French CHAT transcriptions, the strings c', d', j', l', m', n', qu', s', t', and y' must be obligatorily followed by a space. Presently, this has only been done with some transcriptions.

In hyphenated words like *abat-jour,* the hyphen (-) must be replaced by a plus (+): abat+jour, in order to avoid confusions with suffixes. In French, the hyphen symbol is sometimes used between words, like in *est-ce que;* in these cases, the hyphen symbol must be omitted and replaced by a space to yield *est ce que* to ensure that all words are included in frequency counts.

In order not to create an unreadable transcript and in order to avoid overinterpretation often inherent in error analysis, a decision was made to rely on the %pho tier for the definitive form of words. It is then possible to revise interpretations on the main line without returning to the videotape.

Table 106: Champaud Files

File	Date	Age
greg01.cha	16-FEB-1988	1;9.18
greg02.cha	1-MAR-1988	1;10.3
greg03.cha	22-MAR-1988	1;10.24
greg04.cha	19-APR-1988	1;11.21
greg05.cha	3-MAY-1988	2;0.5
greg06.cha	22-JUN-1988	2;1.24
greg07.cha	28-JUL-1988	2;3.0
greg08.cha	29-SEP-1988	2;5.1
greg09.cha	11-OCT-1988	2;5.13
greg10.cha	25-OCT-1988	2;5.27

An additional directory called GREGX contains observations and notes of the parents or investigator for which no audio recording is available and no double-checking can be done. These files begin when Grégoire is 1;9 and run for about 28 months, but the later ones are not yet transcribed.

French – Leveillé

Madeleine Leveillé
Laboratoire de Psych. Experimentale
28 rue Serpente
Paris 75006 France

This directory contains files from a longitudinal study of a single French child. The study was conducted by Madeleine Leveillé and Pat Suppes of Stanford University. The data was donated to CHILDES by Patrick Suppes in 1985. The data are in CHAT format without English glosses. The target child was an only child of academic parents in their thirties. He was in close association with only native French speakers. His parents were willing to submit to the rather demanding rule that all they said, as well as what their child said, would be recorded for 1 hour a week over an indefinite period of time.

Philippe was born on March 3, 1969. In the first visit, Philippe was 25 months and 19 days old. He was a sociable little boy who was not shy, even with strangers. During the period of data collection, he often went to the Faculty of Sciences with his father who taught there. He also visited his mother in a laboratory of psychology where she worked, and he occasionally participated in experiments in the laboratory. Usually he attended nursery school; when he did not stay there the whole day, a lady in her forties stayed with him at his house. Both his mother and father talked a lot with him and provided him with a verbally and intellectually stimulating environment.

The first observational period, April 22 through June 24, 1971, twas completed before summer vacation began. After an interruption of nearly three months (83 days) when Philippe went to the country, the sessions continued at the same frequency through December 18, 1971. There was a lapse of 14 days between September 30, 1971 and October 14, 1971 due to a strike on the Metro, which paralyzed Paris. At that time 21 hours had been recorded. Then the visits became less frequent. Between March 23 and May 6 a total of 63 days elapsed because Philippe was on vacation. Session 33 was the last one, because Philippe was leaving Paris for his summer vacation. The complete schedule of recording sessions was as follows.

Table 107: Philippe Files

File	Date	Age	File	Date	Age
phil01	4-22-71	2;1.19	phil17	11-4-71	2;8.1
phil02	4-29-71	2;1.26	phil18	11-11-71	2;8.8
phil03	5-6-71	2;2.3	phil19	11-18-71	2;8.15
phil04	5-13-71	2;2.10	phil20	11-25-71	2;8.22
phil05	5-20-71	2;2.17	phil21	12-2-71	2;8.29

Table 107: Philippe Files

File	Date	Age	File	Date	Age
phil06	5-29-71	2;2.26	phil22	12-18-71	2;9.15
phil07	6-3-71	2;3.0	phil23	1-6-72	2;10.3
phil08	6-10-71	2;3.7	phil24	1-20-72	2;10.17
phil09	6-17-71	2;3.14	phil25	2-3-72	2;11.0
phil10	6-24-71	2;3.21	phil26	2-10-72	2;11.7
phil11	9-16-71	2;6.13	phil27	2-24-72	2;11.21
phil12	9-23-71	2;6.20	phil28	3-9-72	3;0.6
phil13	9-30-71	2;6.27	phil29	3-23-72	3;0.20
phil14	10-14-71	2;7.11	phil30	5-6-72	3;2.3
phil15	10-21-71	2;7.18	phil31	5-18-72	3;2.15
phil16	10-28-71	2;7.25	phil32	6-1-72	3;2.29
			phil33	6-15-72	3;3.12

For practical reasons, recording sessions always took place in the morning, generally not long after Philippe had awakened. Each session, with a few exceptions, lasted 1 hour. Although the recording periods were relaxed and informal, Philippe was asked not to leave the room in which the tape recorder was installed for any significant time. Usually the tape recorder was set up in the living room, which was at the center of the apartment. Only the microphone was moved to the kitchen during breakfast. If Philippe wanted to play in his bedroom, the tape recorder was taken there and Philippe was asked not to go into the other rooms too often or too long.

Publications using these data should cite:

Suppes, P., Smith, R., & Leveillé, M. (1973). The French syntax of a child's noun phrases. *Archives de Psychologie, 42*, 207–269.

French – Montréal

Helga Feider (deceased)
Centre d'ATO-CI
University of Quebec
Montréal, PQ Canada

Madeleine Saint-Pierre
Centre d'ATO-CI
University of Quebec
Montréal, PQ H3C 3P8 Canada

This directory contains a set of dialogues produced in a task of role play recorded by Helga Feider and Madeleine Saint-Pierre in a Montréal public school. The children are playing "Veterinarian" and "Assistant" and are trying to cure various sick stuffed animals. The corpus is closely transcribed for the use of a variety of speech acts as described below. The corpus consists of 36 files of from three age groups:

1.   Kindergarten —5;6 to 6;8

2.   Grade 3 — 8; 5 to 9;6

3.   Grade 4 —10;6 to 11;6

Table 108: Montréal Kindergarteners

# of dyad	Gender	Duration (min:sec)	Rate/Min Vet.	Rate/Min Asst.
01	Male	05:30	16.55	12.73
02	Female	14:00	11.29	07.14
03	Female	18:00	09.33	07.44
04	Vet: M Asst: F	12:00	08.25	09.92
05	Male	14:00	12.00	06.00
06	Male	07:00	06.86	05.29
07	Male	06:50	03.22	05.71
08	Male	05:00	09.60	12.00
09	Male	12:30	18.96	17.76
10	Male	10:00	12.10	17.78
11	Female	09:00	04.11	05.33

Table 109: Montréal Grade Three

# of dyad	Gender	Duration (min:sec)	Rate/Min Vet.	Rate/Min Asst.
12	Male	16:00	02.87	03.81
13	Female	11:00	13.82	06.00
14	Male	12:00	11.42	06.92
15	Female	06:00	10.17	02.33
16	Female	12:00	25.75	03.00
17	Male	09:00	10.56	09.44
18	Male	14:00	12.79	03.64
19	Male	09:00	14.0	06.56
20	Vet: M Asst: F	07:00	12.57	00.71
21	Male	05:00	06.20	03.80
22	Female	09:00	02.78	02.00
23	Male	18:00	15.22	04.98
24	Female	06:30	08.62	02.00

Table 110: Montréal Grade Four

# of dyad	Gender	Duration (min:sec)	Rate/Min Vet.	Rate/Min Asst.
25	Male	11:30	17.13	07.22
26	Female	06:30	14.62	15.54
27	Male	07:30	15.07	17.87
28	Female	13:11	12.52	02.58
29	Male	09:22	19.22	06.4
30	Female	06:33	10.38	04.43
31	Male	14:30	14.14	07.45
32	Female	21:08	10.36	03.83
33	Vet: F Asst: M	08:00	12.50	09.50

Table 110: Montréal Grade Four

# of dyad	Gender	Duration (min:sec)	Rate/Min Vet.	Rate/Min Asst.
34	Female	17:00	22.59	09.18
35	Male	09:00	11.22	04.33
36	Female	08:00	09.45	02.91

On the %spa tier, the following speech act codes are used. Type 1 are assertive acts of definition or description. Type 2 are directives. Type 3 are suggestions. Type 4 are commissives. Type 5 are expressives.

Table 111: Montréal Speech Act Types

Code	Description	Example
1a	unmarked assertive	J'ai fini. J'ai oubli
1b	prediction	Il va.
1c	description	Son coeur bat.
1d	evaluation	Il est triste.
1e	information	son num
1f	confirmation	c'est
1g	self-correction	Pas lui, le lapin; oui c'est
1h	disconfirm	Non, il n'a pas de fi
1i	assent	Oui, sa patte est bris
1j	dissent	Je ne le crois pas
1k	dispute	Tu dis "aux yeux" c'est les oreilles.
1l	metaphor, irony	J'ai bien commenc
1n	supposition, assumption	Ca peut
1p	fabulation	Il fait minuit
1q	action regulation	3-9-8-7-5-3-4 (while dialing)
2a	permission request	Je l'appelle?
2b	information request	Qu'est-ce qu'il a, le chat?

Table 111: Montréal Speech Act Types

Code	Description	Example
2c	order	Apporte-moi le chien.
2d	prohibition	
2e	polite request	Peux-tu me passer la seringue?
2f	self-directive	Bon, m'as y donner une piq
2g	confirmation request	C'est l'ours?
2h	attention request	Regarde.
2i	justification request	Qu'est-ce que tu fais là?
2j	reflecting on a course of action	Qu'est-ce qu'on fait?
3a	grant permission	Il va pouvoir sortir demain.
3b	proposing a course of action	On va y donner une piq.
3c	propose an action by authority	Faudrait qu'il reste á l'hôpital.
4a	proposal	Je vais m'en occuper de lui.
4b	offer	Tiens, le thermometer.
4c	compliance with request	O.K.
4d	refusal of a request	Ben, on ne sait.
5a	verbal acknowledgment	Bonjour, madame.
5b	emotional reaction	Oh, mon doux!
5c	reaction with explanation	Zut, c'est qu'il est tannant, lui!
6	playful speech	Halo, monsieur ours.
7	other speech act	
0	incomplete, no obvious function	

Additional non-CHAT codes used on the main tier and sometimes on the %com tier include:

[% r]:   laugh
[% re]:   the preceding word is repeated

[% sol]:	monologue
[% sim]:	simulated speech
[% aff]:	head nod to indicate agreement
[% idem]:	non verbal action corresponding to previous verbal request
[% h]:	high voice
[% g]:	low voice
[% f]:	loud voice
[% p]:	low vocal intensity
[% a]:	fast speech
[% l]:	slow speech
[% chu]:	whisper
[% cha]:	chanted speech
[% ri]:	speech emitted while laughing
[% sac]	staccato voice
[% al]:	the preceding syllable is lengthened

This classification system was developed and validated by the authors on the basis of these two articles:

Bach, K., & Harnish, R. M. (1979). *Linguistic communication and speech acts.* Cambridge, MA: MIT Press.

Dore, J. (1977). "Oh Them Sheriff": a pragmatic analysis of children's response to questions. In S. Ervin-Tripp & C. Mitchell-Kernan (Eds.), *Child discourse.* New York: Academic Press.

Publications using these data should cite:

Feider, H., & Saint-Pierre, M. (1987). Elementary school children's pragmatic skills: What children learn between five and ten. *Lenguas Modernas, 14,* 57–67.

Saint-Pierre, M., & Feider, H. (1987). Etude psycholinguistique des capacités pragmatiques du langage chez les enfants de cinq a dix ans. *Revue Québécois de linguistique, 16,* 163–186.

French – Rondal

Jean Rondal
Laboratoire de Psychologie
Boulevarde du Rectorat, 5
Sart-Tilman
B-4000 Liège, Belgium
jarondal@vm1.ulg.ac.be

This corpus was contributed by Jean Rondal of the University of Liège. This directory contains a set of 120 files of interactions between Jean Rondal's son Stephane and his Mother Rene. Stephane was born on 28-JUN-1972 and was the only child during the time of these recordings. Stephane has agreed to the use of his name in the files. Between the ages of 1;2 and 4;3, the child was living in the United States in St. Paul, Minnesota with his parents. The language spoken in the family was French with only a few sentences from English from time to time. Between 4;4 and 4;9, the child was back in French-speaking Belgium with his family. From approximately 3;2 to 4;3, Stephane attended nursery school in St. Paul. His French MLU dropped in the first half of this period of time from 4.50 to 3.25, as he was struggling to learn to speak more English. Not uninterestingly, the mother's MLU stagnated and even dropped about 0.50 MLU during the same period of time.

The transcription and segmentation of utterances was done in accord with the principles discussed in Rondal, Bachelet, and Peree (1985). The files were converted into CHAT in 1992. The bulk of the sentences are produced either by the child (CHI) or the mother (MOT). Occasional sentences from the father or other adults are marked as Other (OTH). The mother's sentences are transcribed in standard French orthography. The child's sentences are transcribed in a nonstandard form in order to capture more closely the actual phonetics of the child's productions. The departures from standard French orthography are as follows:

1. A colon (:) following a vowel indicates lengthening.
2. The tilde (~) following the vowel "e" indicates an oral unrounded vowel with relatively high tongue position, as in the French word for "tea."
3. e= is a lowered front oral unrounded vowel as in "paix."
4. i= is a lowered front nasal unrounded vowel as in "pain."
5. u= is a lowered front nasal rounded vowel as in "brun."
6. o= is a lowered back nasal rounded vowel as in "bon."
7. a= is a low back nasal rounded vowel as in "blanc."
8. oe is a lowered front rounded oral vowel as in "peur."
9. eu is an high front oral rounded vowel as in "peu."
10. o" is a lowered back oral rounded vowel as in "peau."
11. o is a lowered back oral rounded vowel as in "part."
12. w indicates a rounded voiced velar semi-vowel or glide, as in "Wallon."

No attempt has been made or will be made to convert this system to UNIBET. Elisions are indicated by the apostrophe. Word stressing and pauses are marked. There are no comments or situational notes.

Publication using these data should cite:

Rondal, J. A. (1985). *Adult–child interaction and the process of language understanding.* New York: Praeger.

Rondal, J. A., Bachelet, J. F., & Peree, F. (1985). Analyse du langage et des interactions verbales adulte-enfant. *Bulletin d'Audiophonologie, 5.*

Italian – Calambrone

Paola Cipriani
IRCCS "Stella Maris"
INPE-Universitá di Pisa
Viale del Tirreno, 331
Calambrone (Pisa), Italy

Giuseppe Cappelli
ILC (CNR)
Via della Faggiola, 32
Pisa 56100 Italy
beppe@icnucevm.cnuce.cnr.it

This corpus includes data on both normal and disordered language development. The normal data come from six participants (2 boys and 4 girls) whose speech samples were collected at home. Each child was recorded bimonthly and every session lasted from 30 to 45 minutes. The data from children with language disorders were collected at the Stella Maris Institute and include longitudinal as well as cross-sectional data on clinical syndromes (developmental dysphasia, genetic and chromosomal disorders). The longitudinal participants are three dysphasic children, observed from the age of three. Their linguistic production was limited to holophrases and few word associations. Their speech was videotaped during monthly 30-minute sessions.

This database is the result of research conducted from 1985 to 1990 in the laboratory of "Fisiopatologia del linguaggio in etá evolutiva" in which many people have taken part: Piero Bottari, Anna Maria Chilosi, Lorena Cittadoni, Alessandro Ciuti, Anna Maccari, Natalia Pantano, Lucia Pfanner, Paola Poli, Stefania Sarno, Luca Surian, and Paola Cipriani as coordinator. Pietro Pfanner is the Scientific Director of the Institute. Giuseppe Cappelli of the Institute for Computational Linguistics (directed by Antonio Zampolli) was responsible for the computational aspects of the project. Data collection was supported by the grant 6 500.4/ICS/62.1/1135 (13/08/85) assigned to the Stella Maris Scientific Institute by the Italian Ministry of Health.

All transcripts were derived from videotaped interactions recorded with a video camera (Hitachi VM 200E or Nordmende V150). Each session was also audiotaped with a Sony™ TCM-6 recorder with Sony™ ECM-150T personal microphone. Transcripts were filed on floppy disks of IBM personal computer by one researcher, and the level of mutual evaluation agreement was checked by two independent transcribers.

The six normal participants were: Rafaello, a first-born boy from a family of high SES: followed from 1;7.08 to 3;3.00 (39 videotapings); Rosa, a second-born girl from a middle-low SES, followed from 1;3.00 to 3;3.23 (43 videotapings); Martina, the only daughter from a family of middle SES, followed from 1;7.00 to 3;0.00 (20 videotapings); Guglielmo, a second-born boy from a family of middle-high SES, followed from 2;1.00 to 2;11.00 (13 videotapings); Viola, a second-born girl from a family of middle SES, followed from

1;10.00 to 3;0.14 (23 videotapings); and Diana, a first-born girl from a family of middle SES, followed from 1;6.07 to 3;0.19 (26 videotapings).

Table 112: Longitudinal SLI Participants

Participant	Ages	Files	Kbytes	Words	Child Words
Marco	6;2 – 9;4	13	296	30587	8027
Sara	4;11 – 6;5	12	257	32735	8216
Davide	5;8 – 6;11	4	73	9191	4490
TOTAL		29	626	72513	20733

Table 113: Cross-Sectional SLI Participants

Participant	Ages	Files	Kbytes	Words	Child Words
Manolo	7	1	5	489	489
Angela	8;2	1	5	307	307
Jessica	10;3	1	6	469	469
Romina	8;3	1	7	497	497
Paola	10;7	1	5	234	234
Ketty	11;10	1	4	270	270
Francesca	7;9	1	11	1179	674
Emanuele	9;3	1	5	654	400
TOTAL		8	48	4179	3420

The language samples from children and interacting adults were transcribed in CHAT format with a minimum context contained in dependent tiers (%act; %gpx; %exp); the main lines of the children contain the real speech produced, with some coding for special forms of lexicon, punctuation, and pauses. At a second stage some new lines were added in order to code errors, omissions, and presyntactic devices. The focus of our first analysis was on lexical and morphological acquisition by normal and language-impaired children, looking in depth for transitional phenomena and stages of global language development.

Publications using these data should cite:

Cipriani, P., Pfanner, P., Chilosi, A., Cittadoni, L., Ciuti, A., Maccari, A., Pantano, N., Pfanner, L., Poli, P., Sarno, S., Bottari, P., Cappelli, G., Colombo, C., & Veneziano, E. (1989). *Protocolli diagnostici e terapeutici nello sviluppo e nella patologia del linguaggio* (1/84 Italian Ministry of Health): Stella Maris Foundation.

Italian – Roma

Elena Pizzuto
c/o Virginia Volterra
Istituto di Psicologia CNR
Viale Marx, 15
Rome, Italy
pizzuto@kant.irmkant.rm.cnr.it

Elena Pizzuto of the CNR in Rome has contributed these data in CHAT from a longitudinal study of a single child originally studied by Antinucci and Volterra. This corpus was collected in 1969 and 1970 as part of a language acquisition project at the Istituto di Psicologia in Rome. The male participant's name is Francesco. He was taperecorded between 1;4 and 4;0. The data is morphemically coded. The data collected had as focus the child's spontaneous language production with adults and the relevant contextual information during interaction. The transcription was morphemic rather than phonological and no attention was given to other features, such as paravocal.

Francesco was a bright, healthy child of middle-class, university educated parents living in Rome. Francesco's mother worked part-time as a biochemist. During her absence, Francesco was cared for by a working-class maid. The maid spoke a lower-class Roman version of Italian and this might be considered as a possible influence on Francesco's speech. Francesco attended preschool during the morning in the period from 2;6 (2 years, 6 months) through his fourth birthday. Francesco was a first-born child. His sister was born slightly before his third birthday. The mother's pregnancy is an issue that clearly concerned him and is discussed several times in the records from about 2;6 to 3;0.

Francesco was studied from 1;4 to 4;0. He was visited in his home approximately every two weeks, and two-hour audio recordings were made at each visit. The observer was well known to the family, and the children were accustomed to the recording equipment. Sessions were for the most part spontaneous and unplanned, although the adults present tended to initiate games or other activities that encouraged the children to talk. Because both were highly verbal children, such encouragement was rarely necessary.

Transcriptions of the recording sessions include all child speech, all adult speech relevant to the child's utterances, and information concerning the nonverbal context. The latter includes descriptions of the child's play activities, actions by the adult which prompt comment by the child, and any contextual or background information clarifying the child's communicative intentions. In Francesco's case, observer Virginia Volterra was also a family friend present on many occasions outside the research periods. Hence her background notes and interpretations are a particularly rich and accurate source.

When coding the transcripts into CHAT, several simplifications were made. First, a variety of types of data were noted on a %cri line. The abbreviation "cri" here stands for "context-relevant information" including gesture, situation, proxemics, and so forth. Second, the symbol @ was used without any further extensions for nonstandard forms. In general, these transcripts contain insufficient information to be used to study phonological development, intonation, retracings, or speech acts.

Publications using these data should cite:

Antinucci, F., & Parisi, D. (1973). Early language acquisition: A model and some data. In C. Ferguson & D. Slobin (Eds.), *Studies in child language development*. New York: Holt.

Antinucci, F., & Volterra, V. (1978). Lo sviluppo della negazione nel linguaggio infantile: Uno studio pragmatico. In L. Camaioni (Ed.), *Sviluppo del linguaggio e interazione sociale*. Bologna: Il Mulino.

Volterra, V. (1972). Prime fasi di sviluppo della negazione nel linguaggio infantile. *Archivio di Psicologia, Neurologia e Psichiatria, 33,* 16–53.

Volterra, V. (1976). A few remarks on the use of the past participle in child language. *Journal of Italian Linguistics, 2,* 149–157.

Volterra, V. (1984). Waiting for the birth of a sibling: The verbal fantasies of a two year old boy. In I. Bretherton (Ed.), *Symbolic Play*. New York: Academic Press.

Portuguese – Batoreo

Hanna Batoreo
Departamento de Linguística
Faculdade de Letras Univ. Lisboa
Lisbon 1699 Portugal
hb@di.fc.ul.pt

This corpus of narratives in Portuguese was collected in the context of work by Hanna Jakubowicz Batoreo on a doctoral dissertation in linguistics entitled "Towards the Characterization of the Interface Between Linguistic Expression and Spatial Cognition in European Portuguese: A Psycholinguistic Approach to the Expression of Space in Elicited Narrative Discourse" supervised by Professor Isabel Hub Faria at the Laboratorio de Psicolinguistica, Faculdade de Letras da Universidade de Lisboa, Lisboa, Portugal, 1996. This dissertation was supported by two funds of Junta Nacional de Investigacao Cientifica e Tecnologica: FMRH/BD/241/92 and PRAXIS XXI/BD/5260/95.

The two stories used for elicitation are the "horse" story and the "cat" story. For each story 60 narratives were elicited — 30 from adults and 30 from children. The children were ages 5, 7, and 10 with 10 children in each age group. The total number of elicited narratives is 120. The file names indicate the story ("h" or "c") followed by the age of the participant (5, 7, 10, or "ad") and the serial number of the participant within the group. After the numbers, is either the letter "f" for female or "m" for male.

The dissertation focuses on the linguistic knowledge of space. The language studied is the European variety of Portuguese. The study of space raises basic epistemological questions in a number of different fields (e.g., Cognitive Science, Philosophy, Social Sciences, the Arts). The characterization of the interface between linguistic expression and spatial cognition involved a strong experimental component, with a psycholinguistic methodology, namely with respect to production and acquisition. A moderate Whorfian assumption underlies the investigation undertaken, namely that languages differ from one another with respect to their semantic structures and that the latter are reflected on the ways speakers conceive the world. Given the general aims mentioned above, research was carried out along the following lines:

1. Demonstration of the relevance of cognition to the study of language, in particular to the interface between linguistic expression and spatial cognition;

2. Definition of the scientific scope of cognitive linguistics relative to other linguistic currents in cognitive science, given the assumption of localist theory, establishment of space primitives (both cognitive and linguistic) within Leonard Talmy's theoretical framework.

3. Analysis of the interactions among the grammatical, lexical, and contextual mechanisms of the linguistic expression of space in European Portuguese, taking into consideration spatial, temporal, and aspectual references.

4. Proposal of a parametrization of the space typology in European Portuguese and establishment of linguistic constraints on cognitive primitives of space.

5. Establishment of the spatial parameters of the production of elicited narrative discourse by European Portuguese native speakers (both children and adults), adopting the psycholinguistic methodology developed in the 90s in particular by Melissa Bowerman, as well as by Maya Hickmann and Henriette Hendriks.

The Cat Story:

Picture 1: A bird is sitting in a nest which is on a limb of a tree.

Picture 2: A bird flies away and a cat comes up to the tree.

Picture 3: The cat sits watching the empty nest.

Picture 4: The cat climbs the tree as a dog watches.

Picture 5: The dog pulls the cat's tail, as the bird flies back.

Picture 6: The dog chases the cat away, as the bird hovers at the nest.

The Horse Story:

Picture 1: A horse is running in the field near a fence.

Picture 2: The horse looks across the fence at a cow.

Picture 3: The horse jumps the fence. Cow in the background and a bird on the fence.

Picture 4: The horse stumbles on the fence and falls. The cow and bird watch.

Picture 5: The cow bandages up the horse's leg. The bird brings a first aid kit.

The dissertation contains two volumes (over 1,000 pages). Volume I includes seven-chapters which deal with the five topics listed above. Volume II, the Appendix (Chapter 8), includes in particular (Chapter 8.3) the Corpus of 120 narratives (60 adults and 60 children) elicited according to Hickman's technique. The corpus is transcribed and codified in the CHAT format.

Publications using these data should cite:

Batoreo, H. (1996). *Towards the characterization of the interface between linguistic expression and spatial cognition in European Portuguese: A psycholinguistic approach to the expression of space in elicited narrative discourse*. Unpublished doctoral dissertation. Faculdade de Letras da Universidade de Lisboa, Portugal.

Portuguese – Porto Alegre

Ana Maria Guimarães
Rua Carvalho Monteiro, 446/503
Porto Alegre RS 90479-100 Brazil
anaguima@vortex.ufrgs.br

Since 1991, a group of Brazilian researchers in Porto Alegre has been working to establish a database on the language development of children from 5 to 9 years of age. This research focuses on language development in the period of the acquisition of literacy. The project is named "Language development in children during the literacy period." The main goal of this project is to establish a data archive for doctoral students. The data are collected both cross-sectionally and longitudinally. However, only the cross-sectional data are currently in CHILDES. There are 180 cross-sectional participants, divided into 9 groups with 20 participants in each, sampled at 6-month intervals. There are 10 participants in the longitudinal study who have been followed five times a year, since 1992. All of the participants are middle-class students from private schools in Porto Alegre, Brazil. Porto Alegre, the capital of the state of Rio Grande do Sul, is located on the left bank of the Guaibaís river. With a territory of 497 square kilometers and nearly 3 million inhabitants, the metropolitan area has an intense cultural life built around two universities, museums and several theaters.

The longitudinal data are in the directory called "alegre-lo". The cross-sectional data are in the directory "alegre-x." The age ranges of the 9 cross-sectional groups are:

1. 5;0 to 5;5,29
2. 5;6 to 5;11,29
3. 6;0 to 6;5,29
4. 6;6 to 6;11,29
5. 7;0 to 7;5,29
6. 7;6 to 7;11,29
7. 8;0 to 8;5,29
8. 8;6 to 9;0
9. 9;0 to 9;6

The seven children in the longitudinal corpus are given in the following table:

Table 114: Porto Alegre Children

Child	Gender	Age
ALE	female	4;8.7 to 8;10.11
CAM	female	4;11.14 to 8;9.17
CAR	female	4;3:7 to 8;5.1

Table 114: Porto Alegre Children

Child	Gender	Age
GAB	male	5;9.19 to 9;0.17
MAT	male	6;2.3 to 9;0.2
NAT	female	5;4.2 to 8.9.24
ROD	male	5;5.1 to 7;7.2

All data were collected in interview situation between a female adult and the child. All interviews took place in the school the child was attending or in the home, and lasted approximately 30 minutes. There were three elicitation tasks that were designed to provide a representative sampling of the child's linguistic capabilities:

1. Dialogue between the investigator and the children during which the experimenter asks questions about school, home, or significant events in the child's life (like his or her birthday).

2. Personal narrative (oral and written) in which the aim was to encourage the child to report on a meaningful event, at school or at home.

3. Narrative from sequential pictures.

For 20% of the participants there are also data from two additional tasks:

4. Free conversation between children (dyads), and

5. Retelling of a story the child had listened to before.

There are two master's dissertations in progress based on this data. One of them looks for the emergence of narrative voices and the other analyses the use of aspect to distinguish narrative foreground and background. We are also developing a new project on spatial expression in children's narratives, in collaboration with Drs. Faria and Batoréo of the University of Lisbon in Portugal.

Publications using these data should cite:

Guimarães, A. M. (1994). Desenvolvimento da linguagem da criança na fase deletramento. *Cadernos de Estudos Linguísticos, 26,* 103–110.
Guimarães, A. M. (1995). The use of the CHILDES database for Brazilian Portuguese. In I. H. Faria & M. J. Freitas (Eds.), *Studies on the acquisition of Portuguese*. Lisbon: Colibri.

Portuguese – Florianópolís

Leonor Scliar-Cabral
UFSC/LLV
Rua São Miguel 1106
Bairro Saco Grande
Florianópolís, Brazil 88030
isapl@cce.ufsc.br

These data were collected, transcribed, and examined during Leonor Scliar-Cabral's doctoral thesis work in 1974. The records were reviewed during the adaptation at the University of Florianópolís to CHILDES in 1993. They consist of one Brazilian Portuguese child's 5530 utterances in broad phonetic transcription (including intonational patterns) collected in three sessions:

1. Age 1;8.21, MLU 1.45 with 5 hours of recording for 1320 utterances.

2. Age 1;10.20, MLU 2.22 with 6 hours of recording for 2245 utterances.

3. Age 2;2.8, MLU 2.40 with 6 hours of recording for 1966 utterances.

The phonetic transcription was made by Scliar-Cabral, who has phonological training. Three speech therapy students checked the transcriptions. The intonational patterns that were transcribed in the original version were not adapted to CHILDES, but this information will be added in the future. Notes were taken for describing the situational context and/or any relevant information. The child's mother and father were helpful in translating his lexical creations. No videotapes were made. The following measures were computed: MLU, utterance types, utterance tokens, type-token ratio, upper bound, number of imitations, percentage of imitations, lexicon size, number of nouns, verbs, adjectives, locatives, and pronouns, functors required, functors present, and percentage of functors present. Other classes computed were: copulas; modals; pivotal operators; discourse operators; tags; interjections; onomatopoeias; stereotypes. Pronouns were subclassified as possessive, demonstrative and interrogative. MLU was computed using the criteria suggested by Brown (1973) and Bowerman (1973). Utterances were coded only as imitations if they had an identical intonation to the previous utterance, as well as a complete lexical overlap. Omitting imitations and onomatopoeias, the MLU computed by CLAN matched that computed by hand.

The child was a Brazilian Portuguese native speaker, living in an upper-middle class suburb of São Paulo. He attended a part-day upper-middle-class nursery where Brazilian Portuguese was spoken. His parents were of upper-class Jewish background: although the father was a fluent speaker of French, the parents spoke only Brazilian Portuguese with their child. The father was a professor of linguistics at the University of São Paulo; the mother was a psychologist. There were frequent and tight contacts with other relatives, like uncles, aunts, and grandparents who also used Brazilian Portuguese. As is common among Brazilian upper-middle-class families, there was a housekeeper and a nanny who used a lower-class sociolinguistic variety, sometimes from different regions of Brazil. Excluding these inputs, all the other adults used the Brazilian Portuguese variety of São Paulo city and its surroundings.

Spanish- ColMex

Oralia Rodriquez
Estudios Linguisticos
El Colegio de Mexico, A.C.
Camino Al Ajusco No. 20
Mexico, D. F. 01000
orodrig@jupiter.colmex.mx

This corpus includes short samples from 30 Mexican children ages 6;0 to 7;0. Each child performed two tasks. One was the narrative description of a short set of pictures; the other involved providing instructions for a simple task. The files for the narratives are named *nar.cha and the files for the instructions are named *ins.cha.

Spanish – Diez-Itza

Eliseo Diez-Itza
Universidad de Oviedo
Departamento de Filosofía y Psicología
C/ Aniceto Sela
33005 Oviedo, Spain
ditza@correo.uniovi.es

These data were contributed by Eliseo Diez-Itza. They are a small part of a much larger corpus being prepared at the University of Oviedo by Dr. Diez-Itza and his students, with assistance from Verónica Martínez, Raúl Cantora, and Manuela Miranda. This database has provided the basis for several cross-sectional descriptive studies on the acqustion of Spanish, with special focus on phonological, lexical, and narrative issues. The directory currently contains 20 transcripts of dyadic conversations between children (10 girls and 10 boys in the age range from 3;0 to 3;11) and investigators trained in the process of recording, transcribing, and analyzing spontaneous speech samples, using CHAT conventions. The taping sessions were conducted in the participants' homes. Each one lasted approximately forty-five minutes. During this spontaneous verbal interaction, the children had to tell a story. They were also asked to talk about a visit to the doctor, and a birthday party. GEM header lines were used to mark these particular passages. The spontaneous speech parts (HES) were also marked.

Publications using these data should cite one or more of these:

Diez-Itza, E. (1995). Procesos fonológicos en la adquisición del español como lengua materna. In J.M. Ruiz, P. Sheerin, & E. González-Cascos (Eds.), *Actas del XI Congreso Nacional de Linguistica Aplicada*. Valladolid:Universidad de Valladolid.

Diez-Itza, E. (1998). *Nuevas tecnologías para el estudio del aprendizaje del lenguaje desde la perspectiva funcional: El proyecto CHILDES*. Paper presented at the XXII International Conference of Functional Linguistics, Evora, Portugal.

Diez-Itza, E., Martínez, V., Cantora, R., & Miranda, M. (1999). *Procesos fonológicos de metátesis en el habla infantil*. Paper presented at the IV Symposium of Psychlinguistics, Universidad Autónoma de Madrid, Spain.

Diez-Itza, E., & Perez-Toral, M. (1996). El desarrollo temprano de funciones discursivas. In M. Perez-Pereira (Ed.), *Estudios sobre la adquisicion del castellano, catalan, euskera y gallego*. Santiago de Compostela: Universidade de Santiago de Compostela.

Diez-Itza, E., Snow, C.E., & MacWhinney, B. (1999). La Metodología RETAMHE y el Proyecto CHILDES: breviario para la codificación y análisis del lenguaje infantil. *Psicothema, 11*, 3: 517-530

Spanish – Linaza

José L. Linaza
Psicología de los procesos
Universidad Autónoma de Madrid
Cantoblanco
Madrid 34, Spain
jlinaza@ccuam3.sdi.uam.es

Jose Linaza of the University of Madrid has contributed data from a longitudinal case study of his son Juan between ages 2 and 4. Juan's younger brother Jaime also talks in the files collected at the later ages. The names of the files reflect Juan's ages in years and months. The data were reformatted into CHAT in 1992. Most of the files have the father as the major interlocutor. However, the mother and another researcher speak with the child on some of the tapes. Juan's speech is often transcribed in a way that captures phonological deletions. For example, "Orge" is used for "Jorge" and so on. Before doing analyses for lexical items, the researcher should take a good look at these alternative spellings. The marking of clauses or utterances in the original was not always consistent, so counts such as MLU would not be appropriate.

Spanish – López Ornat

Susan López Ornat
Departamento de Procesos Cognitivos
Facultad de Psicología
Universidad Complutense de Madrid
Madrid 28223 Spain
pscog09@sis.ucm.es

This directory contains the longitudinal corpora of a Spanish child, from Madrid, Spain. The child, named María, was studied by Susana López Ornat of Madrid's Complutense University, from 1988 to 1991. María is an only child who was videotaped from ages 1;07 to 4;00, every fortnight in sessions of about 30 minutes. Those took place at home during bath, play or feeding interactions with her parents, who belong to a middle-class professional family. The CHAT version of the database was recoded by María Carrasco, at the Faculty of Psychology (Universidad Complutense de Madrid).

The ID field for file segments has three components: the first digits correspond to age in years and months, "z" stands for this participant, and the following three digits number the file in a chronological order. Example: the ID field 107z001.cha indicates the first segment of the file from age 1;07.

The symbol [= text] stands for the adult version of María's sentence.

The symbol [= ? text] stands for unknown adult version.

The symbol [=% text] stands for the sentence context.

The symbol ( ) indicates an ambiguous phoneme.

The transcription was made maintaining the orthographic rules of standard Spanish, but an apostrophe (') marks the emission of an amalgam, where the child fuses two or more different adult words with no underlying grammatical analysis. For example, "s'a" means the child has fused the clitic "se" with the verb "ha".

Publications using these data should cite:

López Ornat, S. (1994) *La adquisición de la lengua Española*. Madrid: Siglo XXI.

For further analysis of this database please consult:

López Ornat, S. (1997) What lies in between a pregrammatical and a grammatical representation? Evidence on nominal and verbal form-function mappings in Spanish from 1;07 to 2;01. In W.R. Glass & A. T. Pérez-Leroux (Eds.) *Contemporary perspectives on the acquisition of Spanish*. Somerville, Mass., Cascadilla Press.

Mariscal, S. (1996) Adquisiciones morfosintácticas en torno al sintagma nominal: El género gramatical en español. In M. Pérez Pereira (Ed.) *Estudios sobre la adquisición del castellano, catalán, eusquera y gallego* (pp. 263–270). Universidade de Santiago de Compostela: Servicio de Publicacions.

Spanish – Marrero / Albalá

José María Albalá
Departamento de Lengua Española
Universidad Nacional de Educación a Distancia
Senda del Rey s/n
28040 Madrid, Spain

Victoria Marrero
Departamento de Lengua Española
Univ. Nacional de Educ. a Distancia
Senda del Rey s/n
Madrid, Spain 28040
Victoria.Marrero@human.uned.es

These 12 files are the first part of a corpus on Spanish child language in CHAT format. The aim of our work is the linguistic analysis (at the phonic, morphologic, syntactic, semantic, and pragmatic levels) of the language of six normal children, from 1;8 to 8 years old. This longitudinal study started at the end of 1990. Transcription is orthographic, when it is possible. When the child form does not correspond to a standard word, but we can identify the unit, the transcription is as close as feasible to the orthographic representation.

Errors are not marked with [*] on the main line, but are coded on the %err dependent tier, with the following structure:

<locus> nonstandard word = standard word

Files beginning by IDA belong to a child living in the Canary Islands, where a specific dialect of Spanish is spoken (similar, in some aspects, to the Caribbean Spanish). The transcription was made, however, maintaining the orthographic rules of standard Spanish, but indications about the pronunciation of some sounds are attached.

Spanish – Montes

Rosa Graciela Montes
Universidad Autónoma de Puebla
Apdo. Postal 1356
Puebla, Mexico 72001
rmontes@udlapvms.pue.udlap.mx

The data being contributed consist of transcripts of thirteen 30 to 45 minute audio recordings of a Spanish-speaking child interacting with her parents in the child's home. The earliest recording was made when the child was 1;7.20 years of age and the last one when she was 2;11.14.

Biographical data

Koki was the first child of a middle-class professional couple. Both parents were linguists. At the time the tapes were made the parents had research and teaching jobs in a linguistics program in Patzcuaro, Mexico. The mother was out of the house from 9 A.M. to 1 P.M. and then again from 4 to 8 every evening. The father worked mostly at home. At the time the tapes were made Koki was the only child; however, during some of the later tapes, the mother is pregnant with her second child, and reference is made to this baby in some of the tapes.

Language Background

The child, Koki, who is the researcher's own child, was acquiring Spanish as a first language. The father is American, his native language is English and he was learning Spanish at the time that the tapes were being made. However, even when he was not fluent in the language, he usually addressed Koki in Spanish. The mother is Argentine, her native language is Spanish, but she had acquired English as a child living in various English-speaking countries. The parents spoke in English to each other but both spoke mostly in Spanish to Koki. Koki was born in Poland, where her parents were teaching. When she was 6 months old the family left Poland and went on an extended trip to Argentina where they stayed until just before Koki's first birthday. During this time they lived with the mother's family in a Spanish-speaking household. The family lived briefly in the States, for a period of two months (1;1 to1;3) and then moved to Patzcuaro, Michoacan, in Mexico, where the recordings were made. At the time the recordings were started they had been living in Patzcuaro for 4 months (1;7.20).

To summarize Koki's language background: she was acquiring Spanish as a first language. Everybody in the house spoke to her in Spanish, including her father who was learning Spanish. The Spanish spoken in her surroundings was Mexican Spanish; however, the mother spoke Argentine Spanish. Koki's Spanish seems to be mostly Mexican. In the earlier tapes there are some phonological and lexical features from Argentine Spanish. In the later tapes, there are Argentine lexical items, but Koki's phonology is mostly Mexican. Her regular contacts with Mexican speakers included a Mexican woman who came in daily to help around the house and two little girls, slightly older, who lived down the street and with whom Koki played often.

The parents did not keep a diary record of Koki's language development, but notes indicated that her first "words" were at around 10 months. A lexicon of her productive vocabulary drawn up on June 15, one month before the first recording, lists approximately 60 words.

Data Collection

The data were gathered with no particular purpose other than to document the development of the child's "communicative competence." The tape recorder was turned on during "play sessions" or daily routines (lunch, bath, and so forth.) and no attempt was made to elicit any forms or test her competence. The tape recorder was always in full view and was a big source of interest although it did not appear to inhibit the child. However, it did have some influence on the interaction because very often when the child made moves to grab the microphone or the tape recorder the mother attempted to distract her by calling attention to some other objects or would initiate some other activity. These play sessions are "naturalistic," but they are also special child-centered situations. The adults tended to follow the child's lead and the child, in general, is the one who proposed and initiated activities. When both parents were together they tended to each interact with the child rather than with each other. Talk between the parents were tacitly assumed to be some sort of interruption. When the tape recorder was not on the same type of activity often occurred. Thus, the recorded events were felt to be natural or typical of that type of situation. However, unrecorded play sessions were more susceptible to outside interruptions than were recorded ones.

Transcription

The transcripts presented are in CHAT format. Pauses are indicated by # plus seconds and tenths of seconds in brackets. Following suggestions in the literature for conversations with young children, only pauses between utterances greater than 2 seconds were marked. The transcripts were made from audio recordings. During the recording sessions one of the parents (usually the mother) made notes about the context of utterances, concurrent actions, and so forth. However, these notes usually note major, salient actions and details are lost that often are crucial for giving a full interpretation of what went on.

Table 115: Montes Files

File	Date	Age	Duration
k01	21-JUL-1980	1;7.20	30 mins

Table 115: Montes Files

File	Date	Age	Duration
k02	19-SEP-1980	1;9.18	30 mins
k03	26-NOV-1980	1;11.25	30 mins
k04	30-JAN-1981	2;1.29	30 mins
k05	28-FEB-1981	2;2.27	30 mins
k06	22-MAR-1981	2;3.21	10 mins
k07	19-APR-1981	2;4.18	30 mins
k08	25-MAY-1981	2;5.24	45 mins
k09	11-JUN 1981	2;6.10	30 mins
k10	11-JUL-1981	2;7.10	30 mins
k11	10-AUG-1981	2;8.9	30 mins
k12	19-SEP-1981	2;9.18	30 mins
k13	15-NOV-1981	2;11.14	45 mins

K01 and K13 are the end-points of the tapes done with this child, however there are about twenty additional tapes awaiting further transcription.

The author would appreciate receiving a citation notice of any use made of this corpus, and, if possible, a copy of the paper or article.

Publications using these data should cite:

Montes, R. (1987). *Secuencias de clarificación en conversaciones con niños (Morphe 3-4):* Universidad Autónoma de Puebla.
Montes, R. G. (1992). *Achieving understanding: Repair mechanisms in mother–child conversations.* Unpublished doctoral dissertation, Georgetown University.

Spanish – Romero

Silvia Romero-Contreras
University of the Americas
Puebla 223 Col. Roma
Mexico, D.F. 06700

This project has been funded by the researchers themselves and the University of the Americas. This corpus is part of a database that we are gathering of Spanish as a first language in naturalistic contexts, for the development of descriptive studies of the process of the construction of communicative competence in Spanish monolinguals.

Data Collection

Data were collected from the child in daily parent–child interaction at home. Samples were videotaped. Children in this project are selected according to the age range defined (6 months to 7 years). They, as well as their parents, have to be native Spanish speakers, residents of Mexico City for the last 5 years. Participants have to be free of any condition that may suggest abnormal development or a family history that may indicate a language impairment. Children should be free of strong cultural influences other than Mexican; therefore, those children attending bicultural schools are not eligible.

Transcription Procedure

Transcription was done directly from the videotapes with the aid of field diaries for other contextual information. Several passes of the video were often necessary. Regular spelling was the rule, except for unintelligible or child specific utterances. No translation into English has been included. Warning: Contextual information is still limited; copies of videos are available on request.

In the file name, the first and second digits stand for the lower limit of the age range of the child at the beginning of the study, expressed in years (first digit) and months (second digit). The third and fourth digits stand for sex. Twelve children are included in each age range, therefore numbers used are from 00 to 11, odd numbers are females, even numbers are males. The fifth digit stands for the child's school option, that is, the kind of school the child attends or is going to attend: 0 = public school, 9 = private school. The sixth digit stands for the part of the corpus in the file, this data is coded progressively: 1 = first part, 2 = second part, and so forth.

Three @Stim codes are used: Sinclair lógica, Sinclair física, and Sinclair simbólico. These codes refer to specific tasks used with the children in order to assess their cognitive development taken from Sinclair (1982).

Biographical Data for participant in file 200691. Participant's age at the beginning of the study was 2 years. He was a male. He had one older and one younger sisters. He was enrolled in a private preschool. His parents were middle-upper-class. The father was a bio-chemical engineer currently working in the Foreign Trade Division of a Foreign bank. The mother was a Speech and Language therapist. They were Catholics.

All the family, except for the father who grew up in Monterrey, Nuevo León, had always lived in Mexico City. The family lived in an urban home with all facilities: kitchen, three bathrooms, four bedrooms, garage, garden, and so forth. The child, at the moment of the study, shared his room with his older sister (5 years) and had for himself and his siblings a game-room full of toys of all kinds. The child likes to watch movies, the same ones over and over. His favorite activities include ball games, playing musical toy instruments, story telling, book reading and other age appropriate games.

No pseudonyms have been used, nor need to be used. Informants have given consent for the use of their data. We ask potential users of our data to give notice in advance to the authors, outlining the purpose of the study and specific uses to the corpus.

Publications using these data should cite:

Romero, S., Santos, A., & Pellicer, D. (1992). *The construction of communicative competence in Mexican Spanish speaking children (6 months to 7 years).* Mexico City: University of the Americas.

Additional references include:

Sinclair, H. (1982). *Los beb.* Buenos Aires: Gedisa.

Spanish – Serra / Sole

This directory contains the transcripts from the single Spanish-speaking child in the Serra / Sole longitudinal study of 10 children. In the larger study, five children are monolingual Catalan, four are bilingual Catalan-Spanish, and one is monolingual Spanish. The Spanish speaking-child, Eduard, was videotaped from 1;4 to 3;10 from 1986 to 1989. He was videotaped at his homes in spontaneous interaction with his mother, in sessions of 30 to 45 minutes. The family was middle-class.

The research project is entitled "Language acquisition in Catalan and Spanish children" and is directed by Miquel Serra (Universitat de Barcelona) and Rosa Sole (Universitat Autonoma de Barcelona). It has received support from the Spanish research council (Grants DGICYT PB84/0455; PB89/0317; PB91/0851; PB94/0886). The research assistants of the project have been: Montserrat Cortes, Connie Schultz, Elisabet Serrat, Vicens Torrents, and Melina Aparici. Cristina Vila and Montse Capdevila have collaborated in different stages of it.

The authors would appreciate receiving a copy, or a summary, of any work using the corpus. The times for the recording of the 11 files from Eduard are as follows:

10-14.cha	(1;4,8)
10-15.cha	(1;5,16)
10-16.cha	(1;7,15)
10-17.cha	(1;9,19)
10-18.cha	(2;0,30)
10-19.cha	(2;3,4)
10-20.cha	(2;4,28)
10-21.cha	(2;7,10)
10-22.cha	(2;10,0)
10-23.cha	(3;1,12)
10-24.cha	(3;10,20)

Spanish – Vila

Elisabet Serrat Sellabona
Department of Psychology
University of Girona, Pl. Sant Domenech, 9
17071 Girona, Spain
eli@zeus.udg.es

This is a corpus of data from Emilio, a Spanish-speaking boy who was audio recorded (with some gaps) from 0;11 to 4;08. Emilio was born 20-MAY-1980. The project has been partially supported by a grant from Spanish Government (DGICYT PB89-0624-C02-01). The head of the project was Ignasi Vila, and the work was carried out in the ICE (Institute of Educational Sciences) in the University of Barcelona. Associate researchers were Montserrat Cortes, Montserrat Moreno, Carme Muñoz, and Elisabet Serrat. The collection and transcription of the data would have not been possible without the help of Carme Mena, Ana Novella, and Joaquim Romero.

Table 116: Vila – Emilio Files

File	Age	File	Age	File	Age
E01.cha	0;11.09	E13.cha	1;10.11	E25.cha	2;08.27
E02.cha	1;00.10	E14.cha	1;10.19	E26.cha	2;11.07
E03.cha	1;01.20	E15.cha	1;11.12	E27.cha	2;11.24
E04.cha	1;04.09	E16.cha	2;00.02	E28.cha	3;10.00
E05.cha	1;04.24	E17.cha	2;00.29	E29.cha	3;10.13
E06.cha	1;05.19	E18.cha	2;01.22	E30.cha	3;11.25
E07.cha	1;06.08	E19.cha	2;03.00	E31.cha	4;00.09
E08.cha	1;06.19	E20.cha	2;04.16	E32.cha	4;01.00
E09.cha	1;07.11	E21.cha	2;05.23	E33.cha	4;01.12
E10.cha	1;08.13	E22.cha	2;06.17	E34.cha	4;06.00
E11.cha	1;08.26	E23.cha	2;07.08	E35.cha	4;08.15
E12.cha	1;09.19	E24.cha	2;07.24		

8:   Other Languages

Table 117: Other Languages

Corpus	Age Range	N	Comments
Cantonese on page 362	1;05–3;08	8	Longitudinal study; language development of Cantonese-speaking children each recorded for approximately one year.
Estonian – Argus on page 366	1;8–2;5	1	Case study of an Estonian child
Greek – Stephany on page 367	1;9, 2;3–2;9, 1;9– 2;9, 1;11– 2;9	4	Data on Greek acquisition collected in natural speech situations in the home and school
Hebrew – BSF on page 368	1;6–5;11	100	Cross sectional, naturalistic speech samples of Hebrew-speaking preschool children.
Hebrew – Levy on page 374	1;10–4;11	11	Several Israeli children studied for a short period of time, along with a few studied for up to two years
Hebrew – Na'ama on page 375	1;7–2;6	1	Longitudinal study made in the home with or without the mother present
Hebrew – Ravid on page 376	1;8–6;10 (37)	1	Longitudinal study of Hebrew in a naturalistic setting
Hungarian – MacWhinney on page 378	1;5–2; 10	5	Longitudinal study of five Hungarian children in a nursery school environment
Irish – Guilfoyle on page 380	6	2–3	Single sessions from Irish-speaking children
Japanese – Miyata on page 382	1;3–3;0	2	Longitudinal study of two Japanese siblings in their home
Mambila – Zeitlyn on page 386	mostly adults	12	A single conversation from a household in Somie village, West Cameroon with an English translation

Table 117: Other Languages

Corpus	Age Range	N	Comments
Mandarin – Tardif Beijing on page 393	1;9.3–2;2.7	10	Longitudinal study in a naturalistic setting with an English transcription included
Mandarin – Tardif Context on page 396	2 year olds	25 + 25	Cross-sectional study with single observations of 25 Mandarin-speaking children and 25 comparison English-speaking children
Polish – Szuman on page 397	1;5–7;9	10	Diary data collected by Szuman and his students and computerized by Magdalena Smoczynska
Polish – Weist on page 398	1;7–2;6	3	Three children learning Polish with six files for each child
Russian – Protassova on page 399	N/A	1	Longitudinal study of a child learning Russian
Russian – Tanja on page 400	2;5–2;11	1	A child learning Russian in a monolingual environment in the United States
Tamil – Narasimhan on page 402	0;9–2;9	1	Longitudinal study of a Tamil child during unstructured situations with her parents in the home
Turkish – Aksu Koç on page 406	2;0–4;8	34	Cross-sectional data collected during the visit to the children's home or preschool with some follow up four months later
Welsh on page 407	18–30 1;6–2;6	7	Longitudinal study of natural speech from children in the early stages of acquisition of Welsh as a first language

Cantonese

Thomas Lee
Department of English
Chinese University of Hong Kong
Hong Kong
thomaslee@cuhk.hk

This corpus was collected by Thomas Hun-tak Lee (Chinese University of Hong Kong), Colleen H. Wong (Hong Kong Polytechnic University), and Samuel Leung. This database contains longitudinal data on the language of eight Cantonese-speaking children, each recorded for approximately 1 year. The corpus contains 171 files coded in CHAT format and tagged with a set of 33 word-class labels.

These children were observed in their interactions with the caretakers, the investigator, and occasionally other adults who chatted with the children during the visits. Three research students carried out the observations and the recording. Patricia Man recorded Bohuen and Gakie; Alice Cheung recorded Bernard, Tsuntsun and Tinfaan; and Kitty Szeto recorded Johnny, Jenny and Chunyat. The names of the children and the ages during which they were recorded are as follows:

Table 118: Cantonese Files

Name	Sex	Ages	Files
Bohuen (wbh)	F	2;03;23 – 3;04;08	27
Gakei (cgk)	F	1;11;01 – 2;09;09	19
Bernard (mhz)	M	1;07;00 – 2;08;06	26
Tsuntsun (ckt)	M	1;05;22 – 2;07;22	25
Tinfaan (ltf)	F	2;02;10 – 3;02;18	16
Johnny (hhc)	M	2;04;08 – 3;04;14	16
Jenny (lly)	F	2;08;10 – 3;08;09	20
Chunyat (ccc)	M	1;10;08 – 2;10;27	22

Each file name is made up of the initials of the child (the first three characters) and his or her age at the time of recording, in terms of year (1 character), month (2 characters), and day (2 characters). For instance, the file wbh20322.cha contains tagged utterances of Bohuen (whb) when she was 2 years, 3 months, and 22 days old.

The Children

Bohuen was raised in a monolingual Cantonese-speaking working-class family. Her father worked in the warehouse of a mass transport company and her mother was a part-time piano teacher. She had a brother who was about 2 years younger. They lived with the child's grandmother and uncle. The child had already started attending a nursery school when data collection started. After school, she was taken care of by her parents and grandmother.

Gakei was also raised in a monolingual Cantonese-speaking working class family. Her father was a technician in a electronic company and her mother was a housewife. They lived with the child's grandmother. Gakei's parents were both born in Hong Kong. The child was not yet enrolled in a nursery during the whole period of data collection. She was taken care of entirely by her mother.

Tsuntsun was the only son of a Cantonese-speaking family, living in Hong Kong. His father was a Census and Survey Officer working in the government and his mother a secondary school teacher teaching Chinese and Religious Studies. Since his birth, he had been living in his maternal grandparents' house during weekdays and was taken care of by his grandmother. His parents visited him occasionally during the weekday evenings and took him back home on Friday nights to stay over the weekend. They communicated in Cantonese. When Tsuntsun was 1;10, his mother went to study for a year in the United Kingdom. He started to attend a nursery at 2;1.

Bernard was born in Kent, United Kingdom. He was the only son of the family. His father was a lecturer in the Division of Construction and Land Use of the Hong Kong Polytechnic. His mother was a lecturer of the English Language Teaching Unit of the Chinese University of Hong Kong. Bernard's mother brought him back from the United Kingdom at the age of 8 months. He was then taken care of by his maternal grandmother at her house until the age of about 1;1. From that time to the age of 2 years 6 months, he was taken care of by a caretaker during the weekdays. He communicated in Cantonese, though his parents occasionally introduced to him some English terms. He started to attend the nursery playgroups at the age of 2 years 6 months.

Tinfaan was the youngest child in a Cantonese-speaking family living in Hong Kong. She had a sister who was four years older. Her father was an engineer working in the government and her mother was a piano teacher teaching at home. During the first one-and-a-half years from her birth, she was taken care of mostly by a Filipino helper while her mother worked as a school music teacher. After her mother had stopped working in school, Tinfaan was mostly taken care of by her mother, except at times when her mother had to give piano lessons or had to go out, when Tinfaan would be looked after by her Filipino helper. She communicated in Cantonese except when speaking to her Filipino helper, for which she used "something English-like" (as described by her mother). She started to attend kindergarten at the age of 2 years 9 months.

Jenny was the youngest child in the family. She was born in Hong Kong and her family spoke Cantonese. She had an elder brother who was ten years older and an elder sister who was four years older. Jenny's father was a businessman and her mother was a housewife. The family employed a Filipino helper, who spoke some Cantonese and English to the children. She had not started going to a nursery during the period of data collection.

Johnny was the youngest child in the family. He was born in Hong Kong and his family spoke Cantonese. He had an elder sister who was seven years older. His father was an engineer and her mother was a typist. The family employed a Thai helper and she spoke Cantonese to the children. He had not started going to a nursery during the period of data collection.

Chunyat was the only son in the family. He was born in Hong Kong and his family spoke Cantonese. His father was a merchant and his mother taught English in a secondary school. They lived with the child's maternal grandparents. He had not started going to a nursery during the period of data collection.

Codes

Below is a summary list of the syntactic categories used in coding the corpus. The romanizations are based on the Cantonese romanization scheme of the Linguistic Society of Hong Kong (LSHK) (Matthews & Yip,1994, pp. 400-401).

Category	Example
1. adj = adjective	hung4
2. adv = focus adverb	zung6, dou1, jau6, zoi3
3. advi = adverb of intensity	hou3, gei2, gam3, zan1
4. advm = adverb of manner	maan6maan6dei2, ma4ma4dei2
5. advs = sentential adverb	bat1jyu4, gam2(joeng2), jat1cai4
6. asp = aspectual marker	zo2, zyu6, gan2, gwo3, hoi1
7. aux = auxiliary / modal verb	jing1goi1, hang2, ho2ji5, wui, sai2
8. cl = classifier	go3, zek3, bun2, bui1, di1
9. com = comparative morpheme	gwo3 (as in dai6 gwo3), di1 (as in hung4 di1)
10. conj = connective	dan6hai6, tung4maai4, waak6ze2
11. corr = correlative	jut6...jut6, jau6...jau6, gam2...gam3, jat1...jat1
12. ctc = clitic	dak1, dou3
13. det = determiner	nei1, go2, dai6
14. dir = directional verb	lok6, soeng5, ceot1, jap6, lai4
15. ex = expressive utterance	baai1baai3, zou2san4
16. gen = genitive marker	ge3
17. ins=emphatic inserted marker	gwai2 (as in hou3 gwai2 leng3)
18. nn = noun	ping4gwo2, ba4ba1
19. nnloc = locative noun phrase	soeng6mien6, leoi3mien6
20. nnpr = pronoun	ngo5, nei3, keoi3
21. nnpp = proper name	tin1faan4, zeon3zeon3

22. neg = negative morpheme   m4, mai6, mou5
23. prt = postverbal particle   faan1, sai3, can1, maai4, gwo3, ha2
24. prep = preposition   tung4maai2, hai2, bei2
25. q = quantifier   jat1, saam1, sap6, gei2, mui5
26. rfl = reflexive pronoun   zi6gei2
27. sfp = sentence final particle   &la3, &ga1 &ma3, &ge3 &le1
28. vd = ditransitive verb   bai2, bei2
29. verg = ergative verb   dit3
30. vf = function verb   hai6, jau5, hai2
31. vi = intransitive verb   siu3
32. vt = transitive verb   teoi1
33. wh = wh words   mat1, mat1je5, dim2, dim2gaai2, dim2jeong2

Chinese characters

The romanized version is derived from the Chinese tagged corpus by means of a conversion program based on a dictionary. Since a character may have different pronunciations (due to language variation or context), the romanized data files sometimes give more than one romanized form for a single character, separated by ^. Thus, for example, the Cantonese morpheme for "you" can have an alveolar lateral initial or an alveolar nasal initial. The morpheme will be rendered as "lei^nei" in the romanized data. The romanized corpus contains the categorial tags below each romanized utterance, but it does not contain English glosses. In time, we hope to seek resources to enable us to disambiguate the romanized forms, and provide English glosses. The CHAT version now in the CHILDES archive is a version that incorporates the Chinese characters on a "%can" tier, with the romanizations on the main tier. This amalgamation was done first by Brian MacWhinney, whose help and advice in the final stages of the corpus preparation is gratefully acknowledged, and then checked by the research team. This version has passed the CHECK test for format consistency.

The creation of this corpus was made possible by a three-year grant (RGC earmarked grant CUHK 2/91) to Thomas Hun-tak Lee of the Chinese University of Hong Kong, Colleen H, Wong of the Hong Kong Polytechnic University, and Samuel Leung of the University of Hong Kong. The project was supported by two studentships from the Hong Kong Polytechnic awarded to Patricia Man and Alice Cheung, and a studentship from the University of Hong Kong awarded to Kitty Szeto. In addition, funding for the later stages of the project was provided by a direct grant from Faculty of Arts, Chinese University of Hong Kong, a grant from the Freemason's Fund for East Asian Studies, as well as research assistantships from the Hong Kong Polytechnic University. The support of these funding agencies is hereby acknowledged. Further details are given in the following report, which should be cited when these data are used:

Lee, T. H.T., Wong, C. H., Leung, S., Man. P., Cheung, A., Szeto, K., and Wong, C. S. P. *The Development of Grammatical Competence in Cantonese-speaking Children*, Report of RGC earmarked grant 1991-94.

Estonian – Argus

Reili Argus
Ugala 25
Talllinn, Estonia EE0016
T.Argus@crebit.ed

Reili Argus of Tallinn, Estonia, has contributed a set of 17 files documenting the language development of a single Estonian-speaking child, Hendrik, between ages 1;8 and 2;5.

Greek – Stephany

Ursula Stephany
Institut fur Sprachwissenschaft
Universität zu Köln
D-5000 Köln 41, Germany
stephany@rs1.rrz.uni-koeln.de

The Greek child data in this corpus were donated by Ursula Stephany. They were collected between 1971 and 1974 in natural speech situations in the homes and Kindergarten from four monolingual Greek children growing up in Athens, Greece.

The boy Spiros was observed at 1;9.
The girl Maria was observed at 2;3 and 2;9.
The girl Mairi was observed at 1;9, 2;3, and 2;9.
The girl Janna was observed at 1;11, 2;5, and 2;9.

File names (e.g., MAI21A1.cha) are structured as follows:

Child's name: SPI, MAR, MAI, JAN
Child's age in months
Period of observation: A (1;9 or 1;11), B (2;3 or 2;5), C (2;9)
Running number of file at period A, B, or C.

The transcription is phonetic/phonemic. Capital letters have been used for the interdental fricatives (D voiced, T, unvoiced) and the voiced velar fricative (G). Grammatical coding is to be found on the %mor line; phonetic detail is indicated on the %phon line; adult correspondences are indicated on the main line or on the %err line.

Publications using these data should cite:

Stephany, U. (1992). Grammaticalization in first language acquisition. Zeitschrift für Phonetik, *Sprachwißenschaft, und Kommunikationsforschung, 45,* 289–303.
Stephany, U. (1995). The acquisition of Greek. In D. I. Slobin (Ed.), *The crosslinguistic study of language acquisition. Vol. 4.* Hillsdale, NJ: Lawrence Erlbaum Associates.

Hebrew – BSF

Ruth Berman
Department of Linguistics
Tel-Aviv University
Ramat Aviv, Tel-Aviv 69978, Israel
rberman@ccsg.tau.ac.il

The materials in this Hebrew data set were gathered during the first phase of a crosslinguistic project on the development of tense-aspect funded by a grant from the United States-Israel Binational Science Foundation (BSF) awarded to Ruth A. Berman, Tel Aviv University as principal investigator and Dan I. Slobin, University of California, Berkeley, for three years starting in September 1982. The first undertaking of this study was to collect as much as possible in the form of naturalistic speech samples for Hebrew preschool children. This was done in some cases by recordings and transcriptions carried out by members of the project team (native speakers of Hebrew majoring in linguistics, including Inbal Gozes, Galia Hatab, Yona Neeman, and Ziva Wijler); in others by typing up transcriptions of students doing seminar and other research papers under the aegis of Dr. Esther Dromi of the School of Education and Dr. Anita Rom of the School of Communications Disorders at Tel Aviv University; and in yet others by materials collected in the course of work on graduate theses by students of Ruth Berman, including Dafna Kaplan, Shoshana Rabinowitch, and Batya Zur. Around 160 transcripts varying from under 50 to over 500 utterances in length were collected and typed up in this way. The ones that allowed for this were then optically scanned and reformatted at CMU for entry on CHILDES, whereas the rest were entered onto an IBM-clone PC computer at Tel Aviv University according to the current CHAT format. The data are without English glosses.

All this material was then reviewed and checked by Ruth Berman (when on sabbatical at Berkeley in 1985 and 1986), and 100 of the best, most reliable transcripts were selected for inclusion in CHILDES, providing a data-set of approximately 100 individual transcripts for each year.

The children all came from middle-class homes and were monolingual Hebrew speakers whose parents were in most cases also native speakers of Hebrew. They come mainly from metropolitan Tel Aviv and its environs, and are from urban and rural backgrounds, where "rural" refers to children who are raised on the communal settlements (kibbutzim) or in the cooperative villages (moshavim) which constitute part of the middle- to upper-middle-class stratum of Israeli society.

Table 119: BSF — Ages 1;6 to 1;11

File	Investigator	Present	Utterances	Comment
alita18.cha	M. Hirsch	INV	280+	problematic
gadi111.cha	E. Dromi student	INV	350	few combinations
keren11.cha	E. Dromi	MOT	60	early one-word
keren13.cha	E. Dromi	MOT	150	rich one-word
keren15.cha	E. Dromi	MOT	120	few combinations
*liro111.cha	A. Rom student	FAT	125	basic syntax
mixal16.cha	E. Dromi student	INV	109	combinations
noa111.cha	A. Rom student	INV	132	some syntax
ran19.cha	E. Dromi student	INV	63	few combinations
uris11.cha	Y. Strassberg	CHI	48	mainly one-word
uris12.cha	Y. Strassberg	CHI	15	several strings
yifat11.cha	E. Dromi w/mother	INV	300+	mainly input
yifat14.cha	E. Dromi student	INV	56	
yifat16.cha	E. Dromi student	INV	108	mainly one-word

Table 120: BSF — Ages 2;0 to 2;11

File	Investigator	Present	Utterances
adi26.cha	D. Kaplan	INV	198
asaf26.cha	A. Rom student	INV	105
chen211.cha	M. Hirsch	INV	320
eran26.eng	A. Rom student	INV	135
hay21.cha	N. Shoham	MOT	203
hay22.cha	N. Shoham	MOT	225
hay24.cha	N. Shoham	MOT	180
kobi21.cha	E. Dromi student	INV	203

Table 120: BSF — Ages 2;0 to 2;11

File	Investigator	Present	Utterances
maya29.cha	A. Weiss	MOT	-
nimro22.cha	E. Dromi student	INV	141
nimro23.cha	E. Dromi student	INV	101
ori20.cha	L. Dganit	MOT	61
ori21.cha	L. Dganit	MOT	71
ori22.cha	L. Dganit	MOT	186
ori23.cha	L. Dganit	MOT	60
ori24.cha	L. Dganit	MOT	72
roi23.cha	A. Rom student	INV	129
ronit20.cha	B. Zur	CHI	61
sharo20.cha	A. Rom student	INV	80
tomer27.cha	M. Hirsch	INV	-
urik25.cha	D. Kaplan	MOT	112
urik26.cha	D. Kaplan	MOT	86
urik211.cha	D. Kaplan	MOT	-
yahel23.cha	A. Rom student	INV	75
zohar26.tem	Z. Wijler	INV	72
tomer27.cha	M. Hirsch	INV	265
maya29.cha	A. Rom student	INV	242
urik211.cha	D. Kaplan	MOT	220
yael211.cha	Z. Wijler	MOT	90
yahel23.cha	Hadas	MOT	-
zohar26.cha	Z. Wijler	INV	-

Table 121: BSF — Ages 3;0 to 3;11

File	Investigator	Utterances
amit30.cha	B. Zur	50
avi36.cha	B. Zur	31
aviad31.cha	Mirit / Rom	153
boy36.cha	Sara / Rom	102
chen31.cha	M. Hirsch	253
dani311.cha	A. Rom	46
debby35.cha	S. Rabin	
dotan31.cha	S. Rabinowich	103
guy311.cha	Z. Wijler	239
inbar36.cha	D. Kaplan	78
keren36.cha	S. Rabinowitz	128
limor311.ch	M. Hirsch	159
limor40.cha	M. Hirsch	78
*mayan39.cha	Y. Neeman	204
merav38.cha	G. Hatab	582
mixal33.cha	B. Zur	52
mor310.cha	M. Hirsch	265
*mor311.cha	M. Hirsch	100
moti311.cha	B. Zur	50
rafi211.eng	D. Kaplan	157
rafi30.cha	D. Kaplan	198
ravit38.cha	B. Zur	49
reut32.cha	M. Hirsch	208
shlom36.cha	D. Kaplan	323
smadr37.cha	Z.Wijler	201
yael32.cha	S. Rabinowich	80
yotam30.cha	Smadar / Rom	151

Table 122: BSF — Ages 4;1 to 4;11

File	Investigator	Utterances	Comments
adi43.cha	S. Rabinowitz	67	long narratives
adit41.cha	A. Rom	32	
arel42.cha	A. Rom	11 +18	
avi47.eng	A. Rom	32	
barux42.cha	A. Rom	21	
dana41.cha	S. Rabinowitz	83	
dudi41.cha	A. Rom	19	
elad43.cha	A. Rom	26	long utterances
eran43.cha	I. Gozes	275	
girl46.cha	B. Zur	45	some narrative
ido46.cha	S. Rabinowitz	104	
keren44.cha	B. Zur	43	
or411.cha	Z. Wijler	330	long utterances
oren410.cha	B. Josman	15	
oshra41.cha	A. Rom	43	
saa47.cha	A. Rom		
shar411.cha	A. Rom	32	
shay410.cha	A. Rom	37	
tali46.cha	B. Josman	190	
yaron42.cha	A. Rom	28	
yifat42.cha	B. Zur	40	narrative
yoni44.cha	S. Rabinowitz	123	
yonit45.cha	B. Josman	178	
yuval46.cha	Z.Wijler	197	
ziv41.cha	B. Zur	45	narrative

Table 123: BSF — Ages 5;0 to 5;11

File	Investigator	Utterances	Comments
amnon53.cha	S. Rabinowitz	168	plus narratives
*ari56.cha	S. Rabinowitz	65	
aron511.cha	A. Rom	23	picture description
asaf51.cha	S. Rabinowitz	88	
ben51.cha	S. Rabinowitz	79	
david55.cha	B. Josman	15	story retelling
elad56.cha	B. Josman	15	story retelling
gil52.cha	A. Rom	29	long utterances
gilad54.cha	B. Zur	42	stilted
girl52.cha	B. Zur	31	narratives
idit58.cha	A. Rom	19	picture description
*keren50.cha	G. Hatab	160	
*oren52.cha	B. Josman	15	long utterances
shar510.cha	A. Rom	29	
tal54.cha	A. Rom	29	long utterances
yifat54.cha	B. Zur	32	narratives
*yonat56.cha	B. Josman	23	part narrative

* Files marked with asterisks have English glosses for the Hebrew.

Publications using these data should cite:

Berman, R. (1985). The acquisition of Hebrew. In D. I. Slobin (Ed.), *The crosslinguistic study of language acquisition*, pp. 255-372. Hillsdale, NJ: Lawrence Erlbaum Associates.

Berman, R., & Dromi, E. (1984). On marking time without aspect in child language. *Papers and Reports on Child Language Development, 23*, 23–32.

Hebrew – Levy

Yonata Levy
Department of Psychology
Hebrew University
Mount Scopus
Jerusalem, Israel
msyonata@mscc.huji.ac.il

These data were contributed by Yonata Levy of Hebrew University in Jerusalem. The samples were collected in naturalistic settings, mostly in the children's homes by the experimenter with sometimes one other member of the family present. The data were transcribed and coded by the experimenter who had collected the data. The following table gives the list of pseudonyms and ages:

Table 124: Levy Files

Child	Age	#Files
Bar	2;4	4
Erez	2;3–2;5	3
Keren	2;10–2;11	3
Maor	2;3–2;5	3
Mika	3;1–3;6	2
Noya	3;1–3;7	9
Oren	2;7–2;8	3
Rotem	3;4–4;4	8
Ruti	1;10–2;4	29
Sigal	3;0–3;1	3
Xamtal	2;11–3;8	10

For further information regarding these children, please contact Dr. Levy.

Hebrew – Na'ama

Ruth Berman
Department of Linguistics
Tel-Aviv University
Ramat Aviv, Tel-Aviv 69978, Israel
rberman@ccsg.tau.ac.il

This corpus contains files from a Hebrew-speaking child between ages 1;7 and 2;6. Na'ama was the firstborn child of middle-class, fairly well-educated, native-speaking parents. She was recorded by Dafna Kaplan, a friend and neighbor of the family, as part of Kaplan's M.A. studies in linguistics at Tel Aviv University in 1983. The recordings were all done in her home, with or without the mother present.

Table 125: Na'ama Corpus

File	Age	File	Age
1	1;7.8	10	2;2.12
2	1;7.27	11	2;3.2
3	1;8.25	12	2;3.23
4	1;9.2	13	2;4.14
5	1;10.0	14	2;5.4
6	1;11.0	15	2;5.8
7	2;0.10	16	2;6.0
8	2;0.24	17	2;6.4
9	2;1.12		

Hebrew – Ravid

Berman, Ruth
Department of Linguistics
Tel-Aviv University
Ramat Aviv, Tel-Aviv 69978, Israel
rberman@ccsg.tau.ac.il

This directory contains 37 files collected by Dorit Ravid from her daughter Sivan between the ages of 1;8 and 6;10. The recordings were made between May 1980 and April 1985 Sivan (SIV), was a first-born female, born June 14, 1978. Her brother Asaf (ASA) was born July 30, 1979. The mother (MOT) is a linguist. The father (FAT) is Arik. The family lives in an apartment in a high rise building in a provincial town called Yahud in the center of Israel (Tel Aviv metropolitan area). Their mother is a (second generation) native Hebrew speaker, their father came to Israel as a small child, and the children were definitely monolingual Hebrew speakers throughout the period of the recordings. The family background and lifestyle is typical of well-educated, literate Israeli middle-class salaried professionals. The recordings were made by the mother when the children were playing at home in their bedroom or the living room — sometimes just the two of them, most of the time one or both of them with one or both of their parents, occasionally with (maternal) grandparents or with another child from the same neighborhood. Sivan, the older child, was linguistically highly precocious with an unusually developed metalinguistic feel for language, and in these recordings she did not often give her brother much floor space! Asaf was 0;9.16 in file 111a. There is not much speech from him until file 206b when he is 1;4:8.

Table 126: Ravid Corpus

File	Age	Utts	File	Age	Utts
111a	1;11.2	600	304d	3;4.17	229
111b	1;11.12	87	304e	3;4.18	377
202a	2;2.18	223	306a	3;6.11	371
202b	2;2.19	264	306b	3;6.21-29	209
203a	2;3.5	112	307a	3;7.9	40
203b	2;3.12	195	307b	3;7.18	197
204a	2;4.3	848	307c	3;7.21	499
205a	2;5.7	1075	404a	4;4.22	188
205b	2;5.24	1036	404b	4;4.24	390
207a	2;7.20	495	404c	4;4.24-29	547
207b	2;7.29	501	407a	4;7.17	116

Table 126: Ravid Corpus

File	Age	Utts	File	Age	Utts
300a	3;0.23	1100	407b	4;7.21	511
301a	3;1.2	156	410a	4;10.6	482
301b	3;1.27	147	410b	4;10.9	442
303a	3;3.26	66	505a	5;5.12	572
304a	3;4.5	41	505b	5;5.25	192
304b	3;4.10	200	506a	5;6.11	754
304c	3;4.14	308	603a	6;3.22	542
			611a	6;11.4	405

Hungarian – MacWhinney

Brian MacWhinney
Department of Psychology
Carnegie Mellon University
Pittsburgh, PA 15213
macw@cmu.edu

These data were collected by Brian MacWhinney in Hungary during the 1970 academic year. They were donated to CHILDES in 1985. The children studied were Zoli, Moni, Andi, Gyuri, and Eva at the National Institute for Nursery School Methodology (BOMI). The children all came from middle-class families with two working parents. The recordings were made by using a wireless microphone and a radio receiver. The microphone was sewn into a pocket in one of the standard nursery school aprons worn by the child. The particular apron used had the figure of a fox on it and the children often competed to be allowed to wear the "fox apron." Recording began in November when it was already too cold for the children to go outside for long periods and continued through March. There was a one month break during April. When recording resumed in May, the children were often outside playing in the garden.

Activities at the nursery school were very highly structured. Each child had a symbol that identified a particular closet, a particular chair, a particular towel, and so on. There were only a few children under the age of 1;3 in the school. Those children were kept in cribs in a special room. The children between 1;3 and 2;0 were in a second play group. Zoli, Andi, and Moni were in that group. The older play group had children from 2;0 to 3;0 and Eva and Gyuri were in that group.

Table 127: Zoli and Moni

Sample	Age	Hrs.	Utts.	MLU	Dates
Zoli1	1;5.2-5	4	51	1.10	Dec 7-8
Zoli2	1;6.29-30	6	228	1.58	Feb 3
Zoli3	1;8.6-8	8	2675	1.60	March 11-16
Zoli4	1;10.0-6	7	1911	1.87	May 5-11
Zoli5	2;0.0-5	6	835	2.58	July 1-7
Zoli6	2-2-0-3	7	1826	2.50	Aug 31-Sept 3
Moni1	1;11.18-27	8	1478	1.53	
Moni2	2;2.0	8	576	1.28	
Moni3	2;4.16-17	5	797	1.15	
Moni4	2;5.10-13	8	700	1.03	

Table 128: Andi, Éva, and Gyuri

Sample	Age	Sample	Age
Andi2a	2;1.22	Eva3f	2;10.27
Andi2b	2;1.27	Eva3a	2;10.20
Andi2c	2;2.4	Eva3b	2;10.21
Andi2d	2;8.4	Eva3c	2;10.22
Eva1a	2;7.12	Eva3d	2;10.25
Eva1b	2;7.18	Gyuri1	2;3.7
Eva1c	2;9.0	Gyuri2	2;3.8
Eva2a	2;9.19	Gyuri3	2;3.11
Eva2b	2;9.20	Gyuri4	2;3.12
Eva2c	2;9.21	Gyuri5	2;3.13
Eva2d	2;9.22	Gyuri6	2;3.14
Eva2e	2;9.24	Gyuri7	2;3.21
Eva2f	2;9.25	Gyuri8	2;3.22
Eva3e	2;10.26	Gyuri9	2;3.23

Most of the interactions are with a dyad of children and the investigator. Some of the interactions, particularly those with Zoli, involve only the investigator and the target child. The nursery school teachers only rarely engaged the children during the recordings. The investigator is not a native speaker of Hungarian and, particularly during the first few months of the recording, the investigator's use of Hungarian was fairly weak. Listening back to the tapes, it is difficult to detect any influence that this had on the children who seemed more interested in the investigator's moustache and the toys that he was carrying than in the rather nonstandard nature of his language.

MacWhinney (1975) conducted a detailed analysis of the syntactic patterns for Zoli, Moni, and Andi with particular emphasis on the relative contributions of word-based positional patterns and general topic-comment patterns to word ordering. MacWhinney (1974) provides additional information on data collection and transcription. Zoli was born July 5, 1969. Samples 1 and 2 are not complete. They were kept in a separate notebook which now appears to be missing. Publications using these data can cite:

MacWhinney, B. (1974). *How Hungarian children learn to speak.* Unpublished doctoral dissertation, University of California, Berkeley.
MacWhinney, B. (1975). Pragmatic patterns in child syntax. *Stanford Papers And Reports on Child Language Development, 10,* 153–165.

Irish – Guilfoyle

Eithne Guilfoyle
Dun Laoghaire Institute
Kill Avenue, Dun Laughaire
Co. Dublin, Ireland
guilfoyle@hotmail.com

This corpus is made up of 5 recordings made in Ireland in 1992, each approximately 45 minutes long. The children are native Irish speakers, aged between 1;7 and 2;9 years including one pair of twins. The children were recorded on audio and videotape in the presence of a parent and a researcher. The conversation is entirely in Irish, however all of the data is translated into English, and the child's data is glossed on a %mor tier. The children played with a number of toys and the conversation primarily focuses on the toys.

The data were gathered by E. Guilfoyle, University of Calgary, under the auspices of a grant from the Social Sciences and Humanities Research Council of Canada (grant 410-91-1956). The transcripts were typed up by Nóra Welby and verified and translated by Fiona Coll. The transcriptions were glossed and checked by Eithne Guilfoyle and Síle Harrington, assisted by Leah Bartolin, Hooi Ling Soh, Erica Thrift, Grace Randa, and Sean Mac Lennan.

The data were coded with a view to studying the children's syntactic and morphological development, however, some of the child and adult data may be of interest to people interested in borrowing, language change as all the adults are bilingual, and the children have varying exposure to English.

Table 129: Guilfoyle Children

File	Child	Sex	Birthdate	Recording	Age
1	CAI	F	01-DEC-1990	5-JUL-1992	1;7.4
2	SEA	M	01-FEB-1990	16-JUL-1992	2;5.15
3	MAI	M	14-FEB-1990	17-JUN-1992	2;5.3
4	CIA	M	06-OCT-1989	16-JUL-1992	2;9.10
4	LAO	F	06-OCT-1989	16-JUL-1992	2;9.10
5	RON	M	05-JUL-1992	05-AUG-1992	2;1.0

Japanese – Ishii

Takeo Ishii
Department of Foreign Languages
Kyoto Sangyo University
Motoyama, Kamigamo, Kita-ku, Kyoto
Japan 603-8555

Jun is a third child in the family with a brother Ken and a sister Yasuko. The family lived in Kyoto City and moved to Kusatsu City, Shiga Pref., where Jun was born. The family speak Kyoto dialect. Dialect and family words are listed in the file dialect.cdc.

The Jun corpus is made public to child language researchers. Any researcher interested in child language acquisition may use these data freely. More data will be added in the future. Some warnings concerning the corpus are: (1) Reliability was not checked, (2) The length of the observational sessions differ, (3) Some of the movies, especially earlier ones, are not very clear due to the weather, and (4) UNIBET symbols are used, especially for earlier sessions when child utterances are unclear. The data include only the utterances of participants with few situational descriptions, as it was very complicated to describe the situations fully.

The database currently contains 61 files and each recording lasts about 15 minutes. The resulting movie files are between 300 and 590 megabytes in size. The first 31 files cover the ages between 0;8 and 1;11 at a roughly bimonthly frequency. The second set of 31 files cover the period from 3;5 to 3;8, but each session lasts nearly one hour and is divided into about 4 periods of 15 minute recordings.

If you use this data or parts of it, please send one printed copy of your article/publication to Takeo Ishii. Please cite Ishii, Takeo 1999, The JUN Corpus, unpublished. Movies on CD-ROM are available upon request (only for Macintosh now). Each includes a movie file, a chat file. If you want copies of movie files, please send blank CD-Rs together with a return addressed envelope and postage stamps. About 630MB is recordable on one CD-R. Please be sure to specify the file names you want.

Japanese – Miyata

Susanne Miyata
Aichi Shukutoku Junior College
23 Sakuragaoka Chikusa-ku
Nagoya 464 Japan
smiyata@asjc.aasa.ac.jp

If you use this data or parts of it, please send one printed copy of your publication to Susanne Miyata.

Warnings

1. These data are not suitable for the study of the mother's overall language behavior, except for questioning and answering behavior. The Aki and Ryo data were originally sampled for the study of the child's question development and many remarks of the mother are not transcribed. These omitted parts are unfortunately *unmarked*.
2. Reliability was not checked.
3. The length of the observational sessions differ. The actual length is noted in the @Warning header of each file,

History

Aki and Ryo are children from two unrelated families, both living in Nagoya. Both children's parents gave their kind consent for the publication of this data. Although they consented to the use of their actual names, all last names in these files are replaced to preserve privacy.

The children were observed once a week for about one hour at their home while playing with their mother. The homes were both 4-room apartments in the center of Nagoya. In the previous observations it had proved convenient for both mother and observer to fix weekday and time. As Aki and Ryo were quite late risers, we decided to start each session after 10 A.M. After a short period of excitement, the child would settle down to play. The videotapings started usually about 10:20. For the recording I held the camera in my lap (rather than in front of my face), a method that had proved effective in prior observations. The setting was free indoor play. The mother was instructed to "make the child speak," but there were no regulations concerning the kind of play.

The transcription was done in Romaji (Hebon) rather than in Japanese script, in order to better preserve the actual pronunciation. The transcription often uses UNIBET symbols, especially when the meaning of the utterance was unclear. For slightly deviant items with clear meaning no phonetical transcription is provided. The transcription was done in

JCHAT 1.0 Hebon, using WAKACHI98 (Oshima-Takane& MacWhinney, 1998; Miyata & Naka, 1998).Situational cues were provided to a certain extent, to make it possible to follow the conversation without visual cues.

Codes

Question intonation was coded using $FIN (falling intonation) and $RIN (rising intonation). Where unmarked, assume rising intonation. Wa-questions were marked with the following four codes from Miyata (1992, 1993):

$WAP wa-Question (Place)   papa wa? where is Papa?
$WAN wa-Question (Name)   kore wa? what is this?
$WAE wa-Question(Educational) gomen ne wa? what about "sorry'?
$WAG wa-Question (General)   papa wa ookii. mama wa?
                Papa's big,what about Mama?

The final particles "no" and "wa" which are homophonic to case particles, have been marked as "no@fp" and "wa@fp." Calling has been marked as @v (vocative). Interactive words (yes, no, greetings) are marked by @i .

MLU Computation

There are three different bimonthly MLU values: Jiritsugo-fuzokugo-MLU (Ogura, 1998), Morikawa-shiki-MLU, and Minami-shiki-MLU. The first one counts words and particles, the second one all morphemes except PRES, and the third one includes PRES. For details see Miyata (1998).

Biographical Data

Aki was born on 27-SEP-1987 in Nagoya, the firstborn child. His mother was 31 years old at the time of his birth. Pregnancy and delivery were normal. Aki's birth weight was 2870 g. His physical development was normal, aside from a 6-day hospital stay (2;4.30 to 2;5.4) due to a small operation (surgical cut of a short thumb sinew), and he was healthy throughout the observation. Aki was an active, curious, fearless child, very interested in books and stories. However, his concentration span was quite short, and he would soon grow weary. His pronunciation was very clear. He uttered his first word at 1;8. In February 1995, he was an average student in the first grade of primary school.

Ryo was born on 15-Aug-1985 in Nagoya, the second-born child. His mother was 32 years old at the time of his birth. Pregnancy and delivery were normal. Aki's birth weight was 3325 g. His physical development was normal, and he was healthy throughout the observation. Ryo was an active, athletic, curious, fearless, and talkative child. He did not show much interest in books, but started out to play video games ("famikon") at an age of two. His pronunciation was very clear. He uttered his first word at 1;7. In February 1997, he was an above average student in the first grade of primary school.

Aki Participants

AMO, Mother, called "Okaasan," 32 years, pianist, part-time lecturer in the piano section of a senior high school in Nagoya, and gives private lessons, and concerts.
AFA, Father, called "Otoosan," associate professor for biogenetics at a University in a nearby town to Nagoya
REE, 2-year-old younger brother Ree, called "Reechan," born 22-AUG-89 (Aki's age: 1;10:26)
OBA, baby sitter, called "Obasan," 61 years, no university degree
BAA, Grandmother, maternal), called "Baaba," former primary school teacher
OOB, Grandmother, paternal, called "Obaasan," housewife
SUZ, Investigator, called "Suuze(san)," friend of AMO, AKI, AMO, AFA, REE live together. Occasionally BAA and sometimes also OOB come to visit.

Ryo Participants

RMO, Mother, called "Mama," 32 years, pianist, part-time lecturer in a music school in Nagoya, giving also private lessons at home.
RFA, Father, called "Papa," clarinetist, part-time lecturer in a music school in Nagoya. He too gives private lessons at home, and concerts.
YUK, 6-year-old elder sister Yukari, called "Yukarichan," (Yukari's age at RYO birth: four years)
SUZ, Investigator, called "Suuze(san)," friend of RMO.
RMO, RFA, YUK live together.

Situational Descriptions

The apartments consisted of:
B   bath, called "ofuro")
T   toilet, called "toire"
H   long hall, called "rooka"
P   piano room, called "piano no heya", normally closed
TA   tatami room, called "tatami no heya", open to living room, sleeping room at night,
L   living room, called "ima" or "oheya", room where Aki's toys and books are stored
K   dining kitchen, called "daidokoro", open to living room
kk   kitchen counter
TT   dining table
V   balcony (called "beranda", in front of piano room, tatami room, living room)

Publications using these data should cite:

Miyata, S. (1995). The Aki corpus — Longitudinal speech data of a Japanese boy aged 1.6-2.12 -, *Bulletin of Aichi Shukutoku Junior College, 34,*183–191
Miyata, S. (1992) Wh-Questions of the Third Kind: The Strange Use of Wa-Questions in

Japanese Children, *Bulletin of Aichi Shukutoku Junior College, 31,* 151–155

Additional relevant publications include:

Miyata, S. (1993). *Japanische Kinderfragen: Zum Erwerb von Form-Inhalt-Funktion von Frageausdrücken,* Hamburg (OAG)

Miyata, S. & Naka, N. (1998). Wakachigaki Gaidorain WAKACHI98 v.1.1. *Educational Psychology Forum Report* No. FR-98-003, The Japanese Association of Educational Psychology.

Miyata, S. (1998). Nihongo Kakutoku to MLU keisan: Slice MLU, paper presented at the 9th meeting of JSDP, March 1998.

Oshima-Takane, Y. & MacWhinney, B. (1998). *CHILDES Manual for Japanese,* McGill University / Chukyo University.

Mambila – Zeitlyn

David Zeitlyn
University of Oxford
Institute of Social and Cultural Anthropology
51 Banbury Road
Oxford OX2 6PE England
zeitlyn@vax.ox.ac.uk

These data have been prepared as part of an ESRC-funded project "Kinship and language: a computer-aided study of social deixis in conversation" (grant no R000233311) which supported Andrew Wilson. Dr. David Zeitlyn, the project director, is a British Academy Research Fellow at the Institute of Social and Cultural Anthropology, Oxford and a Research Fellow at Wolfson College, Oxford.

Introduction to Mambila

The Mambila lie on either side of the Nigeria/Cameroon border, the bulk of them living on the Mambila Plateau in Nigeria. A smaller number (c. 12,000) are to be found in Cameroon, especially at the foot of Mambila Plateau escarpment, on the Tikar Plain. The fieldwork was restricted to these latter groups, and in particular to the village of Somie. Self-sufficient in food, the villagers have grown coffee as a cash crop since the early 1960s. Cameroonian Mambila on the Tikar Plain have adopted the Tikar institution of the chiefship, yet their social structure otherwise closely resembles that described for the Nigerian village of Warwar by Rehfisch (1972) based on fieldwork in 1953. Nigerian Mambila did not have the same type of institutionalized chiefship as is found in Cameroon. In Nigeria, villages were organized on gerontocratic principles, and largely lacked political offices. The system of exchange marriage described by Rehfisch (1960) has now vanished, and with it the two sorts of named group which recruited through different combinations of descent, marriage type (exchange or bridewealth), and residence. Marriage is viripatrilocal, and is increasingly on the basis of courtship although bridewealth is still a major factor. However, bridewealth may be paid in installments over a number of years. It is not cited as a reason for the failure of young men to marry. Most people in the village are members of either the Catholic or Protestant church. Zeitlyn (1993) gives some information about the kinship terminology. A short transcript from that paper plus digitized audio recording may be found at the following URL using gopher rsl.ox.ac.uk within the anthropology corner or at the following URL for the World Wide Web: http://rsl.ox.ac.uk/isca/mambila/mambila.html.

Introduction to the Data

The Mambila transcript that accompanies this file has been transcribed according to CHAT guidelines, with the following exceptions and constraints. First the utterances have been segmented according to the principles described in Stiles (1992). We note that this is controversial and for many other purposes we feel the turn or the phase may be safer albeit harder to define. A spoken phrase may be crudely understood to be a turn or an utterance beginning and ending either with a turn transition or a pause.

Developmental psychologists familiar with CHAT should note that the data were not collected and coded with developmental issues in mind. It is hoped that they may still find them of some interest nonetheless. The transcription of Mambila follows Perrin's work on the phonology with some modification for the village of Somie. Characters are used with their standard IPA values. In addition, the following characters have been redefined to create the Mambila font:

Table 130: Mambila Font Values

ASCII value	Phonetic value
198	velar nasal "ng'
239	Upper-case velar nasal "Ng'
191	Mid-low back rounded vowel "aw'
207	mid-central vowel "schwa'
96	Low tone
94	High-low tone
171	High tone
164	Mid-low tone

The database includes a copy of the Mam-Times font which is a Macintosh composite postscript font created by David Zeitlyn that assumes you have Times-Roman installed in your system (if you want high quality printing). Even without Times-Roman installed, it should display adequately on screen. The Mam-Times font needs to be installed in your system.

The transcript records a conversation in the house of Michel Sondue on 15-DEC-1990. The recording was made, in Zeitlyn's absence, by Sondue and comments made during the course of the conversation show that those present were not unaware of the presence of the microphone. Neither Zeitlyn nor Sondue can ascertain any significant difference between this conversation and others which were not recorded. The transcription procedures deserve some mention. Soon after making the recording, Zeitlyn went through it with Sondue. At this stage, they made some contextual notes and copy of the recording. Sondue repeated each utterance into a second tape recorder, speaking slowly and clearly. To do this he used both his understanding as a native speaker and the fact that he was an actor in the conversation to understand parts of the recording that were (and remain) extremely indistinct. In the course of making this second recording, Sondue explained various idioms and vocabulary items that were new to Zeitlyn. Zeitlyn subsequently transcribed the second recording in the UK and then returned to the original recording. The transcript was then coded in the UK following a scheme developed in a pilot study by Blum-Kulka and Snow (1992), elaborated in Wilson and Zeitlyn (1995). In the course of the coding, the English translation was revised so that the use of pronouns and names was parallel to their use in the Mambila original, although there are obvious problems in this such as a gender neutral third person and some (rare) compound pronouns. The coding process turned up some further problems that were resolved during a further fieldtrip in May 1994. The result is a robust transcript. This is not to say that it is not theory-laden (Ochs, 1979) and inevitably it could be improved, in particular the absence of a visual channel combined with the free passage of children (and adults) in and out of the house makes it uncertain just who the nonparticipating audience is at any one time. In addition there are often the voices of children at play in the background. Most of the time these have proved too indistinct to be able to transcribe. Almost any recording one makes in Somie includes children playing somewhere in the background!

Header Tiers and Background Information

The conversation is taken from a household in Somie where a taperecorder has been left with the father of the household (MIS — Michel Sondue) to minimize any effects due to the presence of the investigator (DZ — David Zeitlyn). The participants are predominantly family of MIS and his wife TBL, with the exception of two visitors, DAN and MBM. Most of the family members are co-resident with MIS and TBL, except for their eldest daughter ANG and her young child NKB. Throughout the conversation there is a general procession of participants in and out of the house. These tend to consist of the younger children who are playing outside. This causes two problems: a) it is often unclear who is speaking or what is being said when the voice comes from outside the range of the microphone, and b) without a visual record of what is happening, it has proved difficult to track the whereabouts of the participants, hence causing difficulties with the address tier. In particular cases of doubt or confusion, the file has been checked and re-checked with the participants themselves.

Main Tiers

Many turns in this conversation have been segmented into several distinct utterances that are coded individually. The motivation for this segmentation comes from our own research interests and the need to have a conceptually viable unit of conversation over which to score frequencies over certain linguistic and illocutionary items. The criteria by which we performed this segmentation comes from the work of Stiles (1992) and his concept of speech act. Stiles has presented a taxonomy that he claims is an improvement on the traditional attempts in being based on principles of classification whereas "most other systems have been developed empirically-by examining samples of a particular domain of discourse" (p.31). This will not only ensure that the taxonomy is both mutually exclusive and exhaustive (every possible utterance is categorized uniquely) but is more likely to be applicable to all languages, a feature of great interest to anthropologists doing cross-cultural comparisons, so long as the principles themselves are universally applicable. This will depend on the theoretical underpinnings of the taxonomy.

Stiles (1992, p. 14), a clinical psychologist, conceives every utterance (1) to concern either the speaker's or the other's experience, with experience understood broadly to include thoughts, feelings, perceptions, and intentional actions, (2) to either make presumptions about the other's experience or not to presume anything of the other's experience, and (3) to represent the experience either from his or her own personal viewpoint or from a viewpoint that is shared or held in common with the other. These three principles of classification he calls "source of experience," "presumption about experience," and "frame of reference," respectively. These principles are dichotomous in having the value "speaker" or "other." Hence we have a possible eight categories (2 X 2 X 2), or Verbal Response Modes (V.R.M.s for short), which he labels Disclosure (D), Edification (E), Advisement (A), Confirmation (C), Acknowledgment (K), Interpretation (I), and Reflection (R). He is careful to make clear that these names are only for convenience and the category classification should not be confused with their everyday connotations, although he uses the considerable overlap with natural categories as evidence that his principles are salient. This is further discussed in our review of Stiles (Wilson & Zeitlyn, 1995). Applying these criteria often requires that what seem to be normal sentences are split into two or more phrases that constitute separate utterances. On the main tiers we have paid little attention to tonal and prosodic information, but have incorporated information such as interruptions, pauses, overlaps and retraces. Retraces are further discussed below.

Dependent Tiers

%eng: Each main line has a free English translation. These tiers look like main tiers in that they preserve the main line information in CHAT format (except for the ID code). This will permit certain analyses to be completed on the basis of the English translation alone. In particular, the translation attempts to preserve the person referring expressions (i.e., pronouns, names, kin term) used.

%spa: All utterances are coded for their speech act. The taxonomy we have adopted for this purpose is the VRM taxonomy of Stiles (1992), which is easily applied to natural conversations. See Wilson and Zeitlyn (1995) for a full review.

%add: Addressee. This conversation is a multi-party conversation, so most utterances have several candidates for addressee, as there are several people whom can reasonably be expected to hear the utterance. Coding this aspect is achieved by a series of hierarchical cues that, when applied, will cut down the set of potential addressees to the set of actual addresses. The cues are as follows (Wilson & Zeitlyn, 1995):

1. Physical constraints that determine the candidates who are within earshot.
2. The presence of vocatives that will uniquely identify the addressee.
3. The subsequent turn, if it follows appropriately (i.e., is an answer to a question) reveals addressee, even though it may have been "negotiated" or unintended.
4. Informational content: the addressee is the set of persons for whom the utterance is maximally informative (e.g., telling a story to a visitor, because the rest know the story already). The addressees are coded by the ID code. If there are more than one ad-

dressee, the codes are split by a colon; the names are always coded in the order as they are introduced on the header tier.

%top: This tier records any changes in the topic or content of the conversation. Notoriously hard to pin down, we have adopted a rather intuitive approach to this aspect, coding on each utterance a change ($new) or reversal ($rev) of topic as it occurs.

%fta: Face threatening act. An attempt to capture the intuitions of face work and linguistic politeness (Brown & Levinson, 1987) within this natural conversation has led to our coding of any utterance that is reckoned to threaten the face of others (addressee or not, we have not included face threats, e.g., insults, to absent third parties). Each code is presented in the following order: the face threatener, usually the utterer, though not always, the threatened, the imposition of the face threat, and whether the face threatened was positive or negative (Brown & Levinson, 1987; Wilson & Zeitlyn, 1995). A weak threat is coded as 1 and a strong threat is coded as 3. Thus the code $mis:gun:2+ve tells us that in that utterance, MIS has threatened GUN's positive face to a value of 2.

%nte and %ftn: These tiers provide additional information that might be of help in understanding the significance or meaning of certain parts of the conversation. For example, reference to third parties are elaborated upon, along with some general ethnographic information, as well as any breaks in the tape recording.

%pre: This tier provides a code for all person referring expressions that occur in any one utterance. Three aspects of person referring expressions (PREs) have been coded for the category of expression, the actual linguistic form, and the status of the referent relative to the utterance. These three aspects are coded together and separated with colons.

We have distinguished the following five categories of expression: pronoun, kin terms, names, titles, and descriptive expressions. The distinction can be operationalism both on semantic grounds and on syntactic grounds (Wilson & Zeitlyn, 1994). For each category, the linguistic form is coded in a different way as follows:

1. Pronouns ($pro): The Mambila system of pronouns is roughly comparable to the English system, that is there are three persons (first, second and third) that can be either singular or plural. We have marked these by a number followed by "s" (singular) or "p" (plural). In addition we noted if the pronoun is a possessive (e.g., $pro:2spos). In addition there are other pronouns that do not have simple translations in English. For example, "Bubu" is a compound pronoun that refers to two persons, and "nyi" is an anaphoric pronoun used to refer to the speaker of reported speech. In these cases the Mambila form has been maintained in the coding tier.

2. Names ($nam): With names the actual linguistic realization is maintained on the tier to allow immediate inspection without reference to the main tier from which it came. There are some cases in which the form of the name is often varied, possibly to act as a mitigator (e.g., "Celistine" and "Celi"). These changes have been coded in the following way. The "unmarked" version of the name is determined by examining which is the most common version. Thereafter any variation of that name

("marked" forms) are coded with a (+) or (-) depending on whether they appear to be marked in a positive, more intimate, direction, or a negative direction. For instance, DAN is sometimes addressed as "Dan-e" This has been coded as $nam:dan-e(+).

3. Kin terms ($kin): The linguistic form of kin terms are coded in the same way as names, that is by preserving the original form and adding any intimacy marker where necessary.

4. Titles ($tit): The linguistic form of titles is maintained on the coding ti= er.

5. Descriptive expressions ($des): These expressions too are preserved on the coding tier. Often a descriptive phrase will be made up of two or more words. In these cases the words are linked on the coding tier with a _ (e.g.$des:b`¿_ntaar_dï). This preserves the expressions when conducting any FREQ searches. Some linguistic expressions are made up from combinations of these simple expressions. These can either consist of a series of simple expressions that refer to the some person which we term compound expressions (e.g., Aunt Sally, or Sir Brian) or a series of simple expressions which achieve ultimate reference by referring to others, termed oblique expressions (e.g., my brother's daughter). These combinations are coded by coding the simple expressions connected with an & sign (e.g., $kin:tele:abs&$pro:1s:utt). In the case of compound expressions, where only one person, or set of persons, are referred to, the conversational status (explained below) is included only once.

The third aspect of this %pre tier is the conversational status of the referent, and requires coding the referent according to how he or she stands in relation to the utterance. This code rests on the following distinctions:

1. Utterer (utt): the expression can refer to self (e.g., "me")

2. Addressee (adr): the expression can refer to the addressee (e.g., you or an explicit vocative).

3. Participant (cnv): the expression can refer to someone in the conversation who is not being addressed with that utterance.

4. Overhearer (aud): the expression can refer to someone within earshot, though not participating in the conversation.

5. Baby (bby): the utterance can refer to someone or something who does not have the ability to comprehend or reply. This category includes pets or small babies.

6. Absentee (abs): the expression can refer to someone who is absent (or dead).

7. Rhetorical (rhe): the expression can refer only in a rhetorical sense.

It is, of course, possible to refer to more than one individual with any simple expression (e.g., "they", "sisters" etc.). Thus it is possible for the referents to have different conversational statuses. For instance, "we" will often refer to utterer and addressee or utterer and absentee. This outcome is coded by combining the status codes in the order given above, separated with a + sign. For instance, $pro:1p:utt+cnv+abs.

One final piece of information required when coding the person-referring expressions is to whether the expression was uttered as part of a retrace or not. If any p.r.e. is then re-traced or coded, it is flagged with a dash at the end of the code. This allows the analyst the choice of considering attempts to refer (an illocutionary concept) or with linguistic data exactly as uttered. For instance:

    *TBL: \<Dan-o ke ka\> [/] Dan-o, ke ka!
    %eng: \<Dan-o Look\> [/] Dan-o Look!
    %pre: $nam:dan-o:adr- $nam:dan-o:adr

Publications using these data should cite:

Wilson, A. J., & Zeitlyn, D. (1995). The distribution of person-referring terms in natural conversation. *Research on Language and Social Interaction, 28,* 61–92.

Additional relevant publications include:

Blum-Kulka, S., & Snow, C. (1992). Developing autonomy for tellers, tales, and the telling in family narrative events. *Journal of Narrative and Life History, 2,* 187–217.
Ochs, E. (1979). Transcription as theory. In E. Ochs & B. Schieffelin (Eds.), *Developmental pragmatics*. New York: Academic.
Stiles, W. B. (1992). *Describing talk: A taxonomy of verbal response modes*. Newbury Park: Sage.

Mandarin – Tardif Beijing

Twila Tardif
Department of Psychology
Chinese University of Hong Kong
Hong Kong
ttardif@harp.psy.cuhk.edu.hk

These data were recorded in Beijing between August 1991 and January 1992 and were analyzed in Tardif (1993). The data were collected from 10 families and their toddlers who were selected from immunization records. The criteria were that: (1) the children should be between 20 and 22 months of age at the beginning of the study; (2) their parents should be native speakers of Mandarin and, preferably, native to the city of Beijing; and (3) both parents should have received formal schooling which was either high school level or below for the "workers" group and college level or above for the "intellectuals" group. All children were firstborn and only children. This was a necessary consequence of China's one–child policy and not explicitly a feature of the design. An effort was also made to equate the age and gender distribution of the participants in each of the social class groups. Thus, each group had a total of five children with four males and one female, and the average age of the two groups differed by only 3 days. Overall, the children's mean age was 21 months, 24 days at the time of the first visit.

Table 131: Ages at Visit 1 and Visit 5

Child	Gender	Visit 1	Visit 5	Social Class
BB	M	1;10.12	2;2.7	Intellectual
CXX	F	1;9.25	2;1.18	Worker
HY	M	1;9.10	2;1.4	Intellectual
LC	M	1;9.21	2;1.4	Worker
LL	M	1;9.6	2;0.27	Worker
LXB	F	1;9.3	2;1.9	Intellectual
TT	M	1;9.3	2;0.28	Worker
WW	M	1;10.28	2;3.2	Worker
WX	M	1;9.27	2;1.20	Intellectual
YY	M	1;10.20	2;2.18	Intellectual

The caregivers were not always the children's parents, nor were they always the same from one visit to the next. In general, caregiving in China is unlike what one might find for many Anglo-European families in the United States. Rather than having a single caregiver who stays at home with the child during the day, Chinese children are exposed to multiple caregivers who each play significant and overlapping roles in the child's daily life. Thus, caregivers may include not only the children's mothers and fathers, but also grandparents or great-grandparents, live-in nannies, aunts who came to the house everyday for lunch or dinner, neighbors, or any adult who felt it necessary to intervene in the child's activities. The definition of a "caregiver" used in this project was anyone of school-age or above who addressed at least five utterances to the target child in a single visit or who performed caregiving activities such as feeding, dressing, bathing, and playing with the child on a regular basis. In further analyses of adult–child speech with this corpus, I would suggest pooling across all active caregivers in each visit.

All visits were conducted by Twila Tardif (Chinese name: XiaLing), a nonnative but fluent speaker of Mandarin, who was accompanied on at least two of the early visits to each family by a native Beijing research assistant who helped explain the purposes of the study and to ensure that everything would run smoothly. The families were told that the researcher was interested in children's language development and wanted to collect data that were as naturalistic as possible by recording the children in interaction with whomever they normally interacted. They were not told until the very end of the study that the study also looked at the effects of adult speech on children's language learning.

Each visit was scheduled at the convenience of the child's family with the only condition that the visits were to be spaced about 2 weeks apart and that the family was asked to do whatever they normally did at that time of day. The actual activities that the families participated in varied dramatically, but included the usual range of activities that we would consider "normal" for a two-year-old child and his or her caregiver(s): indoor toy play, watching television, cleaning up, feeding, talking and playing with neighbors, and even a trip to a local amusement park. In all cases, the researcher asked the families not to interact with her during the recording time and to try to ignore her presence as she stayed off to the side taking notes on the context of the interactions. In practice, interactions between the researcher and the family frequently occurred, particularly towards the end of the study when she was a familiar presence to not only the children and their families, but also to their immediate neighbors.

Visit 1, or the 22-month visit, was the second or third visit made to each of the families whereas Visit 5/6, or the 26-month visit, was the eleventh or twelfth recording session. Families were paid a total of 200 yuan (at the time, the exchange rate was 6 yuan to 1 United States dollar), approximately one month's salary, at the completion of their participation in the 6-month longitudinal study.

The tapes from each visit were first transcribed into the pinyin system of romanized Chinese spelling by trained undergraduate and graduate students (all native speakers of Mandarin, most also Beijing natives) from one of three Beijing universities. The transcribers were asked to not only write down the words that they heard but to also pay close attention to who the speaker and intended listener for an utterance was, as well as utterance boundaries, changes in loudness, and any errors, mispronunciations, or dialect words that occurred. After initial transcription, the tapes were then listened to by the researcher and entered into the computer for analysis. Any disagreements between the researcher and the student transcribers were resolved by playing the segment to at least one other native Mandarin speaker and entering the form that was agreed upon by at least two of the listeners. If no agreement could be reached, the segment was deemed uninterpretable.

Words were coded according to the parts of speech described by Chao (1968). Speaker code IDs have the format *SP-LI, where the first two letters refer to the speaker of an utterance and LI refers to the intended listener.

The main findings that have been gathered from these transcripts thus far focus on these Mandarin-speaking children's early vocabularies. Specifically, the children in this sample do not demonstrate a noun bias in their productive speech, but instead show more verb types and tokens than noun types and tokens (Tardif, 1993; Tardif, 1996). Examination of the caregivers' speech has shown that Mandarin-speaking caregivers also use more verb types and tokens in their ongoing speech (Tardif, 1996) and that they use a much higher proportion of verb types and tokens in their speech than do Italian- or English-speaking caregivers. Moreover, verbs tend to appear in the highly salient utterance-initial and utterance-final positions in Mandarin adult-to-child speech that is also different from the pattern shown for English and other languages. Ongoing analyses of these data include an examination of adult use of pronouns and other address terms when speaking with their children and an examination of the discourse of negotiation in parent–child conflicts. In addition, Anat Ninio and her colleagues at Hebrew University are coding the children's utterances in order to examine issues in the theory of dependency grammar.

Publications using these data should cite:

Tardif, T. (1993). *Adult-to-child speech and language acquisition in Mandarin Chinese.*Unpublished doctoral dissertaion, Yale University.
Tardif, T. (1996). Nouns are not always learned before verbs: Evidence from mandarin speakers' early vocabularies. *Developmental Psychology, 32,* 492–504.

Additional references include:

Chao, Y. R. (1968). *A grammar of spoken Chinese.* Berkeley, CA: University of California Press.

Mandarin – Tardif Context

Twila Tardif
Department of Psychology
Chinese University of Hong Kong
Hong Kong
ttardif@harp.psy.cuhk.edu.hk

This corpus is a cross-sectional comparison of 25 Mandarin-speaking children and 25 English-speaking children in different language contexts. The data from the English-speaking children are in the English database.

Polish – Szuman

Magdalena Smoczynska
Department of General Linguistics
Jagiellonian University
Aleja Mickiewicza 9/11
Krakow 31-120 Poland
ulsmoczy@vela.filg.uj.edu.pl

These data were collected by Szuman and his students at the University of Krakow in the years following World War II. In most cases, the children were studied by their parents, many of whom were graduate students in developmental psychology, working with Szuman. In many cases, the public library of Krakow preserves additional materials on this project, including photographs, related treatises by Szuman, and examples of the children's artwork. Magdalena Smoczynska computerized the Szuman notebooks and contributed her transcripts to CHILDES. The ages of the 10 children are given in the following table.

Table 132: Szuman Children

Child	Birthdate	First Session	Last Session
Basia	12-DEC-1952	1;5	7;9
Inka	-	0;10.0	7;7
Jadzia	-	4;1.0	5;1.0
Janeczek		4;2.0	7;3.0
Jas'	3-JUL-1947	0;11.0	6;6.0
Kasia	17-DEC-1957	1;3.0	3;11.0
Krzys'	14-MAR-1943	2;0.0	3;0.0
Michal	19-JAN-1949	2;0.0	6;8.0
Piotrus'	22-FEB-1943	2;0.13	2;9.0
Tenia	16-APR-1955	1;5.0	2;0

Polish – Weist

Richard Weist
Department of Psychology
SUNY Fredonia
Fredonia, NY 14063 USA
weist@a12t.cc.fredonia.edu

Richard Weist has contributed these data from three children learning Polish. There are six files for each child. The children were tape recorded at the following ages: Marta at 1;7, 1;8, 1;8, 1;9, 1;9, and 1;10.2; Bartosz at 1;7, 1;7, 1;8, 1;8, 1;11, and 1;11; and Kubus at 2;1, 2;2, 2;2, 2;4, 2;4, and 2;6. All of the children were from middle-class families raised in the urban environment of Poznan, Poland. In general, their parents were highly educated. The children were recorded in their homes (typically an apartment) by two experimenters. One of the experimenters carried a small bag containing the tape recorder and the other took context notes, which were integrated during transcription. In addition to the three child language data sets, we have included a description of the coding. The basic unit of data was a text line, a gloss, and a translation. Context notes are included where available. Because of the use of morphemic glosses, the data are coded morphemically in a way that is very useful for comparative analysis.

This project was supported by NSF BNS 861777, NICHHD, and the Kosciuszko Foundation. Zbigniew Nadstoga and Emilia Konieczna-Tou entered the data. Publications that use these data should cite Weist, Wysocka, Witkowska-Stadnik, Buczowska, and Konieczna (1984) or Weist and Witkowska-Stadnik (1986). We would like to thank Magdalena Smoczynska and Oscar Swan for their helpful comments on our coding system.

Publications using these data should cite:

Weist, R., & Witkowska-Stadnik, K. (1986). Basic relations in child language and the word order myth. *International Journal of Psychology, 21,* 363–381.
Weist, R., Wysocka, H., Witkowska-Stadnik, K., Buczowska, E., & Konieczna, E. (1984). The defective tense hypothesis: On the emergence of tense and aspect in child Polish. *Journal of Child Language, 11,* 347–374.

Russian – Protassova

Ekaterina Protassova
Pelimannintie 21-23 F 27
Helsinki 00420 Finland

Ekaterina Protassova of the Russian Academy of Education has contributed data from recordings of her daughter Varvara, born on October 1, 1982, in Moscow, the first and the only child in the family. Her father Alexander (Sasha) was a book illustrator and her mother Ekaterina (Katja) was a psycholinguist. The child was brought up at home. Some days of the week grandparents took care of her, sometimes she spent several hours in a family with two children and a dog. Her grandparents lived at the time in the same flat; both were scientists. The girl's name is Varvara, which is a Russian equivalent for Barbara. A more common short variant is Varja; diminutives include Varen'ka, Varjusha, Varjunja, and Varjushen'ka. The appellative is Var', Varjun', and Varjush. At seven months, Varvara used her first word which was to call herself Ain'ka, so sometimes this name is used by parents.

All of the recordings were taken during 90-minute periods in the usual situations at home or in the summer house by a simple recorder and written down immediately afterwards in Russian. The roman transliteration, English translation, and comments were added in 1995. Childish sound modifications and shortenings of the conventional words are usually included, at least until the fourth session. The dates of the files are as follows:

Table 133: Varvara Files

File	Age	File	Age
1	1;6.5	4	1;10.14
2	1;7.13	5	2;0.1
3a	1;8.24	6	2;4.14
3b	1;8.24	7	2;10.14

Russian – Tanja

Eva Bar-Shalom and
William Snyder
Dept. of Linguistics, U-1145
University of Connecticut
341 Mansfield Road
Storrs, CT 06269-1145 USA

barshalo@uconnvm.uconn.edu
wsnyder@sp.uconn.edu

The Tanja corpus was videotaped and transcribed by Eva Bar-Shalom, a native speaker of Russian, in collaboration with William Snyder. The project was conducted in the Child Language Laboratory, Department of Linguistics, University of Connecticut, and was funded in part by the University of Connecticut Research Foundation. The corpus contains fifteen longitudinal, spontaneous-speech samples from a monolingual, Russian-learning girl with the pseudonym "Tanja" between the ages of 2;05.14 and 2;11.20. Tanja was recorded in her home in the United States at a rate of approximately twice per month. At the time of the study Tanja was an only child, and was cared for at home by her monolingual (native Russian) mother and her bilingual (native Russian, ESL) father. The language spoken at home was consistently Russian, and exposure to English was minimal.

Tanja was born on 14-DEC-1993. The dates of the recordings, and Tanja's age at each recording, are as follows:

Table 134: Tanya Files

File	Date	Age	File	Date	Age
Tanja01	28-MAY-1996	2;5.14	Tanja09	20-SEP-1996	2;9.6
Tanja02	10-JUN-1996	2;5.27	Tanja10	25-OCT-1996	2;10.11
Tanja03	18-JUN-1996	2;6.4	Tanja11	08-NOV-1996	2;10.25
Tanja04	25-JUN-1996	2;6.11	Tanja12	11-NOV-1996	2;10.28
Tanja05	23-JUL-1996	2;7.9	Tanja13	15-NOV-1996	2;11.01
Tanja06	12-AUG-1996	2;7.29	Tanja14	22-NOV-1996	2;11.08
Tanja07	29-AUG-1996	2;8.15	Tanja15	04-DEC-1996	2;11.20
Tanja08	09-SEP-1996	2;8.26			

Publications using these data should cite:

Bar-Shalom, E., & Snyder, W. (1997). Optional infinitives in Russian and their implications for the pro-drop debate. In M. Lindseth and S. Franks (eds.) *Formal approaches to Slavic linguistics: The Indiana Meeting 1996*, pp.38–47. Ann Arbor: Michigan Slavic Publications.

Bar-Shalom, E. & Snyder, W. (1998). Root infinitives in child Russian: A comparison with Italian and Polish. In R. Shillcock, A. Sorace, and C. Heycock (eds.) *Language acquisition: Knowledge representation and processing. Proceedings of GALA '97*. Edinburgh, UK: The University of Edinburgh.

Tamil – Narasimhan

R. Narasimhan
Tata Institute of Fundamental Research
Homi Bhabha Road
Bombay 400-005 India

The files in this directory are from a longitudinal study of a single Tamil child conducted by Dr. R. Narasimhan of the Tata Institute of Fundamental Research in Bombay and by R. Vaidyanathan of the Audiology and Speech Therapy School of the Nair Hospital in Bombay. They were contributed to the CHILDES in computerized form in 1984 and reformatted into CHAT in 1986. The files are taken from language interaction between a child and her parents during unstructured caretaking situations. The interactions were audiotaped in her home over a period of 24 months, from the time the child was 9 months old to the time she was 33 months old. The recording relates to 25 sessions in all at approximately biweekly intervals. The typed transcripts of the corpus are about 450 pages. The language is Tamil which is spoken in South India. Transcription has been done phonemically. Complete English glosses and contextual notes are provided.

Participant

Vanitha, the target child in these transcripts, was born on June 6, 1979. She was the first born child. The father was an engineering graduate and worked as a civil engineer. The mother, a graduate of science, worked as a research officer in a forensic laboratory. The child's father was born and brought up in Tamilnadu, and her mother was born and brought up in Nagpur. The family belonged to the middle class.

During the data collection period, when the parents were away working, Vanitha was looked after by a caretaker whose mother tongue was the same as that of the family. The caretaker was the mother of a 15-year-old girl and 12-year-old boy. When at home, during holidays, Kiran, the neighbor's child (girl) used to visit Vanitha and play with her. Although Kiran's mother tongue was Telugu she used to interact with Vanitha in Hindi.

Vanitha's mother was transferred to Nagpur when the child was 20 months old. The mother and child stayed in Nagpur for 10 months. During this period they came to Bombay to visit the father every 2 months, at least. Vanitha joined a nursery class at Nagpur when she was 25 months old. The medium of instruction in the class was English. Sree, Vanitha's maternal uncle's daughter of the same age, also attended the class with her. Vanitha's maternal uncle and aunt worked as doctors in two different hospitals in Bombay. They used to visit Vanitha's family often. Her grandmother used to visit her family frequently also.

Recording Procedure

Data collection of the parent–child interaction was started when Vanitha was almost exactly 0;9. Home visits were made by R.V. for data collection at intervals of approximately 2 weeks (but with some gaps when the child was away from the city). R.V. was a stranger to the household until the start of this field study. The home visits lasted for about 2 hours during which time about 45 minutes of audio recording was made using a portable cassette recorder (Orion, model MC) with a built-in condenser microphone.

The parents were informed that they and the child were being audiotaped for a field-study of parent–child interaction in the early stages of language behavior acquisition. They were asked to interact with the child as they would normally do in the absence of the observer. The recordings were made inside the house while the parents were involved in un-structured caretaking (feeding, dressing, and so forth) and free-play situations. During the recording sessions R.V. was essentially a silent observer of the parent–child interactions. The audio recordings were supplemented by manually written notes. The observer kept a running account of the child's and parents' actions, and of all interactions including the objects and events referred to in them. Comments were noted down on the situational contexts in which utterances were made and also the nonverbal behavior of the interacting partners.

Transcription

Phonemic transcriptions of the utterances from the tapes as well as the manual notes, including intonations (where relevant), were made by R.V. using his linguistic background (R.V. is a trained linguist who works in the Audiology and Speech Pathology Division of one of the major hospitals in Bombay). Initial typescripts prepared by him of his transcriptions were keyed into a computer (DEC 1077 system at NCSDCT) using a text-processing and text-composition software, DIP, developed at NCSDCT. The printouts from the computer were then used as working copies by three research students to verify the completeness and correctness of the transcribed corpus against the original tape recordings.

The corpus consists of transcriptions of the language behavior interaction in the verbal dimension only. Intonation contours are not marked (except rarely, to identify questions), nor are the gestural accompaniments of speech. Clearly both these are important and relevant inputs to language behavior acquisition. They are not included in the corpus, because our primary interest is in the analysis of the corpus in the verbal dimension.

The English translations of the utterances that accompany their phonemically transcribed Tamil originals should be used with great caution. These are primarily intended to give a rough idea of the ongoing interaction. The English translations do not convey the structures and patterns of the originals faithfully. Hence, all inferences about the syntax and semantics of the parent–child interaction should be drawn only from the original Tamil versions. Nursery terms and idioms in Tamil have not been translated into "equivalent" ones in English because such correspondences for the most part are not valid. Many Tamil expressions are very culture-dependent and quite often untranslatable into English "oral speech." In some cases Tamil terms have been left untranslated and a directory of translations has been separately provided.

Segments of conversations between the parents, and of conversations in Hindi (between

Vanitha and her parents, or between Vanitha and her friends) have been omitted in this corpus, except where they blend with and are necessary to establish and maintain context. Also, nonverbal vocalizations, singing and other rhythmic or rhyming vocal behavior have not in general been transcribed except when they form an integral part of the context for the ongoing verbal interaction.

Table 135: Tamil Phonemes

Tamil	English	Example
I	I	pin
ii	ee	sheep
e	e	bed
ee	a	shape
I|	I	children (ibar in the original)
u	u	push
uu	oo	boot
o	o	obey
oo	oa	coat
a	u	but, cup (pronounced as E when word final)
aa	a	car, father
ay	i	kind, island
aw	ou	bound
p	p	pin, spin
b	b	bag
t	t	Tanya (Rus) A name
d	d	DOM (Rus) house
t~	t	table (tip of tongue curled) (tdot in original)
d~	d	dance (tip of tongue curled) (ddot in original)
k	k	kit, sky
g	g	gun
m	m	man
n	n	net

Table 135: Tamil Phonemes

Tamil	English	Example
n~	n	(ndot in original)
S	s	sit
s	sh	ship
c	ch	chain
j	j	jug
l	l	lip
l~	l	(ldot in original)
l|	l	(lbar in original)
r	r	ring
v	v	win
y	y	yes

Publications using these data should cite:

Narasimhan, R. (1981). *Modeling language behavior*. Berlin: Springer.

Turkish – Aksu Koç

Aksu-Koç, Ayhan
Department of Psychology
Bogazici University
80815 Bebek
Istanbul, Turkey
koc@boun.edu.tr

These data were gathered in 1972 and 1973 in Istanbul, under the direction of Dan I. Slobin, with support from The Grant Foundation. All of the children came from urban, professional families in which at least one parent had a college education. They were selected at 4-month age intervals, from 2;0 to 4;4. Some of the children were visited a second time, 4 months later, resulting in a full age range of 2;0 to 4;8. The first visit occurred within 1 week on either side of the day of the month corresponding to the child's birthday. Children were visited in their homes or preschools over the period of a week, during which they were given a battery of cognitive and language tasks, as described in Slobin (1982). The overall study included Turkish, Serbo-Croatian, Italian, and English. The Turkish phase of the study was designed in collaboration with Ayhan Aksu-Koç.

These transcripts represent all of the adult–child spontaneous and guided conversation during the course of those visits. (A number of standardized comprehension questions are interspersed in the conversations.) The interviewer was female (either Ayla Algar or Alev Alatli'); as indicated at the top of each sample, other adults and children took part in some sessions. All words are in lower case; only proper names are capitalized. Uncertain transcriptions are enclosed in parentheses; standard equivalents of child or colloquial forms are given in square brackets. Child utterances are separated into morphemes by hyphens. Diacritics are marked by the apostrophe which indicates umlaut following o and u, dot following I, dotless following i, macron following g, and cedilla following c and s.

These data were entered onto computer and coded with support from the National Science Foundation (BNS-8812854), using facilities provided by the Institute of Cognitive Studies and the Institute of Human Development of the University of California at Berkeley. The transcripts were typed and morphemicized by Abdul Bolat and Mine Ternar; they were checked and grammatically coded by Aylin Ku'ntay. Further information can be obtained from Dan I. Slobin.

Publications using these data should cite:

Slobin, D. (1982). Universal and particular in the acquisition of language. In E. Wanner & L. Gleitman (Eds.), *Language acquisition: The state of the art*, pp. 128-172. New York: Cambridge University Press.

Welsh

Bob Jones
Department of Education
University of Wales
Aberystwyth
Wales SY23 2AX
bmj@aber.ac.uk

This project, (C.I.G for Caffael yr Iaith Cymraeg "Acquisition of the Welsh Language") was funded by a grant from the ESRC. It was based in the Linguistics Department of the University College of Wales, Bangor and Aberystwyth.The Principal Researchers were Dr. Robert Borsley, Dr. Michelle Aldridge, Prof. Ian Roberts (in Bangor), and R. Morris-Jones (in Aberystwyth).

The full-time research assistant in Bangor was Susan Clack and, in Aberystwyth, Gwennan Creunant was employed on a part-time basis. The project was initially to run for 12 months (from January 1996) but a subsequent extension on the basis of unspent monies gave another three months employment for both research assistants. This documentation file was written by Susan Clack on July 17, 1997.

The aims of the project as outlined in the ESRC grant application were:

1. To gather a substantial corpus of natural speech from children in the early stages of acquisition of Welsh as a first language. There were weekly tapes of 30 to 45 minutes over 9 months.

2. To investigate the development of syntax, especially clause structure, and to map out the typical pattern of development.

3. To use recent work on the development of syntax to illuminate the early stages of the development of Welsh syntax.

4. To use the Welsh data to evaluate ideas about parameter setting and functional categories that have emerged in recent work on the development of syntax.

5. To make the corpus available to other researchers through the CHILDES database.

Transcriptions were taken from 45 minute (usually) audiotapes only. Roughly, 9 months of six children (plus 4 months of another) are recorded from approximately 18–21 months to 28–30 months. The purpose was to tape naturalistic, spontaneous utterances and not to do specific elicitation.

Factors of sex of child and position in the family were not considered in choosing participants. The area from which the children were drawn is predominantly Welsh speaking (60–70% and higher in some of the villages). All the parents, (apart from one who learned Welsh from 3;0) were first language speakers of Welsh.

There are two components to this corpus. One is the Bangor dataset and the other is the

Aberystwyth dataset. In Bangor, three participants (one female first child, one male second child, one female second child) were forthcoming. The first dropped out after 4 months. Tapes of a further child (first-born male) previously recorded in 1994 and roughly transcribed for a pilot study (Borsley and Aldridge) were totally redone in CHAT format. The Bangor files were prepared with the CHILDES editor.

Transcripts of a further three children (all first-born female) were prepared simultaneously in Aberystwyth by Gwennan Creunant. These files have been converted to CHAT format by the Principal Researcher in Aberystwyth who had previously worked with his own computer programs (for morphological tagging and glossing) for the analysis of the speech of older children. Tapes were made fortnightly in the initial stages (mainly one wordish) and weekly (holidays and illness permitting) in the later stages.

In Bangor there are 27 tapes in the ALAW Corpus, 26 in the RHYS Corpus. Taping of ELIN ceased after 11 sessions. It was decided to redo 29 of the 42 transcriptions of DEWI into CHAT. This means there are 93 transcriptions of Bangor area children. Transcriptions on the whole follow standard orthography (see below for exceptions) with occasional phonographic representations. Standard Welsh orthography is basically phonetic which makes a phonographic representation feasible. All speakers spoke basically Northern dialects.

The Aberystwyth corpus comprises 75 files. Transcriptions are generally phonographic. In Aberystwyth, on the mid-Wales coast, Southern and Northern dialects are heard and this is reflected in these phonographic transcriptions.

The Bangor Dataset

All the Bangor children live in the Arfon area Gwynedd, North Wales. In this area Welsh is spoken by approximately 70% of the population but this figure is higher in some of the villages where the children live. The education policy of the area is largely monolingual Welsh until at least 7;0. Otherwise, bilingual policies of administration are the norm in the public sector.

For the Bangor tapes the same toys were used in all sessions. These included a suitcase of animals, cars, a Fisher-Price™ parade of shops, Barbie dolls and Action Men with clothes, plus odds and sods. In some transcripts, child's mother, grandmother, grandfather, father and/or siblings are present. The investigator was present on all occasions (but one of Elin and a few of Dewi which were mainly tapes made by parents for various reasons). The participants vary from corpus to corpus and day to day. In the majority the investigator and the child are alone for most of the time. In the case of Dewi, the same toys were also used but the taping was usually done in the investigator's home, Dewi living close by in the same village.

All Bangor transcripts represent at least 30 minutes of tape time (45 minutes of most Kevin tapes). Some are longer for a variety of reasons, such as quality, ease of transcription, unusual quietness of child, sibling dominance in parts of tape, and so forth. All but a handful of tapes were made between 9:30 and 10:30 A.M. Times of the few that were not are noted in the initial headers.

All but a handful of tapes were transcribed on same day as taping. This means that context was fresh. Generally, an attempt has been made to add background and contextual information especially where utterances may be ambiguous. Efforts have also been made at making specific remarks about potentially ambiguous or odd utterances on %com lines, for example, the shaking of a head (when recalled) for negation where the form is declarative.

About 70% of the tapes have been listened to by an independent checker with the transcript available. Comments were made on transcripts. The tapes were then totally listened to again by the transcriber with checked transcripts. Amendments and corrections were then made, elevating best guesses to full status, interpreting xxx's, adding and reiterating %COM especially in relation to intonational status of an utterance.

All transcripts (except Dewi which were second transcriptions) not independently checked have been checked with tape for a second (or third in some cases) by the transcriber. Here we have tried to be true to what is heard rather than what we know to be prescriptively correct. This comment is particularly relevant with regard to mutations (on the nonchild lines).

In the documentation of each corpus, which follows at the end of this file, there are comments for all children except Dewi. These comments were usually made straight after transcribing and are of a general background nature with some impressions as to development.

The Bangor research assistant would like to thank the following: First and foremost the parents of the children for their unstinting cooperation. Also, Bill Hicks of Cysyll for installing the Welsh Spellchecker, Professor Cathail O'Dochartaigh (formerly of Cysyll, Bangor University and now of Glasgow University), Dr. Margaret Deuchar for advice in the early stages, Dr. Michelle Aldridge for her patience and good sense, Gwennan in Aberystwyth for sharing the lows of transcription work, Vivienne Pritchard for cheerfully checking, and many others including the members of the Manchester/Bangor reading group into Child Language, in particular Ginnie Gathercole, Marilyn Vihman, and Elena Lieven.

CHAT Usage

Generally, CHAT conventions have been followed (hopefully) but there are some divergences. These are noted here together with some general points.

1. The text replacement symbol [: text] has been used for a phonographic representation. These should not be considered as text replacements.

2. Words are not morphemicized. However, elided forms have been broken up. For example, "dwim isio" is represented by: dw i øm isio > copula1PS+pronoun+neg isio=want.

3. The trigrams ^w^ and ^y^ have been used for the circumflexed w and y of Welsh, e.g., dw^r = water and ty^= house. All other accents were available in ASCII.

4. The notation [?] has been used for best guess with 80–90% certainty. For less certainty alternative transcriptions [=? text] have been used or otherwise xx or xxx. A single x has also been used sometimes to denote something less than a ? word.

5. Time locations are not consistently marked on all transcripts. One dictaphone did not function correctly for a while and then was replaced by another with different readings. In general, the pattern of notation of @Time Locations reflect a pattern of either pause in the discourse or difficult/interesting utterances (for easier retrieval on tape) and not any regular pattern (although many have been added on checking for ease of retrieval).

6. %com lines have sometimes been used for a target language gloss in the case where there is a degree of uncertainty as well as other comments relating to interpretation. If the %gls is used, the target language gloss is quite certain. These are more common at a stage where there are more two word utterances.

7. Utterances/sentences have been delimited by # on the nonchild lines. ## on these lines would indicate a pause. # on the child lines is used for pauses.

8. Repeats on words by (/) were used in the early stages. In the later stages, as retraced utterances became more common, these were eliminated and all repeats are marked as retracings as they seemed more appropriate.

9. English words are followed by @s (s for Saesneg = English) or are represented by xs, the latter so that they can be included in MLU scores on the child lines. Chunks of English (which can then be excluded from MLU's with -s) are represented by xxs. There will be [= English text] following all xs and xxs, or, if these are not clear [=? English text]. Many English words are spelled with Welsh phonography where it seems appropriate. There are other words where the orthography would be identical. The English words marked with @s are generally those where the Welsh orthography does not seem appropriate.

10. The only postcodes that have been used are: [+ imit] , [+ part imit] and [+ prompt].

Disambiguation Devices

All Welsh/Welsh and Welsh/English homonyms have been disambiguated in the Bangor corpus (for the purpose of aiding glossing in Aber and making word lists). A variety of ways have been adopted to do this and details can be found in the following introduction to the lexicon and in the lexicon itself. The only disambiguation that has not been done is that of the predicate marker "yn" on the non-CHAT lines. The following disambiguation codes for common words are indicated below:

yn	verbnoun follows
yn1	prepositional use
yn2	predicate adjective/noun follows
yn4	ambiguous as to yn/yn2

i	first person singular pronoun following finite preposition or verb
i'	preposition = to/for
o	preposition = of/from.
øo	third person singular masculine pronoun
øna2	elided "dyna" as in "dyna fo": there it/he is
na1	comparative word equivalent to "than"
na3	equivalent to neu = or
na7	"reduced" "mai" for focussed subordination
øta1	"reduced" "ynte"= or
do:	"roof"
do	yes (past) word
(d)dyn	man
(d)tyn	tight
dy	second person singular pronoun (possessive type)
ødy	elided copula "ydy"
di	second person singular pronoun
ødi	elided aspect marker/preposition "wedi"= after
øna	elided locative and existential marker "yna"= there
na	negative (generalised)

Representation of English

The representation of English words in this corpus has posed some problems. Many English words have orthographic Welsh forms that might well be considered part of the Welsh language, for example, doli>doll. Welsh orthography is used where it is seems appropriate. In this sense the transcripts are not strictly phonographic. For example, ice cream is represented by ice+cream@s and not eis+crim (see Aber corpus) whether or not it is pronounced in the English way or the Welsh way.

The specific conventions adapted to address these concerns were as follows:

1. The English derivative appears after ">" e.g., doli>doll, ffrwnt>front.
2. Some forms have identical orthography to the English in which case the English derivative appears after "<=", as in, mat<=mat, top<=top. There is no marking in the text to distinguish such a word as an English word. They may be words which are very common. This is a shortcoming but the emphasis is on trying to retain the phonographic integrity of Welsh.

3. English words with English orthography are marked with @s. In some cases Welsh orthography is inappropriate. For example, we use wee+wee@s and not wi+wi but pi+pi and not pee+pee@s. In some cases it is personal preference of the researcher. e.g., flat@s and not fflat. In other cases distinguishing in this way aids in the elimination of homophonous forms e.g., go@s vs go=adjectival intensifier.

4. Some English will be marked as xs or xxs. Use of these varies from corpus to corpus but in general these strings are used for chunks of language rather than individual words. In these cases the English translation appears in a bracketed string as [= text] or [=? text] in the files.

5. Welsh words with English plurals where not the norm: nple eg blodaus= flowers (where English and Welsh plural is compounded).

6. Engish words with Welsh plurals where not the norm (whatever that is): nplw.

This notation has been used partly to eliminate English for the purposes of analysis, to identify chunks of code-switching and to eliminate homophonous (with Welsh) forms. It will be the case that some words marked with @s will also appear in xs or xxs strings. The main motivation for the policy adopted here is to maintain a constant representation of Welsh phonography/orthography/phonology in contrast to that of English. In mind is the fact that not everyone who may look at this corpus will be as well versed in English as Welsh speakers tend to be in Wales. Often, decisions as to how mark words have felt arbitrary but the preceding guidelines have been followed as far as possible.

Notations and Orthography

The symbols @s, xs, xxs, @o (onomatopoeic words) and markings for homonyms have been added after initial transcription in the later stages. As far as is possible the context in each case has been checked for accuracy. Sometimes something like woofwoof may appear marked with either @o or @c. This is relevant for categorization purposes. The same applies to the words "bang" and "bwm."

Conventional spellings are used in the most part. There are a very few exceptions: isda>eistedd=sit; isio>eisiau=want; plus verbal and prepositional forms noted below.

In the lexicon, the usual dialect form or spoken form occurs after "@". Most of these cases are subject to regular rules: 1) words with "e" in final syllable going to "a"; 2) dropping of silent "f" in words like nesaf, af, and so forth.

In the case of inflected prepositions (especially inflected forms of "gan"), there are different orthographic representations. The same applies to a few verbs such as rhoi/rhoid/rhaed = give.

In the cases where conventional spellings are not used the conventional form (or root form) occurs after a dash. Alternatives, either English or Welsh, occur after slashes. English translations occur after equals signs. Alternative Welsh forms for English words appear after >. If they do not occur in the corpus they are marked with *. If they occur the % follows. Welsh words that appear with the English "s" plural appear in a category: nple. This notation is usually used where a Welsh plural could (and may otherwise) be expected. There will be a handful of plurals where the English plural morpheme is well established. The categories used are: n= noun, vn=verbnoun, a=adjective, av=adverb, wh=wh word, fb=finite be, p=preposition, ip=inflected preposition, fv=finite verb, loc=locative adverb, g=greeting (or like). Soft mutations are indicated by ^, nasal by ^^, and aspirate by ^^^.

Layout

Number of repeats on words appear first. In later files these have almost totally been replaced with retracing symbols. This seemed more appropriate after the early one and two word stages. Proper nouns appear with capital letters. English forms have not been marked on these yet.

Pronunciation Notation

In the CHAT files, only pronunciation forms follow target form in brackets [:]. This is not the usual (text replacement) use of these brackets with CHILDES. These phonographic representations, made possible because Welsh orthography is phonetic to a high degree, are not consistently done but have been added to add a flavor of the child's phonological competence.

Publications using these data should cite:

Aldridge, M., Borsley, R. D., Clack, S., Creunant, G., and Jones, B. M. (1998). The acquisition of noun phrases in Welsh. In *Language acquisition: Knowledge representation and processing*. Proceedings of GALA '97. Edinburgh: University of Edinburgh Press.

9:   Index